MW01253065

This book is exciting, important, generative. Splicing cultural theory, social science, and psychoanalysis, it invites many sorts of readers across the clinical-academic divide. With its nuanced takes on intimacy's living and emergent diversity, it's a volume that, it turns out, we've been waiting for.

Muriel Dimen, Adjunct Clinical Professor of Psychology, Postdoctoral Program in Psychotherapy and Psychoanalysis, New York University

The sphere of intimacy is where we live our lives most intensely and passionately. Not surprisingly, it is a highly conflicted zone. This important book seeks to explore intimacies in all their complexities, by setting up a dialogue between sociohistorical approaches and psychoanalysis. The result is a book that is never less than illuminating, and at its best is revelatory and often deeply moving. This is a collection of essays that will become indispensable to our understanding of the significance of intimacies in the contemporary world.

Jeffrey Weeks, author of The Languages of Sexuality (2011)

This collection of essays—moving, exhilarating and trenchant—will fundamentally alter how academics, psychoanalysts, activists, and culture theorists approach 'intimacy'. An important agenda is to unsettle normative discourses around intimacy, while revealing how the state, the legal and the economic systems are forces in the scenes of intimate life. Queer theory, psychoanalysis and political theory co-exist with intense personal narratives. The book is a great argument for multi-disciplinary dialogues and encounters.

Adrienne Harris, Clinical Associate Professor of Psychology, Postdoctoral Program in Psychotherapy and Psychoanalysis, New York University

Intimacies is both a surprising and unsurprising book. It is unsurprising because it engages central discussions in anthropology, sociology, psychoanalysis, and philosophy organized by how to understand the knots, projections, and inconstancies of the intimate ties on which we rely. It is surprising because the essays are so intimate. A compelling, engaging read.

Lauren Berlant, George M. Pullman Professor, Department of English, University of Chicago

Intimacies

In the last decade or so, there has been a shift in the popular and academic discussion of our personal lives. Relationships—and not necessarily marriage—have gravitated to the center of our relational lives. Many of us feel entitled to seek intimacy, an emotionally depthful social bonding, rather than simply security or companionship from our relationships. Unlike in a marriage-centered culture, intimacy is today pursued in varied relationships, from familial to friends and to romances. Intimacies are being forged in multiple venues, from face-to-face to virtual, cyber contexts.

A new scholarship has addressed this changing terrain of personal life—there is today a vast literature on cohabitation, parenthood without marriage, sex and love outside marriage, queer families, cyber intimacies and friendships. However, much theorizing and research has focused either on the interior, subjective or sociocultural aspects of intimacies, and not their interaction.

This volume aims to break new ground: *Intimacies* explores the psychological terrain of intimacy in depthful ways without abandoning its sociohistorical context and the centrality of power dynamics. Drawing on a rich archive that includes the social sciences, feminism, queer studies and psychoanalysis, the contributors examine:

- changing cultures of intimacy;
- fluid and solid attachments and intimacies from hook ups, to sibling bonds, to erotic love;
- a politics of intimacy that may involve state-enforced hierarchies, class, misrecognition, social exclusion and violence;
- embodied experiences of intimacy and dynamics of endings and loss; and
- a pluralization of intimacies that challenge established ethical hierarchies.

This volume aims to define the cutting edge of this emerging field of scholarship and politics. It challenges existing paradigms that assume rigid hierarchical approaches to relational life. *Intimacies* will be of interest for psychoanalysts and for students or scholars in sexualities, gender studies, family studies, feminism studies, queer studies, social class, cultural studies and philosophy.

Alan Frank is a psychoanalyst practicing in New York City.

Patricia Ticineto Clough is Professor of Sociology and Women's Studies at Queens College and Graduate Center, CUNY.

Steven Seidman is Professor of Sociology at the University at Albany, SUNY.

Intimacies

A new world of relational life

Edited by
Alan Frank, Patricia Ticineto Clough
and Steven Seidman

Routledge
Taylor & Francis Group

LONDON AND NEW YORK

First published 2013
by Routledge
2 Park Square, Milton Park, Abingdon, Oxon OX14 4RN

Simultaneously published in the USA and Canada
by Routledge
711 Third Avenue, New York, NY 10017

Routledge is an imprint of the Taylor & Francis Group, an informa business

British Library Cataloguing in Publication Data
A catalogue record for this book is available from the British Library

Library of Congress Cataloging in Publication Data
Intimacies : a new world of relational life / edited by Alan Frank, Patricia
Ticineto Clough and Steven Seidman.
      p. cm.
   Includes bibliographical references and index.
   1. Intimacy (Psychology) 2. Interpersonal relations. I. Frank, Alan,
Psychoanalyst. II. Clough, Patricia Ticineto, 1945- III. Seidman, Steven.
   BF575.I5I55 2013
   158.2--dc23
                2012050417

ISBN: 978-0-415-62690-3 (hbk)
ISBN: 978-0-203-07018-5 (ebk)

Typeset in Baskerville
by Taylor & Francis Books

Printed and bound in the United States of America
by Edwards Brothers Malloy

Contents

Illustrations

Figures

Tables

Contributors

John Borneman is Professor of Anthropology at Princeton University. His recent publications include: *Political Crime and the Memory of Loss* (2011); *Being There: The Field Worker Encounter and the Making of Truth* (2009); *Syrian Episodes* (2007); and *Death of the Father* (2003).

Patricia Ticineto Clough is Professor of Sociology and Women's Studies at Queens College and Graduate Center, CUNY. Her recent publications include: *Autoaffection: Unconscious Thought in the Age of Teletechnology* (2000); *Feminist Thought: Desire, Power and Academic Discourse* (1994); and *The End(s)of Ethnography: From Realism to Social Criticism* (1998); as editor, *The Affective Turn: Theorizing the Social* (2007); and as co-editor, *Beyond Biopolitics: Essays on the Governance of Life and Death* (2012).

William F. Cornell is a professional in psychoanalytical therapy, Pittsburgh, PA. His recent publications include: editor, *The Healer's Bent: Solitude and Dialogue in the Clinical Encounter* (2005); *From Transactions to Relations: The Emergence of Relational Paradigms in Transactional Analysis* (2005); and *Explorations in Transactional Analysis* (2008); "Aspiration or Adaptation: An Unresolved Tension in Berne's Basic Beliefs," *Transactional Analysis Journal* Vol. 40; "Searching in the 'Unsaid Seen': McLaughlin's Unfinished Reflections on the Place of the Body in Psychoanalytic Discourse," *American Imago* (Winter 2010); and "SAMBA, TANGO, PUNK: Reflections on Steven Knoblauch's 'Contextualizing Attunement within a Polyrhythmic Weave: The Psychoanalytic Samba'," *Psychoanalytic Dialogues*.

Alan Frank is a psychoanalyst practicing in New York. Affiliated with the National Institute for the Psychotherapies, He is currently writing a book on men, masculinity and intimacy.

Roger Friedland is a Professor of Religious Studies and Sociology at the University of California Santa Barbara. His recent publications include: *The Fellowship* (2007); *To Rule Jerusalem* (2000); and as editor, *Matters of Culture* (2004).

Joshua Gamson is Professor of Sociology at the University of San Francisco. His recent publications include: *The Fabulous Sylvester: The Legend, the Music, the Seventies in San Francisco* (Henry Holt/Picador, 2005); *Freaks Talk Back: Tabloid*

Talk Shows and Sexual Nonconformity (University of Chicago Press, 1998); and *Claims to Fame: Celebrity in Contemporary America* (University of California Press, 1994).

Paolo Gardinali is director of the Survey Research Center at the University of California Santa Barbara. His recent publications include: "L'accesso alla banca dati, I dati sulla struttura economica e produttiva".

Anne Golomb Hoffman is Professor of English and Comparative Literature at Fordham University. Anne is also affiliated with the Institute for the History of Psychiatry at Weill Cornell Medical College and the Columbia Center for Psychoanalytic Training and Research. Her recent publications include: "Is Psychoanalysis a Poetics of the Body?" *American Imago* (2006); "Archival Bodies," *American Imago* (2009); "The Power of Images: Refractions of a Stereotype of the Male Jewish Body," (2010); and *Between Exile and Return* (1991).

Jane Kupersmidt is a psychoanalyst in New York. She is a member of the Faculty of the National Psychological Association for Psychoanalysis, and a Fellow of the International Psychoanalytic Association. Recently she has worked on Freud's "Rat Man", particularly relating to current controversies around anxiety, obsessional states and "perverse" defenses, papers on loneliness and aloneness, long-term treatment with traumatized "anti-analysands," and papers on psychoanalytic structures in literature and art.

Linda Nicholson is Susan E. and William P. Stiritz Distinguished Professor of Women's Studies and Professor of History at Washington University. Her recent publications include: *Identity Before Identity Politics* (Cambridge, 2008); *The Play of Reason: From the Modern to the Postmodern* (Cornell, 1998); *Gender and History: The Limits of Social Theory in the Age of the Family* (Columbia, 1986); as editor, *Feminism/Postmodernism* (Routledge, 1990); and as co-editor (with Steven Seidman) *Social Postmodernism* (Cambridge, 1995).

Jeffrey Prager is Professor of Sociology at the University of California, Los Angeles, and Co-Dean and Senior Faculty Member at the New Center for Psychoanalysis, Los Angeles. His recent publications include: *Presenting the Past, Psychoanalysis and the Sociology of Misremembering* (Harvard University Press, 1998); "Healing from History: Psychoanalytic Considerations on Traumatic Pasts and Social Repair," *European Journal of Social Theory* (2008); "Jump-Starting Timeliness: Trauma, Temporality and the Redressive Community," in Parker, Crawford and Harris (eds) *Time and Memory* (Koninklijke Brill, 2006); and "Melancholic Identity: Post-Traumatic Loss, Memory and Identity Formation," in Elliott and DuGay (eds) *Identity in Question*, 2009.

Leila J. Rupp is Professor of Feminist Studies and Associate Dean of the Division of Social Sciences at the University of California, Santa Barbara. Her recent publications include: *Drag Queens at the 801 Cabaret* (2003); *A Desired Past: A Short History of Same-Sex Love in America* (2002); and *Sapphistries: A Global History of Love between Women* (2009).

Joseph Schneider is Ellis and Nelle Levitt Professor of Sociology in the Department for the Study of Culture and Society at Drake University. His recent publications include: *Deviance and Medicalization* (1992); *Having Epilepsy: The Experience of Chronic Illness* (with Conrad, 1985); *Giving Care, Writing Self: A "New" Ethnography* (with Wang Laihua, 2000); and *Donna Haraway: Live Theory* (2005).

Steven Seidman is Professor of Sociology at the University at Albany, SUNY. His recent publications include: *Romantic Longings* (Routledge, 1991); *Embattled Eros* (1992); *Beyond the Closet* (Routledge, 2002); and *The Social Construction of Sexuality* (Norton, 2006).

Daniel Shaw is Faculty and Clinical Supervisor at the International Association for Relational Psychoanalysis and Psychotherapy, National Institute for the Psychotherapies. His recent publications include: "Enter Ghosts: The Loss of Intersubjectivity in Clinical Work with Adult Children of Pathological Narcissists," *Psychoanalytic Dialogues* (2010); Issue Editor, "The Analyst's Love: Contemporary Perspectives," *Psychoanalytic Inquiry* (2007); "Narcissistic Authoritarianism in Psychoanalysis," in *Power Games: Influence, Persuasion, and Indoctrination in Psychotherapy Training*; and "On the Therapeutic Action of Analytic Love," *Contemp. Psychoanalysis* (2003).

Catherine B. Silver is Emerita Professor of Sociology at Brooklyn College and the CUNY Graduate Center, and a psychoanalyst in New York. Her recent publications include: "The Politics of Paranoia," with Alan Roland, *The Psychoanalytic Review* (2010); "Womb Envy: Grief and Loss of the Maternal Body," *The Psychoanalytic Review* (2007); "Making Emotional Sense of the Proposed Boycott against Israeli Academics and Intellectuals," *Engage* (2007); "Gender and Value Orientation: What's the Difference?! The Case of US and Japan" (2006); "Leaking Affections. A Socio-psychoanalytic View"; and "Gender Identity in Old Age: Toward (De)gendering?" *Journal of Aging Studies* (2003).

Arlene Stein is Professor of Sociology and Women and Gender Studies at Rutgers University. Her recent publications include: *The Stranger Next Door* (Beacon, 2002); *Sex and Sensibility: Stories of a Lesbian Generation* (University of California Press, 1997).

Verta Taylor is Professor of Sociology at the University of California, Santa Barbara. Her recent publications include: *Drag Queens at the 801 Cabaret* (2003); "Culture and Mobilization: Tactical Repertoires, Same-Sex Weddings, and the Impact on Gay Activism" (with Katrina Kimport, Nella VanDyke and Ellen Andersen), *American Sociological Review* (2009); and "Collective Identity in Social Movement Communities: Lesbian Feminist Mobilization" (with Nancy Whittier), in *Frontiers in Social Movement Theory* (1992).

Acknowledgements

The editors are pleased to thank the authors for their contributions to *Intimacies*. We are grateful to each for exploring intimate life in original, compelling and often deeply personal ways. We hope they are as excited and pleased with this volume as we are.

Many thanks to Routledge, especially to Gerhard Boomgaarden and Emily Briggs, for supporting a book project that encourages dialogue between psychoanalytic and sociohistorical scholars.

Introduction

Alan Frank, Patricia Ticineto Clough and Steven Seidman

Intimacies: A New World of Relational Life was initially conceived at a party celebrating the marriage of two of our three co-authors, Alan Frank and Steven Seidman. In their NYC home they brought together some of their closest friends and family. As an academic, Steve's friends were mostly professors—of sociology and women studies. As a psychoanalyst, a great many of Alan's friends were also analysts. They had no idea whether this mix would work, but it did. There was a social and intellectual buzz that infused the event; conversations seemed energizing and exciting, and this had less to do with marriage (of which most of us were deeply ambivalent) than with the intellectual mix.

After the party, Alan and Steve talked about the people who attended this event, and who populate and give vitality to their lives. They noticed two things.

First, in this admittedly very white, professional, mostly over-fifties crowd, there was enormous variation in the personal lives of their friends. There were straight married couples but often enough the women were the primary breadwinners; there were a couple of male hetero-partners who assumed primary responsibility for domestic affairs; there were single women, gay and lesbian couples, friends who were deeply attached to one or both of their parents and others for whom family was not a basis for intimacy; among many in this small social circle, both coupled or single, friends were often counted as primary intimates. In short, what Alan and Steve realized was that their lives, and those of their dearest friends and kin, displayed a multiplicity of intimacies. Indeed, each of us seemed embedded in a rich intimate network, including partners, spouses, parents, children, friends and colleagues, not to mention occasional sex partners, siblings, therapists, clergy, dance partners, animals and even inanimate objects.

As a sociologist, Steve marveled at this intimate variation; not surprising, perhaps, but imagining a wedding party of his parents' generation, this event seemed to signal a big change in American culture. Alan shared this perception, but wondered, too, about the subjective, interpersonal texture of intimacies today. What sorts of psyches, internal dynamics, and unconscious wishes and fantasies drive such a dramatic cultural shift? They began to wonder whether their two worlds couldn't be brought together in a more powerful and compelling way to say something about the psychoanalytic and sociocultural meaning of intimacies in America today.

Fresh off the celebratory high of their marriage celebration, Steve and Alan were disposed towards a sanguine view of such changes. After all, after growing up in a closeted era they were now legally married! Alan and Steve shared their thoughts with their close friend (and third co-editor of this volume) Patricia Clough. She shared their enthusiasm for a volume that aimed to chart some of these changes and that drew on critical social and psychoanalytic perspectives, but Patricia challenged their somewhat sunny disposition in ways that proved pivotal for this book. She made the telling point that intimacy itself is a contested concept; as it becomes a site of discourse and analysis there has also ensued a struggle to define it and deploy it for various normative and regulatory purposes. So, the "intimate" has not only become an arena of multiplicity but its social and ethical-political meaning is indeterminate and contested. Alan and Steve, having read their Foucault and the critical post-Freudians, agreed.

In the course of ongoing conversations, the three of them sketched out the intention of a collection of essays on intimacies. The concept of intimacies would be left open to conflicting meanings and politics; contributors would be encouraged to address a wide range of intimacies and urged to find a personal voice wherever it felt appropriate.

As we reviewed the literature on intimacies, it was obvious that there was a great divide between the social and the psychological. On the one side, there were well-regarded demographic, sociological and historical studies of American intimate life. We also noted, though, that a preponderance of this scholarship focused on either parent–child relations or marriage, and recently cohabitation; there was much less written on friendships, siblings, casual erotic intimates, non-monogamous intimacies, immigrant intimacies, transnational intimacies and so on. This is perhaps understandable in an era characterized by the normative and social dominance of the couple, marriage and the nuclear family, but in our view this intimate order is losing its hegemonic status. Feminist and queer movements, long-term trends linked to gender equality, singlehood, single parenthood, surrogacy, the constitutionalization of privacy, and the elaboration of both a cyber world and a security state, have altered American culture. Many Americans today not only live in a different intimate milieu than their parents and grandparents, but this generation is aware of the multiple, fluid and ambiguous meanings of intimacies in a way that was less possible under a normative regime that stipulated an equation between intimacy and marriage and family. Today we are "postmarital" and "postfamily" in the dual sense of being aware of the pluralization of intimacies and being mindful, as well, of the dark side of intimacies such as violence, power, institutional intrusions into private life, and disciplinary control exercised at the level of the body and desire.

Since all three of us have long histories with psychoanalysis, Alan being an analyst and Patricia and Steve both academics and in psychoanalytic training, we knew that something was missing from the literature on the social and political meaning of intimacies: an analytical perspective on the emotional texture and unconscious dynamics that are the experiential meat and potatoes of intimacy. In much of the current literature, whether we're talking about demographic, sociological or Foucauldian accounts, the psyche is either written out of the story or is inserted, but only as part of biopolitical regulation. However compelling such perspectives may be, they do not recognize what to us is a fundamental point: the deeply affective, unconscious interpersonal dynamics of intimacies. For, in the end, intimacies, of whatever kind, entail selves who have complicated, multi-layered inner lives, and a sense of agency that makes "intimate" experiences meaningful. Accounts of intimacy that write the psyche out of their stories are not just one-sided but also perpetuate a politic that denies agency and denies that, however much "the social" constructs the intimate, there is an irreducible subjective and interpersonal dimension.

Simultaneously, psychoanalysts from Freud to Jessica Benjamin and Steven Mitchell have produced an archive of work that speaks powerfully to the psychology of intimacy and has become part of the indispensable grammar of intimacies. Yet psychoanalysts rarely manage to weave together this rich language of the psyche with an equally rich account of the social fabric.

So, the intention of *Intimacies* is to suggest something of the changing landscape of intimacies in America today; to speak to its agentic possibilities and also its role in a politics of control and exclusion; and to approach intimacies in terms of the interpenetration of the psychic and the social.

Changing cultures of intimacy

To paraphrase Foucault: throughout history there have been many societies valuing close personal relationships but few perhaps that embraced intimacy, at least as Americans and many Europeans understand this concept today. As Linda Nicholson suggests, a "discourse of intimacy" became part of the American public culture in the 1960s and 1970s. Before "intimacy" there were other languages of personal bonds such as those of virtue, filial or gender duty, family alliance, romantic friendship, or true love. Most importantly, there has been the language of marriage. As Steven Seidman argues, by the early decades of the 20th century, a heterosexual, racialized notion of marriage became an inclusive institution, bundling together love, sex, companionship, parenthood and family. All non-marital, cross-racial, close relationships were either stigmatized as potentially sexually and gender deviant, marginalized as bad imitations of marriage, or erased as a part of American culture. So, at the same time that a rigid Victorian gender order was weakening, a new state-enforced marriage-centered relational order was solidifying that disrespected or censored nonmarital forms of relational intimacy.

In the last half century, America and many European nations experienced the declining significance of marriage and arguably the rise of an era of "relationships." Today, marriage is just one option among a spectrum of intimate possibilities. Indeed, the separate components of intimacy that were bundled together and established marriage as an enveloping institution could now be approached as distinct, separate, intimate dimensions to be decided upon by the individual. Somewhat provocatively, we suggest that, in an age of ever-expanding, mutually negotiated relationships, it's not sex, not love, not marriage, not family and not gender roles, but intimacy that is at the heart of relational life. Intimacy increasingly suggests an ongoing process of self and other subjective exploration and mutual self-revelation in a quest to be authentic and forge a rich intimate solidarity.

In short, we believe that Anglo-Western European cultures have articulated a new concept of rights, that of *intimate citizenship*. In principle, selves have a right to personal intimate freedom with regard to partner selection, the social form of intimacy, and its internal organization. Although this right is becoming an important part of the search for personal freedom and happiness, we are also aware that it has been applied unevenly and excludes or inferiorizes many nonheterosexuals, gender-different folk, immigrants and the disabled, among others.

In his contribution, "State and class politics in the making of a culture of intimacy," Seidman emphasizes the formative role of the state in shaping personal life. By the 1960s and 1970s, the state was empowering individuals, at least as it pertained to personal matters. Seidman underscores the significance of the constitutionalization of privacy, which gave selves considerable latitude to deliberately organize their personal and relational lives. In the last few decades, the state authorized relational choice by creating an umbrella of legal protections for personal-relational decisions such as reproductive and contraceptive rights, protection from domestic violence, the recognition of single parenthood and cohabitation, the effective ending of censorship and anti-miscegenation laws, the decriminalizing of homosexuality, and so on. The state has retreated from the restrictive regulation of personal life while lifting many of the legal barriers that prevented a much more fluid, pluralized relational order from taking shape.

Simultaneously, though, the state also withdrew a great deal of its social support for a diversified intimate order. In contrast to many Western European nations, America's neoliberal state does not provide the social conditions that would universalize intimate autonomy, such as family leave, a living wage, universal healthcare, free abortions, legalization of gay/lesbian unions, trans rights, etc. For Americans who lack the capital to buy domestic help, access to surrogacy, healthcare, family leave, or day care, they are often forced to rely on already stressed-out informal, kin relations. Furthermore, for Americans who rely on welfare to support their relational lives, they not only face reduced state support, but Clinton's 1996 welfare reform act made such support contingent on suspending privacy rights. For these Americans, the new intimate citizen has been a mixed blessing. It may lessen the stigma on nonconventional relations and households but it also reduces the available resources for realizing relational choice. Seidman suggests that, as in so many other areas of American life, social class is today at the heart of the politics of intimacy.

In "Let me tell you who I am," Linda Nicholson also sketches a sweeping historical view of changes in American intimate life. In her view, self-disclosure is at the heart of intimacy. So, how has this practice changed over the decades from the mid-1800s through today? She argues that self-disclosure has to be understood in relation to the changing meaning and relations between the private and public spheres.

In Victorian times, at least among the white middle classes, the private and public spheres were sharply differentiated. The former was the domain of women, the latter men; the former was also the sphere of marriage and the family and was the only appropriate place to express deeply personal feelings and ties. In the course of the last century, there has occurred a blurring of the private and public.

There were many reasons for this, for example, the women's and gay/lesbian movements, the mainstreaming of nonwhite populations, the sexualization and gender mixing of the public sphere, the growth of popular culture and so on. Nicholson, though, emphasizes the salient role of psychotherapy in American culture. With its ethos of subjective exploration and self-revelation as liberatory, psychotherapy contributed significantly, even if unintentionally, to bringing self-disclosure into public life. Today, a culture of self-expression and confession informs celebrity culture, electoral politics, popular culture, identity politics, literary practices and so on.

This transformation of relational life took off in the 1960s and 1970s, but accelerated by leaps and bounds since the 1990s. In particular, a new cyber culture has encouraged public practices of self-exploration and identification that challenge the historic association of intimacy, self-disclosure and privacy. Many critics associate such developments with the end of privacy and hence intimacy. By contrast, Nicholson provocatively suggests that the meaning of privacy is changing, not disappearing. There are, for example, forms of communicating (texting, emailing or Facebook) that indeed are personal and public, and these present an odd mix of being both intimate and anonymous. However, these same social media make possible personal communications that are private—intended for an exclusive other or others, and therefore intimate. Of course, as with any such communication media, there can be betrayals, but that is not about technology but social ethics. For Nicholson, the cyber world allows people to be "alone together" but also together alone.

Between fluid and solid intimacies

Solid intimacies are thick, life-sustaining relationships that usually deepen and strengthen over time: husband/wife, husband/husband, parent/child, brother/sister and grandparent/grandchild. By contrast, porous intimacies, some more and some less significant, but less sustaining on an ongoing basis, ebb and flow throughout our life: casual friends, student/teacher, office mates, doctor/patient, college roommates, holiday lovers, fuck buddies. Constant and solid or intermittent and porous, each has been, at one time, clearly definable. It was easier when our intimate choices seemed that cut-and-dried—black or white, with very little gray.

However, with the recent changes in the cultural landscape of intimacies, now seemingly more plastic, there is, too, an ever-broadening gray area. The fluid/solid binary is less reliable as a guide to intimate life in America. Living in this gray space, socially and psychologically, may be unsettling and evoke anxiety and discontent. Yet, it also, we think, invites a nuanced ethical and political discussion about our personal lives; encourages relational exploration and innovation; and would seem to expand choice that is layered and often complex. Undoubtedly, many Americans today are still in the process of adjusting to this changing intimate world. We're exploring ways to mix solid and fluid intimacies, to forge both deep, secure attachments and fashion various meanings and pleasures from our multiple, layered social connections. We should be cautious, however, about judging the myriad ways Americans are inventing personal and relational lives. As many essays in this volume indicate, new freedoms sit alongside empowering and, as well, unsettling forms of social control and surveillance, and loneliness is often teetering at the edge of ecstatic solidarities. However, one thing seems clear: many Americans are fashioning lives that are layered with fluid and solid intimacies. The essays in this section offer compelling evidence of precisely such inventions.

In "Unexpected intimacies," Alan Frank argues that too often intimacy is viewed through a conventionally normative—and often times through a heteronormative—lens. Doing so, he believes, can obscure more nonconventional, but possibly more fluid connections. He challenges assumptions that stipulate what we may consider morally perverse and "normal" behavior, and contends that behavior that most Americans would likely consider the antithesis of intimacy can be a meaningful form of attachment and an anchoring social bond. In his essay, Frank presents a patient, David, to dramatically illustrate his point. One sees clearly, during their 10-year working relationship, if Frank had not struggled with his own thinking and vigorously challenged the often myopic view of David's nonconventional intimate life, both analyst and analysand would have suffered a terrible, irretrievable loss.

In their study of college students, "Hey God, is that You in my underpants?" Roger Friedland and Paolo Gardinali raise important issues about the fluidity of intimacy. In a hook-up culture where conventional dating is a rare occurrence, sex is ordinary and love is improbable, they ask if love has anything to do with erotic pleasure, and what God and religion have to do with the organization of sex and love. Interviews with students at several colleges reveal college men and women are still connecting sex with feelings and relationships. Though sex and intimacy are definitely more fluid and experimental, a big concern is that college-age women and, most especially, college-age men lack a language of love or simply do not embed sex, feelings and relationships in an articulated culture of love. They believe there is one clear exception: students for whom religion is integral are much more likely to align sex, feelings and love. For these students, love is important not only because it binds a relationship, but also, its morality of self/other caring and compassion is a condition of a people in solidarity.

Through extensive in-depth interviews, Leila Rupp and Verta Taylor, in "Queer girls on campus," present a fascinating portrait of nonheterosexual college women. These young women struggle to negotiate a sexual/affectional life that avoids compulsory hetero and a regulative gay/lesbian discourse. They analyze the stories of these women in order to understand this new world of sexual fluidity, the kind of intimacies and identities it fosters, and what kinds of intimacies are possible in a culture that values sexual and gender fluidity.

In his essay, "Intimacy and ambivalence," Daniel Shaw illustrates how individuals and couples mix fluid and solid intimacies. In particular, Shaw depicts the ambivalence that can create enormous tension as one aspires to sustaining loving, intimate relationships. No doubt ambivalence is a multidimensional concept. For Shaw, ambivalence turns on a contradictory desire to be deeply known and, also, to remain hidden. In a series of case studies, he compellingly conveys the challenge, to both analyst and patient, of peeling away defenses to reveal a more vulnerable, accessible self. However, even an emotionally available self may still struggle with ambivalence, though the dance of visibility/invisibility will, hopefully, lessen.

Lateral intimacies

Until recently, intimate life was organized or imagined chiefly in a vertical manner. First, the über institution of intimacy was hetero-marriage and the family. Indeed, so dominant was this model that other intimacies were viewed as pale imitations or preparations for hetero-marriage, or simply erased from public life and collective memory. Second, within hetero-marriage/family, verticality reigned: husbands exercised authority over wives, parents over children, and fathers over families.

The vertical model has not disappeared, but there has occurred a leveling of intimate life. Marriage is today one intimate option among many, including singledom, romantic affairs, fuck buddies, cohabitation, civil unions, domestic partnerships, polyamorous relations and so on. Moreover, the model of marriage as an inclusive institution that took root in the first half of the 20th century has unraveled; today, sex, love, companionship, parenthood and family are no longer necessarily bundled. Individuals make decisions about each of these facets of intimacy—and if and how to unite them. Today, too, more Americans are claiming the independent value and integrity of friendships, kin relations, religious and other civic ties, sex partners and situationally specific intimacies, e.g. sports buddies, bar friends, sewing circles, bowling leagues. Intimate life is increasingly horizontal and layered, making up a mosaic of truly dizzying forms. Joshua Gamson's essay, "The belly mommy and the fetus sitter," beautifully illustrates the layered, horizontal character of intimacies today. Josh and his spouse share their intimate, often convoluted journey to become parents. When these two men, out of sheer necessity, are forced to deal with egg donors, surrogates, legal institutions and the medical profession, this process—at times poignant and emotionally rich, and at other times overwhelming—inadvertently generates layers of intricate and complex relationships.

Of course, verticality within marriage and the family has not ended. While men no longer exercise state-sanctioned authority over their wives, they continue to exercise disproportionate power in the public and private spheres. Still, that's changing as well. Today, family law in Europe and the USA recognizes wives as independent rights-bearing persons and has leveled the status of men and women in American families, even if informal power still favors men. Mixing a rich ethnographic anthropological tradition and a personal story, John Borneman highlights vast differences between cultures of self-disclosure, intimacy, and family across time and space. For example, whereas intimacy remains deeply embedded in kin systems in some Middle East cultures, in Germany and the USA intimacy outside of marriage and heterosexuality has become conventionalized. Indirectly, he also underscores a contrast between vertical kin systems that privilege lines of descent and more lateral ones that privilege individual choice and equality.

In her groundbreaking study *Siblings*, the feminist psychoanalyst Juliet Mitchell makes a powerful case for the importance of siblings, and more generally lateral relations. The preoccupation with Oedipus, and fathers, effectively challenged in the last few decades, has allowed a deepening appreciation of the centrality of the lateral relations between siblings and between individual family members and peers. In his moving essay "Lost and found," William Cornell demonstrates the importance of lateral intimacies by sharing a very personal story—the fracturing of his sibling relations and his struggle, when facing the death of his sister, to forge an intimate connection with his sister and brother after a lifetime of alienation. The poignancy of his struggle to figure out the place of his siblings in his intimate map speaks to the need to bring lateral relations into the center of intimate studies.

Unsettling intimacies

Intimate relations often can be troubling for those engaged in them, especially when intimacy is all but inextricable from anxiety, misrecognition and violence. Further, the way intimacies are unsettling make it necessary to understand intimacy as both a social and a psychic experience; however, the relationship of these two aspects of the experience of intimacy cannot be predetermined. Presenting two of his clients, Jeffrey Prager shows how psychoanalysis often is practiced with the aim of establishing an intimate relationship between analyst and analysand. With this aim, psychoanalytic practice often can evoke in the analysand deep needs, thought to arise first in early childhood, and then later frequently to take a sexualized form, both of which can seek expression in the analytic process. This can bring up anxiety and defensive responses both in the analyst and analysand, which nonetheless is the very stuff of therapeutic action. Prager not only shows how he and two analysands make their way through this demanding experience of establishing a deep intimacy, but he also shows the way sociality can be used to limit the experience of intimacy in a defensive use of socially circulating narratives and identities. Focusing on narratives of child sexual abuse and homosexual identity, Prager suggests that certain uses of narrative and identities can be detrimental to the ongoing process of experiencing intimacy, especially when used unconsciously to defend against the expression of need for or frustration with the analyst.

If for Prager narrative and identity can work against a revelation of psychic needs and against experiencing intimacy, Arlene Stein shows the importance of socially circulating narratives and identities to ensure recognition or to correct misrecognition. Recounting stories about her and her partner becoming parents through artificial insemination by a male friend, Stein makes clear how queer families have to negotiate recognition as well as manage misrecognition in their relationship with social institutions such as hospitals and schools. Often these negotiations occur around filling out forms that institutions require; these institutional records affect family narratives of origin and development. Stein shows that, even with the gains recently won for queer families, they still are negotiating socially dominant scripts in the creation of family stories in ways that seriously affect intimate relations, such as those between parents and between parents and children.

In Patricia Clough's exploration of family violence in her relationship with her sister, the socio-historical conditions of ethno-racism and the harshness of immigration are shown to affect intimacy over generations. Clough links these socio-historical conditions shaping intimacy to what she describes as biopolitical governance, or the uneven distribution of capacities among populations, including the capacity for intimacy. She goes on to propose that the intimacy of lateral relationships, first experienced among siblings, is becoming more relevant to bio-political imaginaries. Recognizing the indeterminacy of the relationship of the psychic and the social in such imaginaries, Clough's writing style, its aesthetic form, breaks up the narrative both of life story and social psychological theory, offering an unsettled and unsettling understanding of herself and her sister, an unsettled and unsettling realization of family sociality and intimacy.

Phenomenology of intimacy

Perhaps it is in the ending of a relationship that we can fully experience the intensity of its intimacy. At least it might be at the end of a relationship that we look back and take full stock of what the relationship has meant to us. The way relationships end is important; the ending can affect how relationships will be remembered and how they will go on affecting us. Not only have psychoanalysts long recognized that termination is a process central to the analysis, but they also recognize that the intimation of an ending may be felt throughout the analysis, often around negotiating boundaries between analyst and analysand. Perhaps the link between boundaries and intimacy is intense because it carries the weight of the inevitability of loss. The losses suffered by analyst and analysand during the analysis and at its termination may be a reminder of the loss of life itself, our own life and the lives of loved ones. As in analysis, in life, there is work to be done to mourn rather than deny, to suffer loss and thereby gain the strength to go on living, living well.

Jane Kupersmidt and Catherine Silver each tell of their work with patients where the career of the analysis is fated by the patient's capacity for intimacy and the analyst's response to these limitations and affordances; they tell of struggles between analyst and patient over the affective excesses around boundaries. Through these struggles, the patient and the analyst are drawn into enactments of past intimacies, where intervals of rupture and repair are suffered unconsciously and where what is most desired by the patient is moved along to ends often not imagined at first by either analyst or patient. Sometimes these ends are the very end of an analysis where struggles to contain erotic and aggressive drives as well as coming to terms with separation in intimacy cannot be accomplished, where self-awareness of primary internal objects cannot be tolerated and insight may never come or only come after termination.

Anne Hoffman also writes of the termination of an analysis where, however, a capacity for creativity was successfully restored during the analysis. Hoffman's deeply troubling writing block, the seeming reason for her seeking treatment, is worked out in her analysis through working through the writing block to realizing an unconscious connection between her body and the body of texts. This working through allows Hoffman to re-find the infantile body as the ground of metaphor. Showing analysis to be a work of intimacy, intra-personal and interpersonal, where touching must occur mainly through language and an imagining of embodied presence, Hoffman also reminds us of the rich connection of psychoanalysis, literature and the arts.

While Hoffman explores the very unique aspects of terminating an analytic relationship where one's experience of internal change is an experience with another that nonetheless must come to something of an abrupt end, Joseph Schneider writes about an ending he experiences with the death of his wife. No longer able to touch her, Schneider shows us how objects that can speak of his wife both enable him to experience a final separation from her while internalizing all that has been of their love and lives together. Drawing on a number of current philosophical discussions engaged with reconsidering the divide between nature and matter, the inert and the living, Schneider makes clear that objects do not simply remind us of a lost one but rather objects do so because they are alive enough to enliven what has passed from awake or conscious experience. Schneider, like Hoffman, reminds us that the body to which psychoanalysis refers is not merely the human body; it is the lively bodies of all matter, of all around us that sustains unconscious experience, ghostly experience of dreams, memories and the arts and on which sociality, too, draws to create the ongoing sense of a shared reality.

Intimacies pivots on a simple but compelling observation: we live in a connected world, and its emotional and social texture is enormously complex. Most of us participate in multiple types of intimacies. Many Americans forge long-term, monogamous, quasi-marital relationships, but even these are extraordinarily varied, from marriage to civil unions, cohabitation, coupled without sharing residence, "group" intimacies, polygamous, polyamorous, and on and on. Also, many of us participate in situationally specific or episodic relationships in which intimacies are perhaps more fluid and transient, from casual sex, to affairs, temporary but thick connections, e.g. during travel, at work, with service workers, at a protest or musical event. Whether this layered, changing, pluralized order of intimacies turns into fragmentation, anomie and despairing loneliness, or allows for a rich, layered subjective and interpersonal order is still unclear. Moreover, postmodern irony compels us to place alongside gains in choice costs varying from living with heightened insecurity to social machinery deploying technologies to survey and control selves through the very apparatus of self making.

Part I

Changing cultures of intimacy

1 State and class politics in the making of a culture of intimacy

Steven Seidman

Many Americans navigate an intimate world that is postmarital. It's true that marriage is still privileged as the preferred intimate arrangement by the state, and it's also the case that most Americans still want to marry, will marry, and that gaining the right to marry is at the top of the gay/lesbian agenda. Yet, marriage today is no longer compulsory; it is one relational option. Like other intimate relationships, we freely enter and exit marriage; we negotiate how to balance autonomy and solidarity; and many of us form close, sustaining relationships chiefly in order to realize intimacy. The latter concept, for the purposes of this essay, refers to an historically unique kind of emotional and social closeness featuring the depthful sharing of inner lives, negotiating the conditions and dynamics of the social bond, and aspirations to sustain a sense of personal authenticity in an emotionally thick experience of solidarity.

I will argue that there has been a dramatic expansion of intimate choice in the USA and that the state, especially the federal government, has played a key role by constructing the individual as an "intimate citizen." The latter concept asserts that every citizen is recognized by the state as having a right to privacy and to bodily, erotic and relational autonomy. At the same time, the government has failed both to recognize fully a reality of intimate diversity (the state "establishment" of marriage), and provide the resources that would make intimate citizenship a reality for many Americans. Despite an emerging field of expanding erotic-relational choice and variation, intimate life in contemporary America remains heteronormative, marriage centered and class inflected. Thus, Americans possessing high levels of economic and cultural capital, especially if they are straight and married, can more fully exercise their intimate autonomy than citizens with fewer material and cultural resources and opportunities, especially if they are not heterosexual and married. These Americans navigate erotic-relational life as a sphere of insecurity, vulnerable to disrespect, marginalization, and at times criminalization.

The heteronormative, marriage-centered organization of American institutional and intimate life has been much commented on (Canaday 2009; Coontz 2005; Ingraham 2008). I add little to this discussion. Instead, I wish to "decenter" a marriage-centered perspective by situating this institution in a context of changing patterns of personal and relational life.

In the first three sections, I sketch broad changes in American intimate life from roughly the early 19th century to the present. In the final section, I address a dimension of personal-relational life that is often obscured by a popular culture featuring personal choice and romantic love, namely the class politics of intimacy. In the course of this historical-critical sketch, I highlight the formative role of the state in shaping a marriage-centered culture and its recent transformation. For the purposes of this essay, my focus will be erotically oriented intimacies. I do not consider a multiplicity of nonsexual, nonromantic intimacies such as friendships, kin relationships, workplace, cyber, and machine-and-object-related intimacies, and so on.

The Victorians: marriage as a status regime

Between 1800 and the 1860s, marriage was the only state-recognized, church-sanctioned sexual arrangement, and it was exclusively for opposite-sexed, same-race couples, and legally free American citizens.

At the heart of Victorian marriage was a specific gender-based status order. Men and women were understood as different but destined by nature and God to form a union. Men were rational, competitive and sexually driven; they were expected to be the protectors of kin and the rulers of public life. By contrast, women were spiritual, moral and maternal; they were supposed to organize lives around domestic and religious matters. Women would provide the right moral-spiritual environment for the making of a respectable family and a virtuous citizenry, while men governed inside and outside of the family. Through marriage, each sex could realize its gendered nature while also creating a moral foundation for the family and society.

Although Victorians didn't necessarily marry for love, it was expected to grow during marriage. However, this was less a romantic and passionate love than a sympathetic bond based on shared religious and family values. Sex was expected but chiefly for family making; sex oriented to carnal pleasure was condemned by the guardians of Victorian America as corrupting the moral-spiritual sanctuary of marriage and the family (Seidman 1991; D'Emilio and Freedman 1998).

No doubt, a certain intimacy accompanied a life shared over decades. However, intimacy, in the sense of a process of ongoing self-revelation and the forging of a depthful, enveloping companionship was not expected and did not serve as a yardstick of a good marriage. To the extent that intimacy was expected, it was during the courting process and as a strategy to determine the moral character and suitability of a potential spouse (Rothman 1987; Lystra 1992). Once betrothed, a good marriage was less about intimacy than fulfilling gender and kinship obligations, family making, maintaining civic respectability, and securing domestic and social order.

Intimacy seems to have flourished chiefly outside of marriage, especially among friends of the same sex. As we've noted, women and men occupied separate spheres and social roles, which no doubt shaped different psyches and sensibilities. Victorians often found a deep moral and psychological affinity with persons of the same sex.

Consider that men's lives were centered in an exclusively male public world; men worked and socialized together, and often shared sleeping quarters when they traveled. Men's friendships were supported by exclusively male associations and clubs (Rotundo 1994). Similarly, women shared lives organized around domestic tasks and moral and religious instruction. Women also enjoyed exclusively female associations. At times, friendships among women were emotionally thick, even romantic, and paralleled marriage as long-term, committed relationships (Smith-Rosenberg 1986; Faderman 1992). Same-sex intimacies, especially among women, were tolerated because they didn't threaten heterosexual marriage. Not only were women said to lack sexual passion, but also marriage was their taken-for-granted destiny.

The intimate culture of Victorians has often been maligned as rigid and intolerant. However, looked at from the vantage point of governmental policy and law, the truth is considerably more complicated.

Across the nation, governments enforced the principle of "coverture." Instead of stipulating marriage as an association of two separate and equal persons, this principle held that, despite its contractual origin, marriage transformed the status of two separate individuals into a publicly recognized legal and social unit. Married persons assumed new identities: husband and wife (Hartog 1991: 2, 13).

Marriage was understood as a public status regime. The laws of nature and God dictated the respective roles, rights and duties of husband and wife (Hartog 1991: 13; Regan 1993: 11; Singer 1992: 1456–63). Because men were viewed as naturally superior in reason and rulership, they were the sole legal representatives of the family. They were also responsible for financially supporting their wife and children. Coverture was embedded in a patriarchal culture that gave to men the exclusive right to vote, hold office and possess family property. Wives were obligated to obey and serve their husbands through their domestic labor and sexual accommodation. They could not enter into contracts, own assets, execute legal documents, or enter the labor market without their husband's consent (somewhat relaxed after mid-century). In short, a wife's legal personality was absorbed or "covered" by her husband (Cott 2000: 11–12, 54).

Despite approaching marriage as a permanent arrangement, Victorians did separate and sometimes divorce. Contrary to contemporary American conventions, separation was not necessarily a step towards divorce but often an occasion to modify the marital arrangement. Without a separation agreement, a wife could not live alone, negotiate a property settlement, use her own funds and earnings, or claim custody of her children (Hartog 1991: 7); also, even after establishing a separate household, she remained married.

States varied as to the conditions of divorce and its consequences, for example, whether the "guilty party" could remarry. Generally, to the extent that marriage was a status regime, divorce was not approached as a private, individual decision; rather, the state alone could grant divorce and only if a spouse failed to fulfill gender-based marital duties. Unfit or unsuitable husbands or wives were viewed as threats to the institution of marriage (Regan 1993: 12). "If a spouse was divorceable, it was because he or she had committed a public wrong against the marriage as much as a private one against the partner; the public wrong justified the state's interposing its authority" (Cott 2000: 49). Divorce, then, was not about reclaiming a right of intimate choice, but about punishing individuals incapable of participating in the institution of marriage (Hartog 1991: 11). Finally, because states made divorce difficult, many Americans simply abandoned their marriage and some remarried. Despite the Morrill Bill of 1862, which made bigamy a federal crime, "bigamy was rife in early America" (Hartog 1991: 11).

Although the government sought to protect marriage by claiming the exclusive right to dictate its form and its dissolution, by enforcing a rigid gender-based institution, and by prohibiting and often criminalizing nonmarital sexualities, its success was decidedly mixed. The combination of a weak federal government, the lack of uniform state laws, and the power of local nonstate authorities meant that customary law often trumped formal law. The former was local, often contested and at times disregarded.

A strong tradition of individual rights, state rights and religious freedom, along with a national preference for the regulatory authority of the market, yielded a weak federal government. For example, despite a moral panic whipped up by politicians and Christian leaders, which associated polygamy with barbarism and moral chaos, this practice, linked especially to Mormonism, was largely unregulated until the end of the 19th century. At this time, the US Congress (Edmunds-Tucker Act of 1887) and the Supreme Court, indicative of the beginning federalization of family law, threatened to deny statehood to Utah and dissolve the Mormon Church (Cott 2000: 119–21; Grossberg 1985: 123).

As the federal government ceded authority to states, the power of which was curtailed by church, local notables and tradition, the state had little power to enforce uniform norms of personal-relational life. For example, while restrictive antiabortion statutes passed in many states in the antebellum period, abortion remained a widely practiced birth control method. One historian estimates "that in midcentury there was one abortion for every five or six births" (cited in Grossberg 1985: 170). "Neither statutory revisions nor judiciary concessions stemmed the tide of women seeking abortions" (Grossberg 1985: 167). Grossberg concludes that "in many ways abortion was like prostitution which neither should nor could be admitted, legalized or eliminated" (Grossberg 1985: 168).

Often, laws pertaining to personal and family life varied widely between states and were unevenly enforced. A telling illustration is the somewhat unsettled and contested meaning of marriage in antebellum America, as manifest in the ambiguous status of common law or informal marriage ("marriages" lacking a state license). Despite the fact that such marriages occurred outside the law, and despite the wide range of relationships that might count as a common law marriage, they flourished well into the postbellum period (Dubler 1998: 1889). Indeed, the division over the legitimacy of informal marriage exposed a basic division: was marriage a private contract based on individual consent and personal well-being or a public status-based institution (Dubler 1998: 1894–95)? Given this cultural divide, it was hardly surprising that the enforcement of state-based marriage varied considerably across states and regions. "New England ... enacted the earliest and most comprehensive regulations [prohibiting informal marriage]; parts of the south and southwest had the least stringent ... [but] everywhere the law remained dependent on the initiative and competency of local officials and the willingness of couples to adhere to legal forms. To the dismay of

reformers ... common law marriage continued [throughout the century] ..."
(Grossberg 1985: 101).

Further limiting government control over intimate matters was the ambiguity
of Victorian categories stipulating erotic and intimate illegalities. For example,
sodomy statutes were often crafted to address specific "unnatural" acts, especially
anal sex and bestiality. However, such statutes were also used in sweeping, inclusive ways to refer to all nonprocreative sex. However, the courts often found that
enforcing this broad view of sodomy proved impossible. Thus, fellatio, [regardless
of the gender of the participants] was in principle enforceable under the broad
definition of sodomy, yet because it was not typically specified in sodomy laws, it
was almost never enforced (Painter 1991–2005). Making matters even more confusing, sodomy statutes rarely specified "sexual orientation." Although such laws
mostly targeted sex between two men, state statutes typically did not specify same-
sex sexual behavior. Setting aside its statutory indeterminacy, the reality was that
prior to 1900 sodomy laws were hardly ever enforced.

Victorians then relied less on the formal statutory power of the state than on
informal and often local authorities to regulate intimate life. Referring to the laws
and social policies governing personal and familial life in early 19th-century
America, Grossberg underscores "the antiregulatory bias of marriage law's formative era ... In many intimate areas—abortion, prostitution, age of consent,
informal marriage—behavior was regulated less by the state than by customary
law, family, and community ..." (Grossberg 1985: 107–8).

While state laws constructed marriage as a public institution and framed its
ideal gender, sexual and racial makeup, this institution gained its coherence and
authority by its embeddedness in everyday life. Yet, a weak state, one that relied
on local customs and authorities, meant that this institution coexisted with a
diverse world of marital and nonmarital intimacies. There was a fluidity and
plasticity in Victorian intimate matters that belies modern stereotypes. Informal
marriages, polygamy, bigamy, slave marriages, even interracial marriages, cohabitation and same-sex intimacies flourished alongside the rigid scripts of public
Victorian culture.

Modernizing marriage: the making of an "inclusive institution"

Between the 1880s and 1950s, America underwent dramatic changes. A world of
nonurban towns and villages governed by kinship, local customs and small state
governments gave way to an industrial, urban, bureaucratic welfare state. The
USA also became a world power.

Many Americans were unsettled by these transformations. In the pre-World
War I years, there was a pervasive sense of social crisis, and many Americans
believed that at its root was the instability of the institution of marriage.

Critics were alarmed that Americans were choosing to remain single well
into adulthood, divorcing with apparent ease, and tolerating the public pro-
liferation of pornography, prostitution and abortion. The surfacing of same-sex
cultures in major cities unsettled them. At the heart of a perceived crisis of

marriage was a deep anxiety about gender. Women were enrolling in colleges at unprecedented rates, participating in the wage labor market, mobilizing for the right to vote and participating in what was an exclusively male public nightlife. At the same time, more and more men were employed in bureaucratic organizations and their work lacked the essential features of Victorian masculinity, e.g. self-reliance and physical labor. If the line between women's and men's work and social life was blurring, what would happen to a gender-based heterosexual marital ideal?

In response to this moral and social crisis, some conservatives advised fortifying a Victorian order by enforcing the gender doctrine of separate spheres. Victorian-inspired moral crusaders and critics supported campaigns to fortify hegemonic masculine values while condemning movements and trends that narrowed the divide between men and women. At the opposite extreme, some radicals advocated a free love alternative, rejecting marriage as corrupting a pure love that should be free of all state interference.

Alongside these critics were liberal pragmatists who argued that securing marriage required its modernization. Modernizers claimed that marriage needed to be reformed in light of a changing America. They advocated three sets of changes. First, marriage should be the only legitimate staging ground for erotic-intimate relations. Contrary to Victorians, modernizers sought to denigrate or criminalize nonmarital intimacies. Second, marriage was conceived as an inclusive institution. Modernizers wished to bundle together sex, love, companionship and parenthood as defining of marriage. Third, in a stunning reversal of Victorianism, reformers argued that sexual love should be the cornerstone of marriage. Far from corrupting love and marriage, the sexual instinct was imagined as at the core of being human and should be at the heart of romantic love. The giving and receiving of erotic pleasure, which Victorians condemned, often in severe language, was now promoted as a way to express love, and, because sex was assumed to be natural and primitive, it could truly anchor the marital bond. However, in order for sex to secure love and marriage, men and women had to learn to approach their bodies and sensual desires without shame and guilt; they had to become skilled sexual citizens. In the early decades of the 20th century, mutual erotic satisfaction was proposed as a chief standard by which to judge true love and the likelihood of a successful marriage (Seidman 1991).

The spirit of mutuality and egalitarianism advocated in sexual love was indicative of a new marital ideal: husbands and wives were to become ideal companions. They were expected to fashion a joint life based on shared interests, values, friends and social activities. Passion, reciprocity and companionship became the signature markers of a modern marriage.

However, modernizers faced a dilemma: marriage was in crisis, and, in light of the turmoil of civil society in the early decades of the 20th century, reformers could not rely on civic or religious associations to reestablish its new foundations. They turned to the state (Grossberg 1982: 221, 225).

Between the 1880s and 1950s, the state intervened in specific yet far-reaching ways to enforce a specific marital ideal—heterosexual, racial, gender scripted, male dominated but no longer patriarchal, and as *the exclusive site of adult sexual intimacy* (Cohen 2002: 182–83). At times, the state simply formalized what were previously informal, customary laws. For example, outside of the South few states prohibited interracial marriage through the early postbellum period. Yet, by World War I, 42 states outlawed interracial marriage between whites and blacks and between whites and Asians (Coontz 2005: 213; Cott 2000: 40, 99, 164; Grossberg 1985: 139–40). Indeed, as late as 1967, 16 states still prohibited inter-racial marriage. At other times, the state legislation created new illegal sexualities. For example, whereas the Victorians lacked specific laws against same-sex sexu-alities, in the course of the 20th century, the state became a "straight state," enforcing a narrow hetero-normative nationalism while contributing to the making of a culture of homophobia (Canaday 2009; Eskridge 2002). At still other times, the state criminalized previously tolerated nonmarital intimacies. For example, by the early 1900s, informal marriages were outlawed in most states; marriage now required a state license and registration (Cott 2000: 89; Grossberg 1985: 92–93). Similarly, cohabitation, which was tolerated in the antebellum period, was now illegal. Finally, the state greatly limited who could gain access to marriage. Negroes could now marry within their racial group, but an influential eugenics movement helped to create new categories of people excluded from marriage, for example, the feebleminded, the idiot, epileptic and mentally re-tarded. Indeed, by 1931, the eugenics movement was so successful that 27 states passed mandatory sterilization laws to protect marriage from pollution by inferior and dangerous groups (Grossberg 1982: 221, 24).

However, modernizers aimed not only to secure but also to reform marriage. As we've seen, they advocated bringing Eros into the heart of love and marriage. At the same time, though, they sought to restrict sex to marriage. In this regard, modernizers lobbied the government to suppress and sometimes criminalize sexual representations, information and devices that might tempt the young or the morally weak to experiment with sex outside of marriage. For example, birth control was believed to threaten a slippage between sex and marriage. Moral crusaders like Anthony Comstock succeeded in getting the US Congress to outlaw the advertising and circulation of all birth control materials through the national mail system. By the early 20th century, many states passed laws criminalizing the mere possession of birth control devices (Cott 2000: 126).

Yet, contrary to Victorians, liberal reformers recognized that modern marriage could no longer rest on a rigidly patriarchal order. America was changing and these reformers embraced gender changes as a marker of progress. Modernizers aimed to realign marriage with the new spirit of equality and companionship. A modern marriage had to accommodate women's changing status without entirely upending patriarchy. How was this to be accomplished?

Modernizers turned to the state to take the lead in altering the gender organ-ization of marriage. In court decisions and legislation, the state, especially the federal government, affirmed the husband's ultimate authority in the family while acknowledging that women could no longer be denied basic rights and personal autonomy. In fact, by the early decades of the 20th century, women had gained the right to vote, hold office, own property, participate in a wage labor market without a husband's consent, and to enter freely into contracts (Cott 2000: 168).

The state effort to modify the gender divide contributed to the making of the new companionate marital ideal. Yet the state continued to uphold men's authority as the chief breadwinner and ruler of domestic and public life. For example, the GI Bill of 1944 amply rewarded returning veterans, 98% of them being men, by paying for their college tuition and board, offering cheap mortgage loans, subsidizing their medical care, providing pensions and favoring veterans for civil service jobs. Through the GI Bill and other federal legislation such as the Social Security Act and the Federal Income Tax Reform of 1948, the state reaffirmed a public world ruled by (white, heterosexual) men, despite women's enfranchisement (Cott 2000: 175–78; Canaday 2009: 170–71).

In the course of the 20th century, America became a marriage-obsessed nation. Starting in the 1920s and 1930s, Americans married earlier and more than any other European nation, and this held true across social class and ethnicity. By the 1960s, almost 95% of adults had married at some point in their lives (Cherlin 2009: 70). Historian Stephanie Coontz captures something of the growing power of marriage as an encompassing institution: "Marriage provided the context for just about every piece of most people's lives. It was the institution that moved you through life's stages. And it was where you expected to be when life ended" (Coontz 2005: 226).

The world of relationships

The campaign to modernize marriage rested on an exclusionary politic, as it stigmatized and sometimes criminalized nonmarital, interracial and non-heterosexual intimate practices. Ironically, this exclusionary dynamic set the stage for a reverse sexual politic. Individuals whose intimate preferences were disrespected appealed to a moral language of normality and a right to personal happiness to press for sexual-intimate rights and dignity. By the first decade of the 21st century, a critical identity politic could claim considerable success. In *Loving v Virginia* (1967), the Supreme Court declared the prohibition against interracial marriage unconstitutional. While the government continues to privilege heterosexuality, same-sex relationships are gaining public recognition and legitimacy, even if incompletely. Paralleling a trend towards deregulating intimate partner choice, the state has steadily (if still unevenly) backed women's independence, especially in their personal lives. Since the 1970s, a series of state policies and Supreme Court decisions have recognized a woman's right freely to enter and exit intimacies, to exercise sovereignty over her body and sexuality, including reproductive rights, to be protected from bodily violence, and to participate as an equal in intimate decisions (Singer 1992: 1458–60).

As a critical identity politics was democratizing marriage, the social status of this institution was undergoing a sea change. For many Americans today, marriage is no longer compulsory, even as it retains a privileged alliance with the state. The social compulsion to marry and the fateful consequences of being single have lessened dramatically (Klinenberg 2011). For many Americans, marriage today is one erotic-intimate arrangement alongside singledom, cohabitation, domestic partnership, civil union or coupledom without co-residence.

Despite its continued state establishment, marriage today is less an institution governed by rigid roles and scripts than an arrangement negotiated by two independent persons (Cherlin 2009: 7; Regan 1993: 39). Furthermore, all of the components that were bundled together in marriage—sex, love, companionship, parenthood and property—are independent arenas of decision making no longer inseparably wedded to marriage. The result has been a dizzying variety of erotic-intimate arrangements—for example, sex without love or marriage, intimacy without sex, parenthood without marriage, coupledom without monogamy, and so on.

I would characterize the change in American intimate culture as twofold. First, marriage has shifted from being a state-enforced legal and moral entity, socially compulsory and valued for its social role, to a private association of two equal persons seeking self-fulfillment and intimate solidarity (Cherlin 2009: 88; Singer 1992: 1463–65). Second, a marriage-centered order is giving way to a relationship-centered culture. To be sure, Americans marry at higher rates than any other European nation (for the African-American exception, see Cherlin 2009: 170). Yet, although marriage is still privileged by the state (Metz 2010: 3–4), it is, like nonmarital intimacies, a permanently impermanent arrangement ultimately resting on the private decisions of two independent persons who decide its form, internal organization and duration (Cherlin 2009: 7–9; Coontz 2005: 278–80). The reality is that, at any given moment, a majority of Americans are choosing nonmarital intimacies (Coontz 2005: 276).

In a relationship-centered culture, we feel entitled freely to form and dissolve relationships, but we also assume responsibility for their governance. Furthermore, although erotic relationships are forged and valued for a variety of reasons such as romantic love, economic security, social status and family making, their ultimate value today, for many Americans, is as sites of intimacy (Giddens 1992). For many Americans, too, intimacy is the chief staging ground to realize an authentic path to self-fulfillment along with a secure sense of belonging. Intimacy, however, also carries normative force; it compels selves to share their innermost interior lives and to explore depths of emotional, psychic openness and connection; it demands an empathic, trusting self for whom the sharing of one's inner life is to be treated as a sacred trust.

In contrast to previous marital orders, which relied on fairly rigid gender scripts and roles, relationships rest on a bedrock of ongoing communication. Of course, gender and other social statuses structure relational dynamics but, in principle, their influence can be thematized and made into a topic of deliberation. This condition of interpersonal reflexivity gives to relationships one of their defining features: they are arenas of dense talk and ongoing negotiation. Intimate decision making is supposed to be cooperative because relational partners are in principle equal, and because the grounds of intimate decision making are no longer taken for granted. For example, an appeal to rigid gender norms no longer suffices to regulate decisions about household tasks, sexual practice or career priorities.

A world of relationships is accompanied by its own normalizing regulations and expectations. For example, a certain level of competence is assumed in navigating intimacy. Relational partners are expected to be able to access their inner lives, communicate feelings, needs and desires, listen empathically, and skillfully negotiate the practical demands and disputes of routine intimate life. Likewise, intimate norms compel selves to be socially and emotionally capable of entering and exiting depthful relationships without "falling apart" or suffering a paralyzing rage or remorse. The norms, expectations and demands placed upon individuals by this culture of intimacy create their own performative tensions and failures and produce new forms of shame, anxiety, denigration and inferiorization.

Class politics in the age of relationships

The decline of marriage as a status regime was in part set in motion by state policies that empowered the individual as an intimate citizen. This transformation was made possible by the constitutionalization of privacy. Beginning in the 1960s and 1970s (*Griswold v. Conn.* (1965), *Eisenstadt v. Baird* (1972), *Roe v. Wade* (1973)), the state steadily recognized a personal sphere of decision making and behavior relating to one's body, sexuality and intimacies that deserve legal protection from arbitrary state or citizen interference (Cohen 2002: 41–44). The core juridical unit of the private realm is no longer a marital or family entity but the individual (Regan 1993: 11; Cohen 2002: 38–44; Glendon 1989; Singer 1992: 1510–14). From this perspective, erotic-intimate relations (between consensual adults) are approached as a contractual association between two independent individuals, rather than a marital system of statuses and roles, e.g. husband, wife, parent and child (Cohen 2002: 187; Regan 1993: 39). As Chief Justice Brennan famously wrote in *Eisenstadt v. Baird*, "The married couple is not an independent entity with a mind and heart of its own, *but an association of two individuals each with a separate intellectual and emotional make-up*" (cited in Cohen 2002: 186). The juridical construction of privacy as a site for the individual to exercise decisional autonomy established a safe and secure personal space. This made it possible for individuals to be psychologically vulnerable and innovative in their intimate choices. A new "intimate citizen" stepped forward: a reflective, ethical agent entitled to fashion her own personal-relational life (Cohen 2002: 28, 51).

This citizen is not just an abstract construction of the law. The state has in fact enacted laws protecting the individual's intimate decision making, for example, from arbitrary citizen and state discrimination or from domestic violence. Simultaneously, the state empowered the individual to exercise relational autonomy by granting her rights, e.g. reproductive rights, basic civil rights (e.g. gay men and lesbians), and access to sexual information and images. Intimate autonomy would be seriously compromised if the state didn't also recognize a plurality of intimate behaviors and arrangements that previously were either lacking legal protection or occupied an inferior legal status, e.g. cohabitation, domestic partnership, common law marriage and many forms of adult consensual nonmarital sex. Although the state has been a driving force of intimate variation, it continues to privilege heterosexual marriage, even if it is no longer compulsory. The contradictory role of the state as enforcing the normativity of heterosexual marriage while legitimating the pluralization of intimate life is at the heart of the current politics of same-sex marriage (Calhoun 2003; Metz 2010: ch. 5; Seidman 2002).

The other side to the enfranchisement of an intimate citizen has been the steady withdrawal of the state from wide swatches of personal-relational life. Two aspects of state deregulation of intimate life are noteworthy.

First, despite the ongoing "establishment" of marriage, the state no longer enforces one model of marriage. Apart from licensing, the state has ceded authority to private individuals to determine just about everything else about the social organization of marriage, e.g. partner selection (ending restrictions for the mentally retarded, prison inmates, guilty divorcees and persons of different races), domestic roles, and whether or not to have children, be monogamous, cohabit and so on. The dissolution of a marriage, which until recently depended on gender role violations by the husband or wife to be adjudicated by the courts, today requires only the decision of either party to initiate proceedings (Singer 1992: 1497–1508). The passage of no fault divorce in virtually every state by 1985 effectively authorizes spouses to negotiate privately the end of a marriage (Regan 1993: 38–39; Singer 1992: 1471–75). Prenuptial agreements, as a civic contract between two individuals, have sidelined the state's role in property distribution in the event of marital breakup. Even more telling of a trend towards the privatization of intimate life is the elimination of a two-centuries-old state enforcement of marriage as a condition of legitimate parenthood. Previously, a child born out of wedlock could not legally make economic claims on her biological father, could be taken away from her biological mother and given up for adoption, or could not recover debts owed to her mother or father (Coontz 2005: 257). In *Levy v. Louisiana* (1968), the Supreme Court ruled that children of unwed parents should enjoy the same Fourteenth Amendment rights as those of married parents. Today, the state recognizes the parental rights of biological parents, whether they are single or married. Similarly, US courts recognize the right of children to be supported by their biological parents, including a right of inheritance, regardless of the parent's marital status (Coontz 2005: 256–57; Singer 1992: 1448). Underlying this legal shift in the status of parenthood and childhood is the reality that almost as many children are born to cohabitating couples as to married ones (Coontz 2005: 264).

Second, the state has lifted many restrictions on nonmarital sexualities and intimacies. The trend in American jurisprudence has been towards blurring the distinction between marital and nonmarital sexual intimacies (Regan 1993: 122–23; Singer 1992: 1446–55). On the one hand, laws criminalizing a wide range of sexual-intimate practices that were perceived as encouraging nonmarital intimacies have been abolished or greatly weakened. Abortion, birth control, pornography, cohabitation, fornication, adultery, sodomy and in many respects homosexuality are today either legal or decriminalized. On the other hand, state recognition and rights that were previously restricted to heterosexual marriage have been extended, even if unevenly and often unequally, to nonmarital behaviors. For example, as a status regime, marital law recognized a set of rights, benefits and obligations attached to married persons that were denied to cohabitants, e.g. the latter could not avail in the courts of divorce proceedings to end a relationship.

> In the past several decades the courts have narrowed the divide between married and cohabitants. e.g. courts recognize cohabitants as having the right to adjudicate the dissolution of their relationship and, like marriage, the courts can impose financial and other obligations on cohabitants; equally telling, domestic partnerships extend benefits to partners that were previously restricted to family members such as health insurance, pensions, family leave, or survivor benefits.
>
> (Regan 1993: 123)

One consequence of state recognition of nonmarital practices is the social legitimation of a culture tolerant of a multiplicity of forms of intimate life (Cohen 2002: 7, 28). The state, especially the federal government (with the qualified exception of homosexuality), has enfranchised adult Americans as intimate citizens by providing strong constitutional and legislative protections for a personal life that gives to individuals considerable decisional autonomy with regard to bodily, sexual, relational decision making. It is in part the retreat of the state as a moral agency regulating personal affairs that accounts for the rise of the New Right and the politicization of evangelical Christians (on the dissociation of law and morality, see Singer 1992: 1527). Although the struggle over state power remains an important site of current sexual politics (e.g. same-sex marriage, reproductive rights, welfare reform), the shape of sexual and intimate life is increasingly dependent on the forces of civil society, e.g. social movements, churches, medical-therapeutic institutions, civic associations, unions and political parties.

There is another aspect to the privatization of sexual-intimate life: the state is not obligated to provide the kinds of social support such as family work leave, access to inexpensive birth control, universal healthcare, comprehensive sex education, or the full enfranchisement of nonheterosexual intimacies that would allow all Americans to exercise fully their intimate rights (for other critiques of privatization, see Cohen 2002; and Singer 1992: 1540–56). In fact, since welfare reform during the Clinton years (Personal Responsibility and Work Opportunity Reconciliation Act of 1996), there has been a concerted effort to reduce social benefits (e.g. the "family cap" that prohibits the state from increasing cash benefits to welfare mothers who give birth) and to tighten eligibility requirements (e.g. mandatory paternity identification).

The reduction of state support seriously compromises the intimate autonomy of Americans receiving social welfare. In *Welfare Reform and Sexual Regulation*, Anna Marie Smith argues: "we are witnessing the State's withdrawal from the poor where redistribution is concerned. *At the same time, however, the state is intervening quite intensely in the intimate lives of the poor*" (Smith 2007: 4, my emphasis). To illustrate the latter point, consider that, to qualify for TANF (Temporary Assistance for Needy Families), applicants must identify the biological father *and* cooperate with the state in enforcing his child support. If the alleged father denies paternity, he and the mother may be required to provide sworn testimony detailing their sexual histories in order to determine the credibility of her accusation. If this doesn't resolve the issue, the mother, child and father must undergo genetic testing as a condition of maintaining eligibility (Smith 2007: 120–21). In effect, welfare recipients, disproportionately young, poor, nonwhite and mothers surrender their full constitutional right of privacy and sexual autonomy. Whereas higher-income, resource-rich citizens can purchase access to family planning, therapists, private physicians and clinics, and legal services, welfare recipients are routinely compelled to expose their intimate lives to scrutiny by the state; their intimate decisions may be shaped by a need to maintain eligibility.

Arguably, welfare reform can be understood in part as a strategy to enlist the state in securing a hetero-marital regime that is being challenged. Thus, TANF provides funds to promote sexual abstinence while unmarried women are encouraged to postpone child bearing, limit family size, and to align sex and parenthood to marriage. Considering the individual components of TANF—family cap, family planning services, paternity identification, teen pregnancy prevention programs, sexual abstinence education and marriage promotion campaigns—welfare policy today authorizes strategies of state intrusion into the personal lives of its recipients aimed at pressuring disadvantaged Americans to normalize their intimate lives by adopting a hetero-marital, monogamous and nuclear family norm.

Intimate relationships are, then, a field of expanded choice but also are burdened by scarcities, insecurities, and state-imposed dependencies and intrusions. This dialectic of intimate freedom and constraint is unevenly distributed across America. Those with economic capital can purchase domestic labor, daycare, good schools, private counseling, healthcare and legal services; they can afford to take a family leave or pursue paths to parenthood through expensive alternatives such as surrogacy and adoption. Suggestive of the class politics of intimacy, consider that college-educated Americans marry at relatively high rates, which allows them access to a court system to resolve relational conflicts around finances, bodily protection and child custody. By contrast, less-educated Americans cohabit at higher rates than their better-educated counterparts, and are more likely to bear children out of wedlock. Lacking a marital status, cohabitants have less access to courts to resolve intimate disputes (Cherlin 2009: 166–70). Many lower-income Americans can neither rely on the state, which has been steadily reducing aid, nor draw on private capital to underwrite a support system for their intimate choices. Instead, they are dependent on an already stressed-out informal network of kin, lovers and friends. If lower-income citizens do receive government benefits, they are subject to forms of state intrusion into their personal lives of which resource-rich citizens are free.

Class dynamics are then at the heart of intimate politics today. Economic inequalities translate into unequal opportunities for exercising intimate choice, but cultural disparities also result in the unequal distribution of the sensibilities and competences to negotiate intimacy effectively. Broadly speaking, college-educated, middle-class individuals have wide access to the cultural resources that enable them to acquire the dispositions and capacities to be skilled in intimate relationships. By contrast, lower-income, less-educated Americans will likely have less access to cultural environments such as psychotherapies, countercultural or new age cultures, high-brow humanistic cultures, and feminisms. I'm suggesting that these Americans will lack the symbolic capital for cultivating the specific kinds of psycho-social sensibilities and competences (mutual depthful self-disclosure, egalitarian negotiation of roles, communicative-based solidarity) that would enhance their prospects at succeeding in a relational order organized around the norm and ideal of intimacy.

There is, then, a disparity between an emerging intimate cultural ideal and the inequality of material and cultural conditions that shape relational capacities. Burdened already by status deflation by working in low-prestige and -income jobs, these individuals may also suffer cultural devaluation and inferiorization because their relationships lack the signature indicators of intimate fulfillment, e.g. depthful sharing, processing of feelings, and a communicative-based, egalitarian-oriented ideal of intimate solidarity.

Why, though, has this *specific idea and norm of intimacy* become a moral yardstick to judge our relationships? After all, for a very long time, marriage, the exemplary intimate institution, was valued for enacting a natural gender order, for family making, or for securing domestic and civil order. Intimacy, at least its current articulation, hardly figured in defining a good or successful marriage through most of the 20th century. If intimacy is being promoted today as the über norm of a good relationship, it is, I submit, partly explained by the cultural authority of a segment of the middle class that came of age in the 1960s and 1970s. A baby-boomer generation and their immediate successors achieved adulthood having absorbed in some manner countercultural, therapeutic and feminist cultures, which value personal authenticity, self-realization, egalitarianism and an ethic of mutuality. This middle-class generation sought to bring these ideals into their close personal relationships, whether friendships or romances. Furthermore, this middle-class segment entered adulthood precisely at an historical moment that saw the unprecedented expansion of the helping professions, healthcare, the humanities, teaching, the academy, and the world of art and entertainment—institutional sectors that incorporated something of this cultural sensibility. I'm arguing that a segment of the baby-boomer middle class, initially coming of age during the cultural shifts in the 1960s and 1970s while claiming full adulthood precisely as these cultural sensibilities and ideals were gaining institutional traction in the world of work, family and popular culture, has been a driving force in promoting a cultural norm and ideal that today claims moral authority (Bell 1996; Binkley 2007; Martin 1981; Bourdieu 1984).

It is not possible for me to address the broader context that shaped this intimate ideal and contributed to its current salience. To cite the obvious, long-term trends associated with changing gender dynamics, the "triumph of the therapeutic" and the emergence of the erotic as an autonomous sphere of value, along with social movements associated with the counterculture, feminism and gay/lesbian liberationism, and a wave of sexual "enlightenment" discourses associated with sex reformers, played a formative role in promoting a new culture of intimacy (Seidman 1992). In a very preliminary and speculative way, I wish to sketch one thread of this story: the role of class anxieties and ambitions. To simplify, this baby-boomer middle-class segment leaned heavily on its appeal to this relational ideal, and its claim to intimate virtuosity, to assert its class identity and project its moral authority in a world where it saw itself as losing ground.

Championing its charisma as intimate citizens is one way this class sought to differentiate itself from blue-collar Americans. The latter is denigrated as relationally underdeveloped and therefore psychologically and morally inferior. Their relational incompetence undermines blue-collar aspirations to middle-class status, regardless of their material life.

The assertion of intimate charisma is also a way this middle-class faction aims to differentiate from other sectors of the middle and upper class. Although the latter may have higher economic and cultural capital, they too are judged lacking because their relationships are said to be mired in traditional models of marriage. These movers and shakers of America are said to lack a meaningful connection to countercultural, therapeutic and feminist cultures. For example, purveyors of intimate fulfillment believe that the workplace in finance, big business, engineering and the law are not friendly to a culture that pivots around vulnerability, emotional openness, egalitarianism or gender flexibility. So, while these power brokers may own high-end art, support museums and cultural organizations, and conduct cosmopolitan lives, such cultural capital does not necessarily translate into sensibilities and skills that cultivate intimacy-oriented relationships.

To summarize, I am suggesting that a sector of the middle class, one that imagines itself as a cultural vanguard, has attempted to elevate a specific culture of intimacy, one featuring a grammar of authenticity, mutual depthfulness, and a quest for an intense, egalitarian, communicative-based solidarity, into a primary marker of class identity and a moral ground for claiming social authority. Anxiously looking backward as blue-collar workers claim equal social status, and glancing sideways and above as a financial-corporate elite accumulate considerable wealth and power, this middle-class segment has staked out a claim for moral and cultural superiority based, in part, on their relational charisma.

The new politics of intimacy ultimately goes beyond class. To the extent that a specific intimate norm has gained broad cultural authority, it creates a layered order of social divisions and hierarchies. Those social classes, ethnicities, sexual and gender populations, nationalities, or disabled populations, whose close relationships do not exhibit psychological openness, inner depthfulness, empathy, dense reciprocal communication, and whose relationships are not articulated in a grammar of authenticity, self-realization and relational growth, will be culturally devalued, perhaps disrespected or even pathologized. These citizens will be vulnerable to suffering a sense of cultural inferiority and marginalization.

Admittedly, this new relational politics has not yet moved into the frontline of sexual politics. The power of the New Right to project the politics of marriage into the forefront of public debate, and also the rallying of the gay and lesbian movement around same-sex marriage, has perpetuated a misleading perception that marriage is still at the center of American intimate life. However, as the social issues focus of the New Right gives way to the economic class agenda of the Tea Party, and as this is echoed on the left in the Occupy Wall Street movement, we might expect that the class politics of intimacy may also receive long-overdue scholarly and political attention.

Acknowledgements

I am grateful for the helpful and generous comments by Alan Frank, Jeff Alexander, Patricia Clough and Linda Nicholson.

References

Bell, Daniel. 1996. *The Cultural Contradictions of Capitalism*. NY: Basic.
Binkley, Sam. 2007. *Getting Loose*. Durham, NC: Duke University Press.
Bourdieu, Pierre. 1984. *Distinction*. NY: Routledge.
Calhoun, Cheshire. 2003. *Feminism, the Family, and the Politics of the Closet*. NY: Oxford University Press.
Canaday, Margot. 2009. *The Straight State*. Princeton: Princeton University Press.
Cherlin, Andrew. 2009. *The Marriage-Go-Round*. NY: Alfred A. Knopf.
Cohen, Jean. 2002. *Regulating Intimacy*. Princeton: Princeton University Press.
Coontz, Stephanie. 2005. *Marriage, A History*. NY: Penguin.
Cott, Nancy. 2000. *Public Vows*. Cambridge, Ma.: Harvard University Press.
D'Emilio, John and Estelle Freedman. 1998. *Intimate Matters*. Chicago: University of Chicago Press.
Dubler, Ariela R. 1998. "Governing through Contract: Common Law Marriage in the Nineteenth Century." *Yale Law Journal* 107: 1885–920.
Eskridge, William Jr. 2002. *Gaylaw*. Cambridge, Ma: Harvard University Press.
Faderman, Lillian. 1992. *Odd Girls, Twilight Lovers*. NY: Penguin.
Fineman, Martha Albertson. 1995. *The Neutered Mother, the Sexual Family, and Other Twentieth Century Tragedies*. NY: Routledge.
Giddens, Anthony. 1992. *The Transformation of Intimacy*. Stanford, Ca.: Stanford University Press.
Glendon, Ann. 1989. *The Transformation of Family Law*. Chicago: University of Chicago Press.
Grossberg, Michael. 1982. "Guarding the Alter: Physiological Restrictions and the Rise of State Intervention in Matrimony." *The American Journal of Legal History* XXVI (July): 197–226.
——1985. *Governing the Hearth*. Chapel Hill, NC: University of North Carolina Press.
Hartog, Hendrik. 1991. "Marital Exits and Marital Expectations in Nineteenth Century America." *Georgetown Law Journal* 95.
Ingraham, Chrys. 2008. *White Weddings*. 2nd edn. NY: Routledge.
Klinenberg, Eric. 2011. *Going Solo*. NY: Penguin.
Lystra, Karen. 1992. *Searching the Heart*. NY: Oxford University Press.
Martin, Bernice. 1981. *Sociology of Contemporary Cultural Change*. London: Palgrave.
Metz, Tamara. 2010. *Untying the Knot*. Princeton: Princeton University Press.
Painter, George. 1991–2005. "The Sensibilities of our Forefathers: A History of Sodomy Laws in the United States." www.glapn.org/sodomylaws/sensibilities/introduction.htm.
Regan, Milton Jr. 1993. *Family Law and the Pursuit of Intimacy*. NY: NYU Press.
Rothman, Ellen. 1987. *Hands and Hearts*. Cambridge, Ma: Harvard University Press.
Rotundo, Anthony. 1994. *American Manhood*. NY: Basic.
Seidman, Steven. 1991. *Romantic Longings*. NY: Routledge.

——1992. *Embattled Eros*. NY: Routledge.

——2002. *Beyond the Closet*. NY: Routledge.

Singer, Jana. 1992. "The Privatization of Family Law." *Wisconsin Law Review*: 1442–1567.

Smith, Anna Marie. 2007. *Welfare Reform and Sexual Regulation*. Cambridge: Cambridge University Press.

Smith-Rosenberg, Carroll. 1986. *Disorderly Conduct*. NY: Oxford University Press.

2 Let me tell you who I am

Intimacy, privacy and self-disclosure

Linda Nicholson

For many in the contemporary USA, including myself, self-disclosure is an important means by which we establish and measure intimacy. Many of us measure how close we are with another human being in large part by how much they know about us: how much we have revealed about our pasts and how much we have disclosed about our inner hopes and desires.

To be sure, there are other ways in which many of us establish and measure intimacy: through sex and other forms of physical contact, and through sharing experiences and time with another. However, while self-disclosure is not the only means by which intimacy is established and measured, it is today in the USA a very important means. However, running counter to this almost obvious fact is another important phenomenon of contemporary life: self-disclosure about our inner selves, the kind of self-disclosure that has been associated with intimate relationships, now also can be found in many contexts that are public and occupied by strangers. On daytime television shows, in the self-confessions of prominent figures in book memoirs and magazine articles, and on Facebook sites where many make public the details of their daily lives, self-disclosure about the "intimate" details of one's "private" life also flourishes. Thus, on the one hand, many of us believe in an inner self that can and should be revealed only to some in circumscribed contexts. We define intimacy in large part by who is allowed access to this part of who we are. On the other hand, the world we inhabit is also increasingly populated by the public presentations of the "private" lives of strangers.

In this essay, I want to address this complex relationship among intimacy, privacy and self-disclosure in the present moment in US history. I want to address the question of how disclosure about certain deep and important aspects of who we are, aspects of the self that have been understood as "private," both functions as a means and measure of intimacy for some, yet is also accepted by many others as legitimately present in non-intimate settings. I want to clarify how the relationship among intimacy, privacy and self-disclosure has come to be so complex in our own time.

I will claim that the meanings of intimacy, privacy and self-disclosure, and their associations with each other, have travelled a curious path in the USA from the 19th century to the present. During the 19th century, particularly for an emerging middle class in the northeast of the USA, private life became significantly, though not exclusively, associated with domestic space and with the family unit that occupied such space. This association of privacy with the domestic/familial unit intensified in the early 20th century as the domestic family unit became more nuclear and as companionate marriage undercut the importance of homosocial relationships among middle-class women and men. In the first half of the 20th century, this understanding of private life as principally centered within the family became elaborated as a narrative about how the private, i.e. the familial, part of the self, can cause dysfunction in our adult selves. At this time, members of the middle class increasingly explained problems in the behavior of poor and working-class people by appeal to deficiencies within the early family lives of members of these groups. This narrative was also used in less extensive ways by members of the middle class to explain problems in their own lives that they could not handle themselves. In both cases, this early 20th-century narrative allowed for the construction of new "private" spaces where self-disclosure was legitimate: the spaces of professional mental health workers whose job was to repair the problematic consequences of early private lives. This migration of self-disclosure to the offices of mental health workers did not challenge the association of self-disclosure with privacy; it did, however, begin to mark the disassociation of self-disclosure with intimacy.

By the 1960s and 1970s, as a new generation of an expanded middle class began to question older forms of family life, so did members of this generation also more publicly scrutinize and talk about their own inner lives. This discourse was symptomatic of a greater openness towards disclosure of "private" life. The "personal" had not only become "political"; it had also become more public. This growing "publicity" about what had been thought of as "private life" not only continued an earlier disassociation of self-disclosure with intimacy, but it also began to challenge the association of self-disclosure with privacy.

The "publicization" of private life has intensified in the last several decades aided by continued questioning about the nature and meaning of close human relationships and by the growth and expanded use of new technologies of communication. This increase in the publicization of private life has caused some critics to question whether there still exist realms of privacy and intimacy at all. I urge caution about such claims. For one, while private life has become more public, many still employ criteria distinguishing what should and should not be made available for general view. Indeed, the co-existence of very disparate ideas about privacy and intimacy in our present social world is largely responsible for our present confusion about privacy, intimacy and self-disclosure. Also, however, I suggest that what we see as the simple erasure of privacy and intimacy at least partly reflects changed meanings of both. When we read the intimate details about a famous person's family history or create zones of privacy within such Internet spaces as Facebook, we are moving away from an understanding of privacy and intimacy rooted in older forms of a separation between private and public to understandings of privacy and intimacy based upon newer forms of this separation.

The 19th-century background

As I claimed in the above, part of our present understanding of "private life" originates in the 19th-century association of "privacy" with the family: with sex and with interactions among close family members. This particular understanding of private life is itself the historical legacy of changes in the meaning of "family" occurring over the early modern period, where "family" shed both its inclusion of domestic servants and also came to accentuate immediate family ties (Nicholson 1986: 105–30). By the 19th century, and particularly for members of a new middle class that was developing in the northeastern part of the USA, this evolution resulted in a declining importance of extended kin and community in constituting emotionally significant relationships and a drawing inward of such relationships to immediate family ties.

This inward turn for members of the 19th-century middle class meant that family life came to represent a kind of "hidden lair in which men and women bound up their wounds, recouped their forces and acted out their passions with manageable risks" (Gay 1984: 459). This hidden lair became depicted in the word "home," a word that captured the emotional significance former aristocrats had placed in the word "house." Whereas "house" had depicted a family's lineage and social networks outside of the nuclear family, and was associated with such emotions as honor and dignity, "home" referred to the space occupied by one's closest family members and was associated with the emotions of intimacy, privacy and affection (Coontz 2005: 164). The narrowing of emotional connections to one's immediate family during the 19th century was exemplified in a variety of ways. Honeymoons, for example, became less often vacations a newly married couple shared with friends or other relatives to an event strictly limited to the newly married couple. Holidays such as Thanksgiving and Christmas became less community and more family focused and augmented with celebrations that focused on events within the individual family, such as birthdays and anniversaries (Coontz 2005: 166–67).

However, privacy and intimacy, while increasingly centered for the 19th-century middle class within the home, was not exclusively centered there. "Private life" also included domains where women and men interacted in close relationships. Close emotional connections were allowed among adult female friends. Even men were permitted such closeness with other non-family-related men, though with men such intimacies were more expected to conclude upon marriage (Coontz 2005: 184–85). While feelings of connection to nuclear family members did intensify in the 19th century, people still felt a greater sense of connection to members of their birth family than would be the case in the 20th century (Coontz 2005: 183). In short, as "private life" was not strictly limited to the 19th-century household, so privacy, intimacy and self-disclosure were not limited to interactions among those family members sharing a domestic space.

However, while the realm of "private life" was not limited to the domestic/ family unit, the family had become a very important site of the private. As Peter Gay states, "No other class at any other time was more strenuously, more anxiously devoted to the appearances, to the family and to privacy, no other class has ever built fortifications for the self quite so high" (Gay 1984: 403). Ironically, one sign of the constraints put upon self-disclosure was the flourishing of a certain form of self-disclosure: diary and personal journal writing. The secrecy associated with diary writing meant that self-disclosure was to be kept under wraps. Diary writing is found outside of the 19th-century middle class; however, what is distinctive here is the extent to which diaries and personal journal writing were encouraged and employed. For many, the diary became a kind of personal friend: the "person" one could entrust with one's most private thoughts (Gay 1984: 445–52). One might say that diary and personal writing functioned as the 19th-century version of blogging and tweeting. The one important difference, however, is that the former, unlike the latter, were kept under lock and key.

There is another arena of 19th-century self-disclosure that, like diary writing, ironically points to the constraints placed *upon* self-disclosure: middle-class courtship letters. As Karen Lystra's analysis of such letters reveals, the writers of such letters understood themselves and each other as possessing an inner, more idiosyncratic self not accessible through observations of public behavior. Indeed, they understood such behavior as potentially concealing a more hidden but "truer" self (Lystra 1989: 32–38). One of the important functions of their letter writing was to reveal to the other this truer self, since it was only upon a foundation of such knowledge that a true marriage could be built (Seidman 1991: 46, 60). Thus, these letters served to bridge the gap that existed between one's public and private self in the construction of a new family unit.

As the above suggests, the 19th century did not give rise only to a separation between private and public spheres of society; it gave rise also to the idea of a separation between private and public parts of the self. This point is reinforced by the claims of many intellectual historians that it was in the late 18th and early 19th centuries when new ideas began to emerge about a deep inner self that can only be reached through inward reflection. Charles Taylor, for example, while noting an orientation to inwardness in such early modern thinkers as Descartes and Montaigne, and in practices of moral and religious self-exploration, argues that it was not until the late 18th century that this inner self was understood as possessing an inexhaustible depth (Taylor 1989: 389). Associated with this idea of a deep inner self was also the idea that access to this deep inner self could be found in our powers of expression.

> This concept of an inexhaustible inner domain is the correlative of the power of expressive self-articulation. The sense of depth in inner space is bound up with the sense that we can move into it and bring things to the fore. This we do when we articulate ... This notion of inner depths is therefore intrinsically linked to our understanding of ourselves as expressive, as articulating an inner source.
>
> (Taylor 1989: 390)

Taylor uses the term "expressivism" to describe this worldview. Others have used the category of "romanticism" to describe overlapping phenomena. The romantic movement commonly refers to that group of 19th-century writers and artists who reacted against the enlightenment belief in the transparency of mind and of what the mind reveals. Against such transparency, romantic writers postulated an inner self that is accessible only through deep exploration. The division between what appears on the surface and what exists underneath was understood by romantics as reflecting a separation between a public self governed by convention and a deep inner self that is both more "natural" and real, and yet also potentially threatening to the social order.[1]

As I have been emphasizing in the above, this separation of private from public spheres and of a private and public self was a middle-class phenomenon. Certainly, elements of similar changes in the relationship of private to public life can also be found in working-class families of the latter part of the 19th century. As has been often noted, the 19th-century middle-class separation of private and public was heavily gender coded, with the wife's retreat from public spaces serving as an important sign of the family's ability to keep their private life private. Working-class families—though white working-class families to a greater degree than black working-class families—also maintained a gender division between private and public life as they similarly tried to keep married women at home. Working-class families in the cities also tended to become more nuclear in form and, like middle-class families, drew firm lines of separation between home life and work life (Coontz 1988: 256–63).

Yet there also existed many important differences between middle-class and both black and white working-class experiences of "private life." Whereas members of middle-class families tended to withdraw from extended kinship networks and community by the latter part of the 19th century, both black and white working-class families continued to rely heavily on extended family and community ties for both economic and social support. Black families, in particular, took into their families the elderly, and those without means of support, rather than institutionalizing them (Coontz 1988: 306–16). Also, both black and white working-class families lived much more of their nonwork lives with similar others in crowded living conditions, on the street, or within community associations. This meant that "private life" was less centered upon the domestic family unit and more shared with those to whom one could turn in need. One consequence is that, among such groups, the distinction between "private" and "public" would be less experienced as a sense of separation between a private self centered within the home and a public self that one showed outside of the home.[2] It would instead be experienced as the difference in one's sense of self in different social spaces.[3]

The early 20th-century psychological self

The 19th-century separation between private and public life and of a private and public self was transformed in the 20th century in complex ways. More people emigrated to the cities to live in new kinds of households and to participate in new types of social recreation, social institutions and jobs. One aspect of these shifts is that the meaning of marriage changed, as a growing number of advice givers pushed an ideal of marriage as based upon friendship and love. As Steven Seidman has argued, an idea of marriage as based upon love and companionship had been an important part of middle-class Victorian culture. Yet, as he notes, a sharp division of gender roles, a norm of large families, and women's social, economic and political subordination to men had made this ideal often hard to achieve. In the first half of the 20th century, with changes in women's education

and social roles, with a dramatic decline in family size and with the commercialization of many family tasks, the ideal became more reachable for many (Seidman 1991: 81). Moreover, as couples were finding it more possible to create
marriages based upon friendship and sexual intimacy, so also were they giving less
attention to extended family ties and to same-sex friendships (Coontz 2005: 207).

Associated with this greater emphasis on the importance of emotional ties
among the members of a more nuclear family unit was also a greater sense of
immediate family interactions as the source of the self. During the 19th century,
economic success or failure had often been attributed to poor parenting (Coontz
1988: 252), and, as I have noted, it was in the 19th century that there developed
the idea of a private, inner self that could potentially disrupt one's public behavior. However, in the early 20th century, both this emphasis on the home and
immediate family as the source of the self and the idea of one's private self as a
source of possible disruption to one's public self became strengthened and elaborated through the growing importance of dynamic psychology as a framework
through which many came to understand themselves and others: as beings whose
"inner self" is largely formed by the experiences one has as a child within the
family and which can potentially influence one's public behavior.

One obvious example of this new way of thinking about the self can be found
in the ideas of Freud, ideas that gained wide currency in the early part of the
20th century. Freud fairly early in his career moved away from looking for the
causes of mental disturbances in the body and towards searching for such causes
in the mind. Thus, like 19th-century mind cure practitioners, Freud began
searching for the underlying mental rather than physiological causes of disturbed
behavior. However, unlike such 19th-century predecessors, Freud soon came to
think about the "private" and "inner self"—or what he came to call the
"unconscious"—as an underlying cause of much human behavior.[4]

At first, adherents to Freudian theory were mostly situated in the large cities of
the northeast and were members of a new professional middle and upper class
(Hale 1995: 75–76). However, during the 1930s and 1940s, some of the basic
tenets of Freud became more widely dispersed through popularizations in widely
read media. Among the tributes at Freud's death in 1939 was a picture of Freud
on the cover of *Time* magazine (Hale 1995: 79). This popularization was aided by
the growth of a vast new regime of mental health professionals, some of whom
saw in Freud's writings a science-based theory to counter those who appealed to
religion and tradition.

> Psychoanalysis became a player in the cultural wars that pitted those who
> continued to defend "civilized" sexual morality, which prescribed continence,
> intercourse only for procreation, monogamous, lifelong marriage, and reti-
> cence about sex, against those who advocated birth control, divorce by
> mutual consent, and frank sex education.
>
> (Hale 1995: 80)

Not only did Freudianism provide support to some mental health professionals,
but such professionals also gave support to Freudianism. Freudianism achieved a

significant amount of popularity in the early 20th-century USA because it was part of a larger movement of those who stressed the importance of early childhood experiences in the making of the adult self. During the progressive era, a growing army of social reformers began challenging older ideas on how best to deal with social deviancy. Instead of looking to punishment and warehousing as the best means to deal with criminals, school rebels or the poor, these reformers advocated changing the beliefs and attitudes of members of these groups, beliefs and attitudes that they identified as the root causes of such social problems (Moskowitz 2001: 30–68). According to such reformers, it was a problematic early home life that generated such ill-adaptive beliefs and attitudes.

> Like their Victorian forebears, progressive era reformers viewed the domestic realm as a critical area of intervention. But in direct contrast to their forebears, they saw the home, not as a haven, but as a source of social pathology. In the new therapeutic theory, the home warped the psychologies of its members.
>
> (Moskowitz 2001: 55)

In the 1920s and 1930s, such reformers were joined by experts in the mental hygiene movement, as well as by experts in such growing fields as marriage counseling and industrial psychology (Hale 1995: 84–85; Illouz 2008: 66–104; Moskowitz 2001: 30–99). Members of all of these groups began focusing on the task of transforming disruptive beliefs and attitudes acquired early in life into more adaptive ones. Thus, marriage clinics spread during the 1920s and 1930s (Moskowitz 2001: 81). Accompanying this spread was the expansion of marriage counseling as a field within higher education, high schools, social welfare agencies and private philanthropic organizations (Moskowitz 2001: 98). The growth of marriage counseling as a legitimate area of inquiry in turn gave rise to an explosion of books, journal articles and even the development of new journals devoted to this topic. Within such books and journals, authors appealed to both sociological and psychological causes of marital discord and marital harmony (Moskowitz 2001: 82–99).

This growing emphasis on childhood experiences as a cause of adult dysfunction can also be found in the area of industrial psychology. Whereas, up until the 1920s, those who sought to "rationalize" the workplace looked at the organization of work as a type of social system requiring social engineering, in the 1920s, psychologists began to take over the field. Beginning with World War I, psychologists had begun to create a new subfield known as "personnel psychology." Following the war, this body of knowledge spread from the army to society at large as US universities began offering doctoral degrees in industrial psychology (Illouz 2008: 66–88). In industrial psychology as well as in the many other ways in which dynamic psychology was influencing American society, it was the family that became the focus of attention in the search for the causes of problematic public behavior. Thus, Elton Mayo, an important leader in the new field of management theory, put the family at the center of his investigations:

> Mayo revolutionized management theories because just as he replaced the moral language of selfhood with the dispassionate terminology of psychological

science, he replaced the engineers' rhetoric of rationality that had hitherto prevailed with a new lexicon of "human relations." By suggesting that conflicts were not a matter of competition over scarce resources but rather resulted from tangled emotions, personality factors, and unresolved psychological problems, Mayo constructed a discursive continuity between the family and the workplace.

(Illouz 2008: 72)

In short, in the myriad ways that dynamic psychology was transforming the USA in the early 20th century, early family relationships were becoming increasingly understood as the source of the public self.

If early childhood relationships were increasingly becoming understood as the source of the public self, though, this did not mean that all such sources should be *made* public. In the first half of the 20th century, dynamic psychology, while theoretically about how we all become who we are, largely reached the public through its therapeutic dimension. Thus, for example, while an important segment of Freudian theory is about how we all progress from infancy into adulthood, many of his ideas that reached a wide public, such as the popularization of the phrase "inferiority complex," were about development "gone wrong." Similarly, in such other widespread applications of dynamic psychology as industrial psychology and marriage counseling, the emphasis was on resolving individual or interpersonal problems. Even today, when scholars talk about the popularization of Freud and other psychological theorists over the course of the 20th century, such popularization is often described as "the triumph of the therapeutic."[5]

However, this intermingling of dynamic psychology with therapeutic cure had important implications for the issue of the relationship between privacy and self-disclosure. If self-revelation was mostly associated with the disclosure of inner sources of problematic behavior, then self-disclosure should only be done in circumscribed settings, among those professionally sworn to secrecy or among those, such as close family members, whom one could trust. Moreover, since the goal of much of the therapy initiated by social reformers in the first half of the 20th century was to eliminate "social deviancy," the practice of therapy was often not seen as something appropriate or desirable for professionals to enact upon themselves. Even when therapy was understood as appropriate for members of the middle class, as, for example, in marriage counseling, the need for therapy was still understood as limited to the few who for whatever reasons could not work out their problems on their own. In sum, therapeutic interventions were often understood as something one was pressed into by professional others or voluntarily undertaken in circumscribed contexts. While such interventions were not necessarily associated with the intimacy of family life, they were still confined to the realm of "the private."

The discourse of intimacy

By the middle of the 20th century, psychological ideas had become deeply entrenched in many areas of social life, from the regular presence of social workers in special courts developed to handle "juvenile delinquency," to the kinds of advice regularly found in the columns in popular magazines on how best to "save one's marriage." However, still in place was the idea that psychological help was primarily needed for the troubled few whose problems should be dealt with only by those with professional accreditation. This began to change in the 1960s and 1970s with the emergence of forms of popular psychology that assumed not only that most people could use some form of psychological help, but also that such help could be achieved outside of the doctor's or therapist's office. It was in the 1960s and 1970s that psychologists such as Carl Rogers began making a public impact with the idea that psychology could be used for purposes of self-realization (Illouz 2008: 159). Other forms of popular psychology emerging at this time, such as gestalt therapy, transactional analysis and EST (Erhard Seminar Training), were based on similar premises. During these two decades, a new generation of young people who were reaching adulthood in this period latched onto a central premise of these and similar therapies, that inner reflection and self-disclosure were necessary and laudable practices for all. Many members of this large baby-boomer generation were part of a middle class that had greatly expanded in the post-World War II era. As these young people rebelled against the music, dress, hairstyles and sexual habits of their parents, so also did they come to reject a view of psychological introspection as only appropriate for the deviant few.

What caused this new acceptance of inner self-reflection and disclosure? Part of the answer lies in changing attitudes among members of this generation towards adult social roles, towards accepting the patterns of behavior they viewed as governing their parents' lives. Feeling that their own lives were open to possibilities unavailable to their parents, many looked to popular psychologies to provide answers and means for realizing such possibilities. As a consequence, psychology became seen less as a tool for remedying idiosyncratic, embarrassing, personal problems and more as a tool for creating a better future self.

This sense of a self with open possibilities is evidenced in this generation's ideas about private life, gender roles, and love and marriage. Whereas love and marriage had earlier been viewed as following certain pre-given scripts—scripts with distinctive roles for women and men and that promised mostly happy endings for all—love and marriage were coming to be seen by many members of this new generation as more precarious projects poorly served by previous understandings of gender roles. This more precarious nature of love and marriage and a greater uncertainty about gender roles required self-reflection and expression to discover who one wanted to be and how one wanted to relate to others.

David Shumway elaborates these ideas in his claims that in this period a "discourse of intimacy" emerged as an alternative discourse to an earlier "discourse of romance." As Shumway argues, an earlier hegemonic discourse of romance followed a plot line that began with a first encounter between two lovers and ended with the promise of the couple cementing their bonds in marriage and then living "happily ever after." The plot line of the discourse of intimacy, however, often began in a conflicted "ever after" and presented itself as a way to end such conflict. Second, while the discourse of romance was premised on highly different gender roles, the discourse of intimacy assumed equality among the participants and demanded a similarity in the behavior of each for discord to end. Third, the discourse of intimacy, unlike the discourse of romance, was heavily dependent upon the language of psychology, and particularly upon a version of it that emphasized the need for internal investigation. While the discourse of romance often depicted lovers overcoming concrete, external barriers—such as the opposition of parents or the intrusion of a competitor for one of the partner's affections—the discourse of intimacy demanded that those involved look within themselves to locate the patterns of belief and emotion that were causing conflict. Communication that entails self-disclosure was deemed central as both a means for couples to attain emotional closeness and a sign that such closeness had been achieved (Shumway 2003: 133–56).

Shumway is not alone in pointing to the 1960s and 1970s as the period when psychological discourse became a more widely accepted means for addressing problems in private life. Eva Illouz and Anthony Giddens have drawn attention to the growth during the 1960s and 1970s of psychological discourse as a widely endorsed medium for thinking about human relationships (Illouz 2008; Giddens 1992). These three and others point to a variety of causes for this widespread adoption of psychological discourse to deal with private life: the growing use of psychology in institutional settings which had begun in the first half of the 20th century; developments within psychology that made interpersonal relationships, rather than internal drives, central to the development of the self; the emergence of second-wave feminism which substituted notions of gender equality for rigid gender roles; and a sharp rise in the prevalence of divorce which made "the happily ever after" story of the discourse of romance less credible.

Certainly, all of these social phenomena contributed to the growing acceptance of psychological discourse in the 1960s and 1970s. However, I believe that a concept that Anthony Giddens introduces, the idea of "the pure relationship," helps us understand some of the more underlying social dynamics that contributed to the appeal not only of psychological talk in general but also of a certain kind of psychological talk in this period.

Giddens argues that the character of intimate relationships underwent an important transformation in the middle part of the 20th century. Familial and other close relationships that previously had been fixed by law, custom and morality became more fluid, less defined by given rules. The open-ended nature of such ties is signified by the emergence of "the pure relationship," that is, a tie between people that is created only for the purpose of satisfying the needs of the parties involved. It has no external support and can be terminated by either partner at any moment in time. Since it has no external support, it exists only to the extent intimacy is created and sustained by those who constitute it (Giddens 1992: 134–40).

As Giddens notes, these claims seem supported by the relatively recent use of the word "relationship" to describe forms of social interaction (Giddens 1992: 55). The word depicts a type of human interaction that has no specified content. Thus, not noted by Shumway but important to this new discourse is that it opens up the possibilities of human closeness outside of heterosexual romance; it does this through use of the open-ended term "the relationship." The latter includes both sexual intimacies between a woman and a woman, or a man and a man, as equally as it describes the sexual relationship between a man and a woman.[6] It describes the interaction of people who live together outside of marriage as well as the nonsexual closeness of friends who do not share a domestic living space. Its only condition is that there exists some form of sustained connection between at least two participants.[7]

Once we accept the point that this new social category of "the relationship" emerges to describe social connection that is indeterminate in content, the question arises as to why such indeterminacy itself became possible. Here I would suggest that an important transformation occurred in the assumed relation between private and public life in the middle of the 20th century. From the beginning of the 19th century, when the idea of separate spheres first began to develop, until the middle of the 20th century, "private" and "public" life were understood as ideally supportive of each other. Thus, the male head of household supposedly worked to support his family, and his success at work was a sign of how successful a head of household he was. In the first half of the 20th century, a good "company man" was necessarily also a good "family man," since the traits that marked the one—stability, loyalty, self-discipline and responsibility—were all necessary in the description of the other. As Barbara Ehrenreich has argued, in the first half of the 20th century, middle-class men proved their masculinity and adulthood by getting married and an unmarried man of a certain age was regarded with suspicions about both his masculinity and his maturity, traits that, if lacking, undermined his desirability in the world of work (Ehrenreich 1983: 14–20). Similarly, middle-class women of a certain age were expected to be absent from the workforce since their presence in the workforce was deemed incompatible with what it meant to be a wife and mother. These roles and expectations about public and private life were assumed to work together to create social harmony.[8]

However, this assumption about a harmonious conjunction of public and private life had always been a precarious one, functioning more as ideology than description. Poor African and European American women had often been unable to fulfill the criteria that marked one as a "lady." The demands of supporting oneself and one's family made such criteria impossible to meet. Similarly, many poor African and European American men were also often unable to find the kind of employment that fit well with assumptions about being a proper head of household. The story about wife at home, children at home or in school, and husband/father at work was one from which many Americans deviated in myriad ways from the middle of the 19th to the middle of the 20th centuries.[9] Social reformers were well aware of these deviations. Thus, as we saw earlier, one important use to which dynamic psychology was put in the first half of the 20th century was to explain and account for private lives that did not fit within this norm and which were assumed to express social deviancy.

New, though, in the 1960s and 1970s was that the ideal of a nuclear, male-headed private life was increasingly coming to be understood as a problem for even white, middle-class, heterosexual men and women. Married, white, middle-class women, even those with children, were increasingly becoming part of the paid labor force. Younger, white, middle-class women were envisaging a life that included large periods of paid employment. White, middle-class men were finding that being married or a parent was no longer a necessary condition of professional employment; indeed, with many companies and careers now demanding geographical flexibility, such private commitments could get in the way of successful careers.[10] Certainly, many still continued to aim for and applaud what they and others referred to as "traditional" families, but an increasing number of others were finding such aims and accolades unconvincing.

It is this questioning of previously given social scripts by those for whom such scripts were supposed to work that contributed to this greater acceptance of self-examination and self-disclosure. Self-disclosure, while earlier understood as the means to establish better harmony between a private and public self, became necessary now to find out what kind of a private self one wanted, and how to achieve and sustain the kinds of connections one desired in life. The embrace of "consciousness raising" in second-wave feminism exemplifies this turn. Feminists during the interwar and immediate post-war periods had come to question forms of discrimination against women in the labor force, and in the early 1960s constructed a large political movement against such discrimination. However, it was not until a younger generation of women began to question more broadly the existence of "sex roles" that feminists added to their political toolbox the tactic of "consciousness raising." "Consciousness raising" was not about fixing individual problems or the problems of "deviant" social groups. It was about white, middle-class women looking at and disclosing to others aspects of their own lives, aspects that they had previously understood as "private." Self-examination and self-disclosure to those outside of one's family and outside of a doctor's office had become understood as not only acceptable but indeed necessary in the creation of a more desirable life. To be sure, a sense of privacy still lingered within some consciousness-raising groups and other popular self-help groups; restrictions sometimes were made about sharing what one heard within the group with those outside of it. However, as such discussion of private life spread to more public spaces, such as in the writings of feminist authors, and in the writings of others in the public media who described their own progression beyond problematic childhoods, the association of self-disclosure with privacy and intimacy diminished.

Intimacy, privacy and self-disclosure today

The dis-association of self-disclosure with privacy and intimacy has continued over the past 40-year period. In part, this is because the upheavals in private life that first generated "the discourse of intimacy" are still with us. In the above, I talked about the increased use of psychological discourse as a tool to help us figure out who we are and in what kinds of relationships we wish to engage. That means, however, that we have also become very interested in how others have come to be who they are and what psychological lessons we can learn from hearing about their own struggles. One might cynically think of the increased information that we are getting today about the inner lives of strangers as a consequence of the greater fame and money that some are obtaining by writing their memoirs, appearing on the Oprah Winfrey show, or otherwise making public their inner lives. However, that many are obtaining money and fame by making public their inner struggles is possible only because so many of us are acutely interested in hearing about such struggles. In a variety of venues of popular culture, including film, theater, novels and television, stories of romance and adventure are having to compete with stories that illuminate the inner lives of the characters they portray. For many of us, such narratives are intensely interesting because they provide clues as to the many ways in which psychic life unfolds and how new forms of "relationships" are created. As we continue to create new forms of families and new forms of emotional connection to others, so do we also want to learn how others have succeeded or failed at similar attempts.

The continued growth of public self-disclosure is also a consequence of the new forms of technology that have permeated social life since the 1980s. The introduction and expanded use of such means of communication as smartphones, Facebook, Twitter, blogging and Skype have meant that the lives of many of us have become more public. It is not just that we have come to know the private lives of well-known politicians and entertainers through these media; it is also that these new modes of communication have created means for many of us to become known by a wider circle ourselves. The gates separating those who are well known from the rest of us have become open to a wider range of keys, and one means and consequence of making it through those gates is by "publicizing" one's private life. Many people strive to create blogs that are followed by a large number of people, and many of those blogs aim to entice through self-revelation.

Thus, this increased "publicization" of private life through self-disclosure seems revealed in many facets of contemporary life, but how extensive is it, and what are its consequences for our abilities to establish intimacy? Some theorists argue that this increased "publicity" of private life, made possible by new forms of communication, has been obtained at the cost of diminished intimacy. For example, Sherry Turkle argues that such new means of communication, while giving the appearance of broadening our interactions with others, have instead facilitated forms of interaction that are thinner and ultimately less satisfying than older forms.

> Digital connections and the sociable robot may offer the illusion of companionship without the demands of friendship. Our networked life allows us to hide from each other, as we are tethered to each other. We'd rather text than talk.
>
> (Turkle 2011: 1)

Jodi Dean goes even further in her claim that the "publicization" of private life has become so extensive that our very identity in contemporary "technoculture" has become dependent upon such publicity.

> My central claim is that publicity establishes the ideological matrix within which individuals in mediated, capitalist technoculture subjectivize their

condition. People's experience of themselves as subjects is configured in terms of accessibility, visibility, *being known*. Without publicity, the subject of technoculture doesn't know if it exists at all. It has no way of establishing that it has a place within the general sociosymbolic order of things, that it is recognized.

(Dean 2002: 114)

Thus, according to Dean, we no longer *have* "private selves"; there is no "there" there other than the "there" that is created for public consumption. However, if we have lost our private selves, does this not also entail losses in our capacities and means for establishing intimacy? If we reveal all to as many as we can get to listen, does not the value of self-revelation diminish and with it one of the important means of establishing intimacy? If my deepest secrets are no longer secrets, what distinguishes what I tell the world from what I tell members of my family or my closest friends? How are "intimates" possible when there are no details of life that are "intimate"?

These dark claims about the loss of privacy and intimacy within our contemporary "technoculture" contain much truth, but I would like to suggest some caution: while private lives have become more public in our own time, there still exist many of us who share important aspects of our lives only with a special few. Part of our present confusion about norms of privacy is a consequence of the fact that older and newer norms coexist in the present.

Moreover, it needs to be emphasized that lives seemingly lived more publicly does not necessarily entail the diminishment of private life and of intimacy with it; that partly what is changing with the growth of new technologies and with the growing "publicization" of private life through self-disclosure are changes in the meanings of private life and of intimacy themselves. Thus, while older forms of privacy have centered on restricting certain forms of self-disclosure, such as revealing emotion or other aspects of one's "inner self," newer understandings are centered on restricting the revelation of other aspects of one's self, such as the minutiae of one's everyday life.

For example, in the above quote, Turkle claims that "we'd rather text than talk." Since texting eliminates some of the intimacy of a phone call—the listening and responding to shades of emotion revealed in voice tone—and even more the intimacy of a face-to-face interaction, the implication of Turkle's claim is that the increase of texting has meant a decrease in intimacy, but does texting decrease intimacy or does it instead change its meaning? Texting represents less of a bracketed event in one's day in comparison to a telephone call, and even less so in comparison to a physical encounter. Texting can be woven more easily into other activities than communicating by telephone or by a physical meeting. Because it is less of a bracketed event, it can more easily be used for communicating the minutiae of one's day: what one ate for breakfast, who one saw on the way to school or work, etc. Here self-revelation involves less the communication of emotion that one does more easily by telephone, and more the communication of detail that one does more easily by texting. Is there anything inherently more "intimate" in communicating emotion than in communicating the details of one's day? Cannot we say that a zone of privacy can be as much drawn around those who hear about one's day as around those who hear one's emotional tone on a telephone call?

Moreover, even to the extent that email and texting may be revealing personal information on a wider scale than had been true of face-to-face and telephone conversations, they are also creating new forms of "private space": the actual physical and time spaces we occupy. Telephone conversations, unlike physical encounters, do not intrude upon one's physical space. They do, however, intrude upon one's personal time. Unless one is good about ignoring such calls, one's time, if not one's physical space, is interrupted by the ring. However, emails and texts can be answered at any time. While there exist some social norms about the length of time appropriate for answering emails or texts, there is more flexibility granted in the time taken to answer such communications than is given to telephone calls. Therefore, while the line between private and public may be diminishing in terms of *what* we communicate to others, new lines may be being created in terms of where and when we make such communications. "Intimacy" may be expressed not in terms of the content of a telephone call or a text message, but in terms of whether a telephone call is picked up at all or in terms of the speed by which a text is answered.

The above are only speculations about the possible directions in which intimacy, privacy and self-disclosure are moving today; it is difficult seeing with clarity major social changes when one stands in the midst of such changes. However, the confusion we feel about privacy, intimacy and self-disclosure should now at least be more understandable. As many of our present ideas about privacy, intimacy and self-disclosure have their roots in particular, historically specific beliefs about the family and who we are, so it is understandable that these ideas should be changing as those beliefs also change. Therefore, while it is difficult to know with clarity where we are heading, it is safe to say that, 50 years from now, contemporary meanings of "intimacy," "privacy" and "self-disclosure," meanings that have their roots in 19th-century social relationships and views about the self, will likely prove as historically outmoded as the computers we now use to describe these concepts.

Notes

1 See Peckham (1970); Giddens (1992); and Kirschner (1996).
2 While my emphasis in this section is on the 19th-century urban working class, these aspects of reliance on wider networks of community and kin can also be found within antebellum slave life and in 19th-century rural life. For an elaboration of similar points in regard to slave life, see Anthony Kaye (2007). John D'Emilio and Estelle B. Freedman make similar points when they distinguish 19th-century middle-class from rural and working-class courtship in the following way: "In contrast to the continuing public courtship of rural and working class youth, in which young people openly pursued pleasure, between the 1820s and the 1880s, middle class courtship became an intensely private affair" (D'Emilio and Freedman 1988: 75).
3 Thus, for example, while W.E.B. du Bois famously characterizes the American Negro as possessing a double self, there is no sense that this doubling represents a separation between a private and a public self. It is for him clearly a separation between two different social selves (du Bois 1989: 5).

4 In this regard, Freud was not completely innovative. As Nathan Hale points out, both Morton Prince and James Jackson Putnam also understood normality and deviance to exist on a continuum (Hale 1995: 121).

5 This phrase comes, of course, from Philip Rieff's well-known book *The Triumph of the Therapeutic* (1966). Even more recently, though, one can find the spread of dynamic psychology being equated with the spread of therapy in Illouz (2008). The idea of the conjunction of Freudianism with the therapeutic in this period was suggested to me by Gerry Izenberg in conversation.

6 Shumway, in fact, claims that the discourse of intimacy privileges the heterosexual couple (Shumway 2003: 137). On this point, I disagree with him.

7 The open-ended nature of the term is illustrated by the fact that the interaction need not even be between two humans. One can imagine someone saying of another person that that person has a neurotic or a particularly close "relationship" with their dog, or that two dogs have a good "relationship" with each other.

8 To be sure, even before the advent of second-wave feminism in the 1960s, these assumptions about women's proper place were unraveling. Thus, scholars have uncovered the many ways in which an acceptance of women in the workforce was developing in the 1940s and 1950s. See, for example, Meyerowitz (1994).

9 There are many works that show the incompatibility of the ideology of separate spheres with poor and working-class lives. Three that illustrate this point, focusing on different time periods in the USA, are Stansell (1986); Stack (1974); and Coontz (1992).

10 Barbara Ehrenreich describes how in the middle of the 20th century there first began to develop the idea that a man could be both heterosexual and a reliable employee, and yet not be married. Ehrenreich argues that the uncoupling of marriage from masculinity and maturity both made possible and was strengthened by magazines such as *Playboy* and such books as Jack Kerouac's *On the Road* (Ehrenreich 1983).

References

Coontz, Stephanie. 1988. *The Social Origins of Private Life: A History of American Families 1600–1900*. London: Verso.

——1992. *The Way We Never Were: American Families and the Nostalgia Trap*. New York, NY: Basic.

——2005. *Marriage, a History: From Obedience to Intimacy, or How Love Conquered Marriage*. New York, NY: Viking.

Dean, Jodi. 2002. *Publicity's Secret: How Technoculture Capitalizes on Democracy*. Ithaca, NY: Cornell University Press.

D'Emilio, John and Freedman, Estelle B. 1988. *Intimate Matters: A History of Sexuality in America*. Chicago: University of Chicago Press.

du Bois, W.E.B. 1989 [1903]. *The Souls of Black Folk*. New York, NY: Penguin.

Ehrenreich, Barbara. 1983. *The Hearts of Men: American Dreams and the Flight From Commitment*. New York, NY: Random House.

Freedman, Jill and Combs, Gene. 1996. *Narrative Therapy: The Social Construction of Preferred Realities*. New York, NY: W.W. Norton.

Gay, Peter. 1984. *The Bourgeois Experience: Victoria to Freud Volume 1*. Oxford University Press.

Giddens, Anthony. 1992. *The Transformation of Intimacy: Sexuality, Love, and Eroticism in Modern Societies*. Stanford University Press.

Hale, Nathan G. 1971. *Freud and the Americans: The Beginnings of Psychoanalysis in the United States, 1876–1917*. Oxford University Press.

——1995. *The Rise and Crisis of Psychoanalysis in the United States: Freud and the Americans, 1917–1985*. Oxford University Press.

Hutto, Daniel D. (ed.). 2007. *Narrative and Understanding Persons*. Cambridge University Press.

Illouz, Eva. 2008. *Saving the Modern Soul: Therapy, Emotions and the Culture of Self-Help*. Berkeley: University of California Press.

Kaye, Anthony. 2007. *Joining Places: Slave Neighborhoods in the Old South*. Chapel Hill, NC: The University of North Carolina Press.

Kirschner, Suzanne. 1996. *The Religious and Romantic Origins of Psychoanalysis*. Cambridge University Press.

Klinenberg, Eric. 2012. *Going Solo: The Extraordinary Rise and Surprising Appeal of Living Alone*. New York, NY: Penguin.

Lystra, Karen. 1989. *Searching the Heart: Women, Men, and Romantic Love in Nineteenth-Century America*. New York, NY: Oxford University Press.

Meyerowitz, Joanne (ed.). 1994. *Not June Cleaver: Women and Gender in Postwar America, 1945–1960*. Philadelphia, PA: Temple University Press.

Moskowitz, Eva. 2001. *In Therapy We Trust: America's Obsession with Self-Fulfillment*. Baltimore, MD: The Johns Hopkins University Press.

Nicholson, Linda. 1986. *Gender and History: The Limits of Social Theory in the Age of the Family*. New York, NY: Columbia University Press.

Peckham, Morse. 1970. *The Triumph of Romanticism*. Columbia, SC: University of South Carolina Press.

Rieff, Philip. 1966. *The Triumph of the Therapeutic*. New York, NY: Harper and Row.

Seidman, Steven. 1991. *Romantic Longings: Love in America, 1830–1980*. New York, NY: Routledge.

Shumway, David R. 2003. *Modern Love: Romance, Intimacy and the Marriage Crisis*. New York University Press.

Stack, Carol. 1974. *All Our Kin: Strategies for Survival in a Black Community*. New York, NY: Harper & Row.

Stansell, Christine. 1986. *City of Women: Sex and Class in New York, 1789–1860*. New York, NY: Knopf.

Susman, Warren. 1979. "'Personality' and the Making of Twentieth-Century Culture." In John Higham and Paul Conkin (eds) *New Directions in American Intellectual History*. Baltimore, MD: The Johns Hopkins University Press, 212–26.

Taylor, Charles. 1989. *Sources of the Self: The Making of the Modern Identity*. Cambridge, MA: Harvard University Press.

Turkle, Sherry. 2011. *Alone Together: Why We Expect More from Technology and Less From Each Other*. New York, NY: Basic.

Part II

Between fluid and solid intimacies

Hook-ups, sex, love

3 Unexpected intimacies

Moments of connection, moments of shame

Alan Frank

Working with a patient over a period of 10 years, a man seemingly unable to forge an intimate relationship and who used sex to create distance, I examined two unexpected intimate connections.

The first allowed me to recognize a seemingly perverse act between the patient and another, not as repulsive or something to be avoided—unconsciously or, worse, consciously—in treatment, but, instead, as a justifiable moral ground of intimate connection. In this regard, I argue that looking at intimacy through a conventionally, and often rigidly narrow, normative lens can obscure more non-conventional, but possibly adaptive and even life-sustaining connections. More specifically, I challenge assumptions and self-appointed moral arbiters, including many in the analytic community, that stipulate the inherent antagonism between what many may consider perverse behavior and intimacy. I intend to make credible the view that behaviors that most would likely consider disgusting, pathological and the antithesis of intimacy can be a meaningful form of attachment and an anchoring social bond. As analysts, we are faced with behaviors—uncomfortable though they may be—that need to be explored and understood, not dismissed as perverse. I draw on rich psychoanalytic and sociological literature that insists on understanding the moral significance of behavior, especially regarding "intimate or sexual acts" in historical, contextual and psychological terms (Benjamin 1988, 1998; Dominici and Lesser 1995; Duberman 2002; Giddens 1993; Reis and Grossmark 2009; Seidman 1997; Weeks 1995).

The second recognition of unexpected intimacy occurred within the analytic relationship. In my work with this patient, someone I thought incapable of intimate attachments, I became aware of unforeseen and often-powerful moments that could either edge into a deepening connection or, conversely, create a seemingly unbridgeable divide. I illustrate how moments of risk-taking vulnerability, which easily could have triggered past traumas, inducing shame and mistrust, instead forged a new ground of trust and intimacy.

Working from a relational psychoanalytic tradition that recognizes analyst and patient as participants in a mutually influencing relationship, I intend to explore how my own early life experiences and countertransference reactions could have impeded or enriched the emotional bond between analyst and patient. I attempt, as well, to speak to a challenge facing many analysts: When does the analyst's self-disclosure, bending the analytic frame and challenging boundaries, inhibit or enhance an intimate connection?

Gleaning the literature on perversion, it was disheartening to read how this concept has been used by analysts to pathologize and create an "other." I believe that analysts have appealed, often without much reflection, to a notion of "normal" sexuality.

In *Sexuality, Intimacy, Power*, Muriel Dimen (2003) addresses the subject of perversion, a topic, she says, that is rife with anxiety. For example, she cites Chasseguet-Smirgel (Dimen 2003: 258), who holds the view that anxiety around a so-called perversion is often dealt with by demonizing the pervert. Also, she references Kernberg and Bach (Dimen 2003: 258), who believe that anxiety around sexual difference can be quieted within the bounds of heterosexual marriage. Similarly, she comments that, in some of his writing, Khan (Dimen 2003: 259) seems to relieve his own anxiety about sexual difference by excluding it from the treatment room. Many analysts, though respectful and empathic to seemingly perverse practices, still see such a patient through a conventionally normative lens, thereby rendering the patient as an inferior, threatening "other" engaged in disgusting, reprehensible acts. Even in more recent writings, an analyst, clearly relational and empathic in his thinking, in one instance concludes that a young boy struggling with separation anxiety, specifically from his mother, often finds hysterical and *perverse* solutions to this anxiety; and in another instance he concludes that a young boy, unable to recognize his maleness, uses the phallus as a defense, and brings into play narcissistic pathology that often includes *perverse* sexuality (Diamond 2009). In both instances, I question if collapsing sexual difference into pathology could have been avoided by withholding judgment and, instead, allowing oneself a fuller appreciation of the layered meanings of the boys' experiences. Making a similar point, in his critical study of masculinities, Corbett (2009: 8–9) argues, "the complexity that is masculinity goes largely unrecorded; the variety that makes for complexity is only recorded as pathology."

No doubt, there continue to be important shifts in thinking in this area. Still, I wonder why this reductionist, pathologizing way of thinking, which assumes that certain behaviors are deemed normal while others are seen as perverse, is not more vigorously challenged? Perhaps it is simply easier and less anxiety provoking to externalize it—"that's *you*, not *me*." It also tamps anxiety when one is able to identify the norm (me) by quickly comparing it to what one believes to be a perversion (not me) (Dimen 2003). Such normative judgments allow an analyst to avoid the discomfort that would accompany a deeper, more nuanced understanding of specific and often complex sexual behaviors. Avoiding closer examination eliminates all possibility of this same behavior being seen, for example, as a fetish, or a form of compulsivity—both behaviors viewed as less pathological and more acceptable in society than a deviant sexual perversion. However, avoiding examination has a decidedly serious limitation: It eradicates the possibility that a sexual act between two consenting adults, no matter that it may initially trigger revulsion, may be a legitimate source of pleasure, a way of connecting, or a pathway to a deep intimate attachment. If this is so, why should the person or the act be pathologized and polluted?

Fortunately, in psychoanalytic history, there were theorists like Kohut (1987) who believed that any sexual act between two intimate adults, as long as it is part of a varied sex life, cannot be considered a perversion. More recently, Dimen (2003), whose concerns resonate with my own, raises serious doubts about the theoretical, moral and political implications of this category. "I am trying to decipher what sense it makes to call [one's] difficulty with love and intimacy a perversion ... it's awful not to be able to love and be loved. But why call this absence, this suffering, this failure, a perversion?" (Dimen 2003: 281–82). Dimen then draws out the political implication of this critique: "I am concerned ... with psychoanalytic participation in domination—in naming, blaming, truth framing, and shaming" (Dimen 2003: 284).

Let's not forget, sexual acts once considered unacceptable and labeled perverse have, over time, found their way out of the DSM-IV (*Diagnostic and Statistical Manual of Mental Disorders*, 4th Edition) and are now deemed acceptable in our society. Yet, we are still a long way from the time when the category of perversion will be a merely historical artifact.

The conceptual and political issues raised by the category of perversion were powerfully presented to me through my work with David. Ten or so years ago, I remember opening the door to see a tall, ruggedly handsome, virile and imposing man. He was seeking treatment, he said, because of his inability to connect to anyone in an intimate way or to have a long-term, meaningful, loving relationship.

From the start, my sessions with David were sexually charged. At once and with great ease, he told me that he was 42, that he was bisexual, that he preferred *friendships* with women and *sex* with men, especially married men, that he was a successful stockbroker, and that he was also a "hustler," a male prostitute, because "it turns me on to have men pay me for sex." He was also into sadomasochistic sex, and described himself as the "top," the one "in control." He told me, boastfully, "I'm well endowed and I know how to use it," and, finally, that he had consulted with another therapist before seeing me, who was "a lot younger than you and *really* hunky." Concerned about a sexual attraction they might have for one another, he would feel more comfortable working with me. "OUCH!" I thought. Simultaneously, a memory (just a blip, really) flashed in my head—"hunky" jocks being picked for the junior high baseball team while I, head down and ashamed, was always picked last. I smiled, recovered quickly, and continued listening.

I had the feeling, while listening to David, that I was hearing a patterned speech that had rolled off his tongue many times before; a need to make crystal clear his hypermasculinity and extraordinary sexual prowess. However, my sudden countertransference reaction, eliciting feelings of shame and vivid decades-old memories of painfully struggling with issues around my own masculinity, and in deep denial about my sexual identity, also made me wonder about David's repressed feelings of shame, his mantle of hypermasculinity and his ambiguous sexual identity. I questioned, as well, whether he felt he had to desexualize me, or minimize me, in order for him to safely risk connecting.

David said he was an only child. He remembers, from early on, his mother being demanding, intrusive and emasculating, but never loving and nurturing. He said, "She had a commanding presence that obliterated everyone else's … Her needs always came first." His father, he said, was "a good egg with no balls … but I loved him." His parents, he said, had "a miserable and loveless relationship. My father was never good enough, or ambitious enough, or man enough to please my mother. She pushed, and she pushed, and she pushed … until he died."

As a child, David was sickly, pale and scrawny. He said that he looked "undernourished," or at least his mother thought he did, and she gave him medication no matter what ailed him; and, tellingly, she routinely examined all of his bowel movements. David said, she would literally "rate" them. If he ever flushed the toilet without her checking first, she would become enraged, would chastise and berate him, screaming or spitting through her teeth, "Shame on you!" He said that she was always saying "Shame on you" for one reason or another. Eventually, the phrase ceased to have any meaning for him. I believed those words impacted greatly and remained deeply embedded in David. "If my stool didn't 'pass the test'," he said, "she would give me an enema." This happened almost daily. David's stools became a toxic barometer for him of how healthy or unhealthy he was. When he resisted the enemas, his father would secretly give him money and would encourage him to acquiesce to his mother's demands. David said, "There was no intimacy in our family and really no real connection … except around shit." In time, he began secretly to enjoy the enemas, learning how to master the intake and retention of fluid and output of feces; once again, he felt in control. The enemas, with their accompanying erotic sensations, and "even the sick thought of my father pimping me out to pleasure my mother," became increasingly pleasurable for him. He remembers these rituals going on for years, stopping, he thinks, at the time of his father's death when he was 12.

One can see the family's dynamics—each playing out dominant and submissive roles—initiating an ongoing pattern of sexual objectification and role-playing, much of it revolving around shit. Shit played a mediating role in family bonding, setting the stage for David's sexualizing and using shit to establish intimacies as an adult.

His parents also used him as a container for their disavowed feelings toward one another and their intense rage. This betrayal by both of his parents, engendering a lack of trust, manifested later in his inability to connect to another person except as an object and often as a container for his own disavowed and rageful feelings. An absence of good enough parenting, one that had the capacity to encourage and affirm David's healthy narcissism and to mirror for him an idealized and intimate connection, instead created a disconnected and unsafe environment. It also led early on to the establishment of a deeply embedded organizing pattern: "If I separate feelings of caring and desire for intimate attachments from bodily pleasures, I won't feel shame, I won't feel vulnerable, and I won't feel unloved." David learned to render his body and sexuality as a vehicle for pleasure, power and control.

David's father died of heart failure just days before David turned 13 and right before his Bar Mitzvah. The celebratory event was canceled, except for a somber religious ceremony. A constant reminder of the sad event was a photograph he secretly kept hidden in a drawer, taken on the day of his Bar Mitzvah—his mother looking stoic, David looking miserable and sad, and his father painfully missing. His father's death was traumatic for him. David remembers his father being in bed at home for weeks. He knew he was ill (his mother kept screaming at him to be quiet), but he was never allowed to enter his father's room or to see him. He remembers an aunt going in and out of the room, caring for his father, and he remembers his mother yelling a lot and giving orders to others, while never seeming directly to care-give his father. In the middle of one night David heard a commotion, but afraid to be in the way and be chastised, he pretended he was asleep. "The next morning the door to my father's room was open and his bed was empty and stripped to the bare mattress." All of his father's pictures around the house were removed. "I never saw my father again. It was like he never existed." David feels guilty that he was unable to protect his father from his mother and prevent his death, but he also felt enraged that his father could not protect him from his horrific mother … and now never would. This further reinforced for David the inability for one to have a loving, trusting and safe relationship.

In high school David was often alone and isolated. He began to masturbate frequently to a recurrent fantasy: having sex with a woman and a heterosexual male, both older than he, and simultaneously "servicing them both and obeying their every command." This ongoing masturbatory submissive fantasy was for David both erotic and shame inducing as he struggled secretly with his homosexuality and his sadomasochistic urges.

David started to mature physically. He began going to the gym to work out and was becoming taller, well built and increasingly good looking. David was becoming a man. "To be a man," as Corbett (2009: 176) says, "is to be big … [and] to achieve phallic power." Indeed, David was becoming increasingly confident of his raw sexuality and his homoerotic appeal to other men. In college he dated women but knew that he was also attracted to men. His ongoing fantasy of a bisexual ménage à trois eventually became a reality. For David, engaging in bisexual ménages, usually with married couples, allowed him to connect sexually, to disconnect emotionally, to avoid intimacy and to deny his homosexuality. These sexual encounters became more and more sadomasochistic, and David increasingly took on the dominant role. For David these encounters were at once pleasurable and humiliating. In time, his sexual encounters became more frequent, more anonymous and more ritualistic, often involving equipment, whips, leather clothing, masks, dildos, etc., and the encounters became increasingly homosexual. The use of ritualistic equipment heightened the objectification of body parts. A mask, making one faceless, hid expressions of pleasure but it also masked displeasure, warding off feelings of rejection or feelings of love, both feelings which, for David, were difficult to tolerate.

David said he had been in therapy for most of his adult life and that all of his attempts at therapy were short lived. All of his therapists were male, some had said they were gay, but, he said, "a lot of them just couldn't deal with my S&M shit," or, he said, he would often terminate treatment when he thought that the therapist was sexually attracted to him. "I could tell that my therapist was 'turned on.' He'd become fixated on my sex life, so eventually I'd 'stick it to him' and leave. *I* got paid for sex, not him."

He talked about his sex life often. Session after session he would talk openly about his frequent and anonymous encounters with men, most of whom paid him for sadomasochistic sex. He would vividly describe these encounters: the elaborate role-playing, the exquisite reciprocity between dominance and submission, pleasure and pain, gratification and humiliation, surrender and control. For David, as the humiliation became more intense and feelings of degradation heightened, sex was becoming more impersonal, and he was becoming more emotionally detached, leading, I believe, to more nonconventional sex.

Eroticism almost always defined our sessions. When it did, I began to see that we each had a role: David talked and I listened; he was dominant and I was passive. In time, during these graphic, erotic tales, and true to our roles, I began to fantasize being physically bound and shackled, or submitting to him sexually, or being verbally and sexually humiliated.

In the beginning, these fantasies were quite unsettling for me. I thought, "Am I, in fact, fixated on his sexual exploits? Am I turned on? Is this simply my erotic countertransference?" In time, I began to realize that metaphorically "my hands *were* tied." I *was* in "a bind." I was "bound and gagged" by David's edict that *he* could focus on his sex life, *but I could not*! If I did, if I asked too many questions, if I got too specific, he would, as he had done to his former therapists, "'stick it to me' and leave!" We were reenacting in the treatment room the same sadomasochistic relationship he'd had with countless others including his parents. I was avoiding David's overt and powerful sexuality by remaining silent. I wasn't going to be cajoled like all those other "shrinks," seduced and shamed and then tossed aside!

The treatment was at an impasse. David was using his sexuality, his frequent, anonymous sexual encounters, and sexual objectification to avoid connecting to another in an intimate and meaningful way, and it was used in our sessions in much the same way, as a defense to avoid more difficult, more painful and more emotionally charged feelings. How was I to get beyond the flood of sexual talk and bravado to reach the man behind the sex? If I couldn't, I'd eventually be "tossed aside" anyway. I had to make a move and somehow shift the dynamic of the treatment or it would fail.

I think it's important for me to note that when David wasn't talking about sex, which was rare, when we were discussing other issues, we did so with far more ease. David was personable, witty, extremely intelligent, and socially engaging. In these fleeting moments, there were glimpses of an emerging intimacy between us, but little more. I was baffled and frustrated. Something had to shift.

It did. Right before Christmas, in our third year of treatment, David gave me a gift. I could tell that it was a fairly large book, and he acknowledged that it was a book of photographs. He said that he'd chosen it for me because he'd imagined from the eclectic artwork and furniture in my office that I would appreciate such a gift. After he left, I unwrapped the book, an anthology of mostly nude and often provocative photographs taken by a well-known photographer. As I thumbed through the pages, I lighted on a stunning photograph of a beautiful nude male, dramatically lit and mostly in shadow, except for his very large and very erect penis. It was David. Photographed 20 years ago, but unmistakably it was David. I suddenly remembered him saying some time ago that as a young man he had modeled for a famous photographer but I had forgotten. Obviously, I was taken aback by this overtly provocative and carefully chosen gift. What was David trying to communicate? I thought, "Boy! He certainly has *balls!*" Maybe he was asking me if I had balls, too. Or was I, like his father, just "a good egg with no balls?" Was this book a test? Would my response to his gift be proof for him of whether or not I had the balls to tolerate his "shit?" Or would I judge, retaliate and use his shit as a barometer for how good or how bad he was, like his mother had? Or collude with him, like his father had? Or use him as a scapegoat, like they both had? Was he challenging me and saying, "Open your fucking mouth and show some balls?" If so, this made the book a very real and very powerful gift. I knew I had my voice back!

Looking at his photograph, I also began to question my envy of David: his youth, his looks, his allure and his daring. He was the "bad boy," living out all his fantasies, and he seemed to relish them. Unlike David, I was the "good boy," just like my mother taught me to be, so I just fantasized. David's life was wild. Mine was not. These were not incredibly strong feelings, but they were feelings none-theless and worth noting, and I'm sure that my intervention in our next session was somewhat informed by this new awareness.

In that session, David asked immediately if I liked the book. I told him that I did like the book and I particularly appreciated this photographer's work. I also commented that it was "an odd but interesting gift." He smiled. Then I said, very offhandedly, "You know, David, you really take *great* pics. I *never* do. I take really *lousy* photographs!" Somewhat taken aback by my deliberately provocative com-ment—reducing a work of art to a snapshot (and also, playfully but pointedly, reducing David to a photograph of a penis)—he recognized the irony as well as my tease. He began to laugh. So did I. In the midst of this shared experience I said, "David, how did you think I'd react to that photograph?" He said, "I'm not sure." And I responded, "Are you *sure* you're not sure?" "Maybe I just wanted to get a '*rise*' out of you," he answered. "Well, you certainly did that," I replied, "but, now I'm really confused, because you said you left each of your therapists when you thought you were getting a 'rise' out of them. I'm now wondering if, in fact, you left them because you *didn't*. And maybe you didn't because they couldn't get past your sexuality; perhaps, they felt *neutered* and just gave up. It is very hard to get past." "Nobody ever has," he answered. I said, "And that made you feel ineffective. *You* weren't getting a 'rise' out of them. And they may have felt ineffective, as well, because they couldn't get to know you. I know I've felt that way. You have no difficulty letting me see you naked, but great difficulty letting me see *you*." There was a long pause, and I asked, "Who *are* you?"

This intervention was a turning point in our relationship. I feel that it served us both in numerous ways. It leveled, somewhat, the analytic tilt and reinforced the mutuality of our relationship. My teasing, my reducing a photographic work of art to a dime store snapshot, I think, helped to avert a reenactment of his earlier experiences. I believe that the irony of my comment—you take good pictures, and I don't—illumined for him my awareness of my flaws. It validated, for him, both my appreciation of beauty *and* my capacity for lust, that I was capable of both and that I was also capable of separating beauty and lust. It allowed me, as well, to share with him my vulnerability and frustration by identifying with his other therapists' possible dilemma. It expressed my genuine wish to know David the *man*, not just David the hustler or David with the big dick. I also think it showed him that I, too, had balls, and try as he might he couldn't neuter me. That put us on a level playing field, and we were speaking the same language, which then allowed me to comment on the disparity: his overt nakedness in the photo and his fear of exposure in the treatment room. A camera takes pictures, so inherently it objectifies its subject. This kind of exposure, for David, is safe. It shows his power and his manliness. Exposing feelings is what makes him feel truly naked.

Our sessions began to change. He still talked about his sexual encounters, and still in explicit detail, but he talked less about his own sexual prowess and more about how he experienced these encounters—his need to objectify men and to be objectified by them, his fear of intimacy, his feelings of loss. He also talked touchingly at times about his longing to love someone and to be loved, to be able to connect to another in an intimate and meaningful way. I was no longer seen as just an object. David and I were becoming two subjects in a mutual, inter-subjective relationship. Dialogue was replacing monologue. I was able to ask questions, often detailed inquiries, and he would respond in kind. We were slowly peeling away, like the skin of an onion, his defense mechanisms, to better understand how and why he used them, and to understand, as well, how his deeply embedded organizing patterns, originally installed to protect him from painful experiences and traumas, were now disconnecting him from other people.

Within a short period of time, he said that he needed to share a specific sexual behavior that he'd feared discussing; he was certain that I would find it abhorrent. When I asked him what I might find so repugnant, he said, simply, "I eat shit." I paused briefly and asked, "Why?" David paused, and then said, "That's such a simple question, yet nobody's ever bothered to ask me that."

I had asked David a direct and unambiguous question, one that I realized, in its directness, had the potential to induce shame. However, the question "Why?" was not dissimilar to my asking him, "So, who are you?" in the session following the one where he'd given me the book. At the time, that simple question, I felt, communicated, without ambiguity, my genuine wish to know him—and he understood that. My rationale this time was similar. I felt that straightforward questions would provide reinforcement for him of my ability to tolerate whatever he had to tell me. I hoped it would reinforce, as well, that his importance to me would override any behavior he might engage in short of harming someone or himself. I also thought, at the time, about his earlier challenge to me: Could I tolerate his "shit?"

At first, David's graphic descriptions of scatological sex were difficult to listen to. He was right. The thought of anyone defecating on someone, allowing someone to defecate in one's mouth, or smearing feces on one another, was repulsive to me. How could I continue to engage David when his behavior was so repugnant? Somehow, I needed to get past the behavior to the person and to the contextual meaning it had for him (Goldberg 1995). My being able to separate the person from the behavior, to focus on David's experience during the act and what it meant to him, rather than on the act itself, was key. For David, my ability to do this seemed to foster in him a trust in me and a sense of safety in our relationship. I could tolerate his shit and, together, we could contain it. This, in turn, encouraged an open-ended dialogue, a mutual exploration of extremely difficult subject matter. We talked, often in explicit detail, of what he experienced while engaging in scatological sex. I found myself asking questions that I would never have imagined I'd be able to ask. It might very well have been impossible for me to do this with David, and too shameful and humiliating for David to respond, had our relationship not been developing into a mutually, and unexpected, intimate one. We were no longer talking about shit, even though, in fact, we were.

According to David, ingesting someone else's feces involved an elaborate process for him and his partner: proper hygiene, a regimented diet and an acute awareness of one's state of wellness. It also assumed a deep sense of trust as the anus of one's partner is placed directly on the mouth of the other. As David described the relationship, each person is keenly sensitive to the needs of the other. During the ritual, David reported feeling a deep connectedness; he felt emotionally full, nurtured and loved, feelings he had never felt as a child.

In one session, while graphically describing the awakening and excitation of his various senses during this act, David said, "It's as if my mother is feeding me. I feel this deep, deep hunger, and she feeds me, slowly and knowingly, stopping for a moment and then starting again, until I'm full. It's like a mother eagle forcing food down her baby's gullet, forcing it to eat the innards of some animal she's killed just for her baby, so it'll thrive."

This, for me, was a remarkably visceral and powerful description, rich in symbolism and metaphor, and too complex to process fully in the moment. However, at once, it did give me a profound understanding of the meaning for David of this otherwise abhorrent act. I also remember thinking, at the time, that the shape and texture of a firm stool, essential in this act, was similar to an umbilical cord. So, in some primitive and fundamental way, perhaps it was David's lifeline, his sustenance. The eroticizing and the ingestion of shit gave him a sense of connection with another and a feeling of intimacy that he had not yet realized in other relationships.

There is a long tradition of psychoanalytic thinking that associates non-normative sexual behavior with dehumanization and perversion, but can't these often nonconventional acts that seemingly treat the other as an object, when viewed in their specific, meaningful context, reveal unexpected meanings such as ties of mutual recognition and connectedness? In fact, as David detailed the rituals of scatological sex, at its root were tacit bonds of trust and an empathic view of the other as a subject of integrity and lovability. The complex network of rules that embed and regulate this erotic practice stipulates a moral context of mutual recognition. Ironically, the potential for shame and degradation instead created a heightened sensitivity to how each was affected by the other, as well as a deep sense of trust and solidarity. As odd as it may sound, during this sexual act David experienced a kind of intimacy that was antithetical to his early object relationships.

Aside from his provocative and overt sexuality, which David claimed had often been a deterrent to successful treatment, I now began to wonder if any of David's short-lived therapies had reached an impasse when David's penchant for scatological sex surfaced in the treatment. Could there have been an inducement of shame, or of other unexpressed feelings in David, or in the therapist, or in both that might have played out in the transference and/or in the countertransference enactments?

In a later session, when it seemed appropriate to introduce this notion, we began to revisit some of his earlier treatment experiences and were able to see that not all of them ended for any one specific reason. Most of these treatment failures did not result from someone doing something to David, but some, as David described them, unfortunately did.

In some instances, according to David, when he felt comfortable enough with a therapist to begin to talk about his scatological experiences, once it was verbalized, it was often never spoken about again. Talking about one particularly painful incident, David said, "I finally brought it up, and it was just left hanging there. Now it was in the room, and we didn't talk about it. That made it worse!" I nodded in agreement and said, "I'm sure it did. Now there was shit in the room. You both could see it, you both could smell it, but, for whatever reason, you both couldn't talk about it, and that felt *really* shitty." "It was awful," he said. "Now, I felt like shit. I was sitting in the room with someone, and I was alone, and I felt like shit. I wanted to scream at him, "What I do may disgust you, but it's who I am that disgusts me. I can't connect to another human being. I don't know how to love another human being. Isn't that worse?" Suddenly, the room was deafeningly silent. I was aware of my accelerated heartbeat and of my eyes filling up with tears. I could hear David's shallow breathing, and I'm certain he heard mine. After a while, all I could say was, "Yes, David, that *is* worse."

David's inability to feel an attachment to another human being was far more shameful for him than the shame and humiliation induced by his sexual behavior. From his early childhood to adulthood, David had learned that shit was the only way to connect to another in an erotic and intimate way. Maybe, in time, this way of connecting could become, instead, a transitional object (Winnicott 1986), a link to more expansive and fulfilling intimacies.

In the years that followed, we continued to focus on David's experiences rather than on his behavior. Our work did not involve trying to control the behavior; we worked, instead, to try to deepen our understanding of it. In fact, the frequency of his indulging in scatological sex increased for quite a while, but so did his understanding of it. Interestingly and unexpectedly, as our relationship continued to deepen and become more intimate, his longings to love and to be loved by another intensified. Also unexpected, David began attempts at dating, which for most of his adult life had been anathema, and he has done so, often without sex. Surprisingly, too, his nonconventional sex encounters, as he forges new relationships and attempts more intimate connections, are slowly waning.

Some time ago, on a trip abroad, David brought back another gift for me. This time it was a small package, and he asked that I open it in his presence. It was a life-sized bronze ear. I asked why he had bought me this, and he said, "Because you listen." I turned it over and realized that there was a seashell motif on the back, along with the artist's signature. I looked up and said, "There's also a shell …" And he said, "I also can hear you. It works both ways." The ear, a symbol of an unexpected and ever-deepening intimacy between us, has been displayed prominently and proudly in my office ever since.

Acknowledgements

My gratitude to Janine de Peyer, to Caryn Sherman-Meyer and, most especially, to Steven Seidman for their insightful and invaluable critiques.

References

Benjamin, Jessica. 1988. *The Bonds of Love*. New York: Pantheon Books.
——1998. *Like Subjects, Love Objects: Essays on Recognition and Sexual Difference*. New Haven: Yale University Press.
Corbett, Ken. 2009. *Boyhoods: Rethinking Masculinities*. New Haven: Yale University Press.
Diamond, Michael. 2009. "Masculinity and its Discontents: Making Room for the 'Mother' Inside the Male—An Essential Achievement for Healthy Male Gender Identity." In B. Reis and R. Grossmark (eds) *Heterosexual Masculinities: Contemporary Perspectives from Psychoanalytic Gender Theory*. London: Routledge, 23–53.
Dimen, Muriel. 2003. *Sexuality, Intimacy, Power*. Hillsdale: The Analytic Press.
Dominici, Thomas and Lesser, Ronnie C. (eds). 1995. *Disorienting Sexuality*. London: Routledge.
Duberman, Martin. 2002. *Cures: A Gay Man's Odyssey*. New York: Basic Books.
Giddens, Anthony. 1993. *The Transformation of Intimacy: Sexuality, Love and Eroticism in Modern Societies*. London: Blackwell Publishers.
Goldberg, Arnold. 1995. *The Problem of Perversion: The View from Self Psychology*. New Haven: Yale University Press.
Kohut, Heinz. 1987. *The Kohut Seminars: On Self Psychology and Psychotherapy with Adolescents and Young Adults*. Miriam Elson (ed.). New York: W.W. Norton & Company.
Reis, Bruce and Grossmark, Robert (eds). 2009. *Heterosexual Masculinities: Contemporary Perspectives from Psychoanalytic Gender Theory*. London: Routledge.
Seidman, Steven. 1997. *Difference Troubles: Queering Social Theory and Sexual Politics*. London: Cambridge University Press.
Weeks, Jeffrey. 1995. *Invented Moralities: Sexual Values in an Age of Uncertainty*. New York: Columbia University Press.
Winnicott, D.W. 1986. *Playing and Reality*. London: Tavistock Publications.

4 Hey God, is that You in my underpants?

Sex, love and religiosity among American college students

Roger Friedland and Paolo Gardinali

"This boy called and asked me if I wanted to go with him to dinner," a mother recounts her conversation with her daughter, a 20 year old at an eastern college. The boy had promised to drop by her dorm room beforehand.

That was sweet, her daughter thought; they would eat together at the dorm cafeteria.

The boy walked her right past the dining commons and into town to a local restaurant. When the bill came and she pulled out her purse, the boy put out his hand. He would pay; he insisted.

"Mom, it was a date!" her daughter shouted ecstatically on the phone. "I got asked out on a date!"

She'd been at the university for two years. It was the first one.

A date is a rare phenomenon, not unlike seeing a California condor in the Sierra Mountains during the 1980s. These days, undergraduate men typically have more of what they call "fuck buddies" than dates. We know more or less who does what sexually to whom in the university and under what relational conditions, having researched the love lives of university students through interviews and survey work for several years now.

Normally, you have to pay kids to take surveys. When we began at a handful of universities in 2006, we did not have much money. All we could muster was a knowing invitation. Our first banner ad on Facebook ran as follows: "When was the last time you got laid? Prayed? Said I love you? Tell us about it." In a couple of weeks, more than 1,000 students in California and Texas had taken the survey, a quarter of whom wanted to be interviewed personally about it. We have now surveyed thousands of students both through Facebook and in large university classes at the University of California, Santa Barbara where we both work.[1]

The generation that launched the sexual revolution of the 1960s and 1970s sought to unleash its pleasures through joints and window pane acid, but they were powered by a hunger for truth, for a rawness of experience, guiltless at the limits of social convention. Erotic pleasure was, of course, a central part of that repressed truth. Sex was politics. It is important to remember that the Parisian events of May 1968 began as a student protest at the University of Nanterre, led by Daniel Cohn-Bendit against parietal rules that forbade boys being able to visit girls in the university dormitories. That generation still identified love as the highest form of truth, a reality beyond, and indeed against, social forms (Allyn

2001: 101). "When the truth is found to be lies and all the joy within you dies," Gracie Slick belted out the lyrics to "Don't You Want Somebody To Love?" on Jefferson Airplane's *Surrealistic Pillow* in 1967, "you better find somebody to love." Love was an answer to social untruth.

In the USA, the Christian right reached for power in response to that sex, what they saw as a horrible Babylonian debauchery. Jerry Falwell began his Moral Majority in the wake of the 1973 Supreme Court decision legalizing abortion after stumbling into a Led Zeppelin concert where young people were grinding, fondling and slithering together on the floor. The two were linked. "There," he reports, "they witnessed a horrifying scene. Thousands of young men and women were lying on the floor, engaged in every filthy act imaginable ... On the stage the rock star hero of thousands of American young people stood with out-stretched arms in front of a cross, with psychedelic, fluorescent lights twirling around him." Falwell reported feeling "the tremendous weight of sin that was placed on Jesus Christ at the cross ... He resolved anew to help young Christians turn this country upside down for Christ" (Harding 2000: 120, 195).

For more than three decades now, there has been a religious political obsession with what goes on in young people's underpants, with their sex, that they do it and with so many, that they produce children that they do not want, that their pleasurable combinations of organs are immoral and obscene.

They are concerned with their sex. We are not. It's their love lives that have us worried. The generation that lived the sexual revolution took love for granted; sex was the great uncertainty, the adventure. The new generation has reversed the equation. For them, sex has become ordinary; what is uncertain, frightening, and for an increasing number of them unbelievable, is love. It has become easier for a lot of young women to put a man's penis in their mouths than to hold his hand. That is the real obscenity we want to explore.

In this paper, we want to give you a quick snapshot of who is doing what to whom on college campuses. Then we want to ask, what's love got to do with erotic pleasure? Finally, we want to ask, what's God got to do with the organization of sexuality and love?

In our surveys, we ask each university student about their last sex act. Through social networks and big lecture hall surveys we have now accumulated information about several thousand carnal encounters—what they did, how they felt, who they were, the nature of the relationship in which their sex took place. We begin with the basic coordinates of students' sexual cartography.[2] One could easily conclude, based on media reporting, and even scholarly studies of casual forms of sexuality that all huddle under the rubric of "hooking up," that non-intimate, functional forms of sexual encounters are ubiquitous (Bogle 2008). It is not true.

First, a lot of students come into college not having "had sex," which in the Facebook survey means using something beyond hands, concretely that their or their partners' sexual organs have not penetrated a bodily orifice: vagina, anus or mouth. About a third of university students had their first sexual experiences at college. Almost 40% of the males and 36% of the females who are 18 years old, the freshmen, have not had sex, while, by the time they are 22, that is graduating seniors, those proportions have dropped to between 4% and 6%.

Table 4.1 Sex activity by age and gender

Gender			Age of respondent					
			18 N	19 N	20 N	21 N	22 N	Total N
			Col %	Col %	Col %	Col %	Col %	Col %
Male	Engaged in	Yes	35	43	50	54	32	214
	sexual activity		60.3%	75.4%	82.0%	88.5%	94.1%	79.0%
		No	23	14	11	7	2	57
			39.7%	24.6%	18.0%	11.5%	5.9%	21.0%
	Total		58	57	61	61	34	271
			100.0%	100.0%	100.0%	100.0%	100.0%	100.0%
Female	Engaged in	Yes	91	105	117	108	46	467
	sexual activity		64.5%	73.9%	83.0%	85.0%	95.8%	78.0%
		No	50	37	24	19	2	132
			35.5%	26.1%	17.0%	15.0%	4.2%	22.0%
	Total		141	142	141	127	48	599
			100.0%	100.0%	100.0%	100.0%	100.0%	100.0%

Source: (Facebook 2007)

When you look at the sexual behaviors of first and second-year students in large sociology lecture courses at UC Santa Barbara and break their sexual activity into different acts, you again discover that virginity is not dead, even at a school known for its hard partying and drinking. A third of all students in large introductory sociology classes—and there is no difference between males and females—have never had sexual intercourse.

Second, there is a considerable amount of first-time sexual encounters among students. We asked students who were having sex whether it was the first time with this person or had they done it with her or him before? First-time sex is overwhelmingly loveless: 80% of the respondents having first-time sex said they did not love their partners. However, if you look at the whole population, whether or not they are having sex, less than a quarter of all students were having sex for the first time with their partner. In contrast, little more than half of all students had their last sexual encounter with somebody with whom they had had sex at least once before. A little more than a fifth of the total sample was not having sex at all. That means that if we look at all students, whether or not they are having sex, there is just about as much chastity as first-time sex. Between the media hype and the not infrequent shame of the chaste, the data make it clear that the media, the general public and students themselves, from what we have gleaned, tend to overstate the extent of truly casual sex.

Third, there's a big gender gap in the incidence of first-time sex. Men are much more likely to be having sex for the first time with a partner than are women (Chi square = .000). Some 41% of all male sexual encounters were first-time affairs, while just one-quarter of the female sexual encounters were the first time with the partner. How could this be? Who are they doing it with? Are they lying? We don't think so.

There are two pathways by which men can be having more one-night stands than women: either some women are very sexually active and/or men are able to go

Table 4.2 In which acts have you ever engaged?

	Gender		
	Male *N* *Col%*	Female *N* *Col%*	Total *N* *Col%*
Talking intimately	431 92.1%	859 91.8%	1,290
Holding hands	431 92.1%	884 94.4%	1,315
Kissing	426 91.0%	872 93.2%	1,298
Hugging	453 96.8%	902 96.4%	1,355
Manual stimulation of my genitals by a partner	374 79.9%	720 76.9%	1,094
Manual stimulation of my partner's genitals	370 79.1%	701 74.9%	1,071
Received oral sex	350 74.8%	620 66.2%	970
Given oral sex	305 65.2%	620 66.2%	925
Vaginal sex	315 67.3%	588 62.8%	903
Received anal intercourse	19 4.1%	112 12.0%	131
Given anal intercourse	88 18.8%	15 1.6%	103
None of the above	8 1.7%	15 1.6%	23
Total	468 100.0%	936 100.0%	1404 100.0%

Source: (UCSB 2008–11)

Table 4.3 Cross-tabulation of recent sex by gender

	Gender		
	Male *N* *Col %*	Female *N* *Col %*	Total *N* *Col %*
Not having sex	57 21.0%	132 22.1%	189 21.7%
Having first-time sex with a partner	88 32.4%	118 19.7%	206 23.7%
Having repeated sex with a partner	127 46.7%	348 58.2%	475 54.6%
Total	272 100.0%	598 100.0%	870 100.0%

Source: (Facebook 2007)

Table 4.4 How many sex partners have you had?

		Gender		
		Male N Col %	Female N Col %	Total N Col %
Number of partners	1–2	77	164	241
		36.0%	35.5%	35.7%
	3–4	49	97	146
		22.9%	21.0%	21.6%
	5–10	55	141	196
		25.7%	30.5%	29.0%
	>10	33	60	93
		15.4%	13.0%	13.8%
Total		214	462	676
		100.0%	100.0%	100.0%

Source: (Facebook 2007)

seriatim from woman to woman. Both things are going on. We asked respondents how many sexual partners they had had over the course of their lives. If we look, for instance, at all college students through the Facebook surveys, women, on average, have had significantly fewer partners than men (6 versus 7.8, t (806) = 3.32, P = .001).

The conventional understanding of this gender difference in reported number of sexual partners is that men inflate their reported sexual activity. However, if we decompose those averages into actual counts, there is a large portion of women who have had many partners. When you get up to the higher numbers of sexual partners people have had, there were actually more women than men with big body counts. Some 44% of the women have had sex with half a dozen or more partners. Indeed, a larger percentage of women than men have had more than five sexual partners.

Our interviews suggest one of the ways this might occur. At UC Santa Barbara's sororities there is, for example, a tradition of the "frat loop," where young women try to have sex, and at least make out, with a fraternity brother from each and every fraternity on campus before they graduate. Other girls just choose one house and see how many boys in that house they can "hook up" with before graduation. While young university women, on average, have fewer sexual partners than young men, a lot of young women are playing according to *Sex and the City* rules.

The other source of this gender difference in one-night stands is that the hook-up has become a pathway to the formation of relationships (England and Thomas 2006). Some guys are able to go from flower to flower in part because a large majority of women are hoping that a relationship will bloom from first-time genital contact. It is the women who are disproportionately hoping for this. We found that 60% of women who are having sex for the first time with a guy are hoping a relationship will develop from it after it's done. The problem is that a much lower proportion of guys want that, a 20% gap. Indeed, a majority of the guys who have just had sex for the first time with those women do not even want to see them again, even just to have sex one more time.

Guys do it this way, as President Clinton admitted, because they can. There's an erotic ecology here. Among other things, between female university attendance ratios kissing 60% in some places, with men more likely than women to drop out over the course of their college careers, and the much larger proportion of men who are gay compared to women who are lesbians, there is a growing shortfall in male heterosexual supply. Remember what happens to your demand curves in this situation: The price goes up.

If we consider the gendered order of preferences, women's market position is even worse. If we remember that most women are hoping that a relationship will develop from a first-time sexual encounter and most men with whom they are having that sex do not want a relationship to develop, then it would be rational for some women to generate a diversified portfolio of short-term investments to increase the probability that one will pay off. Further examination is required, but what appears to men through the sexual double standard as wholesale "slut-dom" of which they get to partake may be—at least in part—the outcome of rational female romantic strategists. Many of these women are looking for intimacy, if not love. Of course, it is also possible that some girls just want to have fun, but, as we shall see, the odds of much female erotic pleasure in these encounters are too long to make that a rational explanation. The data suggest that a lot of men are getting into women's underpants by riding on women's romantic hopes.

This situation also enables a lot of men to misread the meaning of female sexual availability. Men can be players because they assume women are too. It is not hard to find the instrumental and disparaging male braggadocio that accompanies this posture. A guy at the UCSB campus recently posted the following article: "Isla Vista: 7 Ways to Spot the Slut." In it he advises the men to zero in on women smokers, especially of cigars. Such women are risk takers. "If she smokes a stogey, she'll probably smoke your dick, too." The contours of male sexual predation have changed since 1949, when Arthur Miller wrote *Death of a Salesman*, in which Hap seduces and, thereby "ruins," the fiancées of executives, even going to their weddings afterwards.

A lot of college men are getting their sex hot while keeping their hearts cold. We asked students to describe the nature of the relationship in which their last sex occurred, using their own categories. In a "hook-up," for instance, there is no meal shared, no movie or concert, no intimacy that might smack of courtship, just flirty words at a bar, a kiss on the dance floor, a text message late at night. Then let's go hook up. It's a physiological function against the wall in the parking lot behind a club, on a park bench, on the bathroom's cold porcelain, or more commonly in whoever's bedroom is closest, known as the "home bedroom advantage." It's usually the male's room—in part because they tend to throw the parties—from which girls walk home alone afterwards in what is known as the "walk of shame" (Hamilton and Armstrong 2009). "Friends with benefits," "fuck buddies" and "no strings attached," on the other hand, involve carnal congress with people you know.

A number of analysts argue that "hooking up" has become the dominant form of sexual interaction on campus. Kathleen Bogle, in her ethnography on hooking up, for example, argues:

There may be individuals who abstain from hooking-up, however, there is no obvious alternative for them if they are interested in sexual interaction with the opposite sex on campus. Although some students were able to find a relationship without hooking up, most students see hooking up as "the only game in town." Due to the lack of alternatives, most students either adapt to the hookup scene or get left out.

(Bogle 2008: 71)

This is not the case. In our surveys of large introductory sociology classes, we found that hooking up, per se, was the occasion for one-fifth of all students' last sex acts. Indeed, the proportion of sex taking place in non-romantic contexts is equal to that taking place in boy–girlfriend relationships (around 45%). Casual sex, even if we include sex with friends, is still not the only game in town.

The gender differences in the relational context of sex are stark. Only a little more than a third of the guys had their last sex with a girlfriend or boyfriend. The overwhelming majority of males had their last sex just as sex, without any emotional meaning: as "hook-ups," "booty calls," "fuck buddies," "no strings

Table 4.5 In what kind of relationship did you have your last sex?

	Gender		Total *N* Col %
	Male *N* Col %	Female *N* Col %	
Friends with benefits	54 13.8%	89 11.8%	143 12.5%
Hook-up	91 23.3%	144 19.1%	235 20.5%
No strings attached	32 8.2%	48 6.4%	80 7.0%
Boyfriend/girlfriend	145 37.1%	354 47.0%	499 43.6%
Husband/wife	3 0.8%	9 1.2%	12 1.0%
Lover	15 3.8%	47 6.2%	62 5.4%
A date	7 1.8%	17 2.3%	24 2.1%
Booty call	16 4.1%	7 .9%	23 2.0%
Fuck buddies	18 4.6%	12 1.6%	30 2.6%
Other	10 2.6%	26 3.5%	36 3.1%
Total	391 100.0%	753 100.0%	1,144 100.0%

Note: The UCSB surveys involved a small change in the definition of a sexual encounter, including manual genital stimulation, whereas the Facebook survey did not include this activity.
Source: (UCSB 2008–11)

attached," or "friends with benefits." In contrast, over half of all female sex acts took place in romantic relationships.[3]

There is a little problem in this economy of bliss. Almost half of all sex acts take place in nonromantic relationships. In their talk students do not easily connect sex and love. Recent ethnographic work suggests that college students talk a lot about sex, but rarely about love, and that, when talking about romance, they almost never associate it with erotic behavior or feeling (Freitas 2008).

However, how they talk and how they feel are two different things. We asked students to describe how easy it is for them to dissociate sex and love. Only a minority of students—less than a third—find it easy to have sex without feelings of emotional attachment. The gender differences are large and very significant (Chi square = .000). A large majority of women find it difficult. Males are around three times more likely to find it very easy (M: 17% vs. F: 6%), and almost three times less likely to find it very difficult (M: 10% vs. F: 28%). Women have much more difficulty disconnecting their hearts from their genitalia than do men.

One 18-year-old female put it to us this way: "For me, sex is synonymous with the word love. My sex life arose from love, as an extension of it, and though I have not experienced this myself, I believe having sex without being in love with your partner would be completely empty and well ... good exercise and that's about it." Another 19-year-old woman said that it was "very difficult. I've done it but sex was way better with the one guy I was in love with. I felt more comfortable with the guy I was in love with ... therefore, I came out of my shell in the moment (if you get me) ... Sex without emotional attachment makes me feel like I'm just a piece of ass ... plain and simple."

The question is, why the gender difference? There are two dominant ways to parse this difference. Some, particularly those who study the biochemistry of

Table 4.6 How easy is it for you to separate sex and emotional attachment?

		Gender		
		Male N Col %	Female N Col %	Total N Col %
Sex without emotional attachment is ...	Very easy	37 17.2%	29 6.2%	66 9.7%
	Somewhat easy	51 23.7%	81 17.3%	132 19.4%
	Indifferent	51 23.7%	84 18.0%	135 19.8%
	Difficult	55 25.6%	144 30.8%	199 29.2%
	Very difficult	21 9.8%	129 27.6%	150 22.0%
Total		215 100.0%	467 100.0%	682 100.0%

Source: (Facebook 2007)

attachment and sexual arousal, and the evolutionary psychologists who attempt to theorize sex differences in terms of the advantages in reproductive fitness they confer, argue that females will be more likely to be physiologically programmed for the pursuit of long-term mating strategies and that romantic love is, in fact, a motivational system designed to sustain them. From an evolutionary point of view, given the relative scarcity of eggs, the relative shortness of fertility, and the need to secure paternal support and protection during infancy, females should be more inclined to long-term mating strategies and more likely to conjoin sexuality and love. Given the hormonal linkage between sexual arousal, orgasm and infant nursing, there is likely a physiological basis for these gendered differences in the mechanisms of attachment (Fisher 2004; Puts 2010).

Others argue that there is a sexual double standard, that we are socialized to believe that men's sexual drives are greater and more urgent, that men are expected to be more agentic than women, and that women are both socialized against and negatively sanctioned for wanting and seeking their own sexual pleasure outside of a romantic context (Hamilton and Armstrong 2009; Armstrong *et al.* 2012). In this context, Armstrong *et al.* argue, "[t]hese views about men's and women's sexual natures may also be internalized by men and women as personal preferences and deeply felt desires. Women, more than men, may come to connect love and sex ..." (Armstrong *et al.* 2012: 10). Thus, women will be more likely to feel comfortable soliciting partners' sexual acts that give them pleasure in a romantic relationship and will be better able to experience pleasure. Women connect sex and love because sex outside of a loving relationship is a source of shame and guilt, not to mention consciously or unconsciously coded as unwomanly behavior.

Whatever the source of these gender differences, a lot of casual sex is taking place that does not comport with female preferences. Only 20% of the women even claim that sex without love is easy or very easy. We know that first-time sex is overwhelmingly loveless. This means that a lot of casual sex acts are being performed by women who are doing things that are not easy at all.

First-time sex is much more likely to be drunken sex for both males and females. The hook-up scene at parties and bars is associated with high levels of inebriation (Bogle 2008). For first-time sex, freighted as it is with uncertainty, risk and indeed some measure of guilt, particularly if there are no expectations of its leading to something else, alcohol provides both courage and—especially for women—exculpation. A woman who is not drunk while having sex, one female informant explained, is presumed either to be "a real slut" or involved in a serious relationship.

If we look at first-time sexual encounters, we find that, for women, the relationship between the difficulty of affectless sex and sobriety is strong and monotonic. The more difficult it is for women to separate sex and emotional attachment, the more likely they are to have been sober in their last sexual encounter. However, it is also the case that women who are having casual sex and say it is easy are precisely the women who take their sex with booze, often lots of it.

The results are consistent with two possible interpretations. One is that women who drink and who enjoy sex without attachment are sensualists, seeking sensuous experiences through both alcoholic and carnal stimulation. The other possibility—the one we believe is correct—is that women who say sex without emotional attachment is easy are most likely to be inebriated during that sex because it is *not* easy. As one female student recounted, the "last hook-up was … stupid. I was under the influence and not thinking about what I was doing. It was stupid that he was sober and took advantage of the situation because he definitely could not get in my pants otherwise." For young women, "hooking up" sober is incredibly daring, a sign, as another female informant put it, "that you care. You are out there and there is nothing to hide behind." Alcohol allows them to anesthetize their moral and emotional sensibilities, particularly when a love that could moralize sexuality is absent. They drink to cope. Their easy sex likely isn't.

Most young women don't get love from first-time sex, but they don't get much pleasure either. In any sexual encounter, women are much less likely to orgasm than are men. The most systematic national survey found that 70% of men aged 18–24 reported always having an orgasm, whereas 22% of young women in that age range did so (Laumann *et al.* 1994: 116). The orgasmic odds for women who hook up are much worse. In their study of the "hook-up" culture, England and Thomas found a major orgasm gap in students' last such sexual encounters, 40% versus 14% (England and Thomas 2006). "The orgasm disparity is much worse than [the] sex gap in pay in the labor market," they report. "[W]omen have less than half the orgasms of men on hook ups, but women earn more than three-quarters as much as men!"

A lot of women tell us that it is not about orgasm, but you should keep in mind that, if you are a woman and it is orgasm you are after, you should be a lesbian. Not only are their orgasm rates much higher than that of heterosexual women, but also they are more sexually satisfied (Coleman *et al.* 1983; Thompson 1995).[4]

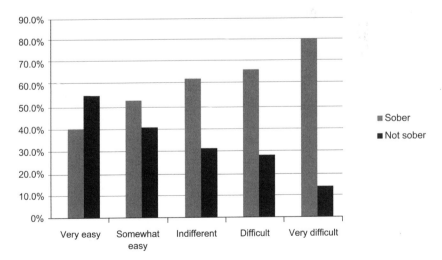

Figure 4.1 Difficulty for women of separating sex and love and alcohol consumption during last sex, first-time sexual encounters

Source: (Facebook 2007)

Lesbian lovers know their partners' bodies; there is no risk of pregnancy and almost none of sexual violence; and lesbian sex tends to take place in the context of intimate relations. Male sexual incompetence, exploitation, sexual practices and female sexual guilt all play a part in heterosexual women's low orgasm rate in casual sex. If you are only going to have sex once, for a man to take pains to give a woman an orgasm is like tipping at a truck stop.

However, love also matters—a lot.[5] Those students who say they loved the person with whom they last had sex were more likely to orgasm. As you can see in Table 4.7, 83% of the men who loved their last sexual partner reported an orgasm, as opposed to only 60% of those who did not. In survey research, a difference of this magnitude is considered substantial. For women, the orgasmic effect of love is even greater: 58% of the women who loved their partner had an orgasm, whereas only 26% of those who did not love them had an orgasm (Chi square = .00). Not surprisingly, the female orgasm rate in first hook-ups is very, very low, around 11% (Armstrong *et al.* 2012: 24).[6]

Romantic love is in trouble. Such love is not just an emotion, it is a code, a set of practices, an ontology, indeed an institution. Romantic love is an historically specific medium of communication linked to marriage. Over the last three centuries, in the West, the institution of love has increasingly ordered exclusive, intimate world making through marriage as a private relation between individuals, "shifting the basis of marriage from sharing tasks to sharing feelings" (Coontz 2005: 156). Love is a symbolically constituted institution, to which one must be committed as a prerequisite to its enactment. "One loves loving and, therefore, a person whom one can love," remarks the systems theorist Niklas

Table 4.7 Orgasm and love

Gender			Did you love this person at the time?		
			Yes N Col %	*No* N Col %	*Total* N Col %
Male	Did you achieve orgasm?	Yes	118 83.1%	148 60.2%	266 68.6%
		No	24 16.9%	98 39.8%	122 31.4%
	Total		142 100.0%	246 100.0%	388 100.0%
Female	Did you achieve orgasm?	Yes	208 58.1%	102 26.2%	310 41.5%
		No	150 41.9%	287 73.8%	437 58.5%
	Total		358 100.0%	389 100.0%	747 100.0%
	Total		500 100.0%	635 100.0%	1,135 100.0%

Source: (UCSB 2008–11)

Luhmann (2010: 32). One falls in love, he notes, "because of loving love." Luhmann argues that it is the limits of intersubjective communication that make sexuality—"the impassioning" of love—essential to its operation (Luhmann 2010: 58–59, 47, 37).[7] This passionate love, experienced as "risky fate," also requires a medium of proof. "How is one ever to be certain that this sole and unique instance of luck has come to pass, that one loves and is loved in a way that can never be otherwise?" This problem of proof, he argues, is "solved" by the decision to marry (Luhmann 2010: 65–66).

The institutionalization of love requires individuals to be in love with love. Yoked, as love has been to marriage, a belief in and a desire for the solidity of marriage would sustain romantic love as a value.[8] Both are increasingly in question. It is one thing to discover that a large proportion of students do not expect love-based marriages to last over the course of their lives. With even odds of marital dissolution, this is not surprising, but we found that significant proportions of young people don't even want a romantic bond to last over their lives. More than a quarter of the men don't want or are not sure they want to stay with the same partner all their lives.

Marriage, of course, is no guarantee of love, but, in that marriage has been a medium through which romantic love diffused as a basis of mate-selection, it is not surprising that its de-institutionalization is associated with an erosion in its believability. A large proportion of students question love as it is now constructed. Not a few young women we interviewed equate love with weakness. "It's so

Table 4.8 Do you want or expect to stay with the same person all of your life?

		Gender		
		Male *N* *Col %*	*Female* *N* *Col %*	*Total* *N* *Col %*
Do you want to stay with the same person all of your life?	Yes	337 72.5%	762 81.2%	1,099 78.3%
	No	37 8.0%	46 4.9%	83 5.9%
	Not sure/ Do not know	91 19.6%	130 13.9%	221 15.8%
Total		465 100.0%	938 100.0%	1403 100.0%
Do you expect to stay with the same person all of your life	Yes	316 68.0%	667 71.1%	983 70.1%
	No	40 8.6%	73 7.8%	113 8.1%
	Not sure/ Do not know	109 23.4%	198 21.2%	307 21.9%
Total		465 100.0%	938 100.0%	1403 100.0%

Source: (UCSB 2008–11)

girly," one outspoken and self-possessed young woman recounted. It means, she said, admitting that you are "weak," vulnerable to what a boy feels about you, giving him the power to destroy your sense of value, your very power to act, to take control. It means, she added, that you are just like your grandmother used to be, that, after all, we have not come very far.

Love is a metaphysical order fashioned out of the doings of pagan gods, Greek citizens who made it the motor for access to truth, the strivings of Christian mystics after divine union, the passionate expression of a human relation with the one God, an idiom of attachment for young women and women who were thereby enabled to choose their mates themselves. The angry temptation is to pull back its curtain to reveal the sad old man who is the real Wizard animating Dorothy's dream world.

Increasingly, there are those who wish to give up on love as outmoded, a crippling form posing demands that few of us can meet. While some feminist thinkers point to the ways in which patriarchy cripples our capacities to love (hooks 2001), other feminist thinkers have led the charge against love, arguing that women's search for it weakens them, making them vulnerable to male demands; that it functions like Nietzsche's slave morality, getting in the way of a woman getting ahead; that it keeps women down. Laura Kipnis, a media studies professor at Northwestern known for her deep-throated analyses of pornography, is their beguiling cheerleader. In her acerbic polemic *Against Love*, Kipnis derides love as an impossible ground for matrimony (Kipnis 2003).[9] Hers is a classic peep show. After God, she contends, romantic love has emerged as our last metaphysical frontier, a form in which it is too terrifying not to believe. As a result, hundreds of millions of us willingly endure a progressive anesthetization of our every complicating desire, and sexual desire above all, in order voluntarily to imprison ourselves within the order of domesticity, which produces compliant workers who are convinced that it is necessary for them to work at marriage just as we do at the plant and the office.

De-institutionalization involves denaturalizing regionalized ontologies, "uncovering" them as ideologies that legitimate interests (Friedland 2009). The modal feminist critique of love is that love, as currently constructed under conditions of gender inequality, legitimates male domination. We asked students whether they think romantic love brainwashes women and forms the basis for their subordination. Not many students, the results reveal, resolutely stand behind romantic love. Just over half either disagree or strongly disagree with the statement. A large proportion think that romance is or might be a sexist construct. Imagine if this many students said American democracy was just an ideological cover for capitalism. Democracy would be in serious trouble.

So who loves? Nobody, except for J.K. Rowling, seems to be worried about that. The religious right, and evangelical Christians in particular, have been preoccupied with young people's sexual abandon, pushing through abstinence-only forms of sexual education, which made it once again into President Obama's health reform bill in 2009. Sex outside of a sacramental marriage is a sin, they say. Only a return to God can contain our lusts.

Does God matter? A huge amount of social science research has now been conducted on whether religious belief and practice constrain the onset and promiscuity

Table 4.9 Does romantic love brainwash women?

| | | Gender | | |
		Male N Col %	Female N Col %	Total N Col %
Does romantic love brainwash women?	Strongly disagree	160 34.8%	293 31.6%	453 32.7%
	Somewhat disagree	103 22.4%	196 21.1%	299 21.6%
	Undecided	97 21.1%	180 19.4%	277 20.0%
	Somewhat agree	80 17.4%	223 24.1%	303 21.8%
	Strongly agree	20 4.3%	35 3.8%	55 4.0%
Total		460 100.0%	927 100.0%	1,387 100.0%

Source: (UCSB 2008–11)

of young people's sexuality. American sociologists have found that really religious young people have intercourse a bit later and with fewer partners (Bearman and Bruckner 2001; Burdette *et al.* 2009; Crockett *et al.* 1996; Hardy and Raffaelli 2003; Jones *et al.* 2005; Regnerus 2007; Thornton and Camburn 1989). However, the more people have looked, the less religion seems to matter.

Nor does religion show up in the way students talk about sex and love. When ethnographer Donna Freitas trekked across America looking for the relation between university students' faith and their love lives, students—including those at Catholic colleges—couldn't even relate to the question. "In interview after interview," Freitas reports, "students laughed out loud when asked what their faith tradition might have to say about these matters. They laughed at the idea that their faith had anything to say about sex—especially to gays—other than not to have it. They laughed because they see religious views about sexuality … as outdated and irrelevant. And they laughed because they were confused about the prospect of their faith having anything useful to say about these things" (Freitas 2008: 196). It was only at the Christian evangelical colleges that students talked God to sex and religion actually shaped their love lives.

We found that belief in God had no impact on young people's sex lives. Those who believe in God, for example, are no more likely to be virgins than those who do not. Even those who took a virginity pledge are not sexually different than those who did not, except they have had a little more oral experience.

Researchers have been looking in the wrong place. God is not working in students' underpants, but God, it turns out, does matter—to their love lives. Belief in God was strongly associated with whether students conjoin sex and love. As you can see in Table 4.11, young people who definitely believe in God are much more likely to make love, as opposed to just having sex (Chi square = .000). More than half of those who definitely believe in God had their last sex with somebody they loved, whereas only slightly more than a quarter who believed in nothing beyond the physical world did so. Those who believe in God, and even more so a loving God, it turns out, are much more likely to have romantic sex and to find it difficult to separate out sex and love. If you want a lover, one of the best places to look is among those who believe in God.

Table 4.10 Cross-tabulation of virginity, statement of personal belief about God

		I have no doubts about the existence of God N Col %	*I have doubts about the existence of God* N Col %	*I believe only in a higher power / cosmic force* N Col %	*I don't believe in anything beyond the physical world* N Col %	*Total*
			Statement of personal belief about God			
Virginity	Not virgin	114	97	70	27	308
		63.7%	66.9%	68.6%	67.5%	66.1%
	Virgin	65	48	32	13	158
		36.3%	33.1%	31.4%	32.5%	33.9%
Total		179	145	102	40	466
		100.0%	100.0%	100.0%	100.0%	100.0%

Note: We only report one year, 2009, because the scale measuring one's belief in God varied across years.
Source: (UCSB 2009)

Table 4.11 God and erotic love

		I have no doubts about the existence of God N Col %	*I have doubts about the existence of God* N Col %	*I believe only in a higher power / cosmic force* N Col %	*I don't believe in anything beyond the physical world* N Col %	*Total*
			Statement of personal belief about God			
Did you love your last sexual encounter partner at the time	Yes	80	47	38	9	174
		53.3%	38.2%	44.7%	27.3%	44.5%
	No	58	64	42	19	183
		38.7%	52.0%	49.4%	57.6%	46.8%
	Not sure/ Do not know	12	12	5	5	34
		8.0%	9.8%	5.9%	15.2%	8.7%
Total		150	123	85	33	391
		100.0%	100.0%	100.0%	100.0%	100.0%

Source: (UCSB 2009)

Why might this be so?[10] Why might belief in God promote the making of love? Why does religious belief shape students' ability and willingness to love their bedmates? There are various possibilities.

The first is that our monotheisms make love into a sacred value, even defining the godhead as a lover. Some social theorists make love the very source of divinity. Weber, for example, argued that religions of salvation posit an eternal, personal, loving—and loved—God, a love that transposes and displaces the generalized material reciprocities of the sib and neighbors in times of need (Weber 1958: 328–29). Freud understood religion as an aim-inhibited sublimate of the force of genital love, God an ego-ideal formed out of the projection of unrealizable and forbidden erotic—both hetero- and homo-erotic—desires to which one develops a passionate attachment and identification (Freud 1946, 1959, 1961, 1962; Butler 1997).

Both Judaism and Christianity promote love as a sacred value. In the Judeo-Christian tradition, the Abrahamic relation with God is built on and out of heterosexual love. Alone among the Near Eastern peoples, the Israelites understood their God as a husband and themselves as his often unfaithful lover (Eilberg-Schwartz 1994: 99). One loved one God. To do otherwise was whoring, adultery and harlotry (Gaca 2003). The Jews understood themselves as God's bride; Paul's Christians as Christ's bride. Despite the difference in marriage partner, in each, love is central. People who believe in God learn to value love.

Perhaps a relationship with God prepares individuals, through normative declaration, a non-discursive habitus (Bourdieu 1990) or through passionate identification, for the vulnerability, the faith, the dependence that one can have with one other person, in this case a lover, or more specifically a beloved. However, perhaps the relationship between religiosity and love is just a linguistic artifact. Love from this point of view would be a kind of appropriate talk; people who talk divine love being more likely to talk human love. If love were just a genital wrapper, a linguistic medium for other purposes, a kind of talk one uses when having sex, you wouldn't expect women who use the category of love to describe their experience to orgasm so much more than those who don't talk the talk. Love's words do physiological work. The words of erotic love are performative: they help create the social bond to which they refer. The question returns to the relationship between the performativity of pious and romantic language.

The second possibility is that these religions proscribe sexual relations before and outside of the marital rite. If you are caught between God and a hard or wet place, you may need another reason, another transcendental value, to justify your sex. Many students, we discovered, still feel there is something morally wrong about premarital sex. Perhaps those who believe in God, whom they believe to disapprove of their sex, can only have sex because they love to counter their religious guilt.

The third possibility is that love, like religion, is a parallel and primordial making sacred. The sacred, as the Hebrew term *kadosh*, or holy, indicates, involves a setting apart, a separation. As Emile Durkheim argued, the sacred is a representation that is set apart and sets the members of a clan apart, thereby forming them into a collectivity. Durkheim's theory of collective representation is based on Trinitarian architecture: collectivity, symbol and an energy mediating the two.

The totem, the god, is a symbol of society because, Durkheim argues, the experience of society is the basis for the experience of god, the experience of the collectivity being the anonymous power that outlives us, one to which we bend without regard to our personal benefit or cost, one that penetrates our very being, that is in us, but not of us (Durkheim 1995: 213–14; Friedland 2005). Perhaps the love of a pair-bond, the making of one flesh from two bodies, operates like an elementary form of totemic representation, the making of a "we." Participation in one may be conducive to participation in the other, or perhaps those who participate in one may also be more likely to participate in the other for independent reasons. Whatever the case, we can ask whether the sources and processes of sanctification, of sacralization, have a commonality and/or a relationship between intimate and religious life.

The fourth possibility is that these monotheistic religions prepare you phenomenologically for love, not just normatively, categorically, or even practically, but as a structure of experience, indeed a form of subject-hood. There are phenomenological parallels between a relationship with God and with a lover. A relationship with the divine is one in which you acknowledge your lack of sovereignty and self-control, in which you admit that you are not your own basis, your own source, that you depend on forces that you will never understand or control, that you rely on forces outside yourself for your being. Monotheism and monogamy parallel each other as exclusive loves.

The phenomenology of Catholic philosopher Jean-Luc Marion makes eroticization of the flesh critical to love, to an individualization through flesh and oaths received from and given to the other (Marion 2007: 126–29, 176). It is from another, from such others, that one is given one's flesh, one's individuality, one's person, one's "proper ipseity," indeed an assurance that one's being is lovable because one is and has been a lover (Marion 2007: 195). In erotic love, one is given one's individuality through the medium of one's flesh, giving oneself up to an unsubstitutable other with whom one is transported out of the world of objects and beings, into what Marion calls the "privilege of worldly inexistence," where all one can share with the other is "this exceptional nothing" of "climactic enjoyment" (Marion 2007: 145). The language of erotic love stages an oath that "allows each love to take flesh" (Marion 2007: 147).

Matters of love

Does love matter? How? Passion is not dead on American campuses. The data make that clear. However, its erosion ought to be a feminist issue. Among college students, the pursuit of erotic pleasure unhinged from love is predominantly a masculine preference. While there are forms of intimacy other than romantic love, women who love their sexual partners are much more likely to obtain these pleasures. If we care about women's pleasure, then we must be both concerned with the conditions under which love flourishes and whether and how love might be refashioned in a more egalitarian gender order (hooks 2001; Firestone 1970). After leaving college, young people do return to traditional romantic forms of coupling (Bogle 2008). Whether their previous experiences of casual sexuality affect their desire and capacity for intimacy and relational commitment has yet to be examined. Given that most adult roles are prepared through primary socialization—work, authority, gender, discipline and skills of every sort—one would not be surprised if they did.

Although it is beyond the empirical warrant of this essay, we want to suggest the possibility that the erosion of love, not the presence of sex, may be the real political problem in the USA. Nothing seems more singular, more revelatory, of who we are than who and how we love. An alchemical mix of one and another; through the making of love one both expresses one's individuality and negates it, yet produces oneself anew through the relationship. One gives oneself over to another human being in order to be given oneself by that other, by her or his touch, vision, words, his or her saving grace, a person who one will never possess, but who will define one by being the very being that one cannot have, who will indelibly etch one's very lack. In loving, we acknowledge that we are not sovereign, that we are not whole, that we can neither define, nor create ourselves by ourselves. In loving, one daily gives oneself and accepts the gift of the other. This mutual self-offering is the experiential core of love. Through love, each of us is not only revealed, but also formed. In choosing to love, we count on the possibility of eternity. One cannot, as Marion points out, say I will love you for this week. Love depends on a structure of faith, on a belief in something beyond sense and reason that we will never touch or know by reason. It depends on the possibility of a promise.

Romantic love is an historical achievement; it is one of the central ways we moderns constitute ourselves as individuals. Love is not simply an ideology, a justification for the arrangements by which we organize mate selection and reproduction. Love is a substance in which one must believe in order to be the kind of subject who can organize one's life in this way. The desire to give oneself to another, to be entrusted with another's being, to hear the call and respond, may serve as a font from which social solidarity, equality and justice all derive (see, for example, Derrida 1998b; Borradori 2003; hooks 2001).

Passion may be a public good. That possibility is there, for instance, in the thought of Jean-Jacques Rousseau. Rousseau's writings—*Julie, ou la nouvelle Heloise* (1761), *Emile* (1762), and *Du Contrat Social, Principes du droit politique* (1762)—all played a critical role in preparing the ground for the French Revolution. For Rousseau, the very concept of the Revolution was first a turning towards erotic love. It is the aristocratic Julie's turn towards sexual love with her socially inferior tutor, to what Rousseau understands as love's powerful, but vital, illusion, linked to a turning towards a refigured God, that was the initial referent for what was to become a people's capacity and demand to be solidary and sovereign. "Rousseau's revolution," as Matthew Maguire puts it, "… is the radical and explicit attribution of value, beauty, and attachment among human beings in love, in common life with others, and with God, to illusion or the possibility of illusion …" (Maguire 2006: 124). Passionate love was a template for the moralized will necessary to the love of a lover, a god and a people, all driven by a desire to be given oneself through the eyes of an other.

Love is an unlikely, even impossible, life course, but nonetheless may have been an essential driver of much that is great in an historical world where we must freely form a solidary "we" to which we bind ourselves, where we must make promises and forgive in order to maintain social solidarity, where we offer ourselves to care for and defend those we will never know, where we periodically dare seek to create the social world anew. Private love may be a prerequisite of our kind of public history. When we no longer believe in it, we cripple our capacity to make it.

To us, it is more frightening that there are increasing numbers of young people who doubt the existence of love than that of God. Love's vulnerability to decay seems more threatening to our political union than that sexual acts are objects of divinely dictated prohibitive legislation. To put it boldly, without love, there is no freedom. Nor can there be justice.[11] Without the possibility of these, it is not much worth living. We need to be less concerned about how and when our sons and daughters cover their genitals, and much more about whether they can uncover their hearts. God's guardianship of what goes on in our underpants may be the least of our worries.

Acknowledgements

The authors would like to thank Patricia Clough in particular, as well as Pernille Arenfeldt, Hannah Bruckner, Jose Cabezon, Arianne Conty, Alan Frank, Leila Rupp, Steven Seidman, Verta Taylor and Howard Winant for their comments, and John and Janice Baldwin for sharing their own survey results. We would also like to thank colleagues both at the University of Sharjah and the Humanities and Arts Colloquium at New York University-Abu Dhabi for their responses to an earlier version of this essay.

Notes

1 This work began in 2007 with a pilot survey for which we ran a banner advertisement on Facebook: "When was the last time you got laid? Prayed? Said I love you? Tell us about it." In the Facebook survey, in spite of the absence of any form of compensation, in a couple of weeks, more than 1,000 students had taken the survey. Sampling through a social networking site (SNS) offered an inexpensive way to access large populations of young people. At UCSB, Facebook claims a high penetration ratio, estimated at 85% (Facebook, 2007). Because we advertised longer at UCSB, took out advertisements in the campus newspaper and spread the word from Professor Friedland's courses on the subject, over half of the respondents came from UCSB. There is no reason to assume, however, that the SNS sample was random either with respect to demographic background variables, religion or sexual behavior. Fortuitously, John and Janice Baldwin, two campus sexologists, drew a random sample of UCSB students for a web-based survey on student sexuality in the same year, indeed just a month before our own survey (Baldwin and Baldwin 2007). The Baldwin survey was fielded using a traditional direct email approach, targeting a representative sample of UCSB students selected from the Office of the Registrar's list, and using $5 gift cards as incentive. Their final response rate was 40%. We were thus able to compare our survey results for UCSB students (n = 615) with theirs (n = 1,073), as well as with the demographics of the UCSB campus. Our sexual behavior reports were remarkably similar. Our primary interest is the behavior of those students who are of college age. For purposes of statistical analysis and to meet human subject restrictions, we used only those respondents who were between 18 and 22, the normative college age group. This yielded a sample of close to 900 students.

2 Gay and lesbian respondents are not analyzed separately here because there are insufficient numbers to be able to say anything meaningful. Of the 1,415 respondents in the UCSB survey, 1,350, or 95%, identify themselves as heterosexual. However, as Rupp and Taylor (this volume) show in the emergence of fluid sexualities among college students, the coincidence of identity, desire and act cannot be assumed. In our sample, for example, of the 22 students who identified themselves as bisexual, 45% had never had sex with a person of the same sex, while the reciprocal percentage of the heterosexuals who had had sex with a person of the same sex was 2%.

3 These are, of course, based on a respondent's categorization of the relationship. Part of the gender difference may be due to the ways they classify the relationship in which their sex took place, such that women are more likely to understand the relationships in which they have sex as noncasual, whereas for men it is the reverse. Lacking dyadic data we cannot address that possibility.

4 In her ethnography of high school erotic cultures, Sharon Thompson reports: "Orgasms—as rare as hen's teeth in the heterosexual narrative—were reported in every lesbian account" (Thompson 1995: 184).

5 Previous work showed that the relational context and expectations in which sex takes place—whether the couple live together, whether they imagine marrying the partner, and whether they are interested in a relationship before first sex takes place—affects the probability of female orgasm (Armstrong *et al.* 2012). These "indirect" measures of love tap neither the emotional state of love, nor the willingness to describe one's state as "love."

6 In our UCSB survey over three waves, we also found that 12% of females had an orgasm in sexual encounters they categorized as "hook-ups."

7 "Sexuality forces one into a non-dissociable mode of involvement. It bars the way to withdrawal into 'pure love', which distances the lover not only from themselves but also from the self that the other sees and desires and therefore, also, from the self by whom the other feels themselves seen and desired. Only in this multiple reflexivity of conscious living and feeling is the other loved as subject and not merely as substance" (Luhmann 2010: 59).

8 It is this historical institutional connection between love and marriage that makes the exclusion of non-normative erotic communities from the rites of marriage so hurtful and wrong.

9 Shulamith Firestone opens her chapter on love in the following manner: "A book on radical feminism that did not deal with love would be a political failure. For love, perhaps even more than childbearing, is the pivot of women's oppression today" (Firestone 1970: 113).

10 The significant net effect of religiosity on erotic love remained in a model in which we controlled for what psychologists call "attachment styles," gender and mating strategies (Friedland and Gardinali 2011).

11 We would not argue that love is a sufficient condition, nor that it must take marital form, or else one would be at a loss to explain the persistent commitments to social justice in northern Europe as the incidence of marriage declines. However, we would argue that it is worth pondering both historical and individual relationships between the affective ordering of intimate lives and the kinds of solidarities that obtain in the body politic.

References

Allyn, David. 2001. *Make Love, Not War: The Sexual Revolution: An Unfettered History.* New York: Routledge.

Armstrong, Elizabeth A., Paula England and Alison C.K. Fogarty. 2012. "Sexual Practices, Learning, and Love: Accounting for Women's Orgasm in College Hookups and Relationships." *American Sociological Review* 77(3): 435–62.

Baldwin, John and Janice Baldwin. 2007. *Survey of Sexual Attitudes and Practices.* Santa Barbara: UC Santa Barbara.

Bearman, Peter S. and Hannah Bruckner. 2001. "Promising the Future: Virginity Pledges and First Intercourse." *American Journal of Sociology* 106: 859–912.

Bogle, Kathleen A. 2008. *Hooking Up: Sex, Dating, and Relationships on Campus*. New York: New York University Press.

Borradori, Giovanna. 2003. *Philosophy in a Time of Terror: Dialogues with Jurgen Habermas and Jacques Derrida*. Chicago: University of Chicago Press.

Bourdieu, Pierre. 1990. *The Logic of Practice*. Stanford: Stanford University Press.

Burdette, Amy, Chris Ellison, Terrence Hill and Norval Glenn. 2009. "'Hooking Up' at College: Does Religion Make a Difference?" *Journal for the Scientific Study of Religion* 48: 535–51.

Butler, Judith. 1997. *The Psychic Life of Power: Theories in Subjection*. Stanford: Stanford University Press.

Coleman, Emily M., Peter W. Hoon and Emily F. Hoon. 1983. "Arousability and Sexual Satisfaction in Lesbian and Heterosexual Women." *The Journal of Sex Research* 19(1): 58–73.

Coontz, Stephanie. 2005. *Marriage, a History: How Love Conquered Marriage*. New York: Penguin.

Crockett, L., R. Bingham, J. Chopak and J. Vicary. 1996. "Timing of First Sexual Intercourse: The Role of Social Control, Social Learning, and Problem Behavior." *Journal of Youth and Adolescence* 25: 89–111.

de Rougement, Denis. 1983. *Love in the Western World*. Princeton: Princeton University Press.

Derrida, Jacques. 1998a. "Force of Law: The 'Mystical Foundation of Authority'." In Gil Anijar (ed.) *Jacques Derrida: Acts of Religion*. Stanford: Stanford University Press, 230–98.

——1998b. "Faith and Knowledge: The Two Sources of 'Religion' at the Limits of Reason Alone." In Jacques Derrida and Giacomo Vattimo (eds) *Religion*. Stanford: Stanford University Press, 1–78.

Durkheim, Emile. 1995 [1912]. *The Elementary Forms of Religious Life*. Trans. Karen E. Fields. New York: The Free Press.

Eilberg-Schwartz, Howard. 1994. *God's Phallus*. Boston: Beacon Press.

England, Paula and Reuben J. Thomas. 2006. "The Decline of the Date and the Rise of the College Hook Up." In Arlene S. Skolnick and Jerome H. Skolnick (eds) *Families in Transition*. Boston: Allyn and Bacon, 151–62.

Firestone, Shulamith. 1970. *The Dialectic of Sex*. New York: Farrar, Straus and Giroux.

Fisher, Helen. 2004. *Why We Love: The Nature and Chemistry of Romantic Love*. New York: Henry Holt and Co.

Freitas, Donna. 2008. *Sex and the Soul: Juggling Sexuality, Spirituality, Romance and Religion on America's College Campuses*. New York: Oxford University Press.

Freud, Sigmund. 1946. *Totem and Taboo*. New York: Vintage.

——1959. *Group Psychology and the Analysis of the Ego*. New York: W.W. Norton.

——1961. *Civilization and Its Discontents*. New York: W.W. Norton.

——1962. *The Ego and the Id*. New York: W.W. Norton.

Friedland, Roger. 2005. "Drag Kings at the Totem Ball." In Jeffrey C. Alexander and Philip Smith (eds) *The Cambridge Companion to Durkheim*. Cambridge: Cambridge University Press, 239–73.

——2009. "Institution, Practice and Ontology: Towards a Religious Sociology." In Renate Meyer, K. Sahlin-Andersson, Marc Ventresca and Peter Walgenbach (eds) *Ideology and Organizational Institutionalism, Research in the Sociology of Organizations*. Bingley, UK: Emerald Group, 45–83.

Friedland, Roger and Paolo Gardinali. 2011. "Attachment, Evolution and the University Hook-Up Culture: A Preliminary Examination." Unpublished, UCSB.

Gaca, Kathy L. 2003. *The Making of Fornication: Eros, Ethics, and Political Reform in Greek Philosophy and Early Christianity*. Berkeley: University of California Press.

Grello, Catherine M., Deborah P. Welsh and Melinda S. Harper. 2006. "No Strings Attached: The Nature of Casual Sex in College Students." *The Journal of Sex Research* 43: 255–67.

Hamilton, Laura and Elizabeth A. Armstrong. 2009. "Gendered Sexuality in Young Adulthood: Double Binds and Flawed Options." *Gender and Society* 23: 589–616.

Harding, Susan Friend. 2000. *The Book of Jerry Falwell: Fundamentalist Language and Politics*. Princeton: Princeton University Press.

Hardy, Sam A. and Marcela Raffaelli. 2003. "Adolescent Religiosity and Sexuality: An Investigation of Reciprocal Influences." *Journal of Adolescence* 26: 731–39.

hooks, bell. 2001. *all about love*. New York: Harper Perennial.

Jones, R.K., J.E. Darroch and S. Singh. 2005. "Religious Differentials in Sexual and Reproductive Behaviors of Young Women in the United States." *Journal of Adolescent Health* 41: 369–91.

Kipnis, Laura. 2003. *Against Love: A Polemic*. New York: Vintage.

Kirkpatrick, Lee A. 1998. "Evolution, Pair-Bonding, and Reproductive Strategies: A Reconceptualization of Adult Attachment." In J.A. Simpson and W.S. Rholes (eds) *Attachment Theory and Close Relationships*. New York: Guilford, 354–93.

——2005. *Attachment, Evolution, and the Psychology of Religion*. New York: Guilford.

Laumann, Edward O., John H. Gagnon, Robert T. Michael and Stuart Michaels. 1994. *The Social Organization of Sexuality: Sexual Practices in the United States*. Chicago: University of Chicago Press.

Luhmann, Niklas. 2010. *Love: A Sketch*. Cambridge: Polity.

Maguire, Matthew W. 2006. *The Conversion of Imagination: From Pascal through Rousseau to Tocqueville*. Cambridge: Harvard University Press.

Marion, Jean-Luc. 2007. *The Erotic Phenomenon*. Chicago: University of Chicago Press.

Puts, David A. 2010. "Beauty and the Beast: Mechanisms of Sexual Selection in Humans." *Evolution and Human Behavior* 31: 157–75.

Regnerus, Mark. 2007. *Forbidden Fruit: Sex and Religion in the Lives of American Teenagers*. New York: Oxford University Press.

Rupp, Leila J. and Verta Taylor. 2013. "Queer Girls on Campus: New Intimacies and Sexual Identities." In Alan Frank, Patricia Ticineto Clough and Steven Seidman (eds) *Intimacies* (this volume).

Shaver, Philip R., C. Hazan and D. Bradshaw. 1988. "Love as Attachment: The Integration of Three Behavioral Systems." In R.J. Sternberg and M. Barnes (eds) *The Anatomy of Love*. New Haven: Yale University Press, 68–99.

Stepp, Laura Sessions. 2007. *Unhooked: How Young Women Pursue Sex, Delay Love and Lose at Both*. New York: Riverhead Books.

Swidler, Ann. 2001. *Talk of Love: How Culture Matters*. Chicago: University of Chicago Press.

Thompson, Sharon. 1995. *Going All the Way: Sex, Romance and Pregnancy*. New York: Hill and Wang.

Thornton, Arnold and Donald Camburn. 1989. "Religious Participation and Adolescent Sexual Behavior and Attitudes." *Journal of Marriage and the Family* 51: 641–53.

Weber, Max. 1958. "Religious Rejections of the World and their Directions." In Hans Gerth and C. Wright Mills (eds) *From Max Weber*. New York: Oxford University Press, 323–62.

5   Queer girls on campus

New intimacies and sexual identities

Leila J. Rupp and Verta Taylor

Once upon a time, there was a standard lesbian coming-out story that went something like this: "I knew when I was five that I was a lesbian"; or, "I realized after 30 years of marriage that I was really a lesbian." What was standard was that, although behaviors and identities could change, coming out involved recognizing one's true essence. No longer. As more and more research points to the lack of fit among desire, behavior and identity, and popular culture embraces the concept of sexual fluidity, certainty about sexual desires and identities is fast disappearing. What does this mean for the kind of intimacies young women in the USA are forging? We analyze the stories of diverse undergraduate college students who embrace the identity of "fluid" or "pansexual" or who refuse to adopt an identity at all on one campus, the University of California, Santa Barbara, in order to understand this new world of sexual fluidity and the kind of intimacies and identities that it fosters. The way these women describe their intimacies brings to mind the final comment of the bisexual narrator of John Irving's novel *In One Person* (Irving 2012: 425), echoing a line uttered by his first love, the transsexual Miss Frost: "... please don't put a label on me—don't make me a category before you get to know me!"

Historians of sexuality have emphasized the complex relationship between the publications of late 19th-century sexologists and the sexual behavior and identities of women and men with same-sex desires (Chauncey 1989; Terry 1999; Duggan 2000). Rejecting the notion that the doctors and psychologists created labels and categories that individuals then adopted, scholars have shown that theories of gender inversion and homosexuality were based on knowledge of the emerging communities of people with same-sex desires, and that, as knowledge of sexological analyses spread through popular culture and word of mouth, the subjects of research and the scientific and popular purveyors of information influenced one another in an intricate back-and-forth exchange. This is what Anthony Giddens (1987) calls the "double hermeneutic," the two-way relationship between the concepts and identities people use to make sense of themselves and social scientific theories, categories and research. We see a very similar dynamic at work today in the creation of fluid intimacies and identities, particularly visible on a college campus where research about and discussion of sexual fluidity both respond to and shape sexualities. That is the tale we tell here.

Jessica's story

Consider the story of Jessica, an Asian American athlete from southern California who identifies as "bisexual, fluid, queer," and who launched a bisexual discussion group on campus. She started to experience same-sex attraction in seventh grade, "There was this girl that I found was attractive. I don't know if I had sexual feelings ... I'm guessing I didn't ... but like, she was cute, she had brown hair and I was like, I can only think within binary terms 'cause it's the only thing that I knew myself." She describes trying to figure out if that meant she was a lesbian. "I was like, 'I don't think that I am a lesbian, but I definitely am attracted to her. Cool, whatever.' So that kind of left some space in between." She found it a "little bit puzzling," that, as a straight-identified person, she could be attracted to a woman. Later, after she came out, she remembered that she had always been attracted to female, rather than male, celebrities, and when in elementary school her friends would discuss who was "hot," in order to fit in she would have to make up male stars. When she came to college and joined a sports team generally associated with lesbian players, she then "started to question about whether or not I was some degree of queer." Just before the end of the season, she went to her first queer party and saw a friend there and asked her, "'How do you identify?' ... or like 'What are you?' or something like that" and she responded that she was bisexual, "and I was like, 'I'm bisexual.'" And then they danced together "As if to resolve some kind of tension or, 'Is this what bisexual people do?'" Then in a team ritual at the end of the year, she was put on the "hot seat" where team mates could ask any kind of questions. Someone asked about her sexual identity and "for the first time I said out loud to a group of people that, 'Oh, I'm bisexual.' I said it like out loud. So, that was really cool and I guess, I wouldn't say liberating, but it was kind of a moment of truth to the world, not necessarily me." She had already, she says, accepted this about herself.

She immediately went to check out the Queer Student Union and by the end of her first year "knew the majority of the very-out queers on this campus ... I was really on top of it. I was having a blast. That whole quarter was like my coming out party." Although she is conscious of the ways people reconstruct their pasts, she is pretty sure that her sports experience made her question her sexuality and that claiming an identity out loud was a crucial moment. For six months after she came out she remained single, then she met her boyfriend and, after a time, established an open relationship with him, the rules being that they could hook up with other people unless the two of them were in the same room.

At the point of the interview, Jessica's sexual experiences with women consisted solely of paid commercial encounters. The summer after she came out during her first year, she "got myself a lap dance and so, the first time I kissed a girl was the stripper that gave me a lap dance." It was her first kiss with a woman, "just a kiss on the lips." Then another time she went to a strip club, bought a lap dance, and asked the stripper what girls were allowed to do in the booth. Finding out that the restrictions were only on men (which she found annoying because the policy ignored queer sexuality), "I like fingered her or whatever and then she fingered me and that was like the end of that." Then she went to Las Vegas and hired a call girl and "we hooked up in the hotel room"—hooking up for Jessica meaning "sex or like fondling or something like that."

Jessica thinks a lot about identity. "If I were to name the, if I were to name my identity titles, like, one after another," she says, "with the first one being the most important or the one that I use the most, it would probably be 'bisexual, pansexual, queer.'" Then she says, "I'm actually, I actually am pansexual," which she defines as "I have an attraction to men, women, and any genders that fall outside those two ... I definitely like to acknowledge attraction to other genders that includes transgender people." She then goes on to say, "I'm a blend of pansexual and omnisexual because I'm also attracted to just things in general." But, she explains, the term bisexual "comes to me first," since people are familiar with it. She thinks bisexuality is looked at critically in the queer community because it is binary, "it doesn't include trans," but she uses the term to support the visibility of bisexuals. "I purposely almost sacrifice not calling myself pan in order to create more visibility for letters that are in our acronym that need more attention." She wants it to be all right for people to call themselves bisexual or fluid which, in her opinion, is "the depoliticized version of the word 'bisexual.'" She wants to "redefine it and educate people about non-monosexual people through the term that already exists."

When asked about the relationship of her sexual identity/ies to other identities, she puts bisexual first, then queer, then female, and last her Chinese ethnicity: "I feel stronger with my queer identity than my race, my ethnicity." She describes herself as straight-looking and "basically white-washed," having been born in New Jersey and lived in Massachusetts in white communities without a Chinese upbringing. She describes the UC Santa Barbara queer community as "super mixed, ... there's plenty of people of color, plenty of white-identified people." She contrasts being attracted to white men but to a much broader spectrum of women: "all kinds of women and fem, butch, anything ... attracted to trans, attracted."

Jessica's story introduces the new intimacies and identities that flourish on campus. Although atypical in terms of buying sex, Jessica's experiences resonate in other ways with the stories of women students who reject the binary of gay/straight and even what they tend to see as the binary of bisexuality as attraction to two genders. Students do still embrace the identities of lesbian, gay and bisexual (the latter, in Jessica's case, for political reasons), but women also call themselves queer, bicurious, mostly straight, heteroflexible, fluid, or pansexual, and others, although they are unlikely to adopt the label themselves, are dubbed "lesbians until graduation." What is going on on campus? This is a very different scene from the last decades of the 20th century, when the classic literature on lesbian and bisexual identities and communities appeared. Identities and communities change over time, and the conditions that facilitated the emergence of lesbian feminist and other lesbian communities in the 1970s and 1980s are no longer in place (Taylor and Whittier 1992; Stein 2010). We explore here the experiences of young women who identify as sexually fluid or pansexual or who reject labels altogether, arguing that both the hook-up culture and academic and popular literature on sexual fluidity are shaping new intimacies on campus.

The hook-up culture and sexual fluidity

The university is a good place to explore new intimacies and identities because, despite the existence of different subcultures within the student population and differences in the class and ethnic backgrounds of students, the hook-up culture serves as the dominant structure for sexual interactions. Hooking up, pervasive in the university scene across the USA, involves casual interactions, ranging from kissing to sexual intercourse, with no necessary implications for an ongoing relationship (Armstrong *et al.* 2010; Bogle 2008; England *et al.* 2007; Friedland and Gardinali 2013; Hamilton and Armstrong 2009). Hooking up is an alternative to dating, which may follow a hook-up if both parties are interested, and those who engage in multiple hook-ups with the same person can become what is known as "friends with benefits." If sex without commitment is by no means new, the fact that the hook-up culture is widely acknowledged as the dominant scene on campus represents a new development from the earlier pattern of dating and forming relationships. Although the existing literature on hooking up focuses on heterosexual behavior among primarily white college students, even going so far as to suggest that students of color and queer students do not engage in the practice (Bogle 2008), students at our campus have quite a different experience. The practice of women kissing and making out in public, purportedly for the purpose of attracting male attention, and the acceptability of threesomes between a man and two women, allow for sexual experimentation on the part of women (Rupp and Taylor 2010). Hooking up is pervasive among queer students as well. As Lea, a white pansexual student, explains, "To me hook up means going home with somebody and having sex with them and leaving in the morning. I mean that's definitely big in the queer community."

The hook-up culture opens spaces for same-sex sexual interactions, and the concept of sexual fluidity flourishes in this context. Empirical studies of sexual fluidity date back to the 1970s (Blumstein and Schwartz 1977; Rust 1993, 2000a, 2000b; Peplau and Garnets 2000; Hoburg *et al.* 2004; Golden 2006; Thompson and Morgan 2008). What the literature emphasizes is women's greater openness to bisexual attractions and behavior compared to men, the capacity of women to change their sexual practices and identities across time, and a lack of fit among women's erotic desires, sexual behaviors and sexual identities. Sexual fluidity itself is nothing new, given the fact that, historically and cross-culturally, what women did with their bodies often has had little significance (Rupp 2012). What is new is an increase in same-sex sexual behavior among women in the USA and the embrace of fluidity as a practice and identity.

National sex surveys show the preponderance of bisexual compared to lesbian behavior and identity. The most comprehensive national data on the population at large, from the 1994 National Health and Social Life Survey, reported that, since puberty, 3% of all women had both female and male partners, while 1% had only female partners; 4% of women reported attraction to both women and men, while less than 1% reported attraction only to women; just 0.5% of women identified as bisexual (Laumann *et al.* 1994). A 2002 survey by the Center for Disease Control's National Center for Health Statistics found that 11.5% of

Table 5.1 Sexual identities of women students, total and UCSB, Online College and Social
     Life Survey, UCSB

Sexual identity	Total	UCSB
Heterosexual	92%	94%
Homosexual	3%	2%
Bisexual	3%	3%
Not sure	2%	2%

Table 5.2 Sexual practices of women students, Online College and Social Life Survey

Sexual identity	Given oral sex to woman	Received oral sex from woman	Given oral sex to man	Received oral sex from man	Vaginal intercourse with man
Heterosexual	2%	2%	72%	71%	69%
Homosexual	56%	58%	44%	47%	44%
Bisexual	48%	48%	81%	81%	79%
Not sure	13%	16%	71%	70%	61%

women 18 to 44 and 14% of women in their late teens and twenties reported at
least one sexual experience with another woman, revealing an increase in same-
sex sexual interactions over time (MSNBC 2012). In a follow-up study in
2006–08, 12% of women 25 to 44 reported having same-sex contact, twice the
percentage of men (Chandra *et al.* 2011). Paula England's Online College and
Social Life Survey of over 13,000 female students on 21 campuses, including
almost 3,000 UC Santa Barbara students, reveals that the vast majority of women
students identify as heterosexual. They are most likely to engage in sexual practices consistent with their sexual identities, yet a small percentage of heterosexual
women (2%) and a larger percentage of women not sure about their identity
(13%–16%) have given or received oral sex from a woman, and a large percentage of lesbians (44%–47%) have had oral sex or vaginal intercourse with a man
(see Table 5.1 and Table 5.2). What these statistics make clear is that the
experience of having some form of sexual interaction with both women and men
is more common than is identifying as bisexual. The hook-up culture and the
concept of sexual fluidity, as we shall see, facilitate this kind of sexual intimacy.

Students' stories

The stories we tell here are drawn from 94 interviews with women students who
identify as anything other than heterosexual. About half are white and half students of color (see Table 5.3), and they listed a variety of sexual identities,
including bisexual, lesbian, queer, fluid, pansexual, gay, not straight, uncertain
and none (see Table 5.4). White women were most likely to identify as bisexual or
lesbian, women of color as lesbian or queer (see Table 5.5), but otherwise few
differences on the basis of ethnicity or class origin emerged in the interviews,

Table 5.3 Ethnicity of interviewees

Ethnicity	% of total
White (n=46)	49%
Latina (n=20)	21%
Asian American (n=13)	14%
Bi/Multiracial (n=10)	11%
African American (n=4)	4%
Middle Eastern (n=1)	1%
Total women of color (n=48)	51%

Table 5.4 Sexual identities of interviewees

Sexual identity	% of total
Bisexual (n=28)	30%
Lesbian (n=27)	29%
Queer (n=19)	20%
Fluid (n=8)	9%
Pansexual (n=4)	4%
Gay (n=4)	4%
None (n=2)	2%
Not straight (n=1)	1%
Uncertain (n=1)	1%

Table 5.5 Sexual identity by ethnicity

Ethnicity	Bisexual	Lesbian	Queer	Fluid/Pansexual	Gay	Other
White	39%	26%	18%	15%	2%	0
Women of color	21%	31%	23%	11%	6%	8%

presumably because of the common university culture. The interviews were conducted by undergraduate students enrolled in a course on female same-sex sexuality in 2006, 2007 and 2012, and by undergraduate and graduate research assistants from 2009 to 2011 as part of a project on queer women's intimacies and identities on campus. Students on the course located their own interviewees, and personal contacts and snowball sampling produced the interviewees for the larger study. We utilize students as interviewers because we have found that similarity in age and status facilitates rapport. The semi-structured interviews were recorded and transcribed and covered desire, love, sexual behavior, relationships, identities, the coming-out process, community participation and political involvement. We analyzed all discussions of the concepts of fluidity and pansexuality in the interviews and then focused on the stories of the 16 students who identified as fluid, pansexual, or as having no identity. All the names used here are pseudonyms.

We explore three different meanings of fluidity or pansexuality as articulated by women students: rapid changes in attraction, shifts in identity, and inclusion of attraction to genders beyond male and female. We conclude by analyzing the ways that academic and popular writing about sexual fluidity are shaping new intimacies and identities within the hook-up scene on campus.

The University of California, Santa Barbara

The University of California, Santa Barbara, is a stunningly beautiful campus of just over 20,000 students, 85% undergraduates, perched on the edge of the Pacific. The undergraduate population is slightly under half students of color and about a third first-generation college students. The university has a reputation as a party school, despite the administration's pride in its standing as a research university, in large part because of the life of the adjacent largely student community of Isla Vista. Isla Vista, separated from the campus by a road known as the "four-lane highway to nowhere" and connected to the campus most directly by bicycle paths, is a densely populated area of overpriced apartments where alcohol flows freely at parties, and the streets, especially on the weekend, are filled with students looking for a good time. As Maria, a white bisexual student, put it, "You don't have to drive anywhere and everyone is always partying all the time especially because it's a beach town. It's just acceptable to drink all the time and normally this would be considered alcoholism, but it's the norm here. People go out pretty much every day of the week, there's always something going on."

Although Isla Vista is not always a friendly or safe place for queer students, there is a large, visible and diverse queer community on campus, revolving around numerous student organizations serving various constituencies. The Resource Center for Sexual and Gender Diversity flyer announces that the Center provides a community space on campus for "self-identified lesbian, gay, bisexual, transgender, genderqueer, gender non-conforming, queer, questioning, two-spirit, same gender loving, as well as people with intersex conditions." Student organizations include the Queer Student Union and Associated Students Queer Commission; groups for different ethnicities, including Black QUARE, De Colores and Queer Asian Pacific Islanders; more specialized groups, including Beyond the Binary, Friendly Undergraduate Queers in it Together (FUQIT, pronounced "Fuck It"), Kink University: A Fetish Fellowship (KUFF), and Students for Accessible and Safe Spaces (SASS). There is a residence hall for queer students, Rainbow House, gender-inclusive housing for transgender and genderqueer students, and a queer studies minor, housed in the Department of Feminist Studies. The queer student activists are a diverse group in terms of gender identity, sexual identity and ethnicity.

Class and racial/ethnic differences among students emerged in some of the interviews. Melissa, a white student who prefers women but is also attracted to men and identifies as fluid, connects her sexual identity to race and class: "as a white woman who has had an easy life and a very privileged life, I see it [sexual identity] as a central focus point of my experience because for me it was one of the hardest things I have dealt with." In contrast, Ashley, who identifies as a lesbian despite her embrace of fluidity, does so because the identity "gives me like a solidity and an identity ... that kind of like make sense because like growing up biracially I didn't have one category ... that I fit into ... so having been able to have one strong identity ... has been very important." Liliana, a Latina, refers to her father's "typical Hispanic male mentality" with regard to sexuality, and her interviewer, an Asian American student, says she is not out to her parents as pansexual because "they're Asian Catholics. If you take the Catholic away, they're still Asians," in both cases suggesting particular familial challenges shaped by ethnicity. Liliana, who identifies her class background as "the lowest, lower class," hated UC Santa Barbara her first year because her white suitemates came from wealthy families and spent lots of money on clothes and made fun of the way she talked. "Anyway, it's just weird to come from somewhere where everyone is brown. And then you come here and everyone is white, blond hair, yoga pants, Uggs." Her perceptions reflect the polarized student body on campus. Despite such varied backgrounds and experiences, differences in ethnicity and class origin did not emerge as central in understandings of pansexual and fluid intimacies and identities.

Fluid and pansexual intimacies and identities

What do students mean when they identify as fluid or pansexual? Here are some typical answers. Mai, an Asian American student who identifies as bisexual, says, "Most people I know identify as queer. In a very like fluid, kind of pansexual kind of way." Ashley says, "I don't think I'm exclusively a lesbian even though I use that term, I think my sexuality is more fluid." Another biracial (black/white) lesbian student, Shauna, also calls herself fluid despite the fact that she is interested in relationships only with women. Lynne, a white bisexual student who at the time of the interview had just broken up with her first girlfriend, says, "my idea of sexuality is so much more fluid than it ever was before."

Despite the vagueness of the terms "fluid" and "pansexual," three themes emerge from students' stories. For some, fluidity or pansexuality connotes some real instability in attraction that is somehow beyond what bisexuality suggests. For example, Kim, an Asian American student, says, "I can say I identify with [loving women], and there's this whole other side of me, and it definitely captures why I'm sexually fluid, because I constantly switch all the time ... And my attractions change, it's weird, like 'there I go again!' But I mean, it's cool." Melissa describes much the same thing: "I feel like there were times when I was more, oh, say, all these guys look really attractive or today all these girls look really attractive." Another white student, Alex, believes that "sexuality is fluid and that it changes and progresses throughout life. Um, I feel like for me I'm definitely like very attracted to women. I want to be with a woman. But there are times, especially when I am out on the weekends having fun and stuff that I do find myself very attracted to men." Latoya, a black student, tries "not to identify sexually because I feel like sexuality is too fluid to put a name on, you know? You can, you might wake up one day and feel like you want a guy, and then, you know, after spending time with a guy you could say, 'Hmmm. But maybe now I want a woman.' You know, it depends on what you feel that day ... For a while, I thought you had to choose one. If you choose one, you had to repress the other, you know, and just recently I learned to just go with what I feel." Valeria, a Latina student, started identifying as "straight with lesbian tendencies" because of her Catholic upbringing, but then "I kind of got over it and I quickly was like, you know, this shit is ridiculous, and then I kind of became a bit more fluid and I was like, well, I think I can do whatever I want, I feel like I'm, you know, pansexual." This kind of rapidly changing attraction undermines the traditional pattern of a committed relationship with one person, whether of the same or a different gender. That is, these women envisage multiple intimacies, serially if not simultaneously, in contrast to the standard sexual script of monogamy.

As Valeria's comments suggest, identifying as fluid or pansexual because of rapidly changing attractions does not necessarily mean that women have a lot of sex with both women and men. In fact, some, like Jessica, have had limited or even no sexual experience with women, and others have not had sex with men. Melissa says she only wants to have sex with girls but "I'm like attracted to guys and I've dated guys and I've like made out with guys but I wouldn't have sex with them." For many women, familiarity with the heterosexual script makes it easier to hook up with men than to approach a woman. Liliana, who prefers to be unlabelled but accepts pansexual and fluid as her identities, has never had a sexual experience with a woman out of shyness. "So the reason why I've always had boyfriends is because they come to me ... I'm not going to go and be like all up on a girl because I'm too shy." Carey, a white student who identifies as fluid and also calls herself "primarily straight but with instances of bisexuality," says she will "meet a woman and just be blown over backwards by her beauty and definitely attracted to her and then I kind of shrivel up, I get really scared, I'm like a 16-year-old guy that's like 'I don't know what to do now!'" Her only sexual encounters with other women have been when she was drunk, which she finds unfortunate, but she explains that it is the only way she gets up the courage. "I'm really inexperienced in chasing women, rather more experienced at chasing men, um, so it's kind of like skiing or snowboarding, I do skiing more often 'cause I'm better at it. Still would like to snowboard, still like to, would love to snowboard." For these women, fluid desires are channeled more easily into heterosexual than same-sex intimacies, but that does not cause them to deny their attractions.

What counts as actual sexual behavior is up in the air in the hook-up culture, and same-sex intimacies confuse the picture even more. Lea, who thinks hooking up involves having sex, describes having gone to "second base," which she defines as "above the waist" with a woman but not having lost "the second virginity ... not yet." Like Liliana and Carey, she finds it easier to hook up with men because of lack of experience making the first move. Her use of the base metaphor prompts a discussion with her interviewer, echoed by other students, of what counts as sex between two women. Although there is no agreement about whether hooking up requires sex—some students say yes and some no—Lea thinks that "fingering" and oral sex count as sex, and therefore a hook-up, between two women but not between a woman and a man. Morgan, a white student who identifies as pansexual and who, at the time of her interview, had recently broken up with a boyfriend and begun her first relationship with a woman, says, "now that I'm in a relationship with a woman, sex is, I mean, there's no penis, so obviously my definition of it changed a little bit ... Everything ... counts as sex." As these examples suggest, same-sex intimacies in the hook-up culture prompt a rethinking of the very nature of sexual behavior.

The rapidly changing attractions that students who identify as fluid or pansexual describe are both physical and emotional, sometimes more one than the other in a gendered way. Lea feels "more of an emotional connection" to men and has "gotten more attraction for women over the years." Kayla, a white student who identifies as "fluid/bi," at first says her relationships with women and men are completely the same physically and emotionally, but later admits that "I just don't connect with many men at all, like I tend to connect better with women. That's probably for numerous reasons, most of which is like, well, most dudes just want to fuck me." Although the hook-up culture is often described as featuring sex without emotional commitment, the stories of women students make clear that intimacies exist alongside "just sex." Carey describes what she calls "sexual tension" between her and her best friend, with whom she had a threesome with a man before they became close. She makes clear that she would have liked to explore their sexual relationship, but her friend started dating someone else and she never had the opportunity. Lynne, who is white and identifies as bisexual, tells of falling in love with her close friend. She would stay at her house, sleep in the same bed, and eventually they started kissing, "which led to other things." Her idea of sexuality, she says, "is so much more fluid than it ever was before, and she's helped me in ways that I'll be forever grateful for." Like so many women, falling in love with a friend opened up a new world of relationships.

When students think about their future intimacies, they paint a wide range of possibilities, some heteronormative or homonormative. Carey thinks that "when I'm married I'll be pretty sexually set ... I think that eventually I'll, um, bend in my wants and desires and settle on being straight." Alexandra, a bisexual daughter of Russian immigrant parents and a leader in campus queer organizations, does not like to make assumptions about the future because "I know that I'm very fluid," but "when I really imagine it, someone that I want to have a long-term relationship with, it's often a man." In contrast, Melissa thinks, "I'm going to probably end up with a woman like in terms of marriage, but I think that I can see myself maybe dating guys." In all of these ways, then, fluid or pansexual identities leave open the nature of present and future intimacies. Yet students such as Jessica, who has an arrangement with her male partner that they can hook up with other people unless they are in the same room, raise the possibility that the polyamorous intimacies on campus may prefigure a move away from strictly heteronormative relationships in the future.

A second theme that emerges from the interviews is that fluidity and pansexuality capture multiple changes in identities as well as attractions. Gabriella, an African American student who identifies as genderqueer and protested the lack of a gender-neutral restroom in her residence hall, says, "Sometimes I'm lesbian. And I used to be bisexual. Yeah, I used to be bisexual ... Then after that I guess I was like, I was like fluid. I still am fluid, kind of. And then it's lesbian—it was lesbian, and then I was fluid again. And now I'm just queer." Dana, who is white and identifies as genderqueer, explains, "Um, I first came out as bi because I thought it would be easier. Then became full out butch lesbian, and now back to, like, pan or fluid ... [F]luid is just about, like, whatever the fuck you want." Given changing attractions and the multiple possibilities of identities, fluidity and pansexuality keep open all of the possibilities for sexual desires, behaviors and relationships.

As Jessica's story suggests, pansexuality functions as a critique of a binary perspective on sexuality that bisexuality itself does not disrupt. As Margaret, a white student who identifies as bisexual, put it, the word "bisexual" does emphasize "the whole binary thing ..., which I don't really tend to agree with." Unlike Jessica, most students who identify as fluid or pansexual tended to distance themselves from bisexuality for a variety of reasons. Sometimes it is because of stereotypes of bisexuals. Joelle, a biracial (black/white) student, thinks that people "will be like 'oh, she wants everything or she doesn't know what she wants.'" Sasha, a Middle Eastern student who identifies as bisexual, also thinks "bisexual" suggests hypersexuality: "Like, if anyone finds out, if anyone like at a party in I[sla] V[ista], ... like if a guy finds out I'm bisexual, it's all of a sudden like, 'threesome?'" Kayla also thinks there are a lot of negative associations with the word "bisexual." She does not like to use it because "straight guys will be like, 'all right, that means she likes to kiss girls in front of her boyfriend,'" suggesting the ways that the hook-up culture can facilitate same-sex interactions. Margaret wonders if she should identify as pansexual but settles on "bisexual" as a term other people understand.

Pansexuality and fluidity are also responses to the perception that "lesbian" is a rigid category that will brook no sexual involvement with men at all. Evoking the old standard story, Melissa sees lesbians as "people who always knew since they were like two or like five years old" that they have same-sex desires, whereas she did not know until she was fifteen and so has "lived most of my life as a straight person." Mai says, "I don't really know a lot of academics that actually really identify, who are like women, who identify as being a lesbian," contrasting that to fluidity. Dana critiques the queer community at UCSB as "hyper-lesbian space, ... it's mostly like 'you like girls, you always like girls.'" Lea says, "I still really like guys. Sometimes I question whether I'm bi or straight but I've never like thought that I might be a lesbian." Alex dislikes the word "lesbian," explaining, "I mean historically and all these things and all the connotations ... and I mean like I do have some kind of very like base-level physical attraction to men." Rachel, a white woman who identifies as queer, does not like the "finality" of the word "lesbian," adding, "it seems like there is no going back from there." Fluidity and pansexual, then, function as a critique of the binary of bisexuality and the perceived rigidity of lesbianism. For these students, their shifting identities keep open the possibility of intimacies with both women and men.

Jessica's definition of pansexual as including an attraction to "any genders that fall outside" male and female is the third theme that emerges in the interviews. This is the dominant understanding that emerged in students' stories. A multi-racial (Latina, Japanese, white) student, Missy, who identifies as queer, defines "pansexual" as acknowledging "the possibility of, you know, being attracted to someone that doesn't fall into those two like male or female categories." Liliana, who doesn't like using labels "because I just don't like limiting myself to just one thing," thinks even "bisexual" specifies just women or men "but I feel like if you say sexually fluid, that includes transgender, literally anything." Margaret has not yet been attracted to someone who does not fit into a binary gender category but says, "it could happen. I'm open to it. And then I'm like, 'Well, shit, should I identify as pansexual?'" Adrianna, a Latina student who does not identify sexually, explains that for her that means "I just like whoever I like. It doesn't have to be a girl or boy." At the end of her interview, she wondered "why people don't like to identify when it's obvious they only like a certain sex," in contrast to her openness. Scarlet, who is Asian American, says, "[Fluid means] like people can be all over the spectrum, male or female, gay or straight" and that there are multiple genders, "there's everything in between." A white student, Olivia, who identifies as fluid, says, "I, yeah, I don't, I wouldn't say I'm gay or straight ... Yeah, I mean I've mostly been with men but I've been attracted to women and had physical intimate encounters with women and I would never close myself off to a gender." Missy would agree: "But I guess things get more complicated too, like, if you identify as genderqueer, you know, you don't like fit into either, like, the male or female kind of binary, you know, ... so then that becomes a lot more like, you know, fluid, I guess. Or like people identifying as pansexual, to, you know, acknowledge the possibility of, you know, being attracted to someone that doesn't fall into those two like, male or female categories." Lea describes, "right now, you know, walking across campus, there was a lot of hot people, men, women, people who I can't tell the gender of and I don't really care because they're hot either way." Margaret hesitates about calling herself pansexual because "I've never been attracted to anyone who didn't identify as male or female." As all of these descriptions indicate, fluidity and pansexuality are perhaps most defined by acknowledging the possibility of sexual attraction to people beyond binary genders.

Although some students identified as genderqueer, none of those who spoke of fluidity or pansexuality encompassing attraction to genders beyond male or female talked about intimate relations with genderqueer or transgender people. They did talk about their desires for masculine or feminine partners, but not in any uniform way. Morgan, who calls both herself and her girlfriend feminine, is "only attracted to feminine men," but with women "I don't think it would necessarily matter." Kayla, too, is "attracted to like a more feminine energy in guys" and wonders if her same-sex desires "lead me to have more feminized choices in males." Lea's ideal is a "tall skinny feminine guy," although her current boyfriend she describes as "pretty masculine, ... almost on the border of like bro-ish." Defining herself as a little bit butch, she says she likes women "a little bit more fem but on the border but it really doesn't matter." Liliana, in contrast to Morgan and Kayla, desires masculine men (but "not a bro") and feminine women. "Everything I want in a guy, I do not want in a girl." Potential attraction to multiple genders does not, as these comments suggest, translate into gender not mattering in terms of desire.

Nor is gender irrelevant in terms of sexual behavior. Kayla, whose boyfriend she describes as feminine and probably "at least bisexual," at first denies any difference between sex with a woman or a man. "When I'm in bed with somebody I don't tend to think about gender, aside from the obvious fact that if it's a dude I have a penis in me, and if not, ya know ... Either shit's going in, or shit's being done ... I don't know, I just don't really even think about gender that much." Later she contradicts this by saying, "I feel like with women, there's a lot more, like, I don't want to say foreplay 'cause that doesn't really make sense, but like mental foreplay ... I feel like it's less just about wham-bam thank you ma'am and more about just the experience as a whole ..." Brooke, at the time of the interview in a relationship with a man, says that "girl-on-girl sex" has "always turned me on and hasn't stopped, versus where straight sex has not always turned me on," the difference being that she has to have feelings for a man. At the same time, she describes a threesome with another woman and a man as a metaphor for her sexuality: "I mean I feel like that's the perfect example right there how I feel about my sexuality. I mean I could go either way, I'm right in the middle. I mean, yeah, it was fun." Fluidity and pansexuality, then, connote openness to desire for transsexual, transgender and genderqueer intimate partners, but gender continues to matter in attraction and sexual intimacy.

Conclusion: from the bedroom to the classroom and back

At the University of California, Santa Barbara, and no doubt on other similar campuses across the country, the sexual scripts of the hook-up culture, with the possibilities for same-sex sexual experimentation and an openness to a variety of relationships, provide a context for the development of new intimacies and sexual identities. Women students who identify as fluid or pansexual, or refuse a sexual identity altogether, express rapidly shifting desires, make sense of changing identities, and acknowledge the possibility of attraction to people of genders beyond male and female. This opens up the possibility of intimacies beyond both traditional heterosexual and gay/lesbian committed relationships (Giddens 1992). Brooke, reflecting on her future, says she expects to continue to have fluid sexual desires. It is change that she sees as a constant: "I know that I am going to change over time as I am exposed to other things, and, like, I think I will definitely evolve with it." Eliana, a Latina student who calls herself "unlabeled," like many other students does not want to get married, to either a man or a woman. At least some of these young women seem determined to shape relationships that satisfy their shifting desires and identities, much like the gay men in unconventional relationships Judith Stacey has researched (Stacey 2005). Whether or not they will in the long run be able to do that is, for now, an open question.

How have women students come to embrace the notion of female sexual fluidity? The stories of fluid or pansexual students point to the complex relationship of college coursework and academic research to the emergence of new intimacies and identities. Just as the writings of late 19th-century sexologists, based on familiarity with homosexual clients and communities, spread knowledge of new identities, the concept of the sexual fluidity of women has moved from scholarship based on interviews with young women to popular culture, in particular around the publication of Lisa Diamond's book in 2008. In line with queer theory, with its emphasis on the instability of gender and sexuality, research on women's sexuality increasingly emphasizes fluidity as a strategy for overcoming gender and sexual binaries. In turn, women seem increasingly likely to identify as fluid. Only 1 out of 23 (4%) of the students interviewed in 2006 or 2007 identified as fluid, pansexual or not identified, whereas 15 out of 71 (21%) interviewed from 2009 to 2012 did. The embrace of a new identity, or of an identity-less sense of sexual self, in the case of those who refuse to embrace an identity, is striking.

Students themselves commented on the influence of the concept of sexual fluidity and the college environment more generally on their thinking about their sexuality. Brooke, who first identified as bisexual, explained that "it was the only thing I really knew about." Lea, in discussing the relationship of her sexual and gender identities, commented on the privilege of a college education "to even have access to these sorts of terms and these concepts and a community that backs these sorts of terms." Liliana knew only gay and straight growing up, adding, "it wasn't until I came to college that I found out about all these other different words, and then I was like 'oh, this kind of applies to how I feel.'" Margaret, who also identifies as genderqueer, talks about the way "everything gathers a history and all these associations." That a college student might identify as genderqueer, she says, is no big surprise. Olivia mentioned "taking classes, like women's studies, it helps me just be more open." Alex prefaced her assertion that sexuality is fluid with "I'm a fem[inist] studies major." Without naming Lisa Diamond, Melissa talked about "this book" about sexual fluidity that described her own sense of herself. Jessica did her "Wikipedia research on each of these terms, 'cause, you know, when you come out you wanna make sure that the term is fitting, right?" Students also talked about the impact of their involvement in the queer community on campus on the ways that they conceptualized their intimacies and identities. Valeria, who herself identifies as a lesbian, says about the term "pansexual" that "you've heard it so often, in like so much of the training that you do in different organization." Alex says, "I hear the term 'pansexual' a lot." The campus culture, shaped by queer theory and research on sexualities, is a context in which new intimacies and identities can emerge and be verified in daily life.

The old story of "I was always a lesbian" is increasingly being replaced, at least on campus, with a more complex tale of gender and sexuality fluidity. That this may not be confined solely to college students is suggested by the fact that the most recent study by the Center for Disease Control found that more women who did not graduate from high school had engaged in same-sex sexual activity than did those with college degrees (Chandra *et al.* 2011). In any case, the campus story is an opportunity to see the interaction between emerging concepts and changing behaviors and self-conceptions. As more young women experience and act on same-sex desires, they engage in intimacies and adopt identities that refuse rigid categories and traditional forms of relationship. Along with John Irving's bisexual hero, they demand of the world, "please don't put a label on me—don't make me a category before you get to know me!"

References

Armstrong, Elizabeth A., Laura Hamilton and Paula England. 2010. "Is Hooking Up Bad for Young Women?" *Contexts* 9(3): 22–27.

Bogle, Kathleen A. 2008. *Hooking Up: Sex, Dating, and Relationships on Campus.* New York: New York University Press.

Blumstein, Philip W. and Pepper Schwartz. 1977. "Bisexuality: Some Social Psychological Issues." *Journal of Social Issues* 33: 30–45.

Chandra, Anjani, William D. Mosher, Casey Copen and Catlainn Sionean. 2011. "Sexual Behavior, Sexual Attraction, and Sexual Identity in the United States: Data From the 2006–8 National Survey of Family Growth." *National Health Statistics Reports* 36 (March 3).

Chauncey, George Jr. 1989. "Christian Brotherhood or Sexual Perversion? Homosexual Identities and the Construction of Sexual Boundaries in the World War I Era." In Martin Bauml Duberman, Martha Vicinus, and George Chauncey Jr (eds) *Hidden from History: Reclaiming the Gay and Lesbian Past.* New York: New American Library, 294–317.

Duggan, Lisa. 2000. *Sapphic Slashers: Sex, Violence, and American Modernity.* Durham, NC: Duke University Press.

England, Paula, Emily Fitzgibbons Safer and Alison C.K. Fogarty. 2007. "Hooking Up and Forming Romantic Relationships on Today's College Campuses." In Michael S. Kimmel and Amy Aronson (eds) *The Gendered Society Reader.* New York: Oxford University Press, 3rd edn.

Friedland, Roger and Paolo Gardinali. 2013. "Hey God, Is That You in My Underpants? Sex, Love and Religiosity Among American College Students." In Alan Frank, Patricia Ticineto Clough and Steven Seidman (eds) *Intimacies: A New World of Relational Life.* New York: Routledge.

Giddens, Anthony. 1987. *Social Theory and Modern Sociology.* Stanford, CA: Stanford University Press.

——1992. *The Transformation of Intimacy: Sexuality, Love, and Eroticism in Modern Societies.* Stanford, CA: Stanford University Press.

Golden, Carla. 2006. "What's in a Name? Sexual Self-identification among Women." In R.C. Savin-Williams and K.M. Cohen (eds) *The Lives of Lesbians, Gays, and Bisexuals: Children to Adults.* Fort Worth, TX: Harcourt Brace.

Hamilton, Laura and Elizabeth A. Armstrong. 2009. "Double Binds and Flawed Options: Gendered Sexuality in Early Adulthood." *Gender & Society* 23: 589–616.

Hoburg, Robin, Julie Konik, Michelle Williams and Mary Crawford. 2004. "Bisexuality Among Self-identified Heterosexual College Students." *Journal of Bisexuality* 4(1–2): 25–36.

Irving, John. 2012. *In One Person: A Novel.* New York: Simon and Schuster.

Laumann, Edward O., John H. Gagnon, Robert T. Michael and Stuart Michaels. 1994. *The Social Organization of Sexuality.* Chicago: University of Chicago Press.

MSNBC. 2012. "More Women Experimenting with Bisexuality." www.msnbc.msn.com/id/9358339/ns/health-sexual_health/t/more-women-experimenting-bisexuality/ (accessed July 23, 2012).

Peplau, Letitia Anne and Linda D. Garnets. 2000. "A New Paradigm for Understanding Women's Sexuality and Sexual Orientation." *Journal of Social Issues* 56: 329–50.

Rupp, Leila J. 2012. "Sexual Fluidity 'Before Sex'." *Signs: Journal of Women in Culture and Society* 37: 849–56.

Rupp, Leila J. and Verta Taylor. 2010. "Straight Girls Kissing." *Contexts* 9(3): 28–32.

Rust, Paula C. Rodríguez. 1993. "Coming Out in the Age of Social Constructionism: Sexual Identity Formation among Lesbians and Bisexual Women." *Gender & Society* 7: 50–77.

——2000a. "Bisexuality: A Contemporary Paradox for Women." *Journal of Social Issues* 56: 205–21.

——2000b. *Bisexuality in the United States*. New York: Columbia University Press.

Stacey, Judith. 2005. "The Families of Man: Gay Male Intimacy and Kinship in a Global Metropolis." *Signs* 30: 1911–35.

Stein, Arlene. 1997. *Sex and Sensibility: Stories of a Lesbian Generation*. Berkeley: University of California Press.

——2010. "The Incredible Shrinking Lesbian World and Other Queer Conundra." *Sexualities* 13(1): 21–32.

Taylor, Verta and Nancy E. Whittier. 1992. "Collective Identity in Social Movement Communities: Lesbian Feminist Mobilization." In Aldon D. Morris and Carol McClurg Mueller (eds) *Frontiers in Social Movement Theory*. New Haven: Yale University Press.

Terry, Jennifer. 1999. *An American Obsession: Science, Medicine, and Homosexuality in Modern Society*. Chicago: University of Chicago Press.

Thompson, Elisabeth Morgan and Elizabeth M. Morgan. 2008. "'Mostly Straight' Young Women: Variations in Sexual Behavior and Identity Development." *Developmental Psychology* 44(1): 15–21.

6   Intimacy and ambivalence

Daniel Shaw

Have you ever watched a grown-up play peek-a-boo with an infant? Wanting to be hidden, and wanting to be seen and found starts early for humans. It seems that we have been designed so that intimacy must always include both.

In my psychoanalytic psychotherapy practice in New York City, it has always been the case that almost all the single men and women I see, and almost all the divorced or considering being divorced men and women I see, are struggling with intimacy: loving and being loved. Many people present with depression stemming from painful feelings of loneliness, and with frustration and discouragement about being able to create and sustain an intimate relationship that feels passionate and alive, and at the same time safe and dependable. According to Aron (1991), their analysts have similar struggles:

> I believe that people who are drawn to analysis as a profession have part-icularly strong conflicts regarding their desire to be known by another, that is, conflicts regarding intimacy ... Why else would people choose a profession in which they spend their lives listening and looking into the lives of others while they themselves remain relatively silent and hidden?
>
> (Aron 1991: 43)

Aron is referring in particular to the kind of intimacy that can develop in a therapeutic relationship, but many other sub-categories of intimacy can also be described. In this chapter, I will focus on the intimacy associated with romantic love and partnership. What is true for many analysts, that the longing and need for intimacy conflicts with a wish to hide, is true for people in general. Most of us, whether we know it or not, are ambivalent about wanting intimacy. The desire to be hidden, to avoid vulnerability for fear of emotional pain, is often dissociated. Many people who believe that they desire and are seeking a lasting intimate partnership, but who experience repeated disappointment and loneliness, find their plight incomprehensible. In a therapeutic context, it becomes possible to recognize the dissociated desire to be hidden and to avoid vulnerability—at which point, inhibiting fears can be examined, understood and worked through. What I see as the therapeutic task in the area of intimacy is not leading patients to achieving a particular type or degree of intimate relating, but rather, helping patients sort out and understand what their real desires are—and what their unarticulated fears and underlying beliefs about intimacy really are.

In this chapter, I will present clinical vignettes of people I have worked with in psychoanalytic psychotherapy who have struggled with intimacy. However, one of my intentions in quoting Aron is to be clear that I do not presume to speak from a privileged position as an expert on intimacy, or as a therapist whose personal intimate relationships are so ideal that I use myself as an example. I am speaking from a relational psychoanalytic perspective, and I am speaking also as a fellow human, who has struggled and struggles still with the intimacy of loving and being loved.

Loneliness

We seek intimacy because the alternative, loneliness, is for most people very hard, if not impossible, to bear. Intimacy-seeking is in our blood and bones—the human infant is biologically designed to grow and develop optimally when intimate nurture is provided. One way we know this is that we can draw a bright line from failure to thrive to its cause: failure to provide adequate nurture (Spitz 1964). A thriving baby is one who seeks nurture and receives it. However, humans are very adaptive creatures, and in the absence of optimal nurture, and in many cases in the presence of very poor and inadequate nurture, humans can still develop and function, sometimes very highly. Optimal nurture provides pleasurable experiences of shared intimacy between infant and caregiver—the warmly held, lovingly touched baby is learning the rudiments of tender intimacy in all the daily routines of infant care. Such early intimacy experiences influence, to one degree or another, the development of each person's particular capacities for and means of expression of intimacy, as the person grows throughout the life cycle.

Of course, parents are not always calm, devoted, soothing and comforting when providing nurture. They can be agitated, anxious, depressed, dissociative and many other unpleasant things—either predominantly, or intermittently—and still provide what we would call nurture: basic care that keeps the baby well enough to grow up. So what can we say with any certainty about intimacy? Given the huge discrepancies in how humans are nurtured that we can observe, it would seem that any conceptualizing we do about intimacy must take into account the myriad ways, each different as a snowflake, that romantic intimacy is actually experienced and expressed. From a liberal perspective, in which hetero-normativity is not considered *a priori* and otherness is not pathologized, it follows that there is no one right way to be intimate. There is no set of 7 Steps to achieve healthy, socially acceptable, approved-by-The-American-Psychological-Association intimacy. We think of intimacy generally as a kind of deep closeness, but what that means to any particular person varies infinitely.

The truth of the matter is, we are all making it up as we go along.

The universality of ambivalence about intimacy

Nevertheless, one thing about intimacy that can be said to be virtually universal is the conflict Aron describes in the passage quoted above, between wanting to be known and wanting to stay hidden. For the many people with whom I have worked, for whom loneliness felt unbearable and intimacy seemed unreachable, this conflict was always dissociated at first—that is, desire and longing for intimacy was felt deeply, but the desire to remain hidden and the fear of being exposed was dissociated, split off from conscious awareness. For someone who has dissociated the side of their conflicted feelings about intimacy that wants to hide, failure to achieve lasting intimacy can seem incomprehensible. Of course, the person who longs for intimacy and is repeatedly disappointed would absolutely deny an unconscious wish to avoid it. Again and again, though, in my clinical experience with frustrated intimacy seekers, I discover that there is a dissociated part of the psyche that anticipates only failure and disappointment if intimacy is attempted. Without recognizing it, they are repeating earlier, developmentally traumatic experiences of lonely despair. When their behavior is explored more deeply, it turns out that they are consistently behaving in ways that have led to failure in the past, while somehow imagining that those behavioral choices will, this time, succeed.

This understanding about dissociated conflict has been developed extensively by Bromberg (1993), who put it this way:

> the individual cannot hold conflicting ways of seeing himself … within a single experiential state long enough to feel the subjective pull of opposing affects and discordant self-perceptions as a valid state of mind that is worth taking as an object of self-reflection. The contents of the mind (affects, wishes, beliefs, and so on) are not readily accessible to the reflective capacity of the observing ego; the individual tends to experience his immediate subjective experience as truth and any response to it that contains the existence of data implying an alternative perspective as disconfirming and thereby unthinkable.
>
> (Bromberg 1993: 163)

Bromberg's insight about unconscious conflict stems from his study of trauma and dissociation—in particular, the realization that cumulative, relational trauma leads to dissociative mental organizations (Bromberg 2011). Relational trauma, also referred to as developmental trauma when specifically describing trauma experienced by developing children due to exposure to problematic aspects of the parents, describes the psychological impact on a person who is or has been in an ongoing relationship with a traumatizing other.

Harold

Harold's story gives a particularly striking example of someone who suffered significant developmental trauma and whose conflicts around intimacy were dissociated. Harold is a single gay man about 35 years old who had referred himself to a 12-Step group for sex addiction, and then contacted me for psychotherapy. Harold was brought up by his paranoid schizophrenic mother, whose intense rages and violent physical and verbal assaults he experienced almost daily. When he left home as a teenager, he came out, and since then Harold has experienced a few short-lived romantic relationships. Otherwise, his extensive sexual activity was with anonymous partners, though, since beginning his 12-Step work, he had chosen to eliminate all such encounters. At a point in our third year of working together, Harold had yet to enter into an intimate romantic relationship, and he was expressing feelings of intense loneliness. He admitted to feeling "euphoric recall" for his anonymous, nighttime encounters in Central Park, and I asked him what he especially remembered about those times. His answer surprised me. He said, "I experienced the most tender intimacy I have ever known with those men. We kissed and held each other so intensely, passionately—it felt so deeply loving." I think Harold was surprised by his answer too. How incredibly ironic, he thought, that the most intimate experiences of love he has ever known were with strangers in the park at night, hiding in the bushes. The problem for Harold with relying on these experiences as a fulfilling source of intimacy was that the tenderness was just one part of the experience. There was also the desperation, the insatiability, the danger and the degradation. Yet, when Harold tried to develop a relationship with a man in a more conventional way, he invariably felt overwhelmed, confused, obsessed—and ultimately, he would give up in despair.

It is hard for Harold to imagine how he can be truly close to someone and also feel safe, both at the same time. His mother's insane rage and violence toward him was internalized as a sense of himself as bad, unlovable, disgusting. For a short while, at night in the park, he could free himself of pain, he could feel completely desirable and deeply connected. He could feel safe—because he and his sex partner knew nothing of each other, and never would. They only knew their intense, compelling desires, and the urgency they both felt about those desires being fulfilled.

As was the case with Harold, people who repeatedly struggle with seeking and not finding enduring intimate connection often have a powerful part of themselves, again mostly dissociated, which feels hopelessly convinced of not being good enough. That underlying belief can be expressed variously, as in: "there are no good [men/women] out there"—this would be an attempt to project out the bad feeling within; or, "I must be wrong to think that I'm a good person—I must actually be horrible, unlovable, undesirable"—depressive, self-loathing feelings; or, "I need to learn to play the game, I just have to learn the rules, I need someone to tell me what the rules are"—expressing a sense of being on the outside and feeling helpless; and so on.

These explanations are experienced as facts, but they are actually feelings, examples of the hopelessness of depressive thinking. However, for those people who suffer from a pervasive but dissociated sense of badness about themselves, and dissociated fears of intimacy, no explanation makes sense. Believing that the bottom line is that they are unlovable is at least a way of having some kind of explanation for their pain. It is easy to understand how someone like Harold, who suffered extreme, cruel abuse at the hands of his mother throughout his developmental years, would internalize a sense of badness. It has been literally beaten into him. He makes great efforts to free himself from this sense of badness, but it clings to him in ways that are not always obvious.

All the harder then, for someone who believes that their upbringing was relatively normal, to understand how or why they carry within them some kind of hidden sense of badness, one that does not conform to their more conscious self-image. The sense of badness about the self, which is experienced as shame, is universal to one degree or another. In depressives, it is blatantly obvious; in others, it is less apparent, and not particularly significant, because it plays a relatively insignificant role in the psyche. For many, though, the sense of badness (shame, unlovability) is present but heavily defended against—a situation of dissociated conflict which sets up an internal tension. Especially for people who prefer to think of their upbringing as "normal," recognizing this sense of badness of the self involves recognizing some of the ways their caregivers may have instilled that sense in them. I've never actually met anyone whose family was "normal," unless normal is meant to describe the average expectable neuroticism in families generally. Families are complicated, and even the most loving parents can inadvertently influence their children to carry feelings of guilt and unworthiness. For people in this situation, it may seem safer to go on defending against this feeling of badness than to confront it directly—for one thing, it allows the sense that everything was fine and normal to remain unchallenged. However, working to deny an internalized sense of badness almost always signals that bad aspects of the parents and the family as a whole are also being denied. This leads to a very unstable internal situation, sitting atop a foundation of dissociation. Facing the truth, while painful, can lead to an internal shift that opens the way for therapeutic work that can strengthen and stabilize self-esteem.

Harold's story opens many questions for me about the nature of intimacy. His experiences in the park at night afforded him a kind of intimacy that may have been the most he could tolerate, the most he felt capable of, the most he believed he could get—perhaps all of the above. The intensity of the sexual excitement was amplified by the dangerous and transgressive nature of the encounters, but, coming down from these highs, Harold would feel intense shame, helplessly at the mercy of his addiction. The problem for Harold was not that the intimacy he experienced in these encounters was not real. It was intensely, passionately real for him. The problem was that the intimacy was limited, constricted, without the possibility of developing, deepening and becoming an integral part of his whole life. After many years of thrilling nights in the park, Harold had exhausted his ability to compensate at night for what was missing by day. Harold's loneliness grew more acutely painful, not less, as he came to rely more and more on the availability of strangers.

Safety

Which feels less safe: loneliness or intimacy? The answer is, of course, it depends. For the human infant, too much loneliness can actually be fatal. Even a small amount of loneliness can feel unbearable for an infant, something that I probably knew from my own infancy, but had to learn all over again, the hard way, when trying to put my first child to bed or down for a nap. Like many first-time parents, we were reluctant to let our baby cry it out when being put down to sleep, so we stayed and stayed and stayed until he fell asleep, hoping he would not wake up and start screaming the instant we left the room. We learned our lesson three years later with our second child—we let her cry it out for two nights, making brief reassuring visits every 10 or 15 minutes until she was finally able to sleep, and then my daughter never had trouble going right to sleep again. My son is now a teenager, and far from complaining when we aren't staying with him, he is happy to spend as much time away from our home as he can; and while in our home, he usually prefers to be in his room with the door shut. He has many secrets now, and almost never wants to be touched, let alone cuddle with either my wife or myself. He's had all the intimacy with his parents he needs for a while, and of course that is as it should be, more or less.

My point is that, given the way human development goes, we are generally people for whom too much loneliness is painful, and for whom too much intimacy is often undesirable. We want closeness, and we want distance; we want connectedness, and we want solitude; we want to be taken care of, and we want autonomy. We are a bundle of contradictions when it comes to intimacy. I contend that we attempt to regulate our experience of intimacy based largely on how safe or unsafe we are feeling.

Interpersonal safety has to do with emotional and narcissistic vulnerabilities— how we feel about ourselves. We generally attempt to feel, or hope or expect to feel good about ourselves. We bolster ourselves in various ways—accomplishments, possessions, cosmetic enhancement, fashion sense, moral and religious values, community affiliations—these are just a few examples of ways that we elevate and maintain our self-esteem. Good self-esteem—that is, feeling good about oneself—provides a feeling of safety, a sense of security that allows for confident engagement with the social world.

We also defend ourselves in various ways from lowered self-esteem. Defenses against feeling badly about ourselves, against injuries to our narcissism, or self-love, can get very complicated. The counter-dependent defense is a common one. It can be heard in the casual indifference of the lover who says, "You can come over and spend the night if you want," indicating that she is not the one who needs or wants anything, but she understands that you do. The counter-dependent person arranges for others to do all the desiring in the relationship, while she never seems to need or want anything. The vulnerability involved in intimacy can lead us to seek ways of defending, or protecting ourselves from anticipated pain. A counter-dependent stance is one of the ways of defending against vulnerability. For married people, another kind of defense would be having affairs. In a secret affair, a married person can enjoy exciting sexual intimacy that is completely isolated from all the dull, routine aspects of his domestic life, and he can completely avoid the exposure of and the arguments about all his weaknesses, flaws, bad habits and so on—all the minutiae that is on display in his marital relationship. The affair is a defense against the bursting of the fantasy bubble that says that intimacy can be easy and uncomplicated, that you are and will always be desirable and potent, and that every fuck can be what novelist Erica Jong (1974) famously called a "zipless fuck"—a kind of hot, earth-shaking sex where there is no mundane tedium about the details of reality, before or after.

How each of us understands what interpersonal safety means to us at any given point of time, how defended or vulnerable we choose to be, will influence the extent to which we are willing or not to be intimate, and will also determine the kind of intimacy we seek. The last posthumously published book by Stephen Mitchell (2003), a seminal thinker in the development of what is now known as relational psychoanalysis, was a deeply thoughtful exploration of intimate romantic relationships. Mitchell noted that loving intimately exposed our vulnerability and dependency, and as such was fraught with emotional danger—the fear of loss, the shame and hurt of rejection. He reasoned that marriage was a way of trying to make love safer, a way of being a winner in the mating game, and not a loser; and a way to insure against loneliness. Then he noted the paradox:

> The great irony inherent in our efforts to make love safer is that those efforts always make it more dangerous. One of the motives for monogamous commitments is always, surely, the effort to make the relationship more secure, a hedge against the vulnerabilities and risks of love. Yet, since respectable monogamous commitment in our times tends to be reciprocal, the selection of only one partner for love dramatically increases one's dependency upon that partner, making love more dangerous and efforts to guarantee that love even more compelling.
>
> (Mitchell 2003: 46–47)

Mitchell's point, that depending on one partner is never as safe as we would like to believe, has been demonstrated to me again and again in my work with couples. There is dangerous vulnerability in trusting and depending on one, till-death-do-us-part, intimate other—the more we care, the more devastating unexpected loss or betrayal would be.

The following vignettes describe people with whom I have worked, disguised for the sake of confidentiality, who longed for intimate partnership, and had experienced profound frustration and disappointment in their search. I offer these vignettes to illustrate some of the different ways people become confused and discouraged when safety needs are in conflict with the need for intimacy.

Laura

I have seen Laura for about four years, from the beginning of her relationship with Jimi. They are still together, but there has almost never been a session where Laura hasn't talked about her agonizing dread of learning that Jimi is cheating on her. Laura is 45 years old, very intelligent and intense. Her 17-year-old son from a previous bad marriage lives with her and Jimi, who often has with him his two young sons from his previous bad marriage (there was one previous to that as well). Laura and I worked hard together to try to understand why she was so anxious, almost constantly preoccupied with the possibility that Jimi could cheat on her. We combed through her childhood history—a cold, rejecting mother and an angry, distant father; we looked at her previous marriage in great detail. We talked about Jimi extensively, and, though he had not been honest in his relationships in the past, he was older now, he had suffered a great deal through his second divorce, and what was odd was that the way Laura described him, it didn't sound to me like Jimi was cheating, or that he wanted to. When she was more calm and less agitated, it didn't sound to Laura like he was cheating either. So why couldn't Laura stop being suspicious? I observed that she had an extraordinary ability to interpret the motivation of others, and it seemed that she continually assumed that Jimi was motivated by a desire to be with other women. Yet, in her heart of hearts, she believed that he was faithful; when she told me what Jimi would say to her, she conveyed an impression of him as deeply committed, very intelligent, perceptive and sensitive. Those qualities stood in contrast to her description of his intermittent selfishness and thoughtlessness, but Laura confirmed my sense that both aspects of his personality were true.

In time, Laura also became more honest with me about the fights she had with Jimi. It became clear that Laura was often intensely provocative and accusatory, and could fly out of control into violent rages that stopped just short of getting physical. Eventually, I had to wonder if Laura's unrelenting suspicions and fears of being betrayed might be less about Jimi, and more about her own dissociated conflicts around intimacy. Laura had grown up with extremely emotionally volatile parents, and, though she felt adored by her father, he could be terrifying when he raged, mostly at her mother, but sometimes at her. She learned to be constantly vigilant for the next outburst, the next attack. Laura had also been molested as a child by the husband of her older sister. She did not tell me about this until well into three years of work together. I wondered if Laura was so traumatized while growing up by witnessing the impact of rage, cruelty and betrayal in her adult role models that she had come to feel that it would be impossible to be loved without being devastatingly hurt. Laura was very insightful in many ways about her vulnerabilities, but it just seemed impossible for Laura to feel safe in an intimate relationship. The very experience of feeling safe elicited feelings of panic: the terror that the safety might suddenly, unexpectedly be lost.

Once her loneliness and longing for intimacy had led her to find Jimi, the underlying conviction that betrayal was inevitable seems to have driven her to behave in undermining ways. She returned repeatedly to her suspicions and accusations, almost as if to convince him to leave her. The Patsy Cline song with the refrain "hurt me now, get it over"[1] has a pithy way, typical of the Country & Western song genre, of getting at this kind of self-fulfilling prophesying. I challenged Laura's certainty that betrayal was going to be coming from outside of her. I asked her to consider the possibility that her anticipation of future traumatization was actually a return of her dissociated memories of traumatizations— traumatizations that had already happened, long ago (Winnicott 1974). This is the case with post-traumatic stress disorder, which is characterized by flashbacks, seemingly arising for no particular reason, of prior traumas. Also characteristic of this disorder is a constant state of agitated hypervigilance, as though the trauma might reoccur at any minute and could possibly be sidestepped with enough advance anticipation (Herman 1992).

In her desperation to have a love that could feel safe, Laura was unwittingly generating a continual state of being in danger in her relationship. Her conflict—

between a deep longing for intimacy, and an underlying conviction that love and trust must always lead to catastrophic betrayal—was clear. She could even notice that, when things were going well between her and Jimi, she would often find a way to start a fight. If Laura truly wished to choose partnership as her primary source of intimacy, she would have to find a way to take the risk of feeling safe and intimate at the same time. How she could construct that experience for herself became the focus of our work.

Raul and Carole

While Laura and Jimi seemed to be unable to resist mutual destructiveness, many couples drift further and further apart by "playing it safe," avoiding confrontation and conflict. I've heard many people say that they just don't feel attracted to their partner any more. After deeper exploration, it becomes clear that their supposed "indifference" is actually the tip of a colossal iceberg, one made up of deeply suppressed rage, frustration and resentment. Intimacy, it turns out, cannot be sustained if differences, anger and conflicts are persistently avoided. This was brought home to me very dramatically by a couple, Raul and Carole, whom I saw only once.

Raul's and Carole's respective individual therapists both knew me and referred them as a couple to me. I was warned that things were very bad between them; that Raul had decided he was gay and Carole didn't believe him. Both still in their twenties, Raul was Cuban-born and an associate in a large New York law firm; Carole had grown up in New York City, in a WASP family that had fallen apart, exposing her to divorce and alcoholism at an early age. After being to-gether four years, and married for two of them, Raul was unable to go on hiding from himself the fact that he was gay, and, as much as he loved Carole, he could not go on lying. He was terrified of how his family would react—they were Cuban immigrants whose fervent religious and cultural traditions were extremely antithetical to homosexuality. However, most of all he was miserably guilty for hurting Carole. Though he had yet to have a sexual experience with a man, he had no doubt that he was gay, and that his life and Carole's life would only be further traumatized if he did not face up to it. He wanted Carole to let him go.

Carole had been completely blindsided by Raul, she claimed, and she refused to believe that he was really gay. I found it hard to believe that she had never suspected that Raul might be confused about his sexual orientation; she told me that the sexual passion they shared had removed any uncertainty about that for her. She was enraged and deeply hurt, but she wanted Raul to either realize he wasn't gay, or go and have a gay affair, get over it, and come back to her. The thought of losing him was unbearable, and at one point in our session, sensing that she was going to have to give up the fight, she threatened to kill herself. Raul immediately counter-threatened that the moment he heard that she had killed herself, he would kill himself too.

"Alright, now nobody is going to kill themselves, OK?" I shouted over their hysterics. "That's enough of that nonsense." They quieted down, somewhat abashed. I continued, somewhat abashed at my outburst myself:

"I am truly sorry. I think what you are going through is tragic. But you each have a chance to come through this—if you can find the courage to end the marriage. Raul, that would mean that you will have to begin life as an out gay man; you only risk hurting yourself and others further by not fully coming to terms with your sexual orientation. You will have to find a way to forgive yourself for hurting Carole. And Carole, you will have to grieve your loss, and eventually be ready to meet another man, and start over. You are both young, and you both have every reason to believe that you can find happiness, but only after you have accepted reality and dealt with it. Which is what you will do, what you must do, because any other alternative is simply ridiculous," I finished.

The session came to an end. They were my last patients that night, and when I left my office and walked out into the street, there they were, in a tender embrace, a fine light rain falling, holding each other, looking into each other's eyes with tenderness and deep sorrow.

I heard nothing more of them, until more than a year later when I ran into Carole's therapist. She told me that Carole and Raul had divorced, amicably; that Carole was happily remarried, and had given birth to a baby boy. Raul had come out, left the law firm and moved to Chicago, where he was pursuing his dream of owning an art gallery and representing new artists. They remained friends, but they were also both focusing on their new relationships, and both were doing well. I was greatly relieved. Raul and Carole had loved each other intimately; but each in their way had chosen safety over reality. For Raul, being heterosexual and married seemed a much safer choice than being who he was, that is, a gay man. Carole imagined that she was safer to ignore any suspicions about Raul's sexual orientation, and just cling to him as tightly as she could. In the end, their love was best expressed by granting each other the freedom to pursue the enduring romantic intimacy in a partnership that they both wanted— and could not fully realize with each other.

Carole and Raul loved each other very much, it seemed to me, and there was no question that the intimacy between them was intense and real. However, their mutual dissociation of Raul's homosexuality made it impossible for their intimacy to deepen and grow in the context of their marriage.

Lorraine

Lorraine is an example of someone who clung to an unfulfilling, deadened marriage for decades, for the sake of "safety," unable to mobilize herself in spite of how dangerously destructive the marriage had become. Almost 50, Lorraine and Alan had raised their two boys together, both of whom were doing very well, one in college and the other soon to follow. Lorraine contacted me shortly after Alan announced that he wanted a divorce.

Alan was the man with whom Lorraine fell in love in college, the first man she had sexual relations with, and a man who never lost his sexual attraction for her, even after the divorce. The problem was that Alan was controlling and demanding, intimidating and belittling. Though Alan was dismissive, belittling and resentful of Lorraine's career aspirations, she nevertheless went on to become an accomplished author and professor during the years she was married to Alan and raising their two children.

Lorraine grew up in a fairly conservative family, in which her younger and older brothers had been free to join their father in his authoritarian ways, while Lorraine was raised in the old-fashioned way—to be a good assistant homemaker to her mother, and to stand by her man, no matter what. Lorraine's world turned upside down when, not long after the birth of their second child, Lorraine discovered Alan was having an affair—because she discovered she had contracted a sexually transmitted disease from him. Alan confessed, he was contrite, they went to counseling and eventually Lorraine believed that she had forgiven him. What she only came to realize much later was that, from the point of her husband's affair on, she finally felt she had something she could hold over him. This realization came to Lorraine months after the divorce, but it marked a point for Lorraine where her identification as simply a victim of Alan's domination became more complex.

Originally living out west, they came east when Alan got a promotion that required him to relocate. Lorraine left her tenured professorship, and the house they had built, to move with her family. It was a huge upheaval, but they managed, the adjustments were made. After two years on the east coast, with their oldest son in college and their younger almost through with High School, Alan made his move and announced that he wanted a divorce. As devastated as she was, Lorraine was also relieved not to have to go on feeling so unseen by Alan, so careful to try not to anger him, so pressured to submit to him. By the time the divorce was final, almost two years later, she had sold the old house, bought a new one at a good price in an excellent location with a mother-in-law apartment she could rent out, found excellent, helpful contractors for the needed repairs who were willing to work in her price range, had been given a contract for a second book, had been offered a tenured position at her new job, and was well into some adventurous dating.

Lorraine was someone who tended to forget how capable, strong and intelligent she actually was. Lorraine often missed Alan, often returned in her mind to the possibility that maybe she should have just given in to Alan, maybe it was all her fault. After all, she had been, she realized, passive aggressive in many ways. Maybe her mother was right, she would sometimes think—she should have focused on keeping Alan happy and kept her troubles to herself. She spent months convinced that she couldn't possibly, at her age, meet anyone who would love her. Her aloneness terrified and paralyzed her. She didn't want to get out of bed; she dragged herself along, doing what she had to do, but it was all hopeless, all over for her.

In spite of Lorraine's certainty for some time after the divorce that she would never find someone else, she eventually found Tom, and they began to negotiate the terms of what for both of them was the first important relationship since their respective divorces. Tom was especially appreciative and admiring of Lorraine, which she found deeply gratifying. However, as for conflict and disagreement, Lorraine had never in her life managed either satisfactorily. If she wasn't submitting, either willingly or begrudgingly, clamming up and getting passive aggressive, and/or dissociating to the point of not knowing what she felt, she'd end up feeling out of control and blurting out explosive things she felt horrible for saying. As it turned out, Tom had a stubborn streak, and he sounded, to my ears, rigid and unyielding in many ways. Lorraine was starting to feel déjà vu, the sinking feeling that she was with someone like her ex, to whom she would end up submitting resentfully.

So, on several occasions, we play-acted conversations in which she acted the part of Tom, and I played her. She showed me what it was that Tom did or said that made her shut down, we explored why (in short, he could react with disapproval just like her intimidating, judgmental father), and I acted out how I would be if I were Lorraine—or a version of Lorraine that didn't freeze like a deer in the headlights when she got scared about the possibility of the whole relationship going up in flames.

In time, Lorraine was able to have different kinds of conversations with Tom, even including expressing different forms of anger (irritation, annoyance, resentment, hurt), that began to seem more constructive. Reluctantly, Tom made some changes. While Tom was more loving in some ways than any man Lorraine had ever been with, she eventually could not ignore the extent to which Tom was still dictating the terms of their relationship, and the extent to which she was going along with him whether she liked it or not. Stubborn, rigid habits of his that she had tried to overlook became more pronounced, and more and more she felt unheard and dismissed by him. She also noticed how she positioned herself to feel that she mattered less than Tom, while another part of her became preoccupied with the things about him that made her feel superior to him. For the first time in her life, she realized how much her family of origin, and her relationship to her ex-husband, existed on the binary seesaw (Aron 2006; Benjamin 1999) of complementarity, the relational matrix where only two positions are possible: superior or inferior; up or down. She realized that, from an unconscious conviction of her inferiority and lesser status as a woman, she tried to be what Tom wanted—she tried to be a woman that Tom would want, whether that was actually who *she* was or not. She noticed at these times that she was far more concerned with what Tom wanted than what she wanted. She saw herself slip into the role of Tom's object, and lose the sense of herself as subject.

I asked Lorraine if she could become more aware and self-reflective about when and how she was focused on what Tom wanted or on what she wanted. She became a keen observer of her state shifts and the interplay of her different self-orientations—now object, now subject—and struggled to center herself less on Tom's needs and more on her own thoughts, needs, feelings, wishes. More fully connected to herself, she realized that Tom's unacknowledged ambivalence about intimacy, and his disavowed need to keep their relationship completely on his terms, was more depriving and required more submission than she could now tolerate at this point in her life, after all she'd been through.

The more Lorraine could allow herself her subjectivity without invalidating herself, the more she was able to bring her feelings out in the open and try to work things out with Tom. At first, this seemed hopeful to Lorraine. Maybe they could be more honest with each other, and negotiate ways of dealing with their conflicts that did not require her submission, but the more connected to herself

Lorraine became, the more rigid and shut down Tom became. In the end, she had to ask herself what frightened her so terribly about letting him go? She began to recognize more fully a subjectivity that belonged to her, one that offered freedom that was unattainable as long as she remained subjugated, orientated to herself as the object of others, her subjectivity vacated.

Lorraine tried valiantly, but it became clear that Tom was not willing to be with her if her needs were going to be considered as important as his own. As she described their conversations to me, she certainly sounded like she had been loving, and hopeful that they could resolve their differences, but Tom would have none of it. So Lorraine was ready to move on. She realized that she had probably stayed with Tom twice as long as she would have, if she had not been so terrified of loneliness. I told her that it seemed like, when she was focused on being what Tom would want, she made herself his object. Without being centered in her own subjectivity, being without Tom seemed to mean being unbearably alone, or being "nothing." Her stronger, more connected sense of herself now as subject seemed to make the prospect of being alone far less terrifying. She even seemed to look forward to having some time to herself, and began to take care of herself and stand up for herself in other areas that she had been neglecting. It no longer seemed safer to Lorraine to submit, to accommodate, to mold herself to what she thought the other would require of her. She had done that throughout her marriage, or tried to, and it hadn't made her happy, and it hadn't made her marriage work.

I told Lorraine that I believed that her shift out of the object position to a sense of herself as subject seemed to give her a much better chance of being able to meet someone and build an intimate relationship—because she, the whole Lorraine, would not be afraid to be more fully present.

Conclusion

I have shared these various stories of people with whom I have worked to illustrate the myriad ways that it is possible to be ambivalent about intimacy. Comedians have long joked about playing hide and go seek when they were a child with their parents, the punch line being that the child hid, waited and waited, and the parent never found them—the parents sneaked out and never came back. What is true in this grim old joke is that yes, we want to hide, but we also very much want to be found, we want to be sought. Similarly, we want to be safe, but we want excitement and at least a little danger. Intimacy isn't easy: not for those who find it readily but are then challenged to sustain it over many years; and not for those who find it exasperatingly impossible to ever get it off the ground.

The point I have wanted to make here is that we humans are naturally ambivalent about intimacy, often in ways that are not conscious. Awareness of this ambivalence, and understanding the sources from which it arises, is an important first step for people who are trying to understand why they feel trapped in repetitive situations, in which their efforts to form a lasting romantic relationship with an intimate other are thwarted. Recognizing the inevitable ambivalence we feel about intimacy is important in sustaining intimacy over time, because we will need to be prepared for the oscillation of closeness and distance that naturally occur in any intimate relationship. We will not be as surprised by ruptures in the relationship, because we will understand that ruptures in intimate relationships are inevitable, and that it is possible to feel lonely with someone you think of as an intimate. People who are good at sustaining long-term intimacy haven't eliminated fighting, or clung to each other allowing no distance between them. Rather, they are people who have learned how to repair ruptures well, and how to reinitiate closeness when distance has gone on too long.

Recognizing our ambivalence about intimacy is equally important for those whose longings for it go repeatedly unrequited. Such people can use their consciousness of their ambivalence to make choices that differ from those they've made previously that have not worked out; they can take risks they might not otherwise take. They can learn to be more present and engaged by centering themselves as subject, rather than throwing themselves away to try to be the right kind of object.

Each of the people I have depicted, Harold, Laura, Raul and Carole, and Lorraine, sought to experience intimacy with a romantic partner. The crisis for each of them that brought them into therapy was that they recognized that the ways they were creating intimacy were not fulfilling. Their intimacy was not growing, and they themselves were not growing. They felt that they were stuck—not growing wiser, happier, more trusting, more free to give and take. They hoped that with an intimate partner they would feel safe, and not lonely. What they came to realize was that they also wanted to feel alive and to feel that they were growing, fulfilling their potentials, moving toward a life that in the end they would feel had been worth living. They, like so many of us, hoped that they could achieve this by securing for themselves an intimate partnership, a home base, from which they could go out to the wider world feeling supported and fulfilled, and to which they could return, to rest, to refuel, to find support and comfort. Each discovered that they had put themselves in positions where those desires could not be realized.

Harold easily found intimacy with strangers, but over time he felt his days were lonely and empty, and that he was not growing. His mother's hatred had become internalized as self-loathing, and his sexual encounters, which had at first dispelled self-loathing, eventually added to his self-loathing to an unbearable extent.

Laura, too, had internalized the disapproval and anger of her parents. Her internalized lack of faith in herself took the form of lacking faith in those from whom she sought love. Constantly on the lookout for betrayal, her anxiety and suspicion put Jimi constantly on the defensive, threatening and destabilizing the relationship. Their intimacy could not deepen and grow while they remained in a constant state of upheaval.

Raul thought he could be safe from his shame and fear and the rejection of his family by denying his homosexual desires. Carole thought she could find a safe haven in Raul's love for her, so she denied all the indications that he might be gay. Their intimacy was real, but it could not support their growth in the context of their marriage.

Lorraine stayed in her unhappy marriage out of fear of the unknown, and was devastated when her husband ended it. Lorraine had been taught that the only way to be safe is to be married. To stay married, you made sure your husband was happy, no matter what you really felt. Divorce gave Lorraine a chance to believe in herself, to free herself from objectification and to understand that intimacy cannot grow between two people when one of them is subjugated.

There are myriad, perfectly valid ways of experiencing intimacy, and the psychoanalyst's job has nothing to do with determining what particular form of intimacy should be preferred, or which forms are "right" and which are "wrong." Rather, the analyst's job, as I see it, is to carefully attend to those repetitive patterns and situations for the patient which have led to frustration, hopelessness and despair. Many of those with whom I have worked, for whom loneliness felt nearly unbearable, were people who had come to know the acute suffering of loneliness throughout a traumatic childhood. For the developing child and adolescent, loneliness becomes traumatic when intimacy is not made safe, or when intimacy is not provided, to the point of deprivation.

The potential of psychoanalytic therapy to help those for whom intimacy has become painful is this: by listening carefully, both for what is said, and what is left out of the patient's narrative, the analyst can eventually help bring into awareness the dissociated conflicts and ambivalence about intimacy that the patient has not recognized. The analyst can help the patient discover and become grounded in her own center of subjectivity, so that the patient may become free of unconscious self-objectification. For this to happen, the analyst too has to grow, to have become able in the course of the therapy to understand and negotiate the safety needs of the patient, while at the same time finding ways to keep things opening up and moving forward.

This kind of psychological growth—which happens not just for the patient, but for the analyst in each therapeutic relationship—signals that the analytic relationship itself has become safe and intimate at the same time, that healing and greater self-knowledge have resulted. At that point, it has become safe enough to be more fully oneself, which means that it is possible for intimacy—with friends, siblings, parents, children and lovers—to be more fully realized, and more deeply fulfilling.

Notes

1 From the song "Leavin' On Your Mind," by Pierce, Webb and Walker.

References

Aron, Lewis. 1991. "The Patient's Experience of the Analyst's Subjectivity." *Psychoanalytic Dialogues* 1: 29–51.
——2006. *A Meeting of Minds: Mutuality in Psychoanalysis*. Hillsdale, NJ: The Analytic Press.
Benjamin, Jessica. 1999. "Afterword." In S. Mitchell and L. Aron (eds) *Relational Psychoanalysis*. Hillsdale, NJ: The Analytic Press, 201–10.
Bromberg, P.M. 1993. "Shadow and Substance: A Relational Perspective on Clinical Process." *Psychoanalytic Psychology* 10: 147–68.
——2011. *The Shadow of the Tsunami: and the Growth of the Relational Mind*. New York: Routledge.

Herman, Judith. 1992. *Trauma and Recovery: The Aftermath of Violence—from Domestic Abuse to Political Terror*. New York: Basic Books.

Jong, Erica. 1974. *Fear of Flying*. New York: Secker and Warburg.

Mitchell, S. 2003. *Can Love Last?: The Fate of Romance Over Time*. New York: W.W. Norton and Co.

Spitz, R.A. 1964. "The Derailment of Dialogue—Stimulus Overload, Action Cycles, and the Completion Gradient." *Journal of the American Psychoanalytic Association* 12: 752–75.

Winnicott, Donald W. 1974. "Fear of Breakdown." *International Review of Psycho-Analysis* 1: 103–7.

Part III

Lateral intimacies

Siblings, surrogates, families

7 Intimacy, disclosure and marital normativity

John Borneman

Shortly after I entered graduate school, in 1985, I ran across a book by the Belgian anthropologist Luc de Heusch entitled *Why Marry Her? Society and Symbolic Structures*. Published four years earlier, it was a significantly revised edition of de Heusch's French book *Pourquoi l'épouser?* (Editions Gallimard, 1971), and sought to bring the French structuralist views of kinship into dialogue with the functionalist views of British social anthropology. I always thought the title unusually direct, even provocative, though its central argument confirmed what everyone already knew: that kinship affiliations—systems of descent and alliance—prestructured marriage choices, a point the Belgian-born French anthropologist Claude Lévi-Strauss had already documented across the ethnographic record, in his magisterial *The Elementary Structures of Kinship* (1948). Although Lévi-Strauss was primarily focused on marriage and alliance, he was well aware of the importance of descent systems, in particular the patrilineal descent systems of Africa, which formed the basis for British functionalist theory.

The question "Why Marry Her?" appeared to me as a provocation because I, at the time, was asking the question: "Why am I not allowed to marry him?" For some time, I had posed this question implicitly to my family, refusing to attend the marriages of my numerous nieces and nephews until, I explained to them, I could also marry my partner of choice. Outside of my immediate family, however, I kept my frustration about marriage exclusion largely to myself. Yet I was bothered that it never occurred to de Heusch, who circulated among the Parisian avant-garde, was friends with the founder of surrealism André Breton and student of the renowned ethnographer of myth Marcel Griaule, to think of marriage outside the intimacy of a man and a woman. De Heusch was not alone here. For most anthropologists at the time, despite the frequency of their own fieldwork evidence to the contrary, the basic questions concerning intimacy were restricted to the relationship of a man and woman in marriage.

Already back then, for me, this definition seemed too narrow; today it seems antiquated. In the 25 intervening years, in both intellectual and Euro-American settings, the norms regarding marriage, social and scientific, have been quite radically revised. Nowadays, intimacy is evoked to refer to many kinds of attachments, to relationships with many kinds of things, human and non-human. My topic here will not be intimacy itself, however, but the changing nature of its disclosure in a period of critical challenges to the marital normativity assumed by de Heusch.

When to reveal what to whom? That question has dogged me since the time of my first sexual fantasies, long before I had any experience. Not only the norms of sexual interest or noninterest, or the norms stipulating when and where to "come out" to family, friends, neighbors, co-workers, have shaped the terms of disclosure. Also, throughout the 1970s, my generation and I experimented with these norms, alternately debating, accommodating, challenging and trespassing them—and, often, simply ignoring them, acting on urges as the situations allowed. My focus here will be more narrowly on the norms of marriage. I cannot really overstate their significance in the formative experiences of intimate disclosure of my generation, what one might characterize as the generation that came of age with the feminist, gay and lesbian movements of the 1970s.

I have always thought that if marriage were democratized, if more individuals were enfranchised to take advantage of its rights, my own experiences of exclusion would become historical survivals. Indeed, it may be that my experience in the last half of the 20th century marks the waning of the power of marriage, at least in what we call the West. Nonetheless, we should be wary of assuming any linear narrative of progress and alert to the perverse reversals of history. Once everyone has access to the institution, we might expect that other institutions capable of making yet-unforeseen discriminations will take its place to create comparable social distinctions of person, class and status. In any case, I have the impression that at present the relevant regulatory norms are quite unstable. This does not mean that anything goes. It means only that the occasions for articulation and symbolization of the norms that orient intimacy, the boundaries between privacy and revelation, and the very meaning of the private and the public, are rapidly changing in unplanned and unpredictable ways.

What I have learned since I read de Heusch is that personal intimacy always unfolds within a particular social politics of intimacy. That politics is shaped by balancing both a desire for transparency and a personal need for privacy. For both the individual and the group, there is a wish to be in some way open to the world and at the same time a wish to keep some things for oneself (or within the group) in order to own one's own life (or to own the group's right to self-define), so to speak. These personal needs for transparency or privacy are often traversed and upset by the other's demands of disclosure. Located between secrecy and disclosure, and self and other, norms of intimacy take shape, are enforced, or transgressed. As an anthropologist who has worked in several field sites, but also as a child and youth in a dynamic period of reshaping notions of intimacy, I have actively engaged these norms as both an art and a politics.

By my mid-twenties, I had come to know marriage as a rite of initiation, a point of access to adulthood, a set of economic privileges and cultural approbations, but available to me only if I agreed, as de Heusch succinctly put it, to "marry her." My one brother and six sisters—all older than me—had married, though one initially eloped before marriage. We don't hear much today about "elopement," but it was a common topic of discussion throughout my childhood and youth. Today it is very rare in the USA for straight people who are fully "Americanized" to run away to "live in sin," as we said in the 1960s, either in order to live with or to marry someone disapproved of by one's own kin, or to avoid the embarrassment and humiliation of an unplanned, unwanted pregnancy.

One of my sisters eloped with her fiancé, but there was no scandal. In any event, she ended up marrying him, and they remain happily married with children. One of my cousins, Mary Ann, initially also eloped. When she reappeared a few months later, my uncle and aunt sold their dairy farm, under the implausible pretext of wanting to do something else, and moved to a faraway state, where Mary Ann, it was said, had a baby and gave it away for adoption. Nobody ever spoke about this directly with her or her parents, although we all knew, even I, the youngest of her cousins and only 10 at the time. About a year later, Mary Ann returned, *sans infant*, and my uncle repurchased part of his old farm—at a huge loss. A few years after that, Mary Ann married the wild young man from whom her parents had tried to protect her. They had several kids and, to my knowledge, also still live together, married.

All of my other siblings had big weddings, with large ceremonial banquets at Chet and Emil's Country Club. My father paid for the ceremonies of my sisters— the male side of the family was responsible for financing the daughters. All of them, except the one who eloped, took a dowry into marriage, though they called it, more modestly, a "hope chest," reflecting what anthropologists used to call "survivals," customs that continue in the present but have largely outlived their original utility.

Why neither my sisters nor my brother married because of an unexpected pregnancy remains a bit of a mystery to me. We were not particularly religious as a family, though all raised Catholic, my mother's religion, except for my brother, who was raised Lutheran, the religion of my father. Catholic priests insisted as a condition of membership in the Church that the children of a Catholic be raised in the faith, and my mother submitted, one of her few actual resistances to my father, who, largely to spite my mother, wanted to bring the children up in his church. Ironically, though, my brother later married a Catholic girl, and ended up converting to Catholicism, while several sisters married Lutheran boys, and converted accordingly. This easy convertibility radically relativized my views on the sacred and the sacraments. So much for the theory of the One and True religion, I thought. At the apogee of prosperity theology, in the 1970s, the sister closest to me in age followed her husband into the evangelical fold, to which they both remain faithful in belief and practice. I benefited, as the youngest, from being able to observe the drama surrounding all these rituals, and early on I proposed for myself not to have children, though I did not renounce marriage. At the age of seven, I announced to my family that I was a proponent of the movement ZPG, Zero Population Growth; they reacted with a shrug and went on reproducing.

I married once, in 1976, when I was 24, to Elisabeth, a Swedish citizen who was taking dressage and jumping lessons from me (at the time I worked with horses). We had become friends and I liked her. She proposed we marry so she could obtain a green card in order to work; I thought it would be fun, in addition to doing a good deed. I also arranged for Elisabeth's boyfriend Birger to marry my farrier Rosie. While planning for the ceremony, I told my mother and sisters, who back then still retained the hope that I would join them among the married. Although the idea that their little brother was to marry made them pause, they recovered by asking, repeatedly, "What do you want us to buy you for the wedding?" I couldn't take the question seriously, but I did not want to explain the actual reasons for the union either, so I said, "A toaster." What? "Just a toaster." Having attended all of their weddings, where they received multiple toasters—the gift of default for those who could not think up a distinctive gift, I thought they'd catch the humor in the event. I think they got the drift: I received no toasters.

Both of us couples had civil ceremonies in front of Justices of the Peace, and we staged a joint tying-the-knot social ceremony, attended by a large group of friends and riding students of mine, performed in a field at the stable where I worked, by a friend, the husband of another of my students, who had by chance been ordained by the Universal Life Church. That wedding—and a victory gallop and jump on horses with my bride—was the talk of my students and friends for a long time. The marriage lasted only a year. Each couple had to pass an immigration interview. Mine with Elisabeth went well. Who, at the time, would question the love of an American man for a beautiful European woman? But the immigration officers suspected Rosie of marrying a foreign man without loving him. They separated Rosie from Birger for the interview, and asked her, "What color is your husband's toothbrush?" When she stumbled, they threatened her with jail time for perjury, for claiming to be marrying for love when she was not. Rosie cracked and Birger then was given two weeks to leave the country. Elisabeth and I divorced, and I haven't seen her since.

This experience, or edited versions of it, has come in handy in my subsequent academic life, in introducing myself during fieldwork in different countries as a social anthropologist who was divorced. Intimate disclosure is part of the deal for fieldwork experience of any depth: if I expect others to tell me about their private lives, they also invariably want to know something about mine. However, what that something is varies by context and place, and each disclosure risks producing its own social drama. As the discourses of "gay sex" and "gay marriage" have become ubiquitous, the demands of disclosure have correspondingly changed, and in some sense become trickier. Some people want to know everything; others want to know nothing. Nonetheless, after a certain age—for me it was around 30—the very first question that strangers have asked me has been "Are you married?" To most, my response has been "I am divorced." Curious people find many ways to follow up. I usually interpret the follow-up questions to want from me a parsing out of the meanings and relations of intimacy to sex and to marriage.

I have experienced these demands of disclosure in an academic life across three continents. In 1986, I entered East Berlin in the former German Democratic Republic on a research visa arranged by the International Research and Exchanges Board (IREX, a program for academic exchange in the former Soviet bloc). My project was to examine the use of law to construct alternative (and initially oppositional) versions of the family in the socialist and capitalist-liberal democratic states. At Humboldt University, which was responsible for my affiliation, social or political anthropology did not exist. The ethnology practiced there was either historical or focused on non-Western cultures (to which most citizens were not allowed to travel), and the other humanities disciplines were invested heavily in Marxist-oriented paradigms, making my work difficult to situate among relevant faculty. Not knowing in which department to place me, they assigned me to the division of family law in the law faculty. Within my first week, the professor who was asked to be my mentor (and probably to keep tabs on me) asked if I was married. "No," I replied.

"Do you have any family?" she followed up.

"Of course," I said, defensively, feeling somewhat insulted. "I have family. Just because I am not married does not mean I have no relations with people I consider family." My response seemed to chastise her, which was likely my intent, and she backtracked and mumbled something apologetically. She herself had a husband and a daughter, and seemed satisfied with and proud of her relations with them. Later that year, at her suggestion, we wrote together an article on the legal issues surrounding surrogate motherhood in the USA, a topic that had just begun to enter public discourse widely, and would soon open up debates about new reproductive technologies, adoption and parenting that had hitherto been marginal if even acknowledged as issues. We submitted the article to *Neue Justiz*, the official legal journal of the East German ruling party, in fact the only East German legal journal. The topic was new and exotic both in the former Soviet bloc and in the USA. The editors at *Neue Justiz* heavily edited our final version, omitting any potentially contentious sentences or interesting asides, making our analysis less ambiguous and less dialectical than we intended in order to construe our positions as in firm opposition to surrogate motherhood and in vitro fertilization.

Within a month of beginning this fieldwork, I realized that my fears of revealing too much had been misplaced, especially with my mentor. I became more forthcoming and less defensive about my own friendships and intimate relations. I got to know my mentor well. I met her husband and daughter and, two years later, after the Wall opened, she came to West Berlin, where I had since moved, and I introduced her to some of my friends there. In West Berlin at that time, people practiced all kinds of household arrangements, some legal, some illegal, some in between. On the ground, there seemed to be no single normative pattern of intimacy or sex, and the institution of marriage seemed to have little to do with many of these patterns. I began to share with this former mentor more intimate details about my desires, housemates and friends, as well as my personal histories with short- and longer-term lovers. After I was appointed assistant professor at Cornell University, in 1991, I even obtained a grant to pay her for some research assistance, and in 1994 I invited her to visit Cornell to present some of her work on legal disputes about property ownership following the integration of the socialist East into the Federal Republic of Germany.

My initial reticence to share knowledge of intimacies stemmed from a fear of what disclosure about sexuality might do to my attempt to build the networks of trust necessary for ethnographic research. During the two decades of my friendship with this former mentor, legal scholars in Europe and the USA began to acknowledge and write more explicitly and frequently about intimate living arrangements that had little to do with marriage and therefore escaped both legal regulation and legal protection. In the early 1990s in much of Europe, what

Germans call *Wohngemeinschaften*—the "living together arrangements" of hetero-sexual partners outside marriage—obtained legal recognition (and support), and those same rights were incrementally extended to same-sex partners. Within slightly more than a decade, relationships outside of marriage lost their contentiousness altogether, as did children born out of wedlock.

In 1994, a professor I had met in 1988, Jutta Limbach, who was one of the strongest advocates I had met for legalizing many of these extra-legal relation-ships, became president of the German Constitutional Court. On November 10, 2000, German politicians voted to legalize same-sex marriage (calling them "Life Partnerships"), requiring the change of hundreds of laws that restricted privileges, benefits, or protections to heterosexual married individuals alone. In Germany today, reticence about disclosure of patterns of intimacy such as I exhibited in the 1980s is not only unnecessary but generally considered *verklemmt*, overly inhibited. That openness does not mean, however, that everyone is interested in intimacy, or that sexuality always comes to the fore as a discursive issue in relationships, or that everyone approves of homosexual intimacy. Intimate disclosure is, rather, in my German experience, considered important only within contexts where the goal is to deepen a relationship, to extend a confidence already at hand, and where it is part of a larger exchange at an appropriate or propitious time.

In 1999, 13 years after my first fieldwork project in Germany, I began research in Beirut, Lebanon, and I visited Syria to begin conceptualizing research that began five years later, in 2004. My experience in Germany did not prepare me for this context. While Beirut today (and before the 15 years of civil wars from 1975 to 1990) may in some sense be, as many say, the Berlin of the Middle East—heterogeneous, cosmopolitan, tolerant, exceptional—it is nonetheless part of an Arab-speaking world and situated within Ottoman and Middle Eastern cultures. Its forms of difference and motivations for differentiation, its laws, as well as patterns of kinship and sexuality, are not readily analogous to those in Germany or the USA. The scene I want to recall occurred in my first fieldwork trip, when I was working on the sources of political divisions in Beirut. A friend introduced me to his mother and aunt. The mother's first question was "Are you married?" Somehow unprepared for the question, or perhaps overly emboldened by my experience in Berlin, I replied, "I am gay." The two women were suddenly silent. They looked down as if taken aback or embarrassed, before changing the topic.

My friend, who seemed pretty open about his own sexual proclivities to his mother, smiled throughout the exchange, and that summer repeated the story of his mother's question and my answer to many friends in different settings. His friends always reacted to this story with ribald laughter. He explained to me that my answer translated as: I have anal intercourse with men, or, more directly, I get fucked by men. Moreover, my response did not answer the question they were asking. The two women were not asking, he said, with whom I had sex, or what kind of sex I had. They were merely asking my kinship affiliation—affinity in its most formal anthropological sense. Their next question would have been about the lineage of my father and his social class.

The mother and aunt were trying to place me in a marital relationship and a descent system (in Lebanon, they call it a "good family") that would be

commensurate with my adult status as professor. Sexual patterns are not pre-
dictive of descent and alliance, and I had only told them about sex. Certain
details of my intimate life that I might have thought relevant to their query were,
from their perspective, unimportant. The same division between kinship disclosure and sexual disinterest was true of their own lives also. For example, it did
not matter that the mother had been a widow already for a decade, during which
she had several what might be considered racy but very discreet affairs. It did not
matter that the aunt had led a life remarkably independent of her American
husband and three children, traveling on her own from the USA to Lebanon,
leaving her husband and children behind for periods up to a year. Those facts
were not something they themselves would have disclosed to me. It did not matter
that my friend had told his mother and aunt that they should stop seeking a bride
for him, that he was uninterested in women in this way.

The details of our relationships, in other words, the specific forms of affinity—
residence and household patterns, sexual relations, friendships—were irrelevant to
their question about my marital status. What they wanted to know about me was
my legally and socially recognized affinal ties, pure and simple, whether through
marriage I and my group, clan, or sect had become linked to another. What was
the network of kin? If, in fact, I was unlinked through marriage, then, for them, I
would qualify as an attractive bachelor—tall, mature, reasonably attractive, with
a prestigious job, steady income. This fact might have opened up another set of
imaginative possibilities for me—and them. They might therefore have had the
pleasure of introducing me to possible unmarried girls from their own large networks. In Lebanon, there is nothing that seems to please women of this status,
class and generation more than to arrange a marriage. My subsequent encounters
over the next six years with these two women have been unfailingly polite and
cordial. They adjusted to what I told them, acting as if they have forgotten my
overly transparent response. Perhaps they repressed it. In any event, they never
again asked about my marital status.

In 2004, I began a year-long stay in Aleppo, Syria, as a senior Fulbright
scholar, splitting my time between research and life in the largest and oldest souk,
and teaching at the university. My project was on the waning authority of fathers,
and relations with their sons. Nearly every person I met posed the very same
question to me: "Are you married?" My standard reply then was "I am divorced
with no children." This is, of course, technically true, though misleading. My
divorce had been over 25 years ago, and I did not even then attach that much
personal significance to it. In the USA and Germany, if I ever refer to my prior
marriage, I usually omit the detail of divorce altogether. However, after my
Lebanese experience, I thought that in Syria disclosing this bit of information
might stop greater demands for intimate disclosure. It did not.

Most of my time in Aleppo was spent with young men and women, who tend
to be curious about a man my age and status who does not have a wife on whom
to call. This curiosity is fed equally by new information, by rumors (some planted
by the state security), and by imagining scenarios based on their own wishes of
what kind of ideal I might be for them, that is, by projection. If young people
wanted to sustain a relationship with me, especially in their imagination, they

often avoided becoming aware of some things; for example, they made believe they did not hear rumors about me, such as that I had AIDS, that I was Jewish, that I was gay, or that I worked for the CIA. As I got to know some people well, they were much more prepared to deal with levels of ambiguity about my personal relationships than was the case at the start of our relationships. Some even tried to protect me from the prying interests of others. Some, after knowing me for a while, alerted me to the rumors about me that they had heard. On the issue of sexuality, some simply did not want to know what my interests were. These negotiations and disclosures were often very upsetting, but I learned a good deal from each encounter.

One Syrian man who worked in the souk in which I resided had received asylum in Australia through his male partner, and lived there with him for seven years before returning, alone, to Syria. His large extended family accepted his orientation without question. It undoubtedly helped that several of his older brothers were also primarily interested in men. He was witty and had a wicked sense of humor, which I found infinitely entertaining, and he worked right around the corner from where I lived, so I spent a great deal of time with him. Soon, he knew everything about my personal situation, and much about my own history of intimacy, and he shared with me many details of his ongoing affairs that he shared with no one else, including and especially not with members of his family. When people asked me what he considered too many questions, he would frequently intervene and yell, loudly, "T-M-I." Too Much Information! He said he had learned that from some tourists.

Another response of mine to young men who asked about marriage was to say, "If I were married, I wouldn't be here. My wife would demand I stay home. And then we would never have met." To this I received a nod of agreement, for company with me, the ability to meet an American professor who was interested in them and their situations, and who was not in a position of authority over them, was an obvious pleasure they did not want to be denied. It gave them an opportunity to argue openly with an American, as well as to befriend one.

Young people would often follow up my response about being "divorced with no children" with "And why don't you marry again?" I'd say, "Once is enough." When I was addressing Sunni boys (Sunni groups comprise over 80% of the population), I'd say, "but you should marry several times." Sunnis can legally marry three times, though I met only one man who did so. To be in a marital state itself, however, if one can afford it, is considered highly desirable and natural. To have a son or several sons is also highly desirable. My unmarried state and my lack of sons was, therefore, most confusing to people, especially to young men and women who were just becoming aware of intimate possibilities and the intricacies of accruing status.

Syrians do divorce, sometimes, but nearly all men who divorce try to find another wife. Divorced women, by contrast, often remain in that state, which is generally viewed by children and youth as a state deserving pity. In short, my decision not to remarry struck most young people as absurd, if not deserving of pity. However, how could they pity me, when I was free to travel, had an excellent job and seemed not to lament a life without a wife or sons? Often adults would smile and intervene in my conversations with children or youth to try to explain that I, coming from the West, had a different perspective. They raised their children to think of the legal institution of marriage, which is regulated by the various religious confessions and not by the state, as about creating the conditions for a particular form of sociality. However, they also encouraged tolerance for the other confessions and other norms. (As I write this, and observe Syria in the throes of a civil war, this tolerance has of course disconcertingly and sadly largely disappeared.)

There is an additional reason why some youths found it difficult to accept my unmarried status. Young women could not openly ask about this status, as that might appear to imply an obvious interest in me, but young men did not share this constraint, and for many, my decision not to remarry, if shared by other financially secure men, would mean that their sisters would be unable to leave the home of their parents. Most young men talked fondly of their sisters; they felt an obligation to help secure their futures. These men, in other words, in asking me about why I did not remarry, were not primarily asking me about sex either. Marriage does not provide automatic access to sex anyway, as Muslim women are frequently assertive about their sexual needs and wishes, and I could have found hetero sex in Aleppo without marrying—either with prostitutes or in secretive relations with girls or women, or with visiting European women. Along these lines, what young men also wanted to know was how I explained to myself the shirking of obligatory relations, that is, the obligation "to marry her," as de Heusch wrote, in order to further or cement an alliance between groups. The pressure to think about marriage as a set of kin obligations and not as a matter of personal interest is especially strong among Aleppian Sunni groups, whose preferred marriage remains cross-cousin, meaning that obligations to marry exist between intimate kin.

As a Fulbright professor in Aleppo, I had prepared to give some lectures on the politics of gay marriage in the USA, knowing full well that Syrians would most likely find this idea extremely challenging if not morally wrong. In private, I met individuals who embraced the idea. Many were curious about what kind of living arrangements I had in the States, and they were delightfully amused to find that I live openly with a male partner. At the university, however, the atmosphere is anything but private—all interactions are watched by somebody, or everybody. The ensuing discussion after such a lecture, I had hoped, would reveal to me the limits of their curiosity and of the limits of the cultural relativism that I experienced readily in everyday relations. For various reasons having to do with fears that I was a spy, the university was reticent about and therefore delayed scheduling my seminar—on any topic I proposed. Eventually, I cancelled the seminar plans, and instead through a relationship with the university president went over the head of the faculty and the ruling Ba'ath Party and presented a series of lectures on American anthropology.

I did find a way in one lecture to use as an example the issue of gay marriage in the USA to explore how anthropology, as a secular discipline that researches cultural differences without initially judging them, relates to the study of religion. I explained the various current positions on marriage, religious and anthropological, the critique from the right and the left. People listened attentively. Discussions after lectures usually took place in small groups of friends. A few days later, several students from one group confided in me that they were confused by the issue, which they had never thought about. Most students, however, said nothing about my specific example, although all with whom I had contact later thanked me profusely for my efforts. In the end, it was an act of disclosure with unpredictable effects, a risk or bet that an idea disclosed now might have ripple effects in the future.

Anthropologists have traditionally made an important distinction between the wedding—as a ceremony or rite—and the institution of marriage. Ideally, the wedding rite precedes its institutional life in marriage. A social ceremony is usually necessary to authorize the institutional life of marriage. It activates another set of norms regarding relations of affinity between kin and nonkin. The ceremony, in turn, authorizes the community to regulate sexual intimacy. This order of events—wedding, marriage, sex—was always more ideal than reality, but that is not to underestimate the value of an ideal. The ordering and future orientation of ideals is crucial for any meaningful life. Without ideals we either live out of a sense of instinct, sometimes confusing instinct with naturalized norm, or we live by submitting our practices to instrumental reason, to the calculation of interests or maximization of profit or advantage. In many parts of the world, this ideal sequencing of ceremony and institution is giving way to improvisation, to new opportunities, and therefore also to more narrowly explicit calculation of interests. In addition, new approaches to intimacy also mean the loss of custom and tradition, at least as normatively defined by the groups involved, and thus the loss of one kind of glue that tends to hold generations together in a community.

Because the societies with which I have engaged have made it difficult for someone attracted to the same sex to access intimacy, sex and the institution of marriage, I have been forced into a kind of random resequencing of the relation between these elements. That forced resequencing has also created a certain estrangement from generational and communitarian narratives, and from the social norms that most people internalize. When I arrived at Princeton in 2001, the university had already made considerable progress in recognizing same-sex relationships. It immediately recognized my "domestic partnership" of four years, independent of any ceremony or institutional support, and it allowed my partner to be included in my healthcare plan. A few joint bills and a joint Visa card account sufficed as proof. This recognition did not, however, initially extend outside the university. Nonetheless, it was quite different from my experience at Harvard in 1990, when a lover from Prague joined me after I returned from several years of fieldwork in Berlin. With no possibility to recognize our relationship legally, his only option at the time was to apply for asylum. Two months after his arrival, he suddenly fell seriously ill, and the ends to which I had to resort to obtain medical care for him because he lacked health insurance or any legal right to be related to me in any way was one of the most distressing experiences of my life. The lack of legal and institutional support proved an impossible strain on the relationship, and was one reason why he returned to Prague the following year to what was soon to become the Czech Republic (after the separation from Slovakia).

In December 2007, the New Jersey Legislature passed a "civil union" law that could confer a legal recognition of same-sex intimacy should I partake in a legal ceremony. I did not jump at this opportunity. My need for social and legal recognition had waned over the years. If I still felt discriminated against or socially excluded or the object of abjection, or if I felt insecure about the social status of my relationship, or if I anticipated death or separation, I might see this differently. However, in the intervening years, I have obtained what I consider sufficient social recognition of my relationship with a man, in my different milieux. The reasons for legal recognition have been largely extraneous to both my personal emotional needs and my formal institutional ones. A legal recognition of my relationship with a German citizen would have largely eliminated my partner's visa problems in the USA, but such recognition would not have substantively changed the dynamic of our relationship. To be sure, for immigration purposes, it helps that he is well educated and has a passport from a European rather than African country, not to speak of what problems might appear were he a stateless Palestinian.

That need for legal recognition comparable to "marriage" arose this year, however, in a new context. My partner was awarded a fellowship for a year at the Institute for Advanced Studies in Nantes, France, and the Institute offered to fly over his family and include his spouse in events. I could be included in that category, they told him, if he offered some proof comparable to their "Le Pacte civil de solidarité" (a legalized civil union agreement between people of the same sex), which guarantees for same-sex couples some of the same rights and privileges as marriage does for heterosexual couples. To provide this proof, however, a copy of my own registration of our domestic partnership declaration at Princeton would not suffice. Six years ago, that registration would have been all we could have obtained in the States, but, since 2007, the state of New Jersey offers a more general legal form analogous to France's *Pacte*. Today, we can get "married."

Faced with that choice, we went ahead with an application for a "domestic partnership" declaration in a "civil ceremony" in New Jersey. To enter into this marriage analogue, questions of intimacy, sex, children, even household, were irrelevant. The ceremony required proof only that we were both non-married and shared a residence. I first had to obtain a copy of my divorce, thus rediscovering the family name of my former wife, which I had since forgotten. Then we had to find a witness for our application. We asked a colleague and friend, who is a Moroccan citizen, to serve (basically he had to testify that we are not lying on our forms, that the marriage is a love marriage). The forms were apparently unchanged since 2007, so they still asked for a bride and a groom. After the staff at the courthouse asked me twice who was the bride, I graciously agreed to list myself. We made an appointment with the local judge for a legal ceremony a week later. The wedding required two further witnesses. We asked another colleague and her husband—she is French, he is American—to join us at the courthouse and affirm that they had seen the wedding ceremony before the judge. My colleague brought along her new iPad touch and interviewed us and took pictures. It was early morning. We went for coffee at Small World afterwards.

The judge at the wedding was very pleasant and chatty. She talked about her recent trip to Nantes and a family history of hiding there during the Nazi period, and she raved about how much we would enjoy being there. In the ceremony, we stumbled when she asked if we had rings—we did not, and had not even thought about it. We stumbled when she asked if we wanted to add something to the vows she would utter—we shook our heads no, confusedly. Her vows were simple, asking us to remain loyal to each other throughout our lives. "Until death do us part" had been omitted. We both said yes, and kissed before the judge and the camera.

My partner is a specialist in ritual, and has much more patience with ceremonies of all sorts than I do. I suspect he would have easily agreed to more ritual, to receptions and dinners and gifts. However, he did not tell his mother, sister, or father before the wedding, and I did not tell my siblings either. Ultimately, for me, the ceremony is a private affair. My ambivalence is not about entering into a relationship with this man (why do I want to marry him?). No, I am ambivalent about the need for social recognition (why marry her?), in which I would have gladly basked earlier in my life. I fear that the ritual and the recognition that follows from it will do precisely what ritual is supposed to do: transform our relationship and our lives. In other words, if ritual were to change us so we could reintegrate into society as a married couple, we risk a change in our status quo, but that's not why we committed to a civil union. We are already adults, we already share a commitment and a life. Although our witnesses felt honored, and immediately told others, and although I received emails and calls congratulating us, we did not perform the ceremony for anybody but ourselves.

Once in Europe, we applied to German authorities to recognize our American civil union. That recognition, called "*Nachbeurkundung*" (certification of original documents), proved rather simple, though somewhat expensive. It took less than a month to complete, and the person in charge in Berlin told us we were the very first to apply. (Most binational same-sex couples get married once in Berlin, not before they arrive.) All the authorities wanted to know was whether the legal ceremony in the USA granted rights that were radically different than such a union in Germany offered. Since US law regarding same-sex unions differs by state and is unstable, and in any case offers few concrete rights and few privileges, the local administrators ultimately seemed to be satisfied with the fact that they did not have to grant us more rights than they would have to grant a German same-sex couple. Our friendly reception may also have had something to do with Berlin having an openly gay mayor. With this recognition in hand, we applied for a residential visa for myself as a family member. In the past, I had always obtained visas through research institutions. I was hoping to get a long-term if not permanent visa, and eventually I did. They granted me a three-year visa, on the condition I not remain outside Germany more than six months at a time. In thinking about these experiences, it dawned on me that I was being recognized in a new way as a result of a "marriage bonus," a deferral of suspicion and a kind of blessing that groups grant to others they are willing to consider co-members. As a "foreigner," even one invited by German authorities and awarded prestigious fellowships, I had never before experienced such openness on the part of governmental authorities.

I still insist on saying that I and my partner are not married but only "civil unionized," and somehow I like the fact that it is not a real marriage but merely a marriage analogue. This is not to take away the joy from anyone else, gay, straight, or tran, who wants the whole ball of wax, ceremony, social approval, exact same legal rights as heterosexual couples. For me, though, it's all a bit bittersweet, coming so late after what seems such a long, angry struggle. What I have achieved—and a relationship of love of any duration is under any circumstances a struggle and an achievement—was not accomplished with the help of society but through a history of public and private confrontations to obtain access to some of the very social norms of inclusiveness and privilege that I had criticized. Nonetheless, our marriage analogue does suggest that these societies, at least the one into which I was born, along with German society, have changed, become more inclusive, of me, at least, but I am reluctant to let those societies take credit for finally granting recognition to a relationship of care and love about which it has until now been intolerant.

References

Borneman, John. 1996. "Until Death Do Us Part: Marriage/Death in Anthropological Discourse," featured article: issues in debate, *American Ethnologist* 23 (2): 215–38.
——2001. "Caring and to be Cared for: Displacing Marriage, Kinship, Gender, and Sexuality." In James Faubion (ed.) *The Ethics of Kinship.* Lanham, MD: Rowman and Littlefield.
——2007. *Syrian Episodes: Sons, Fathers, and an Anthropologist in Aleppo.* Princeton: Princeton University Press.
de Heusch, Luc. 1971. *Pourquoi l'épouser?* Paris: Editions Gallimard.
——1985. *Why Marry Her? Society and Symbolic Structures.* Cambridge: Cambridge University Press.

8 Lost and found

Sibling loss, disconnection, mourning and intimacy

William F. Cornell

The opening lines of Justin Torres's novel *We the Animals* stunned me as he captured the passionate and tumultuous relationships of three brothers:

> We wanted more. We knocked the butt ends of our forks against the table, tapped our spoons against our empty bowls; we were hungry. We wanted more volume, more riots. We turned up the knob on the TV until our ears ached with the shouts of angry men. We wanted more music on the radio; we wanted beats; we wanted rock. We wanted muscles on our skinny arms. We had bird bones, hollow and light, we wanted more density, more weight. We were six snatching hands, six stomping feet; we were brothers, boys, three little kings locked in feud for more.
>
> (Torres 2011: 1)

Clearly semi-autobiographical, if not fully so, Torres creates a vivid portrait of three brothers forging a world unto themselves—touched upon by their parents, but largely free of them—until a secret of the narrating brother rends the family apart. The story ends in tragedy, but in the telling is an extraordinary tale of sibling intimacy, with all of its passions, tenderness, competition and violence:

> We wanted more flesh, more blood, more warmth.
> When we fought, we fought with boots and garage tools, snapping pliers—we grabbed at whatever was nearest and we hurled it through the air; we wanted more broken dishes, more shattered glass. We wanted more crashes.
>
> (Torres 2011: 1–2)

The book filled me with delight, excitement, warmth, grief and—most of all—envy.

In a rather strange coincidence, the novel is set in the same area of upstate New York where I grew up, the brothers' mother working in a brewery. In my multiple levels of identification with this novel, I imagined the brewery to be the Utica Club Brewery that was originally built by my maternal great-grandfather's best friend behind his saloon. My great-grandfather dropped dead at the bar of a cerebral hemorrhage, leaving a young German immigrant wife, who spoke no English, with 13 children—my grandmother being the youngest. The brewery's founder went on to make a fortune, offering no help to the family of the man who died at the bar. The Utica Club Brewery was a few blocks from my maternal grandparents' home where I lived my first four years. The rich odors of the brewery filled the neighborhood, as did my grandmother's life-long hatred for F.X. Matt, the owner of Utica Club.

In our professional papers and conference presentations, we tend to tell the stories of our clients' lives, and more recently of our lives with our clients. This essay has at its heart the story of the fracturing of my sibling relationships and the struggle to establish an intimacy with my sister and brother late in our lives. There is an inevitable intimacy offered to unknown readers in choosing to write in this way. This essay is also an act of love and reparation toward my siblings after a lifetime of alienation.

The family therapist Salvatore Minuchin characterizes the sibling "subsystem" within a family as "the first laboratory in which children can experiment with peer relationships. Within this context, children support, isolate, scapegoat, and learn from one another. In the sibling world children learn how to negotiate, cooperate, and compete" (Minuchin 1974: 59).

Juliet Mitchell (2003), the first psychoanalytic author systematically to bring sibling relationships to the center of analytic theory, argues that "the presence and memory of the richness of lateral relationships are an underestimated part of the fabric of psychic and social life" (Mitchell 2003: 171).

Unfortunately, neither Minuchin's nor Mitchell's descriptions, nor Torres's passionate prose was remotely like my own sibling relationships.

It was about 15 years ago, as I was imagining my psychoanalysis to be coming to a close, that my analyst said to me—with no conscious prompting on my part—"Do you ever wonder how it is that while you never mention your brother or your sister, as though they have never existed, that I find them often on my mind?"

"No," was my singular reply.

"Perhaps we could wonder about it together?"

"I'm not interested. My brother and sister have never been a part of my life. Why the fuck are you bringing it up now?"

"I don't know really, it's just that I find them on my mind. And you don't seem to have them in yours. Might you wonder why my question has evoked such anger in you?"

All that I could feel was my anger in response to what I experienced as a stupid, rather ill-timed intrusion. No answer was to come right away. I didn't even want to think about it, but now I was stuck—my brother and sister, or their absences, were now firmly on my mind. Gradually, what I came to realize was that I had come through my analysis to a point of reaching a compassionate understanding and acceptance of my parents and their limitations (which were substantial). When I began to think about my brother and sister, Gary and Debbie, my acceptance of my parents fell into ruins. I found myself hating my parents again, and I didn't want to do that. I would rather sacrifice the psychic existence of my living siblings than lose the connection I had at last forged to my deceased parents.

In my eyes, I had been the fortunate first born. I was the one who had the love, care and stability of my maternal grandparents for my first four years, during which my father had had a post-war depressive breakdown and my mother suffered two miscarriages. When I was four, my grandfather—a young, vigorous and much-beloved man—was diagnosed with terminal lung cancer, and my grandmother and mother slipped into chronic depressions from which neither ever fully recovered.

Years later, I was the one who—off to college—had escaped the final collapse of the family. I was the one who had been able to create a good life. What my parents had to offer, they gave to me. Though only four years older than my brother and six years older than my sister, I grew up essentially as an only child. I recall no particular interest in my siblings; I cannot recall even playing with them. Neither of my parents completed high school. My father worked in a factory, did night school gradually to earn high school and ultimately college credits, and repaired televisions in the basement for extra income. We rarely saw him. My mother worked at home as a seamstress and laundress. Their lives were not easy.

Growing up in rural upstate New York, the center of my life was school, the outdoors and my dogs. My intelligence was idealized by my teachers and parents, and I felt alive in their praise. I lived my childhood years as though I had no siblings. I also had no close friends, and I now have no question but that these two things were intimately linked. All of my close relationships were in the vertical with my teachers. Lateral relationships, such as described by Minuchin, were a mystery to me and remained so until after many years of psychotherapy and psychoanalysis.

In my preparations for this essay, I had hoped, wished to recall moments of intimacy with my brother and sister growing up. I could not find them. Even on the annual family trip to a camp in the Adirondack Mountains, I cannot recall actually playing with my siblings. I cannot recall taking my little brother along with me into the woods and creeks, but then neither did my father. I don't think this had anything to do with my brother and sister, per se; the usual theories of sibling rivalry, hatred and jealousy don't seem to apply. Was I in some way killing off my brother and sister in reaction to the traumatic intrusion of their beings into my life? While this would fit familiar psychoanalytic theories, it does not speak to my experience. Though I could never have known it at the time, it is as if I were fleeing the overwhelming sadness and anguish that permeated the lives of my parents. I was never in the house any longer than I needed to be, and perhaps— rather strangely—my parents never seemed to be troubled by this. I was, perhaps, the only "trouble-free" part of their lives; I was the teacher's pet from kindergarten on and ridiculously independent from a very early age. When I was 11, we moved into a slightly larger house in town, and my father built me a bedroom in the basement with its own entrance. He told me I was old enough to come and go as I pleased. I did. There was no place for my siblings in the world of my childhood and adolescence.

Torres describes the impassioned cabal he and his brothers formed to hold at bay the psychological and economic disturbances of their parents. My brother, sister and I grew up as virtual strangers to one another.

What I had begun to develop, I can now see in hindsight of my psychoanalysis, was a manic defense against loss. I never stopped moving and doing things. I also developed a deep, unspoken (what else?) contempt for my parents' lack of involvement and caretaking in their children's lives. My choice of profession was no accident—I was to be the good parent and the one who would never ignore the distress of another (except my siblings). It took years of psychotherapy and supervision to see both the unconscious, developmental roots of my position (held firmly in the vertical) and the limits of the "good parent" role as a psychotherapist. For all intents and purposes, I bluffed my way through my first two rounds of personal psychotherapy, snowing my therapists with my intelligence and positioning myself as an idealized patient. It was in my first psychoanalysis that the idealizations collapsed (Cornell 2009).

In our psychodynamic theories, we speak of attachment patterns, internalized object relations, script injunctions and decisions, and so forth, all of which emphasize the enduring impact of our relationships with mother and father. However, our childhood family relations are in fact a more complex mix than the vertical forces of parental relations. This essay seeks an exploration of the centrality of the lateral forces of sibling and peer relations and the consequences of their absence. I will argue that sibling relations form essential, unconscious patterns and beliefs underlying our adult intimacies: our capacity for suffering together and sustaining love, vulnerability, aggression, competition, ambivalence and complexity.

I have come to sibling relations as fundamentally formative in relation to collegial, peer and community relations that are organized on more lateral than vertical/dependent grounds. I have had to face that the lack of truly intimate relations with peers through much of my adult life as an enactment of my lack of relatedness or intimacy with my brother and sister when we were kids. I have come to appreciate deeply the prevalence of the lateral dimensions of transference and countertransference relations in my work as a psychotherapist, greatly enriching traditional assumptions of the parental/vertical dynamics in the transference. I have come to face how the intimacies of the life of a psychotherapist (almost always immersed in vertical relationships) compensated for my lack of lateral intimacies with friends and colleagues.

In some family systems, our peer relations seem to provide an escape from or a balancing alternative to parental dynamics. In other families, it seems the sibling relations are the field within which the unconscious forces and disturbances of our parental psyches are enacted. The latter was the case in my family.

Phenomenologists (Heidegger 1962; Needleman 1963; Spinelli 2005) speak of the infant, often even before birth, being *thrown* into roles and functions to fulfill the unconscious needs and fantasies of the parents. "*Thrownness*" is constituted by the unchosen facticity of one's life circumstances:

> The Dasein [*being-in-the-world*] finds itself determined, limited, placed in time and space; it finds in itself what on reflection would appear to be elements of the non-Dasein; in a word, it encounters itself as facticity, as that which already has been determined and fixed without, so to speak, its own consent.

This sense of passivity, of having-been-determined is what is primarily expressed by the term *Geworfen-heit*, being-thrown.

(Needleman 1963: 98–99)

We are each "thrown" into a particular body, a particular place in time and culture, particular family circumstances, particular historical events, etc. that lay the foundation of our unconscious experience and organization. In these matters, at the start (and often for many years in one's unconscious), one has no choice.

As the first born—born immediately after the war—I was *thrown* into all the hopes of my parents, formed in the crucible of those hopes and of unspoken anguish and anxiety. I was also *thrown* into a lifetime of manic over-functioning to compensate for their losses and insecurities. My brother, however, was born following my father's post-war depressive breakdown, my mother's two miscarriages and our grandfather's diagnosis with terminal cancer; he was born into a world of anxiety and fragility. My sister was born a girl—not good news—to be imbued with all of my mother's sense of worthlessness as the sister of a star older brother. My siblings were *thrown* into very different worlds than mine. We were never able to bridge those worlds as children, and we received no help from our parents to do so.

In my memory (and perhaps imagination), everywhere my brother or sister might go, I had already been there. I was the star of my extended family, of the schools, of the small village in which we grew up. "Oh, you're Billy's brother (sister), well then, we certainly have high hopes for you." They were quite simply fucked. How were they to find places, recognitions of their own?

As life ground our parents down, they had little or nothing to offer to Gary and Debbie. My brother and sister suffered for this. The final blow to the life of my family was my mother's diagnosis with terminal leukemia. Although I was away at college, I was deeply involved in my mother's illness through frequent letters and phone calls from my bereft parents. I knew that she would likely die. Though Gary and Debbie were living at home and knew that Mom was sick, my parents never told them *how* sick. Then she died suddenly as the result of a medical error. Her death was a total shock to them. My father collapsed in the face of it all and left his younger children, then 12 and 14, to fend for themselves. I had no idea of this at the time, as no one told me. It would never have occurred to Gary and Debbie to call me for help; it did not occur to me to offer. I, again, escaped in a manic fleeing of the unbearable anguish on my family. I returned to college to complete my studies and prepare for graduate school. I turned to no one. I sustained myself through injecting amphetamines and heroin.

After graduate school, I started a family of my own, but I gave my brother and sister nothing of my life. I left them in the dirt. My children have never met my brother. As adults, Gary's and Deb's lives were broken and isolated. Debbie, still a teenager, married the first man who showed any interest in her and had four children as quickly as she could, imagining that she would die young like our mom and hoping she could live long enough to get them to adulthood. My sister lived in a violently abusive marriage, but was desperate to keep her family together until her kids were grown, believing that she was not worth anything more than the abuse and control her husband heaped upon her. Deb had come, at my invitation, to visit my family in Pittsburgh on a couple of occasions. It was time that we both enjoyed, but our conversations never became personal, and my invitations were never returned. I never met her children.

In the mid-1990s, I received a rare phone call from Deb. She asked directly for my help. She had been beaten by her husband to the point of hospitalization. The hospital moved her directly into a battered women's shelter, where she met for the first time with a psychotherapist. Deb did not see herself as abused; she told the therapist that she deserved her husband's fury. She did not tell the therapist that she made herself the determined target of her husband's rage so as to draw it away from their children. The therapist asked Deb if she would read a couple of articles on trauma and abuse that might help her think about her situation a little differently. Deb took the articles in hand, looked up and said, "My brother Billy wrote one of these articles." I had known nothing about Deb's abuse. The therapist suggested she call me.

I helped Deb leave her husband. He repeatedly threatened suicide, begging to return—a scene so typical of households dominated by domestic violence. Deb could not tolerate the thought that her children would lose their father to suicide. I doubt she felt she deserved anything better, and she brought him back. She did not tell me of her husband's repeated threats of suicide, she simply returned. I was forbidden to talk with her unless her husband was on the extension phone. Once again, I withdrew from her anguish.

My brother lived alone in the Utah mountains—in my eyes an angry, apparently anti-social isolate. I could not face the guilt and shame I felt in relation to my brother or sister.

This was what I could not face with my psychoanalyst. It was a classic example of what the Bowen (1978) family systems model calls an emotional cutoff, as a fundamental defense against my anxiety and guilt.

I was fortunate that my analyst did not buy into my guilt, so with his support and persistence I was gradually able to realize that my guilt was largely a defense against the pain and losses in my family history that I could not tolerate. I also had to look at aspects of myself that I had disavowed and assigned to my siblings. My own submissiveness and masochism was neatly ascribed to my sister—I could feel "sorry" for her and subtly judgmental while disowning those characteristics within myself. Even trickier was to acknowledge the paranoid streak in me, which I had convincingly projected onto my brother. I was gradually able to re-own these disavowed qualities within myself, so I was more able to accept my siblings as a part of my life and psyche. I was also able to accept that my life had in fact moved in a dramatically different direction from that of my siblings. I did have the emotional foundation of my early years with my grandparents, which provided a life-long resilience that my siblings lacked. By the end of my analysis, I began to feel concern and interest in them, but I was still unable to reconcile with them or initiate actual, present-day relations with them. That was to come a few years later. I'll return to this story after we have explored some ideas about sibling relations.

In a compelling coincidence, at the same time, I was invited to write a chapter for this book, I was also invited to give the keynote address for a conference in

Sydney, Australia, the theme of which was "Allies & Enemies: The role of real and metaphoric siblings in our psychological worlds." I felt ill equipped to address the topic in any thoughtful way, but, having decided to attempt the writing of this chapter, I turned—as is my habit—to the literature. This proved to be a considerable challenge in that I soon discovered there was very little about sibling influences in psychological and relational development in the psychoanalytic literature. "A cruel joke this is," I thought to myself, "alone again—where are all the brothers and sisters who have gone before and addressed this topic with wit and wisdom?"

I also turned to thinking about my clinical work. I have long been known as a therapist who works directly and comfortably with his clients' sexualities. I often hear from supervisees, "My clients never talk about sex. How come yours do?" "Perhaps that's because I ask." It may not be such a surprise that my clients rarely talked about their siblings! I have discovered that, much like with sex, there was great interest in talking about siblings, too. All I've needed to do is ask.

There is the question of what constitutes a "sibling." In his study of *Sibling Relationships across the Life Span* (1995), Victor Cicirelli defines full, half, adoptive and "fictive" siblings; others (Colonna and Newman 1983: 303) added the term "social siblings" to denote those who are taken into a family system in sibling roles while biologically unrelated. I would suggest that even for only children there are likely to be cousins, neighbors, friends and others who are inducted into quasi-sibling functions. While the place of siblings is almost universally absent in the psychoanalytic and clinical literature, the child development literature (Dunn and Kendrick 1982; Dunn 1993; Sanders 2004) is replete with research into the importance of sibling and peer relationships—the lateral—as fundamental in our psychological and interpersonal development, with the potential to be among our most enduring protocols for adult intimacy.

Turning to the psychoanalytic literature, I could find but six references to siblings in Freud's 23 volumes of writings, even though he had five sisters and two brothers, one of whom died as a young boy. Further surveys of other central analytic figures, including Winnicott, Klein, Bowlby, Berne and the relational psychoanalytic literature unearthed a dearth of discussions about the psychological and relational influences of sibling relations.

It took Juliet Mitchell's work to bring a serious theoretical focus on sibling relations and their unconscious meanings in our transferential relationships and adult intimacies. She argues that vertical, i.e. parental, relationships are over-theorized in psychoanalysis, at the expense of lateral, i.e. sibling, relationships. Mitchell forcefully challenges the absence of sibling influences in psychoanalytic theories of psychological and relational development, arguing that:

> In all cases, accounts of neurosis are dependent on the vertical framework. The context in which the theory is formed is the private consulting room which echoes the private [I would add, nuclear] family. However, lateral relations exceed this private space—occurring in the wider social world of [sibling,] street, school, and workplace and bring these spaces and their rich occupancy into the family.
>
> (Mitchell 2003: 18)

One often gets the impression from the analytic literature that the mother/infant relationship and the Oedipal crisis are the primary—and perhaps only—crucibles of psychic development. Mitchell demands attention to the lateral dimensions of siblings and peers, the social worlds outside of the nuclear family, arguing that the baby is born into a world of peers as well as parents.

At the heart of Mitchell's (2003, 2006) psychoanalytic theories of sibling dynamics is her concept of sibling trauma:

> But the [newborn] adored sibling, who is loved with all the urgency of the child's narcissism, is also loathed as its replacement—[for] the baby it can never again be … The sibling is *par excellence* someone who threatens the subject's uniqueness. The ecstasy of loving someone who is like oneself is experienced at the same time as the trauma of being annihilated by one who stands in one's place … These qualities, which can be seen in any distressed toddler, seem to me to arise as a response to the trauma of sibling replacement.
>
> (Mitchell 2003: 10)

While I found Mitchell's work to be deeply thought-provoking and intellectually rewarding, I found her ideas to suffer from overgeneralizations and great leaps to conclusions that I have not found in my clinical experience or in the child development literature. While Mitchell celebrates the metaphorical siblings of "the friends and mates at nursery school and on the street with whom I fought and played, screamed and laughed" (Mitchell 2003: 171), there seems not a trace of suggestion that intimacy among actual, biological siblings is a possibility.

I don't believe that every sibling birth has to create a psychic trauma for the older siblings as Juliet Mitchell seems to suggest. The presence of siblings in our lives can enrich as well as diminish our sense of self and provide rich opportunities to deepen our capacities for intimacy. Sibling relations have the potential to create a dialectical tension between loss and love, differentness and similarity that deepens and enriches our adult intimacies.

Prophecy Coles, while acknowledging the importance of Mitchell's work, takes a different perspective, stressing, "I believe siblings can genuinely love each other, and the games they create among themselves may be some of the most precious moments of a remembered childhood" (Coles 2003: 26). She goes on to argue "that to see the parent-child relation as the sole seat of health and pathology is to omit the importance of the sibling/peer relationship, especially when the parent/child relationship is absent or negative" (Coles 2003: 75). This view is much more consistent with the findings of child development research, which delineate sibling factors that are far richer and more complex than single-factor theories, such as sibling rivalry, birth order, reaction formation, or sibling trauma that have predominated the analytic literature (Dunn 1985, 1993; Dunn and Plomin 1990; Hetherington *et al.* 1994; Cicirelli 1995; Akhtar and Kramer 1999; Sanders 2004).

Servaas van Beekum (2009) published the first article in the *Transactional Analysis Journal* in its nearly 40-year history addressing "the lateral," i.e. sibling relationships. Van Beekum (2008) had a year earlier written an article for an organizational management journal that described the ways in which the remnants of sibling relationships are often played out unconsciously within collegial and work relations. That article grabbed my attention, but his 2009 article, "Siblings, Aggression, and Sexuality: Adding the Lateral," had a tremendous emotional impact on me as I was struggling—often poorly—in coming to an understanding of my own sibling relationships and affections.

As van Beekum is one of nine siblings, I think he knows what he's talking about, and so I quote at some length:

> Each new sibling enters a minefield in which she or he has to survive and find his or her own identity ... The sibling is another object in the child's life. These types of early sibling experiences form templates for relationships— carried from infancy through childhood and adolescence into adulthood— that potentially can turn out to be painful, blissful, eroticized, nurturing, disappointing, and/or shocking.
>
> (van Beekum 2009: 131)

Among his varied sibling relationships there was no consistency; each of his sibling relationships carried their own emotional reality. In van Beekum's article, he speaks to the complex dialectic in sibling relationships between the need to find and sustain an individuated identity, on the one hand, and sustain intimacy and inter-reliability, on the other.

Research on sibling relations has emphasized the necessity of sibling "de-identification" (Cicirelli 1995), or sibling "differentiation" (Vivona 2007), as essential for identity development within the lateral, sibling dimensions. Vivona's article, for example, brought theoretical light to my own struggles and those of many of my clients. She writes:

> The lateral dimension, perpetuated in relationships with siblings, peers, partners, and many others throughout life, is structured around a particular challenge: *to find one's own unique place in a world of similar others.* [It is no coincidence that van Beekum also quotes this passage in his article.] ... That resolution, I suggest, may be accomplished through a process of differentiation, an active and *unconscious* process of identity development by which a child amplifies differences with siblings and minimizes similarities.
>
> (Vivona 2007: 1192, emphasis added)

My siblings and I certainly had the "amplification of differences" down pat, but at great emotional expense to ourselves and those around us. However, I think that, in the amplification of our differences and the distancing that resulted, we unconsciously created rigid, defensive beliefs based on emotional cutoffs, rather than resilient identities. For Gary, Debbie and me to find and face our similarities and our needs for one another meant facing the pains that our original family had been unable to contain. Our sibling struggles mirrored the defense of emotional cutoffs emphasized in the Bowen family systems literature (Landaiche 2009;

Kerr 2008; Bowen 1978) as a primary means of managing anxieties, pains and rejections that outstrip a family's capacity to receive and contain this distress.

Van Beekum suggests that there is an essential parental responsibility in this regard:

> Parents are mainly important in the way they are able to contain this [sibling] process, one in which they do not take part. The parental role of containment includes relational and emotional presence through discussion and dialogue, boundary testing, humor, giving in, letting go, and holding on to children lovingly. When such containment is missing, siblings will do what they need to do anyway, although in a less safe environment.
>
> (van Beekum 2009: 133)

My brother and sister suffered much more deeply in this minefield than did I, and our parents were unable to provide anything close to the holding environment that van Beekum describes. Van Beekum's article opened a way for me to begin really thinking about what was happening within my own extended/broken family. The theme of the Australian conference and the invitation to write this essay—now nearly two years in the making—have opened many doors in my understanding of my patterns of intimate awkwardness and avoidance in my life.

So, it is time to return to my personal story. My dad was the third born of four siblings, an older brother and sister, a younger brother. He was seven when his father died unexpectedly of a medical error. His mother quickly became more deeply involved with the man with whom she had been having an affair, leaving the bereaved kids pretty much to manage for themselves. This is not a story ever told to me by my father (his account of his childhood was very different). This was the account told to me by his older sister after his death. Dad was a teenager when he fled the family in favor of World War II. He came back a broken man from the war in which the returning soldiers were hailed as heroes. He endured his anguish in a silent withdrawal, doing his best to earn a living, live a decent life and protect his children from his inner demons. Encased in an anguished silence, his unspoken anguish was nevertheless passed on to his children, but the history and facts of his suffering remained unknown to them.

A brief window to my dad's suffering opened unexpectedly: I had refused induction to the draft during the Vietnam War, filing for conscientious objector status based on political rather than religious grounds. To my utter surprise, this father who rarely spoke wrote an impassioned and articulate letter to my draft board, saying that, as a veteran of World War II, he could never allow a child of his to participate in any war. In spite of my repeated inquiries after his letter to my draft board, he refused to speak of what happened to him (or what he did) during the war.

He was only 40 when he lost his beloved wife, who like his father died suddenly as a result of a medical error. After our mother's death, Dad's life became increasingly unbearable. I twice talked him out of shooting himself. Ten years after the death of our mother, Dad told me that he had decided for certain to end it. In keeping with a now long-standing pattern, he told only me. My brother and sister were left out.

While I was struggling with my father's anguish and his wish to die, I was listening to Bob Dylan, as I often did and still do when I am disturbed. Usually under circumstances like these I prefer his angry songs, of which he was a master as a young man. As I was struggling to write to my father one day, I happened to hear Dylan's "Tomorrow is a Long Time," a delicate and mournful song about a lost love. As I heard Dylan sing, "I can't speak the sounds that show no pain" (Dylan 1963/1973: 42), I was thrown full force into the meaning of my father's desperate, mute pain. Dylan's words clutched at my throat, and I could feel my father's inconsolable anguish. Dylan was a young man singing of his loss of a sweetly loved girlfriend; my dad was a middle-aged man crushed by the unmourned losses of a lifetime, his wife's death being only the most recent and devastating. I could suddenly set my own misery aside as I began truly to grasp what he had lost and accept his inability to come to terms with it. I wrote out the lyrics, mailed them to him, and flew out to be with him.

Once again, I was intimately drawn into his decision to die, while my siblings were left out as bystanders. He insisted that I not tell them. Unfortunately, I honored his request, and looking back I can see now that I felt so estranged from them that it was as though there was no basis for such an intimacy. I could not help them—they were at that time but strangers at the periphery of my life.

I remained horrified and furious with Dad, demanding he take care of himself. He told me to leave him alone—the family's universal solution. I refused. He finally replied, with unforgettable honesty, "You don't have the right to ask that of me. You have not lived my life, and I have had enough of this life." It was a confrontation that would stay with me forever. Even in the last days of his life, he refused to tell me of the war years that still haunted him, but we were able to speak of our lives and losses together in a pained and loving honesty. It was a rare moment of intimacy with my dad, a discovery that we did have the capacity to face hard truths together.

Gary and Deb did not have the privilege of that kind of conversation with him, and they suffered massively in the face of his death and his determined silence with them. Silences have echoed through our family system. Silences are embedded in the family script. Though a hard-working and deeply devoted mother, my sister then lived *her* own suffering in silence, *her* history hidden from her children—following what we might call a family script. I, in my own way, also followed the family script, leaving my siblings to the side as bystanders silenced and in silence.

Our family, on both the maternal and paternal sides, had been scarred for several generations by the sudden deaths of parents (usually the father) early in life. For reasons I'll never know, these families could not grieve. Within the context of the containing functions of vertical/parental relations, there were huge lacunae when it came to death and loss. This is what Debbie, Gary and I were *thrown* into. My mother's family tended to collapse into various forms of depressive symbioses. My father's family tended to fragment into bitter, silent isolation. Our mom was a difficult woman. Our dad was a kind man, and all three of us siblings tended to identify with him, mirroring his patterns of silent withdrawal. His was not a hostile withdrawal, but one that I think he imagined protected us from his inner demons. I have read many stories in the child development literature about how siblings pull together in protective covens like the Torres brothers to ward off violent, psychotic, addicted or absent parents. That was not the case for the Cornell kids. I did not offer a gesture of benevolence toward them until very late in life.

A few years ago, my first psychoanalysis well behind me, things changed yet again. It had been my unhappiness in my marriage and my inability to decide on getting a divorce that had propelled me into my first analysis. My marriage had been based on profound levels of caretaking, in which I felt responsible for everything. This, of course, is another story, but through the course of my analysis I was able to initiate the divorce and after several years as a single parent was able to establish a new love relationship. My new relationship, though I could not have said so at the time, was grounded in the lateral rather than the vertical. Our intimacy was based on a peer relationship of mutual pleasures and support. Mick neither wanted, nor would tolerate, my caretaking tendencies.

Mick, who had known me in our professional circles for quite some time, had come into my personal life following my divorce and his own. We were both fathers. As we got to know one another, he discovered I had siblings. This took him completely by surprise, as he, like most people, assumed I was an only child. Mick, on the other hand, was the eldest of nine siblings, the first eight of whom were born within ten years of one another. Mick, also, it so happened, was on the faculty of the Western Pennsylvania Family Center, a Bowenian training program. He knew something about emotional cutoffs within family systems from both personal and professional perspectives. He took me to task. I articulated my rationalizations with full force and conviction, as I had with my analyst several years before. He was not impressed. I explained that my sister was married to a severely abusive man who listened in when we spoke on the phone and had never let me meet their children. He was not impressed.

Analysts tend to rely on insight and the subtle workings of the therapeutic relationship. Bowenians tend to lean more toward action—actually *doing* things, not just talking about them. "OK," Mick suggested, "let's take a bit of a holiday in Connecticut [where Debbie lived]. We can give them a call on a couple hours' notice and drop by. What can he do, slam the door in our faces?" We were about to step through this history of emotional cutoffs.

It worked. My sister welcomed the two of us into her life with open arms. Her children, now in their thirties, met Uncle Billy for the first time in their lives. In those few years, Deb and I became very close. This was all the more remarkable to me in that Deb's life experience (she worked in a factory) and world view were very constrained. She was a blue-collar Republican and was not ashamed of her racist and anti-Semitic views. She had always known me as a married father of three boys, and here I was showing up at her door with a guy. When I asked her about it, she said that she was so grateful to him for bringing us together that she simply wanted to get to know the kind of man he was. She said she could see the kind of fathers that Mick and I were, and she wanted her kids to get to know us. She could tell I was happy, "and that's enough for me."

However, my brother held himself at the fringes (and I did nothing to change that one).

Then, at 54, Deb was diagnosed with multiple terminal cancers. It was a true blessing that with our reconciliation she did not have to manage her illness and her family's distress by herself. In spite of the odds, she lived two years and remained coherent until a few days before her death.

As she was facing her imminent death, she knew her children needed to know something of her life, her history before she died, but, like our father, she could not speak it to her children, though they desperately wanted to know her better before they lost her. I was shocked to realize how little her children, even as adults, knew about their mother and our family's history. Her children, three sons and a daughter, had turned to each other to ward off their violent father and to care and be cared for by one another. Deb had been a devoted mother and grandmother, the primary financial provider for the family, keeping herself the target of her husband's abuse to protect the children. Her kids loved her fiercely, but they did not know her. They could never understand why she chose to stay with their father.

Two weeks before Deb died, I went to see her alone to talk with her about her funeral. She asked that I speak for her about her life to her children. I told her that I had brought a recorder and we could talk together and I could play her own voice to them after she died. She said, "No, I can't." She wanted to talk to me and for me then to talk to her children for her. She was by this time very ill and blind, so I said to her, "You are fucking blind. I could turn the recorder on, and you'll never know the difference." "If you love me," she replied, "you won't do that. I want to talk to you and you speak for me." I said to her, "You know that's always been my script in the family, Billy will do it." "Well," she said, "Billy is going to do it one more time."

This time I learned a respect for silence, the utter and absolute necessity for my sister of her silence. Though it broke her heart, she could not break the silence for her children. That was mine to do as her big brother—a gift to her and her children and grandchildren. At her funeral, I spoke of and for my sister, bringing in her own words and voice. Her children learned for the first time of their mother's sufferings in childhood and adult life that had come to shape and limit her adult life. They had never heard the story of her own mother's tragic illness or of her father's suicide.

Gary, who had come to visit only once during her illness, had told Deb, "I don't do funerals." He could not bear all that her illness and imminent death evoked in him, and he stepped back into our familiar terrain of an emotional cutoff. I stayed in touch with him, but I could not persuade him to come see her again or even to talk with her. She called him and told him that she understood why he had to stay away and that she loved him. Deb did not cut off.

A week before she died, Gary called to tell her he would come to her funeral. He did not see her alive, but he was there for her funeral. So Gary, too, heard my story of what happened in our family—something of which he and I had never spoken. He collapsed in tears and rose to speak of Deb's death and the death of our parents with a rage and grief that I have never witnessed in my

40 years of practice as a psychotherapist. I then had no question (nor any judgment) of why Gary had found it necessary to live in such isolation. I could finally see in him what I had gradually come to recognize in myself: a dread of being torn to shreds by this grief.

Gary and I have now found each other as brothers in a tentative but genuine relationship. It required our confrontation as a family of a massive tragedy and loss in order for Deb, Gary and I to refashion our sibling bonds, to reestablish a degree of care for one another.

In his brief and poignant essay "On Transience," written in 1916, on the eve of World War I, Freud (1957a: 306) observed "we possess, as it seems, a certain amount of capacity for love—what we call libido," which we attach to certain objects, and that we wish to keep those attachments at all costs. Freud described how, when we lose a loved object, it feels as though we are losing our capacity to love altogether and forever. There can be a ferocious refusal to relinquish the lost one and love anew. There was no one to help Gary, Debbie and me as teenagers and young adults to mourn the losses in the face of our parents' hideous deaths. Distance seemed the best salve. Through the process of mourning—a profoundly painful process—Freud argued that we must release the lost loved one in order to love again and bring our life to another. In this brief essay, Freud contemplated that, once our mourning is over, we learn that we have lost nothing from our discovery of our (or the other's) fragility. My sister, my brother and I learned much about our own and each other's fragilities. We did in fact lose Debbie's life, but, before her death, we had gained a great deal.

"On Transience" preceded and foreshadowed Freud's classic paper "Mourning and Melancholia" (1917). Freud explores the relationships among loss, despair, grief and depression. By the end of World War I, the "Great" War, Freud had come to see that mourning could be so profoundly painful that one could easily be drawn to avoid it, temper it down in the moment. However, he also saw the consequences of this avoidance in the damage to the ego's capacities to engage in life. He saw melancholia (depression) as the result of incomplete mourning resulting in a chronic loss of interest in life, the inability to establish new love relationships, a collapse of initiative toward life, and a sharp diminution in self-regard. In a paper extending Freud's observations and those of Klein (1940), Anne Alvarez (2010) examines the psychological and developmental impact of melancholia and mourning in childhood and adolescence. She observes five "particular states of mind" likely to emerge in reaction to unacknowledged and unresolved loss in childhood: paranoia, manic contempt, narcissistic preoccupation, addictive and perverse chuntering, and a state "which has to do with despair, and with those states which go beyond despair into apathy," resulting in an internal object world dominated by "unvalued, as opposed to devalued objects" (Alvarez 2010: 4). As I read Alvarez's article, I could see the unconscious impact of the losses and isolation in our family system on each of us: my brother falling into a paranoid state of mind in which any form of attachment was a danger, me into manic contempt in which any form of attachment was a burden and a threat, and my sister into an apathy of an unvalued being, driven only by the desire to avert some of the suffering in her children's lives. Alvarez comments that children under these circumstances "have had nowhere to put it except on themselves" (Alvarez 2010: 13). The Cornell kids did not have a family system capable of helping them do much else than spin off into their own private worlds.

It has been more than 40 years since our mother's untimely death and 30 years since our father's self-imposed one. It has taken a hell of a lot of study and psychotherapy, being a father myself, getting a divorce, sending my sons off into their own adult lives, and finally having the firm and vigorous accompaniment of my new partner in life for me to be able to stand alive and open in the face of my sister's death and my siblings' long-neglected sufferings, mourning perhaps not only our own losses but also the unmetabolized losses of the generations preceding us.

As I watch myself mature, my friends mature and my clients mature, I see a shift in primary relationships from the vertical domains of parents and parenting, of authority and dependency, into those of peers, of the lateral. The intimacies of our adult lives are so often found and fed in the lateral relations of colleagues, friends and community members, outside of the once traditional nuclear family. Our childhood sibling relationships provide a deep, unconsciously embedded protocol for lateral relations and intimacy, for better or for naught. I have come to have a profound respect for the enduring developmental centrality of the sibling subsystem—"the first laboratory," as Minuchin so aptly described it, in which "children learn to negotiate, cooperate, and compete" (Minuchin 1974: 59).

References

Akhtar, S. and S. Kramer. 1999. *Brothers and Sisters: Developmental, Dynamic, and Technical Aspects of the Sibling Relationship*. Northvale, NJ: Jason Aronson, Inc.

Alvarez, A. 2010. "Melancholia and Mourning in Childhood and Adolescence: Some Reflections on the Role of the Internal Object." In E. McGinley and A. Varchevker (eds) *Enduring Loss: Mourning, Depression, and Narcissism through the Life Cycle*. London: Karnac, 3–17.

Bowen, M. 1978. *Family Therapy in Clinical Practice*. New York: Jason Aronson, Inc.

Cicirelli, V.G. 1995. *Sibling Relationships across the Life Span*. New York: Plenum Press.

Coles, P. 2003. *The Importance of Sibling Relationships*. London: Karnac.

Colonna, A.B. and L.M. Newman. 1983. "The Psychoanalytic Literature on Siblings." *Psychoanalytic Study of the Child* 83: 285–309.

Cornell, W.F. 2009. "Loves and Losses: Enactments in the Disavowal of Intimate Desires." In D. Mann and V. Cunningham (eds) *The Past in the Present: Therapy Enactments and the Return of Trauma*. London: Routledge, 82–101.

Dunn, J. 1993. *Young Children's Close Relationships: Beyond Attachment*. Newbury Park, CA: SAGE Publications.

——1985. *Sisters and Brothers: The Developing Child*. Cambridge, MA: Harvard University Press.

Dunn, J. and C. Kendrick. 1982. *Siblings: Love, Envy, & Understanding*. London: Grant McIntyre Ltd.

Dunn, J. and R. Plomin. 1990. *Separate Lives: Why Siblings are so Different*. New York: Basic Books.

Dylan, B. 1963/1973. "Tomorrow is a Long Time." In *Writings and Drawings by Bob Dylan*. New York: Alfred A. Knopf, Inc, 63.

Freud, S. 1957a [1916]. "On Transience." In *Standard Edition*, Vol. 14. London: The Hogarth Press, 303–7.

——1957b [1917]. "Mourning and Melancholia." In *Standard Edition*, Vol. 14. London: The Hogarth Press, 237–58.

Heidegger, M. 1962. *Being and Time*. New York: Harper and Row.

Hetherington, E.M., D. Reiss and R. Plomin (eds). 1994. *Separate Social Worlds of Siblings: The Impact of Nonshared Environment on Development*. Hillsdale, NJ: Lawrence Erlbaum Associates.

Kerr, M.E. 2008. "Why Do Siblings Often Turn Out So Differently?" In A. Fogel, B.J. King and S.G. Shanker (eds) *Human Development in the Twenty-first Century: Visionary Ideas from Systems Scientists*. Cambridge: Cambridge University Press, 206–15.

Klein, M. 1975 [1940]. "Mourning and its Relation to Manic-depressive States." In *The Writings of Melanie Klein*. London: The Hogarth Press, 344–69.

Landaiche, M.N. 2009. "Understanding Social Pain Dynamics in Human Relations." *Transactional Analysis Journal* 39(2): 229–38.

Minuchin, S. 1974. *Families and Family Therapy*. London: Tavistock Publications.

Mitchell, J. 2003. *Siblings*. Cambridge: Polity Press.

——2006. "Sibling Trauma: A Theoretical Consideration." In P. Coles (ed.) *Sibling Relationships*. London: Karnac.

Needleman, J. 1963. *Being-in-the-world: Selected Papers of Ludwig Binswanger, Translated with a Critical Introduction to his Existential Psychoanalysis*. New York: Basic Books.

Rodman, F.R. 2003. *Winnicott: Life and Work*. Cambridge, MA: Perseus Publishing.

Sanders, R. 2004. *Sibling Relationships*. New York: Palgrave Macmillan.

Spinelli, E. 2005. *The Interpreted World: An Introduction to Phenomenological Psychology*. London: SAGE Publications.

Torres, J. 2011. *We the Animals*. Boston: Houghton Mifflin Harcourt.

van Beekum, S. 2008. "Erotic Transference as a Social Defense." *Organizational Social Dynamics* 8(2): 154–68.

——2009. "Siblings, Aggression, and Sexuality: Adding the Lateral." *Transactional Analysis Journal* 39(2): 129–35.

Vivona, J. 2007. "Sibling Differentiation, Identity Development and the Lateral Dimension of Psychic Life." *Journal of the American Psychoanalytic Association* 55(4): 1191–215.

9 The belly mommy and the fetus sitter

The reproductive marketplace and family intimacies[1]

Joshua Gamson

Few experiences are more intensely personal and intimate than making a life. When the intended parents, while bringing an extra penis to the mix, lack two of the biological components required for reproduction, the intimacies involved become more complex. When out of necessity the process is approached with intense, self-conscious intention, involving the help of egg donors and surrogates, when it goes against the grain of medical and legal institutions and social conventions, the process yields unusual and intricate relationships. So it was for me. Our first daughter resulted from the egg of a close friend, fertilized by the sperm of either me or my husband Richard—we know which one, but don't disclose that publicly—carried by my college girlfriend, supported by her then husband, and birthed by her near the home of my parents, who helped sponsor the whole expensive endeavor and greeted newborn Reba Sadie, along with several other members of our families of origin, in the maternity ward of Martha's Vineyard Hospital. Our second, Madeleine Blanche, resulted from the egg of a friend, fertilized by the sperm of either me or Richard, carried by a woman from Kentucky who was a complete stranger before we met her through a surrogacy agency, and birthed by her near her own home in Bowling Green, with the surrogate's mother in the delivery room and Reba, my parents and my mother-in-law in the waiting room.

As I will recount, much in these two creation processes was different. One brought together people who already had thick friendship ties to one another, while the second was built largely on a relationship brokered by commercial agents. They also had quite a bit in common. Each involved exchanges of money, facilitated in part by social class, and negotiations with unfriendly or uncomprehending institutional forces. Each engaged a relatively new sort of approach to the deeply intimate process of reproduction, in which key parts of the process were "outsourced" to others. They offer an interesting opportunity to consider the novel forms of intimacy opened up by contemporary reproductive medicine, especially for those for whom the choice to parent remains institutionally and socially controversial, and to consider more broadly the dynamics of intimacy within market-based reproduction.

Indeed, many people, scholars included, see egg donation and surrogacy as quintessential examples of the encroachment of a market mentality into aspects of intimate life that had previously been insulated from commercial forces. For instance, in her recent book *The Outsourced Self: Intimate Life in Market Times*, Arlie Russell Hochschild (2012) details what she calls the "outsourcing" of intimacy, a "strange new emotional capitalism" (ibid.: 13), in which the market has become present "in our bedrooms, at our breakfast tables, in our love lives, entangled in our deepest joys and sorrows" (ibid.: 222). Chief among her examples is surrogacy, in which "a person can now legally purchase an egg from one continent, sperm from another, and implant it in a 'womb for rent' in yet another" (ibid.: 73). She describes a couple who, turning to a surrogacy clinic in India, "saw their relationship with the surrogate as a mutually beneficial transaction," and "imagined themselves as outsourcers paying a stranger to provide a professionally supervised service," establishing with the gestational carrier "the sort of relationship one might establish with an obstetrician or dentist" (ibid.: 83). She describes an Indian surrogate who, "instructed to remain emotionally detached from her clients, her babies, and even from her womb," while doing "an extraordinarily personal thing," entered transactions that were "cursory, businesslike, and spanned differences in language, culture, ethnicity, nation, and, most of all, social class" (ibid.: 93).

Reading that, I wondered: Was that us? Was my family's creation part of the transformation of one of the most intimate human experiences into a commercial transaction, turning conception and childbirth into services, alienating ourselves and the women involved from our bodies and our babies, replacing the personal and the attached with the impersonal and detached? There is certainly something to that; everywhere we turned in our family creation process we encountered market-based activity and rhetoric. Our own class advantages, and to a degree also gender ones, made the whole thing possible in the first place. Like many of the people Hochschild interviewed, all of us involved seemed to struggle with, resist and accommodate ourselves to market logic: trying to "protect the personal from the purchased," to find the line past which intimate life became "too commercial," to hold onto the "spirit of the gift," to seize back intimate moments from the marketplace (Hochschild 2012: 13, 95, 225). To Hochschild, such actions are mechanisms for coping with "the basic imbalance between market, state, and civic life" that shows up in the commercial outsourcing of personal lives (ibid.: 225).

Hochschild's concerns, many of which I share, take their place within a larger body of thinking about the relationship between markets and intimate social life. As Viviana Zelizer has described them, perspectives on this relationship take several forms.

Some see the marketplace and intimate relationships as "hostile worlds," with contact between them leading inevitably to "moral contamination and degradation" (Zelizer 2000: 818). Others suggest that "intimate transfers—be they of sex, babies, or blood—operate according to principles identical with transfers of stock shares and used cars" (Zelizer 2000: 825) and should be understood as simply another transactional type. Still others argue that commercialized intimacy is "nothing but the result of coercive, and more specifically patriarchal, power structures" (Zelizer 2000: 826), serving the interests of the more powerful partners in a gendered hierarchy. Zelizer suggests another, more nuanced approach, which she calls "differentiated ties": intimacy and marketplace are neither hostile, equivalent, nor reducible to coercion, but instead embedded together in social relations, as "people incessantly match different forms of payment to their various intimate relations" (Zelizer 2000: 826).

Pieces of each of these perspectives show up in my family-making stories, but none of them alone quite seems to get it right. As I here tell the stories of conceiving and creating my own family, I want to consider what is and isn't captured in these concerns about market-linked reproduction, and to unravel some of the complexities of outsourced personal life. One is quickly evident just from the fact that I was *able* to build a family as I did. Although I was constantly aware of and wary of the role of the market elements of the process, I was also aware that without those transactions I would remain excluded from biological reproduction. For some of us, facing medical, biological and/or social obstacles, the commercialized aspects of reproduction have been important facilitators of family creation and relationships that were otherwise proscribed. In fact, it is not just capitalist entrepreneurs (for instance, those behind the many for-profit fertility clinics and surrogacy agencies) who have used market transactions to open up parenthood options, but also entrepreneurial activists (like the women who established sperm banks in the 1980s) (Mundy 2007). The expansion of who can become parents, when and how—including, it turned out, by "outsourcing" parts of the process—has resulted not just from commercialization forces, and not just from advances in reproductive medicine, but also from social movements. Without feminism, it is hard to imagine women pursuing parenthood solo (Hertz 2006); without lesbian and gay organizing, the legal and social obstacles to same-sex parenting would have been insurmountable (Lewin 2009). In this context, the marketplace seemed to me neither a moral contaminator nor a coercive force but one mechanism for achieving both a personal and collective goal: the freedom to make the relationships that we want to make, not just the ones that are defined as legitimate by, say, heteronormative social forces and traditional family structures (Stacey 2011).

At an everyday level, my stories suggest, the relationship between marketplace and intimacies is not exclusively one in which the market colonizes personal life and we accommodate ourselves to it or push back against it. In many ways, in the creation of our family, the market indeed pushed against intimacies, replacing connection with commerce; in other ways, it produced intimacies, even as other institutions, such as law and medicine, were hostile or ill-equipped for this kind of family making. In some ways, financial transactions highlighted class differences and undercut the closeness of peers; in other ways, they generated balance and offset differences. Sometimes operating outside of the marketplace was a welcome relief from the ways it pushed people apart; at other times, the detachments it provided were themselves a welcome relief. Sometimes we were suspicious of and resisted the logic of the marketplace; at other times, we sought out and embraced it.

Making Reba Sadie

From the very beginning, considerations of the commercialized aspects of family creation were primary in my and Richard's decision making. For a variety of reasons, some form of biological ties between us and any future baby was very important to Richard, and less so to me. I had no objections to biological reproduction itself, and felt no particular obligation to pursue adoption instead. Instead, my worries echoed the scholarly troubling of commodified intimate life relations. The idea of shopping for eggs, as though procreation was equivalent to a trip to the grocery store, rubbed me the wrong way; the idea of basically renting a woman's womb seemed even creepier, given the degree to which many men have proceeded as if entitled to access women's bodies through purchase, violence, or both. What I wanted, and Richard, too, I think, was something that felt more connected, organic, consensual and intimate.

Then, just after New Year in 2004, I had a dream. In it, my college girlfriend, her freckled cheeks ruddy, her red hair matted with sweat, was having a baby. After my coffee, I gave Tamar a call. We hadn't spoken in about a year, but I told her about the dream and asked her if she and her husband were maybe on the way to a baby.

"Nah," she said. She and her husband Andy had decided against kids. Tamar mentioned only one regret. "I kind of wanted to experience pregnancy and childbirth. I was born into this body, you know, and I feel like I'm missing the chance to experience one of the most amazing things you can do in this kind of body."

"So you're saying you'd like to be pregnant and give birth to a child, but not raise it," I summarized.

"Exactly," she said.

"Have I got a deal for you," I said.

"I'll mull it over," she said. I figured she was kidding.

To my surprise, Tamar called back a few weeks later to discuss the possibility of carrying our baby. She came to our ongoing conversations with lists of discussion topics. Interestingly, among the things she requested was payment, not so much because she needed the money but so that she could treat the experience at least partially as a job, and perhaps because it seemed to balance things, by transforming a pure gift into an exchange of sorts. She also wanted to know how we would feel about her breastfeeding, at least for the first week or two. I'd been reading a lot of surrogacy websites, most of which saw a carrier's emotional attachment to the child she was carrying as the first step towards her decision to screw over the intended parents and keep the kid.

"I'm not worried about getting attached to this baby," Tamar said. "I want to feel attached to this baby. I hope you want that, too." It was exactly what I wanted: attachment and detachment combined. Given the health benefits of breast milk, Tamar also proposed to pump her breasts for the first six weeks and FedEx the milk to California.

"You drive a hard bargain," I told her. I knew she was in.

Not long afterwards, looking for materials to paste into a birthday book for Tamar's upcoming birthday, I found several articles sent to me by her late mother, a psychologist, including an invited address she'd given to the American Psychological Association on Judaism and feminism. In it, she quotes a paper Tamar, then 19, had written about the separation of male and female in the creation story, and their reconciliation through the improbable pregnancies of Sarah (pregnant at 90 with Isaac) and Rebecca (barren for 20 years, only to give birth to twins Jacob and Esau). The logic of the interpretation wasn't easy to follow, but Tamar, her mother reported, "caused pregnancy to represent in symbol that which it is in biological fact, a unification of independent beings who require each other for the creation of new life." Tucked nearby was a letter Nancy had written to me after my break-up with Tamar. "When I think about what 'might have been' between Tamar and you," she said, "it is more often in terms of the large collection of baby items we have squirreled away in our minds for the first grandchild, for which you and Tamar looked like the most likely and most welcome candidates." I made a copy of the letter, and pasted the original onto a page for Tamar's birthday book.

Richard and I set about pursuing both commercial and non-commercial avenues to the egg that might become our baby. I perused egg donors on fertility clinic sites, unhappily, and we began talking to family and friends, one of whom ultimately agreed to donate eggs. All the elements were in place: intimates, together, expanding a family by creating a baby.

In April, Team Baby descended on Northern Virginia, near Tamar and Andy and a reputable fertility institute. The fertility institute was located in a small, bland office park in Fairfax. Checking in at the front desk, we could fit our roles into none of their forms. Mom–kid combos beamed from the shiny covers of parenting magazines. The few waiting women and the receptionist watched us with curiosity and caution, as if our laughter might be mocking them. In the waiting room, we were incongruous, a bunch of fertile people loosed in the land of infertility.

While the donor's eggs were being harvested, I browsed the agency's brochures, one of which advertised the availability, for an additional fee, of eggs from women who "hold or are pursuing advanced degrees in medicine or another academic specialty," known at the institute as "doctoral donors."

"Daddy," I said, in my best spoiled voice, "I want a doctoral donor." No one was amused.

After dinner that night, Andy put Sister Sledge's "We Are Family" on the CD player. We pushed back the table and danced a little. *We are family. I got all my sisters with me. We are family. Get up everybody and sing.*

The doctor—who, by coincidence, Richard knew from medical school, where they were among the few African American students—made no mention of our unusual circumstances, and had no trouble recognizing that Richard and I were the intended parents, and that the egg donor and Tamar were not "staff" but members of a tight little team. When she called the next day, the news wasn't good. Only two eggs had fertilized, and neither of the embryos looked promising. The odds of a pregnancy, she said, were slim to none, which Richard told me was doctor talk for "it's not going to happen." I flew home to go back to work.

Tamar, who for months had been physically and mentally preparing for her role, wanted to follow it all the way through. Otherwise, she said, it would be like she'd trained for a relay race and never been handed the baton. Besides, we figured, we'd already paid for the procedure. That Monday morning, Tamar lay on the table, legs raised, with Andy and Richard on each side. The room was a bit cramped, and on one side was a small sliding window much like you'd find at a Burger King drive-thru. The window slid open, and a voice called out, in a manner that reminded Richard of a short-order cook, "Embryos for Gamson." They all held hands and watched on the ultrasound screen as a tiny dot gently traveled, like a slow-motion spitball, to its destination.

Tamar was told to lie low for the day. Andy went to work, and she and Richard got French fries and watched DVDs.

Two Thursdays later, Tamar called to tell us she was pregnant.

Tamar approached pregnancy with the conscientiousness and grit that I recognized from our college years. She studied fetal development, she researched, she charted. She kept her receipts and tracked her expenses on Excel. She dealt with curiosity-seekers with finesse and smiling bite, disarming them with the isn't-it-wonderful news that she was carrying a baby for dear friends, two guys who could not have one on their own. I imagined she left little space for disapproval. She told me she saw her mission as personal and political.

Still, we had to sue her. We had already decided against having the birth in Virginia, where laws were hostile to surrogacy, let alone same-sex parenting. Our plan was to head up to Massachusetts, hang out at my parents' house on Martha's Vineyard, and have the baby in the one state where Richard and I were legally married. Without legal intervention, the baby's presumptive legal parents would be Tamar and Andy, in which case we'd have to adopt our own kid, or at best Tamar and the one of us who donated sperm would, in which case we'd still have a mess on our hands. Tamar and Andy wanted no legal responsibility for a baby and we wanted all of it, so we decided to get a court order so that, as our complaint to the Probate and Family Court of Dukes County, Commonwealth of Massachusetts, put it, "the child's birth record may be established in accordance with those true and accurate facts regarding the child's parentage." I couldn't help but admire the big balls of a system that so casually insisted our collaboration be recorded as a dispute, and charged us money to do so. What a perfect perversion: generosity reflected back to us as animosity. At least, I thought, we got the pleasure of being difficult to digest.

In mid-December of 2005, we road-tripped it together in Tamar's Subaru from Virginia to Massachusetts, she in the back seat with her ridiculous belly and a body pillow, Richard and I in the front. How strange to be here with them, I thought, these two who had walked in from different lifetimes, now laughing it up and arguing about who could be in the delivery room.

Andy arrived a couple of days later, and we all hunkered down like roosting birds in my parents' small guesthouse to await the baby. The fireplace was lit each morning as the coffee was brewing, and burned itself out after that evening's movie. We read fiction punctuated by meals. We stared spacily out at the bare trees. We entered a sort of group marriage, annoying one another with dishwasher-loading styles and inappropriate whistling; occasionally one dyad would peel off for a walk, an argument, or both. On Christmas Day, Richard cooked an elaborate meal that included mac-and-cheese, collard greens and sweet potato pie; it was also the first night of Chanukah, so we lit several menorahs near the

Christmas lights. We became bored, impatient and a little chubby. We tried every trick we'd heard, or thought we'd heard, to get the fully cooked baby to emerge, but she stayed put, paddling about contentedly in her dark sea of amniotic fluid. Finally, after weeks of waiting, the calm, patient nurse-midwife at the Martha's Vineyard Hospital scheduled an induction.

My mother kept a sort of journal record of our stay, with brief, factual summaries of each day's events, entitled "It Takes Two Fathers, a Surrogate, Her Husband, Three Grandparents, a Dog, Three Cousins, Two Aunts, an Uncle, Four Houses and an Island to Birth a Baby: Notes from a Modern Confinement." It includes entries like this one, from December 19th: "At the guesthouse, Josh washes loads of beautiful hand-me-downs that are probably already clean. J and R deal with the legal procedures that will allow them to be recognized as the legal parents of the baby."

In the hospital, our reputation had clearly preceded us—the Vineyard is a small town in the winter, and we were the talk of it—and the warm nurses knew exactly who was who and what was what. We all did our best to entertain and distract Tamar. We put some country music on the CD player, and Andy and Richard danced a goofy jig. I massaged Tamar's back and Andy quietly sang, a cappella, a Kate Wolf song in which a lilac and an apple converse about "life in another time." When it seemed that no amount of drugs, songs, stories, baths and jigs would get this baby moving—the contractions were regular and painful, but didn't increase in intensity, and Tamar's uterus was barely dilated—we ordered a pizza, wheeled Tamar out to the waiting area, and agreed to try again the next day.

The next afternoon, the nurse-midwife broke Tamar's water. A few hours later, Tamar agreed to an epidural, both for pain reduction and to increase the odds of a vaginal delivery. Several hours later, now into the early hours of day three of her labor, Tamar looked wearily at Cathy. "Do you think it's safe to say we've tried everything?" she asked. "Do you think I've done everything I can to get this baby out?" The nurse-midwife nodded, and picked up the phone to call the doctor.

Richard and Andy and I, in scrubs, masks and caps, stood inside the delivery room. Richard's little sister watched from a windowed room just above us. His mother and mine, who had slept overnight on matching couches in the maternity visiting area, were waiting outside the door; my father was on his way. From where I stood, Tamar reminded me of a woman in a magic show being sawn in half, divided as she was by a waist-level screen. The top half was placid, her eyes blinking slowly, her head turned a bit to look at her husband. It seemed to have no connection to the bottom half, where three men poked away frantically with gloved hands dripping blood, pulling out of it the nine-pound creature we named Reba Sadie, after my grandmother and Richard's great-grandmother. Andy cut the umbilical cord.

One of the nurses asked who was to get her first. Richard and I, teary eyed and exhausted, looked at each other and then pointed to Tamar. Tamar, cheeks ruddy, hair matted, crying, gazed dopily at the swaddled infant, and then the nurse brought her back over to me and Richard. Richard held her up towards the fluorescent-lit ceiling, Kunta Kinte style, crying and chuckling. We took her out to the hallway to meet her grandparents. My mother turned to Richard's. "Look at those lips," she whispered.

The day before we were all to leave, my parents made us dinner and left us to eat it while they babysat. Over fettuccine that night, we talked on video to future versions of Reba. The combination of sleep deprivation, hormones, wine and intimacy proved irresistible, and pretty much anything anyone said made someone else cry. When Tamar reported on our success with feedings ("every two to three hours, we're keeping meticulous records, and one of your daddies is always there"), I filmed the tears coming to Richard's eyes.

"What do you want Reba to know about who you are and who you are to her?" I asked, recording. Just the question made me cry a little.

"I'm not sure who I am to her yet," Tamar answered, drying her tears without interrupting the drama of the moment. "She'll have to figure that out as she grows up. But who she is to me: She's this wonderful little person I helped bring into the world, and I'm really glad she's here. Her dads needed a little help birthing her, since neither one of them has a uterus, and I do, so she got put inside of me when she was two cells big, and she grew inside of me for nine months." She covered her mouth, crying hard now, but readying a punch line nonetheless. "I tried to take really good care of her, and I think I did a pretty good job, cause she came out really, really big."

"Why are you crying?" I asked.

"I'm crying because there's a lot of hormones right now," Tamar said, blowing her nose. "And I'm also crying because I'm going to miss her. I was very glad to help her grow and bring her into this world. It's really hard to let her go now that she's no longer inside me. I want to be part of her life. I will be part of her life." Looking back, it sounds like something you'd hear on *Oprah*, but at the time it was just like listening to the inside of a heart.

Andy cleared his throat, and pushed his long hair back behind his ears. He sang for Reba the song he'd made up earlier in the week. The tune was from the spiritual "Children, Go Where I Send Thee." Andy had inserted lyrics that were equal parts love and cheese. *Children, go where I send thee. How shall I send thee?* Andy sang. *I'm gonna send you one by one. One for the little bitty Reba, wrapped in swaddling clothing, lying in her daddies' arms, born born born on the Vineyard.* Everyone but Andy got a shout out in his song—Richard and me (two), the grandparents (three), Richard's siblings (four), my sister's family (five), the hospital stay itself (six), even the "luck of the embryos" (seven), the nurses (eight), and the Apgar score (nine). He ended not with the apostles, but with Tamar: *Ten for the belly mommy.*

The next morning, the four of us took a walk on the beach with my mother, her dog Rosie and a bundled-up Reba, to say our goodbyes. We didn't talk much. When Tamar and Andy drove off, my mom held the baby while Richard and I chased after their car, waving and crying, like the movie wives of soldiers chasing the train carrying away their husbands.

We flew home to California when Reba was nine days old. In my carry-on bag was her birth record, handed to us the day before by Sandy, a rosy-cheeked hospital records clerk with braces on her teeth. When we'd first arrived at her department, Sandy had not known what to make of the group of us, but over the weeks she had made many phone calls regarding the issue of how the Commonwealth might allow her to provide a birth record that didn't say "mother" and "father." She had gradually become a confederate. The birth certificate she produced listed Parent A and Parent B.

Making Madeleine Blanche

A few years later, when Richard and I decided, over dinner at a casino buffet, that we wanted to conceive another child, we turned very quickly towards market-based surrogacy. Much as she had appreciated the experience, Tamar was not interested in another round; the odds of another friend offering to carry a baby for us seemed slim. Much as we had both appreciated the earlier process, the thought of going through an agency, which would set us up with paid strangers to help us out, gave both of us a surprising sense of relief. I had no regrets at all about the way we had made Reba, but it was filled with exhausting complexities: the weird combination of guilt and gratitude towards the egg donor, the gestational surrogate and her husband; the intense period of group marriage and then the abrupt, painful separation; the ambiguous boundaries of familial relationships; the practical hassles of organizing such an elaborate production, including the medical and legal maneuverings. The thought of doing that again, while parenting a preschooler, just when we were beginning to get some sleep, seemed too exhausting for words. Hiring an agency to help, and working with an egg donor and gestational surrogate with whom we had no past relationship, now seemed not unsettling, cold and overly mercantile, but sensible, clear and clean.

Still, when I looked into surrogacy agencies that had specialties in same-sex family building, I found myself again uncomfortable: with the glossy brochures and high fees, and perhaps with the forced recognition that our way of becoming parents was really only available to us because we had the earning capacity, borrowing power and family financial support to afford it. When I looked at the profiles of egg donors on various websites, I could not feel a connection to any of them. "They're all smiley and young and blue-eyed," I complained to Richard. "Most of them say something like, 'I'm a people person.'" Where were the black women with attitude and the neurotic Jews, or the Jewish women with attitude and the neurotic African Americans?

Thankfully, we knew some of those. So we asked a close friend—a woman with a very sweet, deep attachment to Reba—if she'd consider donating eggs for our next child. She said she'd give it some thought.

We chose an agency, Circle Surrogacy, partly because they were based in Massachusetts—we had vague, naïve notions that they'd be more likely to be connected to surrogates in that state, where we had already established legal parentage once—and partly because their self-presentation was of a small, gay-run agency that viewed surrogates as people rather than as means-to-an-end vessels, and aimed to build rather than limit the relationships between surrogates and clients. That is, they tapped into and comforted the very anxieties about commercialized reproduction that I brought to the table. The first email to us, in early 2008, announced that the president of the agency is "one half of a gay couple and the proud dad to two boys through traditional surrogacy," before mentioning that the agency fees had just increased but if we signed on by the end of the month we'd be under the previous fee structure. We met with the agency president and one of his colleagues a few weeks later in a San Francisco hotel, where they were attending a conference. Some similar agencies, they told us, do not like the surrogates and the clients to have too much contact, and monitor any contact they do have, for fear that they will become too bonded. They took a different approach, they said, encouraging as much contact as possible, under the belief that making a baby together can and should be an intimate bonding experience.

That sounded just right. Plus, we knew this could all take a long time and were ready to get started. We forked over the large agency fee, sent in the 21-page contract, and signed on. Paperwork and emails flooded our way. There was the Timing of Payments notice, the lengthy Explanation of the Matching Process, the Parenting Questionnaire and the separate Father's Questionnaire. We had to send them our wills, choose a plan for purchasing insurance for a surrogate and look for a psychologist to evaluate us. The social worker wanted to talk to us, and then her successor, and then hers. The case manager, and then her successor, offered to answer any questions we might have. We had many.

In March, as I was resignedly narrowing the pool of people-person egg donors, we got a call from the friend we'd asked to consider egg donation. She'd decided, after serious and careful deliberation, that she couldn't do it; among other things, she was concerned that, in order to keep her non-familial relationship to a future child clear, she'd need to distance herself from us and our family. She said we might get a call from a mutual friend, Rachel, from whom she'd sought counsel while thinking it all through. Sure enough, that very evening, Rachel, who was finishing a PhD and had a son a few months younger than Reba, called. She offered us her eggs.

"Are you fucking kidding me?" I said. "A doctoral donor! Do you know how much your eggs are worth on the open market?" Rachel laughed.

Later, Richard asked her if she would feel weird knowing that her son had a genetic sibling, and she had a genetic child, living nearby.

"That's not how I think about it at all," she said, in the direct, self-possessed and no-nonsense manner I'd often admired. "An egg is made up of some cells. I am offering you some of my cells. That's it. Of course, I'd want to know and love any child that comes of this. But that's not my child." Richard and I could not believe our luck—or rather, the kindness of our friends. After the conversation, we cried a little. The next day, I began making arrangements with Rachel for her to see a fertility doctor.

A few weeks later, I received an email from a Circle social worker named Katherine. "We have found a potential carrier that we think will be a great match for you two!; Gail is a thirty-five-year-old single mother of three children, living in Kentucky. She is very excited about helping a couple to create a family as wonderful as hers. She has a very strong support network in Kentucky and feels ready to embark on this journey with the support of her mother, siblings and close friends." She attached Gail's profile and a few photos. Gail, pale with shoulder-length light-brown hair, smiled alone, and then with a baby, and then with a baby and an eight-year-old boy. She was a single mother of three kids, her profile said. She liked "reading, playing games, spending time with family, going to movies and concerts, doing crafts, swimming, many outside sports, and of course shopping." She was of German descent, a high school graduate and a widow. Her father was an alcoholic and her sisters were molested. "I have a really easy pregnancy and I love being a mom but for some people they aren't able to get pregnant so easily," she wrote. "I think if someone wants to be a parent then why shouldn't I help them when it's so easy for me. My family is complete and it wouldn't be my baby. I'd just be carrying it for someone else. It would be my job to protect it until it's born and then they can protect it." She listed her base fee as $20,000. She'd found the agency through a Google search.

Notwithstanding Katherine's enthusiastic exclamation points, there was nothing in particular that made Gail a "great match" for us beyond the fact that she had completed a form and we had completed a form. She was in a state with laws unsympathetic to surrogacy and hostile to same-sex relationship recognition. As it turned out, no one at the agency knew much of anything about Gail beyond what she provided in her profile, and they had no intention of ever meeting her. Still, however careless the matching process, there she was: a woman in Kentucky who would consider carrying our child.

We talked to Gail on the phone the next week. She was nervous and giggling. We mostly made small talk about kids and movies. Towards the end, I asked her what she thought it would be like to carry a child that she wasn't going to raise.

"It's kind of like a babysitting job," she said, giggling. "I figure I'd be babysitting your baby for nine months." Though I figured it might be more emotionally complicated, I liked that: She would be our fetus sitter.

We flew Gail out to meet us in person. She had never flown before. Within a few hours, she had lost much of her nervousness. She was funny and fun loving, with a sense of adventure. I thought maybe that was part of the appeal for her, besides the money and the "why shouldn't I help?" motivation: a taste for something new, different, bigger and weirder than her everyday life in Bowling Green. We introduced her to Rachel, and they seemed to appreciate each other. By the end of the trip, we'd all agreed to try to have a baby together.

The agency, despite their sales pitch, did little to facilitate a relationship between us and Gail, aside from taking over financial transactions. We fought with them over nearly everything, even as their staff members dropped out and new ones popped up in their places. The agency wanted Gail's emotional support to come from a long-distance phone relationship, at a fee of $3,000, with a social worker who was authorized by signed waiver to report to the agency if "there is any threat to the health of the surrogate, if there is any threat to the health of the child, or if the surrogate is thinking of changing her mind." We insisted that she have access to face-to-face support by a mental health professional in her own locale, whose sole loyalty would be to her. The psychiatrist the agency required us to see assured us that was the standard of care according to the American Society for Reproductive Medicine.

"We believe our success in having the highest success rate in surrogacy and having every surrogate relinquish the child is in large part due to [the outside social worker's] extraordinary ability to provide support over the phone and to build a relationship of trust and understanding with the surrogates," the agency's president wrote to us in an email. He offered the example of a surrogate who "developed intra partum depression taking a whole box of Tylenol, trying to kill herself when she was six months pregnant." The social worker had "jumped to the rescue":

> She got in touch with a psychiatrist, who prescribed the one type of anti-depressant that was not dangerous for the baby and we jointly (and nicely) threatened the surrogate with a locked institution if she didn't take her medication every day and show up for every consultation with the psychiatrist we set up. She did both, and delivered a healthy child three months later.

He told another cautionary tale of a surrogate who changed her mind about "releasing" the baby inside of her, revealed this in a "chat room for unhappy surrogates," some of whom were part of the social worker's "remarkable cadre of loyal surrogates." They reported her disclosure to the social worker, who reported it to the agency, and through an "incredible intervention, the surrogate agreed to release the child." He suggested that, while a local therapist might be "by the book," it would "compromise the surrogacy," and could cost much more. "I fear greatly," he said, "that we will lose control." I was not comforted. To him, this was a goal-oriented business transaction; to me, an intimate process. To the agency, she was a service provider, and not one who could opt out once she opted in; to me, she was a person who, much as I hoped would carry our baby, should remain in control of her own body and destiny. The notion that threats, cadres of chat-room tattlers, and incredible interventions would build trust and understanding seemed unlikely; the notion that all that mattered was the "rescue," "control," the "relinquishing" of a healthy baby, and a high agency "success rate," seemed to undermine claims that Gail herself was a priority. We would have to work on trust and intimacy on our own.

Over time, without giving it much thought, we built a friendship with Gail. It made sense to do the egg donation and fertilization in California—and it took two egg donation cycles and four in-vitro attempts to get pregnant—and on each subsequent trip we all relaxed around one another. We were all regulars at the local fertility clinic, where Gail, Richard, our doctor and a nurse, who seemed as invested in our baby as we were, would cram into a tiny laboratory room and wait for the tall, skinny embryologist to present the needle that might contain our future child. For the second pregnancy attempt, we invited Gail to bring her kids, and we took them and Reba on a road trip to Monterey. We were there when Gail's children touched the ocean for the first time; we took them out to dinner, and showed them the Golden Gate Bridge. It was a strange kind of relationship: inherently familial, but also most likely short term; starting and to some degree set to end with a market transaction, but also somehow much more; at once superficial and deep. I was curious about its constraints, but never able really to get past them. She was a single, working mother with limited income, being paid by two men, a doctor and a professor, to conceive and carry a child. Though I had no evidence of it, I wondered if her easygoing persona was in part a means of covering discomfort and even resentment, and of protecting a valuable financial opportunity. For our part, we were loose but also careful, aware of the costs of alienating Gail.

Finally, in early 2008, Gail was pregnant. Unlike Tamar, her approach to pregnancy was unworried and undetailed: she had done it before, and it didn't seem to require much extra attention beyond going to check-ups. She would work in her job as a clerk at a campground/amusement park until the day before giving birth, as she had with her own children. Richard and I had told ourselves not to micromanage the pregnancy, which was just as well, given how hard it was to reach Gail, who sent us short "the baby is doing fine" updates every few weeks by phone and email. On the rare occasions that someone from the agency spoke to Gail, we'd get a sunny, exclamation point-ridden, information-thin email from a caseworker in Boston. Aside from one trip to Kentucky for the 20-week ultrasound, our involvement with the pregnancy was disconcertingly minimal. It really was like having a babysitter for our fetus.

The surrogacy agency had recommended that we pursue second-parent adoption—in which a non-biological parent adopts after the baby's birth—but neither of us liked the idea of adopting our own child. We hired a lawyer to get from a California court a pre-birth order designating us as the parents, as we had done in Massachusetts. Just before the baby was born, after many forms and fees, we were legally deemed her parents by the Alameda County Family Court.

Richard and Reba flew in mid-September to Bowling Green, Kentucky, to await the birth, and I joined them after a week. We had invited Gail to come to Massachusetts or to California for the birth, but, between her work and her kids, that turned out to be too much adventure, even for Gail. I wasn't excited. I figured that Kentucky would be full of homophobia, guns and fatty foods, and maybe not so safe for a black man, a Jew and their black-Jewish daughter. Richard had gone with Gail to meet the obstetrician, who, when faced with the requirements of our surrogacy plan, turned hostile and scheduled her labor to be induced on what later turned out to be a day he would be on a golfing trip. After the meeting, Richard, who is not prone to tears, cried on Gail's shoulder.

Not long after my arrival, while Richard and I were in a matinee of *Zombieland*, our lawyer called to report that the local family court had refused to domesticate the California court order, leaving things in legal limbo. She said she would threaten to sue Kentucky for violating the Full Faith and Credit clause of the Constitution and instructed us to get out of there as soon as the baby was born. I felt vaguely unsafe and out of sorts. People seemed to stare at us. One night I dreamed that the baby was born healthy, and then stolen.

However, when Madeleine Blanche came along a few days later (full head of black hair, long eyelashes, tongue sticking out), that sense of danger had receded. Gail's mother had been with her throughout labor, and held her hand in the delivery room when it got rough. Richard and I had stood behind Gail, watching the obstetrician, a kind, efficient, direct woman, work with Gail, as a forceful nurse ordered Gail to push. My parents and Richard's mother were in the waiting room with Reba. When it was over, we said goodbye to Gail, who went to sleep while we went off to the maternity ward to be regularly awakened by a hungry baby. I wondered if Gail would feel lonely, but couldn't ask.

Our presence seemed to send the staff of women at the Bowling Green medical center into Southern hospitality overdrive: they dispensed diapers, advice and coffeecake. We chatted about four year olds, work and the costs of preschool. Nurse Christie brought a button for Reba that said, "I'm a big sister!" Unfamiliar heads popped in and out. Not homophobia but a kind of homophilic curiosity was swirling around us, turning us into objects of gossip but also of generosity. Anxieties about discrimination were one thing, but my assumptions about homophobia now seemed glib and snobbish.

The problem was getting out of there. One sympathetic young clerk had been instructed by hospital lawyers not to put our names down on the birth forms as parents, but Gail had declined to sign anything that gave her legal or financial responsibility for our baby. The clerk tried the form with just a father's name, but the computer spit it back, saying it required a mother. So she sent the forms, along with a copy of the California court order, to the Kentucky Office of Vital Statistics with neither Father nor Mother listed. Her small act of administrative disobedience was, to me, quite touching. The hospital released us and our legally parentless baby.

On our way out, we went to visit Gail, who had mostly been sleeping since the birth. She was dressed and out of bed. Surrounded by her family, she looked refreshed and ready to get back to her post-fetus-sitting life. She'd called to get help from Richard, since the hospital staff was asking her to wait to be released until "our lawyers get back to us." Gail knew Richard would know how to address this.

"You're not refusing to release this patient, are you?" he asked a blank-looking administrator. "You can't legally keep her here, you know. Get her a wheelchair, please." Minutes later, a wheelchair arrived.

We chatted with Gail, her mother and her teenage daughter about Madeleine, and exchanged a few small gifts. Even as Gail held Maddy for a minute, we kept it light, but beneath it I could feel a strong, thin thread connecting all of us for the rest of our lives, maybe more. I might have made that up.

At the airport, the airline agent refused to allow us to fly with the baby without a note from her pediatrician. "She's three days old and we live in California," Richard said. "I'm her doctor." I watched him dig around for his medical license and then scribble something on a piece of paper. When we boarded the plane, with only a release document from the hospital to identify Madeleine, going home with our children felt like some sort of escape attempt.

Months later, we still had no birth certificate. Smelling discrimination again, I indulged in self-righteous daydreams of lawsuits, but my suspicions proved unreliable. For Kentucky officials the problem turned out to be much more mundane than sexual taboo: they didn't want California telling them what to put on their forms. In the end, they issued a birth certificate saying that Gail was the mother, then sealed it and issued an amended one listing Richard and me as the parents.

Finally, one day the birth certificate arrived. Somehow, with all the lawyering and money that preceded it, I was surprised that it was just a piece of paper.

Then I noticed something: the California judge had directed Kentucky to list one of us as Mother and the other as Father, but Kentucky officials refused. Instead, they labeled us Parent and Parent. Kentucky had out-liberaled California.

We picked up Reba from preschool. She was uninterested in the news, but happy for the celebratory dinner, through which the baby slept, eyelashes fluttering.

Outsourcing, marketplaces and intimacies

Looking back at these experiences of family creation through the lens of market-mediated intimacies, and of the outsourcing of private life, there is certainly plenty of evidence that the marketplace is hostile to both short- and long-term intimacy. In our more overtly market-engaged experience—which resulted in Madeleine—we developed connection, trust and attachments *in spite of* the actions of the commercial agency that made and managed the link between Gail and us. To the degree that we forged intimacy, it was limited and transitory. We came together for a specific purpose, and when that goal was reached, when Gail's "babysitting" job was done, we parted. Even in the case of conceiving Reba, which was much less market-based (though much was still outsourced), the path we took was very much informed by the desire to bypass the commercial surrogacy system, on the grounds that it was likely to be less deeply intimate, as indeed it turned out to be.

It also appears, quite predictably, that the stronger the market involvement, the weaker the intimate ties. For instance, our family's relationship to Gail is, and is likely to remain, a relatively weak, inconsistent one involving very little emotional disclosure. We send her holiday cards every year and photos of Maddy and Reba every few months. She sends occasional news about her kids: last I heard, the older one was deciding to stay in Bowling Green for college so she could be near her boyfriend, the middle one was asking to learn to play piano, and the littlest one was obsessed with horses. Our relationship to Tamar, and also to Andy— they are no longer together—was dramatically strengthened and deepened through Reba's creation. They had been friends, but they became family. Although the relationship with Andy has faded, we see him periodically and he remains in our loose kinship network. Our relationship with Tamar is more intensively and self-consciously present. We see her a couple of times a year, and talk a few more. Although we have been cautious about using "mother" in association with Tamar, which we all agree is both inaccurate and confusing, we sometimes refers to Tamar as Reba's "belly mommy," which reminds Reba that she came into the world like everyone else. More routinely, she is known as Aunt Tamar. For the past two years, Aunt Tamar has taken Reba, without us, to her family reunion in Michigan; that family is already a mix of biological, half-biological and by-marriage kin, and Reba joins the mix as a sort of special guest star.

These experiences are much more complex and nuanced than the critical concerns about the commodification and outsourcing of personal life might suggest. They serve as reminders, first, that the outsourcing of such private, personal experiences is not in itself destructive. Even with payment, these family creation processes produced unusual new relationships, or new depths to existing ones. We did not just arrange for others to provide the service of reproduction. We also brought people *into* our family, expanding rather than simply delegating to others its intimacies. We became connected, literally combining elements of ourselves. Market transactions and agents did not determine the sorts of relationships that we developed, any more than, say, a matchmaker determines the type of relationship between potential romantic partners. We made our own intimate idiocultures, temporary but with lasting effects, facilitated in part by commercial brokers or by financial transactions we chose. Indeed, at times, much as Zelizer (2000) describes, we used, or simply allowed, the market to "mark the character and range of the social relationship" we were enacting (Zelizer 2000: 842): most importantly, payment marked the boundary between a parental and non-parental relationship to the baby, a boundary all of us involved wanted and needed.

Between the adults, the relationships these experiences produced range from minimal intimacy to maximal. I've already weathered dramatic conflict and changes with Tamar since Reba's birth, and the connection has survived; I am not sure I'll see Gail again, or that either of us would feel that as a loss. Yet even we are permanently bound by the creatures we produced. That is its own kind of intimacy—a spiritual one, in a sense, if not always a practical one.

A couple of years ago, when she was four, Reba asked me if Tamar was at my wedding to Richard. She already knew the answer was yes—she regularly asked to hear "the wedding story" before bed and had seen the photos—but she seemed to want confirmation before she continued.

"So I've known her forever," Reba said.

"Yes," I replied. "Since you were an embryo. Maybe even before that. Hard to know."

"Before that," she said with certainty. "Because I was at your and Daddy's wedding. When I was a spirit. I was sitting on Tamar's lap."

Notes

1 A small portion of the material in this chapter is adapted from my piece "My New Kentucky Baby," which appeared in *The New York Times Magazine* (May 22, 2011).

References

Hertz, Rosanna. 2006. *Single By Chance, Mothers By Choice: How Women Are Choosing Parenthood Without Marriage and Creating the New American Family*. New York: Oxford University Press.

Hochschild, Arlie. 2012. *The Outsourced Self: Intimate Life in Market Times*. New York: Metropolitan Books.

Lewin, Ellen. 2009. *Gay Fatherhood: Narratives of Family and Citizenship in America*. Chicago: University of Chicago Press.

Mundy, Liza. 2007. *Everything Conceivable: How Assisted Reproduction Is Changing Men, Women, and the World*. New York: Knopf.

Stacey, Judith. 2011. *Unhitched: Love, Marriage, and Family Values from West Hollywood to Western China*. New York: New York University Press.

Zelizer, Viviana A. 2000. "The Purchase of Intimacy." *Law & Soc. Inquiry* 25: 817–48.

Part IV

Unsettling intimacies

Anxieties, violence, misrecognition

10 Intimacy, lateral relationships and biopolitical governance

Patricia Ticineto Clough

The viscosity, the heat, the oil drips down my cheek, as I sit; my feet barely reach the floor. My mother is performing a ritual, exorcising an evil spirit that she told me was put into me because of some other little girl's jealousy. The exorcism begins with me in a chair up against the kitchen sink. I look up into her face over me, into the small black centers of her eyes. My mother is doing what I know only the ordained were meant to do. I am frightened but fascinated too. I do not move. So it always seemed that *even before I was I, God was displeased with me*,[1] having been found guilty of some sort of receptivity or complicity. If only I could, I would place my big sister there, to sit beside me, hold my hand and insist we both resist my mother. Instead there is only loneliness in my sister's inability to attend to me; her means of psychic survival would seem to be a denial of a mutual infection of wounds.

Even after years of psychoanalysis, I do not yet fully understand the relationship between my sister and me. It is not that psychoanalysis has not offered me profound insights into this relationship. It is that the relationship began in a place and time marked by violence and psychological abuse met with a collusive denial and dissociation. My sister and I lived our early childhoods in post-World War II Corona, Queens, New York, where the civil rights movement was being played out in everyday life. White children and their families were fleeing the community as Corona was becoming defined as having a "psychological quality," suffering from "urban blight," as the planning consultants hired by the city would put it (Gregory 1998: 90). The consultants would formalize what everyone already knew. Running under the elevated train tracks, Roosevelt Avenue had become an informal boundary between South Corona and North Corona. As the consultants described it, "since the 1950s," North Corona "has absorbed a large percentage of Negroes with serious problems of social disorder while the area south of Roosevelt Avenue remains stable solidly white and predominantly Italian" (ibid.: 91).[2]

Although white and Italian, my family lived in North Corona, where the "social problems" outside our three-room apartment resonated with the "private troubles inside."[3] Yet my sister and I did not find refuge in each other; we were not able to support each other in relationship to family or the community. Not only do we have very few shared memories of our childhood, of being sisters growing up together, but also the few memories we do share are anything but loving ones. Although the older one, my sister has admitted that she did not care for me or take care of me and on occasions even treated me badly. My own dissociation left me without much consciousness of my response to her or any certainty of the location from which acts of hatred and violence originated.

In what follows, I want to expand the notion of intimacy beyond the more common understanding of it as pertaining to relationships of trust and openness, authenticity and ultimate belonging. While often enfolding these normative expectations as an idealized form of intimacy, intimacy actually is experienced along a continuum of trust, openness, authenticity and belonging, including the exploitation of these inside the family but also in situations that bring relative strangers into close contact, in sites of biopolitical governance outside the family, such as schools, religious, medical and therapeutic environments, police stations, detention centers, barracks and prisons. In treating this expanded conception of intimacy, I will touch on the familial and community relationships in which my sister and I grew up, still for us a psychic reality, in order to focus more fully on sibling or lateral relations and explore their relevancy to an expanded conception of intimacy befitting the social realities of the times.

I will bring together the work of the anthropologist Ann Laura Stoler and the psychoanalyst Juliet Mitchell with current understandings of what Michel Foucault referred to as biopolitical governance in order to explore the interrelatedness of intimacy and power or the necessity of intimate relations for power to operate and, in its operation, shape what intimacy is perceived to be.[4] What follows also is informed by my being in psychoanalysis over the past six years, during which time I also have been visiting Corona with my students, some of whom are now living there. Together we have been exploring what it is like to grow up in Corona, spending time with various groups of kids who also live there now.[5]

Lateral relationships, violence and sexuality

In what she calls "geographies of intimacy," Stoler means to direct our attention to the way relationships of power work "through tense and tender ties" (Stoler 2006). For Stoler, it is intimate relationships that "serve as transfer points of power"—not as a microcosm of power but as its marrow (ibid.: 9). While Stoler takes as her examples intimate relationships in North American colonialism and empire, her perspective is meant generally to shift the focus on intimacy beyond the domestic, in order that the study of intimacy critically engage sites of intimacy and possible intrusive intervention such as schools, medical and therapeutic environments, and religious institutions.

I take Stoler's point to be that what might be thought of as the darker side of intimacy is not merely a failure of intimacy but part of, if not a constitutive part of, the more idealized and normative forms of intimacy—shown at a scale other than the individual. For Stoler, as for me, the other scale is biopolitical governance with its focus on life itself and its differential distribution of capacities for living—here, the capacity for intimacy—among various populations. These populations are not preestablished ones but are constituted in the very distribution of the capacity for intimacy that might better be understood as a distribution of degrees of freedom or unfreedom in intimate relations. Although this expanded view of intimacy looks beyond the domestic, the domestic is not, however, excluded from analysis. Not only is the domestic or home usually where intimacy is first entwined with power and where both the idealized and the dark side of intimacy can be experienced all of a piece,[6] but it is also where the governance of populations meets the disciplining of the individual's body and psyche and one site where the domestic, personal, private and public are being reconfigured with the ongoing operation of biopolitical governance.

While it might seem appropriate, then, to see the power relationship between doctor and patient, priest and parishioner, teacher and student, therapist and client to be based on the power relationship between parent and child, a broader perspective ought to allow for peer or lateral relations that often are part of the scenes of power and intimacy both in the family and beyond. Mitchell has argued for the importance of a psychoanalytic understanding of sibling or lateral relationships, their link to parental or vertical relations but also their relative autonomy from them, in order to rethink intimacy in relationship to violence, hatred and love, annihilation and survival.

> Of the few memories I have of my sister, this is one that returns me again and again to a scene of nightmarish qualities. It is a scene of punishment for something I had done. I don't remember what but my sister had complained to my parents and I was sent to stand in the corner. My punishment included having to tell my father the time by reading the face of the clock that was on the dresser beside my parents' bed. One side of the dresser made part of the corner with the other part being a wall. I did not yet know how to tell time but it seemed I was expected to since I would not be set free until I did. Even now I can feel the anxiety that I felt, worried that I would not ever be set free. The roman numerals on the clock's face said nothing to me and yet the clock itself was fascinating; it had a pendulum and I became fixed on it, keeping with its regular and mechanical movement, turning one way then the other, as I tried not to experience the worst part: the three of them—my mother, father and sister—standing together at a distance from me, behind me, laughing at me as I made mistake after mistake failing to tell the correct time. The wall was painted a horrid shade of blue.
>
> It was just after the 1954 decision of *Brown vs. Board of Education*, when the informally segregated schools of Corona were desegregated. My sister and I were attending Our Lady of Sorrows School in South Corona. It was a long walk from our three-room apartment in North Corona to the school. Neither my sister nor I now can remember why she would not walk with me, why I walked alone each day to school and back. By the time my family finally left Corona, it was later than most of the other white families we knew. Eventually "70 percent of Corona's White population left the city to Long Island, Westchester, Rockland and other New York counties" (Gregory 1998: 60). I don't know what I heard in those years. I am not sure what meaning I gave to my parents' wanting to leave Corona. I only know that I identified with those they wanted to leave behind. My identification with African Americans eventually flowered into religious commitments and then political ones.

For Mitchell, the lateral relationship of siblings is to be psychoanalytically under-stood in terms of what she describes as "the law of the mother" (Mitchell 2003). This is not the pre-Oedipal mother, the figure of the "primitive" space or the temporal prior-ness of early infancy (ibid.: 52). This is the mother who introduces the child into "seriality," delivering the child to difference and sameness in the lateral relations of siblings or peers (ibid.: 44, 53). She is the mother who turns birth order into a matter of love over violence and hate, modulating the anxiety of annihilation: where I once was now someone else is, displaced, replaced or just no longer there (ibid.: 48). As the child moves from the ecstasy of oneness to dif-ference and near despair, it is the mother or someone else's care that assures the child that there is room for her and others like her too. Without this law intern-alized, or without a maternal care, love and hate remain confused, opening up the possibility of violent abuse between siblings or peers.

However, sibling relations are not merely organized around the arrival of another child, a problem only for a first-born. A second child or third also experience potential annihilation, struggling to comprehend another already born, in my place and yet different than me. In this sense, lateral relations are an early experience in a child's life even if there are no siblings and only playmates, cousins, classmates; it is the experience of difference and sameness in seriality: not a mere adding on to the parental relationship but the working of a different structure. In this sense, lateral relationships are as central as vertical ones in the development of the child as they open the child to the many kinds of relationships with which she or he will be engaged throughout his or her life, those character-ized by annihilation and survival, violence and sexuality, hatred and love. The existence of another child like myself but different than me also can incite in the child the necessity to understand something beyond their cognitive capacity; it can initiate in the child abstract thought and philosophical wonderment, and can create in the child a sense of mind like a womb, giving birth to ideas, numbers and numbers of them (Mitchell 2003: 69).

In taking up lateral relationships between siblings and peers, Mitchell notes that they have not been central to psychoanalytic theory or practice. Reviewing arguments made by Freud and other early psychoanalytic writers, as well as taking up the case studies they presented, Mitchell finds siblings in these accounts who then seem to disappear from the discussion, as the sibling relationship, for the most part, is assimilated to the vertical relations of parent and child. This results, she proposes, in the way sexuality and gender generally have been understood in psychoanalysis over the post-World War I and World War II years. As Mitchell sees it, psychoanalysis in those years is marked by a focus on infant and mother, a shift from the earlier focus in psychoanalysis on the relationship of the father and child. With this shift, sexual difference became central to discus-sions of sexuality at the same time that it was aligned with sexual reproduction. Thus, sexual difference would be understood as a matter of what is lost to each sex—masculine and feminine—or what the other has, necessary to heterosexual union and reproduction (Mitchell 2003: 49).

What Mitchell finds interesting about sibling or lateral relations is that they are about difference and sameness in a series, so that sibling sexuality is not linked to lack and desire against the horizon of reproduction. Instead, Mitchell suggests that sibling sexuality is linked to nonreproductive, nonheterosexual relations of violence: hatred and love, annihilation and survival. Her account of sibling sexuality begins with her understanding of gender in relationship to the law of the mother, the law which, Mitchell proposes, establishes generational difference around who can reproduce and who cannot. Since neither the boy nor the girl child can reproduce, the law of the mother does not yet determine masculinity or femininity for the child. For the child, gender is not structured around sexual difference; "difference is not intrinsic to the concept" (Mitchell 2003: 125). Neither implying genitality nor a fixed sexual object, gender is the characteristic of "the polymorphously perverse child grown up" (ibid.: 125). Underscoring these points, Mitchell troubles Judith Butler's invitation to trouble gender, concluding that "gender, unlike sexual difference, is not constructed as a binary" (ibid.: 127). With this take on gender, Mitchell goes on to treat sibling sexuality as a matter of violence, hate and love.

> When we were older, I asked her why she did it and she replied that it was because I had annoyed her. Another memory takes shape, one that still is hard for me to believe except she said it was true that she had stuck a pencil into my scalp and at another time, she had cut through the skin on my leg with a scissor making a line of blood down my thigh. I can't feel when I remember these incidences; the memory of them, of us sitting together on my parents' bed where these incidences occurred becomes vague, as we two little girls, sisters, seem slowly to disappear into the white crocheted bed spread. It seems to me that we were left there, not allowed to get down from the bed. I couldn't get away from her but I don't know if I tried; I don't know if I cried. I don't know if I called for my mother.
>
> She told me that she remembered a time, when I was two years old or so, when my grandmother was scolding my mother, telling her she had to stop hitting me. My sister said that my mother left her hand print on my face. As a memory begins to take form, I can see my grandmother and my mother but I cannot imagine how hard you would have to hit a child to leave a hand print on her face. I told my sister that I remembered my father punching her again and again in the arm because she wouldn't eat her breakfast. She said that she remembered that. Sitting next to her at the table, I can feel that punch going through her body right into mine.

Not about the resolution of sexual difference, sibling relationships point to the need for a resolution of violence: being able to accept instead of murdering the other who is so like me. In her reading of *A Child is Being Beaten*, for example, Mitchell proposes that the sexuality of the sibling can be shown as being linked to violence. Rather than the usual interpretation that the beating fantasy is about the siblings' rivalry for the exclusive love of the parent of the opposite sex and that the fantasy conflates sexuality and parental punishment, Mitchell suggests that the fantasy also points to the fact that the child's sexuality most likely is awakened in relationship to the sibling or peer, where there often is joint masturbation but also cruelty, torment, torture, even seduction, and the creation of fantasy. What constitutes sibling sexuality in relation to the beating fantasy is its ongoing enactment as fantasy and/or actions, using past events which "have a present significance—they are still exciting" (Mitchell 2003: 98).[7]

Mitchell reminds us that "the ecstasy of killing, the wish to kill or to get under the skin of the other, all seem nearer to echoes of sibling lateral states than to infant–parent ones" (Mitchell 2003: 106). This drive or wish to kill, like sexual difference, Mitchell concludes, is part of psychic formation and becomes crucial to unconscious processes precisely because murderousness towards self or others is prohibited as part of the prohibition against sibling incest. This murderousness is not, however, a matter of envy in the Kleinian sense. For Mitchell, murderousness towards the sibling does not need to be repaired; nor does gratitude seem to be the positive reversal. Rather, hatred and violence can be "reversed into love." As Mitchell sees it, "hatred and violence are ... related not to envy but to trauma. Psychically obliterated by a traumatic experience, the signs of life are fury and hatred" (ibid.: 41).

> Perhaps an important marker of our similarity and difference was the position of our beds, iron cots pulled out each night. My sister's placed right next to my parents' bed, the three of them head to head to head. Mine was placed at the foot of the bed, near enough to touch their feet moving under the sheet. Just beyond, just over their heads, a crucifix hung that my sister could not see from where she lay. It hung there, I thought, only for me: to condemn or protect me I could not be sure from the evil spirits that I thought I saw all around. She with my parents and me left to pray the rosary, counting Hail Marys, against the return of some other little girl's jealousy.
>
> It was hard to find quiet in the tiny three-room apartment where we lived in North Corona. There was a good deal of noise on the streets and my mother screamed frequently enough to unsettle any peace inside the apartment. At some point, I tried not to hear all the noise. My sister has told me I was always by myself, out of it, in a fog, but I had found something like solitude, a world in my head where there was an ongoing conversation about things all around me. There was God and praying, reading, writing and piano playing. These made me feel safe no matter how lonely. When I was 18, I became a Roman Catholic nun. Although I kept the vows of poverty, chastity and obedience, the feeling of being bad persisted, returning again and again. My sister did not become a nun; she got married in her early twenties. Growing up in impoverished Corona left her wanting things—lots and lots of them. She married a man who would make a great deal of money. She and her family have lived in huge homes with furnishings from her travels all over the world. She spends a great amount of money on her appearance and buys beautiful clothes and jewelry.

Lateral relations and identifying with the aggressor

Needless to say, the lateral relationships between siblings, although relatively autonomous of vertical relationships with parents, nonetheless are most likely affected by them. Although Mitchell does not specify just how parents might affect siblings' relationship, it would certainly seem that, to the extent that parents are hateful with tendencies to violence, the relationship between siblings most likely will not fare well, while the origin of the aggression or the actual identity of the aggressor may remain confused. This confusion may be a matter of the child's unconscious identification with the aggressor, not necessarily becoming an aggressor, but something much more complicated, something akin to the intimacy shared between the partners of the aggression.

> My mother was born in Milwaukee Wisconsin in 1909, just two years after her mother and her mother's sister, both teenage girls, arrived by sail from Messina, Sicily, where in 1908 an earthquake killed nearly everyone including my grandmother's mother, father and brother. My grandmother was married in 1908 to an American man also from Sicily, who would hold me in his arms just after I was born, just months before he died from an alcohol-related disease. The first time my mother told me, I was eight months pregnant. She told me that her father beat her mother brutally after they had sex. He also beat her brother and I think my grandfather might have hurt my mother too. She sometimes implied just that but other than the very few and rare exchanges about him and what he was like when he was drunk, my mother seemed to idolize her father, my grandfather.
>
> As adults both my parents refused to talk with their siblings for a number of years at a time; I don't remember why. I found the ongoing family feuds unbearable and tried to avoid any involvement. I especially was affected by my father's relationship to his one and only brother who had been good to me when I was a young child, but my father stopped talking to his brother when they were still young men. My father refused to communicate with him even as my father lay dying. At the age of five my father had been sent back to Italy with his grandmother and grandfather and was not able to return to his parents in the USA until he was 10. He particularly hated his mother for leaving him there, especially since his grandfather had not been kind to him. He also hated his brother, who was born when my father was 14, four years after he had returned from Italy. My father's sense of abandonment became a way of being and when he married my mother, she offered no solace. When married, my parents moved to Corona, then a community mostly of immigrants, mostly Italian immigrants.

Following the work of Sándor Ferenczi, Jay Frankel argues that identification with the aggressor is "a pervasive change in someone's perceptual world" (Frankel 2002: 102). If terrified by adults who are out of control, the child will subordinate him- or herself to the aggressor's will, "to divine each one of his desires and to gratify these" (ibid.: 103). The child "becomes one" with the aggressor, feeling what the aggressor feels or what the aggressor wants the child to feel. As the child makes every effort to be inside the experience of the aggressor, "he fills the void left by dissociation of her own feelings and perceptions with an ever-vigilant, overheated intelligence." "Dissociation clears the way for identifying with the aggressor ..." (ibid.: 110).

What is to be underscored, however, is that the identification is not necessarily with the characteristics of another, the aggressor let us say, but with a pattern of interacting that is not negotiated; rather, it is a pattern of interaction that is imported or imposed. While for the child it is likely that the threatening other is a parent, Mitchell would remind us that the sibling, too, can be threatening, or the sibling easily may be part of the pattern of a repeating abusive interaction. If nothing else, a sibling's failure to recognize the other's distress or help the other sibling may be experienced as emotional abandonment, which Frankel, following Ferenczi, proposes "is the worst trauma" (Frankel 2002: 131). It is trauma that is at issue, when dissociation "takes away the reality feeling from the traumatic reality and instead attaches to it a fantasy feeling, thus serving as a bridge for the introjection of the experience: It allows the actual, outer events to feel like a private, controllable fantasy" (ibid.: 113). Thus, an identification with the aggressor leaves the child confused about his or her own experience, making it possible to introject a sense of badness and guilt that belong to the aggressor.

In her discussion of malignant trauma and what she describes as "the reproduction of evil," Sue Grand addresses this confusion. She argues that confusional states "suffuse all human cruelty"; thus, the traumatized person is drawn back to evil, not necessarily as a perpetrator, but back to the scene of the annihilation desiring clarity or to be recognized in that very experience, the experience of becoming unknowable, the production of a "no-self" and the reproduction of evil (Grand 2002: 3–9). It is evil, Grand concludes, that "seduces with its perverse promise of recognition" (ibid.: 7). This recognition is impossible in that trauma by definition remains unknowable. It also is impossible because the traumatic reproduction of evil often is characterized by a collusive denial and a more general erasure of events by the perpetrator, the victim and bystanders; there is "a shared attempt at metabolizing and redissociating overwhelming affects of hate, shame, despair, and fear" (ibid.: 16). Part of malignant trauma, then, is the refusal, or the inability of the victim's peers, to see and understand what is happening, never mind make an effort to stop it.

> No one knew why I had picked up the large chunk of broken glass that would rip the tendon of the middle finger of my right hand. The cut was bad enough that I had to be hospitalized. Even now, I can remember the operating room, the nauseating smell of the ether dropping down on the mask over my face as I fell into a fog. After the surgery, there was a nurse, a Roman Catholic nun, dressed all in white, who took care of me as best she could. However, for most of the night, no nurses were available and the kids ran around the ward unattended. There was an older girl who frightened me. When the lights were turned off, she would stand over my bed staring down at me just before throwing cups of cold water all over me. Being wet felt terrible but I couldn't move. I didn't call out. I didn't complain. I eventually came down with a terrible, terrible cold. My father sometimes came to visit me in the hospital but neither my mother nor sister ever did. I was just turning five but I remember that. A short time after the surgery, there was a second surgery to correct something that had gone wrong with the first.

Corona is no longer a community of black and white; it is now the home of a number of recently immigrated ethnic groups. It amazes me how much of the physical structures nevertheless have remained the same, even as names of stores change. The colors are as I remember them then and the smells of the flowering shrubs bring me back immediately to that other time walking to the church to pray, terrified of the dogs along the way. Now as I walk those same streets, the sound of music is rhythmically pounding out of the open windows of teenagers' cars and sirens are blasting frequently enough to remind everyone that the neighborhood is still "tough." The kids in Corona tell me of the violence, at home, at school and along the way, everyone stopped and frisked, every one of them wishing to leave but wanting to stay, knowing somehow they never really will get away. I think Corona will remain on their minds and in their bodies. Some of them tell me how much they pray as they clutch the rosary beads, hanging down from around their necks.

In his treatment of identification with the aggressor, Frankel suggests that such identifications are not unusual, although in more extreme cases, such as those involving malignant trauma, there can be more damage. Identification more usually occurs as part of relations where there is the possibility of an asymmetrical exertion of power as in so many social situations there is. Focusing on lateral relationships with their characteristic sameness and difference reminds us that identification with the aggressor may happen not only in vertical relations but also in lateral ones where there are issues of sexuality and violence, love and hate, annihilation and survival.

It would seem that lateral relationships have special relevance today when intimacy is migrating from the demands of heteronormativity, homonormativity, ethnic and racial exclusivity, and where there can be more negotiation between peers in various types of relationships, or at least where there is awareness of all these possibilities as there is in more and more parts of the world and across various populations. Not only is sexuality being separated from reproduction through various biotechnologies and mechanisms of birth control, but heteronormativity, as well as homonormativity, is yielding some space to queer, transgendered and transsexual identities and object choices.

To propose that laterality plays a large part in these intimate relations is to suggest that these relations may be closer to the complexities of love and hate, survival and annihilation, closer perhaps than to the desires of vertical relationships. In this sense, these relations also are closer to those relations where intimacy arises between relative strangers—that is, all the relationships with those who distribute resources for intimacy, health, safety, religious inspiration and personal growth, where each of us often must operate entrepreneurially in the context of neoliberal privatization in biopolitical governance. To link intimacy and lateral relationships with biopolitics is to put an historical and sociopolitical spin on Mitchell's thinking about siblings beyond her own brief remarks about the history of psychoanalysis. It even raises the question as to the status of the law, the law of the mother, thus making room for the sociopolitical and historical contingency of such a law.

Intimacy and biopolitical governance

Biopower as Foucault has described it includes two forms of power meant to bring life into governance: one, discipline, and the other, biopolitics. The former makes the life of the individual a matter for "infinitesimal surveillances, permanent controls, extremely meticulous orderings of space, indeterminate medical or psychological examinations, an entire micro-power concerned with the body" (Foucault 1979: 145–46).[8] The other, biopolitics, turns to the life capacities of populations, or the regulation of the productive economic and biological capacities of human life at a mass scale," and where population is "a sort of technical political object of management and security ... dependent on series of variables, and a statistical analysis that constitutes an actuarialism, potentially productive rather than merely representational" (Foucault 2007: 70). If discipline is power exerted on the individual "to make live" or live in a certain way, biopolitical technologies are a matter of making live, but at the level of the populations. As Foucault put it, "So after a first seizure of power over the body in an individualizing mode, we have a second seizure of power that is not individualizing, but, if you like, massifying, that is directed not at man-as-body but at man-as-species" (Foucault 2003: 243). In the latter, governmentality works its power through technical solutions, making use of samples, data, markets, banks and the like, assembled in genetic codes, identification numbers, ratings profiles and preference listings—that is to say, bodies of coded data (including human bodies as coded data).

While Foucault's remarks seem to suggest a linear progression from individual body to species, or a move from disciplinary to biopolitical society, Foucault more often suggested that biopower always works as the governance of a constituted multiplicity that must also govern in depth, at the level of the fine points and details of the individual or the singular. He argued that sexuality is exemplary of the intersection of these two forms of power: "at the juncture of the 'body' and the 'population,' sex became a crucial target of a power organized around the management of life ..." both of individual and species (Foucault 1979: 147). For example, Foucault suggests that in the 19th century the sexualization of children and the intense attention leveled at the woman or mother's body were on behalf of the species and its reproduction, but the aim was to obtain results at the level of discipline of individuals and the family as well. Here, psychoanalysis played a part; from the 19th century well into the 20th century, it played a part in establishing the mother's role as the pre-Oedipal mother in relationship to the "law of the father," with desire elaborated as Oedipal desire.

However, as Foucault saw it, biopower would increasingly come to dominate power relations when the family no longer can serve as the model of economy and when governance cannot be modeled on the good father who provides. Rather, political economy becomes the stuff of governmentality, increasingly with a focus on the technical management of populations. In terms of biopolitical governance, the family is only a segment of population, even if the privileged instrument of governance, or a privileged resource for data concerning individual family members. What might once have been considered family matters of sexual and physical abuse, and as such matters of discipline, also are a matter of bio-political control through statistical measures, made a normal matter, but where the boundary between the normal and abnormal is not so much at issue. Instead, there is an investment in comparisons of relative normalcies across various institutions such as the school, the church, the medical and therapeutic establishments, just as these very institutions increasingly must bear up under the private, but now widely publicized failures of institutional figures of authority.

The comparison of normalcies constitutes populations in series often marked by differences and similarities along lines of race, gender, sexuality, ethnicity, class, but increasingly less as a matter of identity than as a matter of risk management, with scales measuring the potential for well-being and the capacity for happiness, health, intelligence, and hope.[9] Thus, populations, constituted in the management of risk, also cross through families as well as races, ethnicities, sexes, classes and genders, transforming, if not in some cases dismantling, the behaviors and identities these categories of population have implied. The capacity for intimacy is not determined by race, class, etc.; rather, these are transformed as the capacity for intimacy is distributed in biopolitical governance. While Stoler argues that to treat intimacy in terms of biopolitics "is not to turn away from structures of dominance but to relocate their conditions of possibility and relations and forces of production" (Stoler 2006: 13), it also might be added that biopolitics points to power relations other than those of sheer dominance and its resistance.

In all this, familial relations still haunt, but perhaps it is the relationships between siblings, lateral relations, that are coming to haunt the most. It may be these relationships that are the "strangely familiar" that Stoler argues we experience in the uses and abuses of intimacy, unsolicited and even desired ones (Stoler 2006: 14). In focusing on intimacy and laterality in relation to biopolitical governance, the law of the father is historically and sociopolitically relativized, as is the centrality of the pre-Oedipal mother. As Mitchell suggests, while the pre-Oedipal mother was made central in psychoanalysis with its turn to object relations, the mother's relationship to siblings or lateral relations nonetheless remained invisible (Mitchell 2003: 31). It is this relationship that now is pressing for engagement sociologically but in psychoanalysis, too, where the shift to relationality may necessitate that transference and countertransference be considered a lateral relationship at least as much as a vertical one.

Sociology, psychoanalysis and philosophy: my sister and me

While intimacy is promoted as a matter of optimism, Lauren Berlant argues, it "is also formed around threats to the image of the world it seeks to sustain" (Berlant 2000: 7). This often leaves us with what Berlant calls "cruel optimism," a repetitive seeking of intimacy that is optimistic but which will not, cannot, ever actually be optimistic (Berlant 2011). Nonetheless, these experiences of a cruel optimism are intimate experiences; they are experiences of intimacy that shape perception of intimacy. I began this essay proposing that I do not yet fully understand the relationship between my sister and me, even after years of psychoanalysis. Maybe it would have been better to say that I have not been able to bear what I do know or what I do know remains not yet fully thought. Even though we remain sisters and, as best we can, offer our families, our children and grandchildren a sense of belonging, I still have not found a way to share with my sister what matters to me most or to be recognized by her, as I would like to be, for who I think I really am. She may feel the same way about me. I do not know; nor do I know if our childhood continues to break her heart as it does mine. It doesn't seem so.

I do know my relationship to my sister continues to haunt all my relationships, not least my relationship to Corona. My childhood there opened me to seek alliances with those who are excluded, like those in Corona who, in my childhood, and now too, suffer violence, hatred and loneliness. Corona is for me (and not only me) an icon of those places created by various forces to bear more violence, more hatred and perhaps more love than other places do; it is a place where annihilation threatens but where survival is magnificent for all the effort it takes to survive. I feel grateful to be able to go back to where I once lived, to know again my own struggles to survive. I take the alliances that I seek as providing a way to face once again former identifications with the aggressions in my family, the identifications of my childhood in Corona. Returning to Corona offers the possibility of breaking once and for all with these identifications, although I know this will be a never fully realized possibility.

I therefore recognize that my childhood identifications are mixed up with my identification with those living in Corona today and this mixup frames what I know and what I cannot know about them. It makes it necessary to practice a certain reserve, a certain humility when I write, inviting experimentation in presentation. That is to say, my childhood in Corona has made it necessary to bring sociology and psychoanalysis into contact with each other. While sociology has enabled me to broaden my understanding of my childhood Corona and to have an enriched understanding of present-day Corona, sociology often does not have as its agenda the study of the individual's inner life and therefore has not developed the capacities for entering deeply into an individual's unconscious. I do not mean that sociology has not offered in-depth case studies of subjects. It has, but these case studies do not offer analyses of subjects' unconscious processes. However, I also do not mean that sociology only needs a supplementary dose of psychoanalysis.

Psychoanalysis cannot be meshed fully with sociology because psychoanalysis offers a very different method of understanding than that of an empirical social science and, therefore, and more importantly, it offers a very different relationship to not knowing or what Christopher Bollas calls "the unthought known" (Bollas 1987). Psychoanalysis offers a relationship to the unthought and encourages a style that expresses this in one's scholarship, research and writing. This demands a special kind of openness to experimentation on the part of the scholar, researcher and writer so that the unthought can come through, affectively making its way to the presentational surface, allowing the unconscious to resonate in the writing through style. In this sense, it is my practice of psychoanalysis that has opened me to a philosophical appreciation of an aesthetic of presentation.

Recently, philosophers have returned to aesthetics as a response to their growing awareness of the largely pre-conscious, not yet conscious or unconscious affective relations between persons and persons and things: the way we affect and are affected, without intentionality, more as a bodily matter than a conscious or cognitive one (Shaviro 2009, 2010; Harman 2007, 2009; Morton 2012; Moran 2012; Massumi 2002; Clough 2007). The return to aesthetics is a way for philosophers to ground this move to express or present in ways that are affective, beyond or without words, and thus to recognize the contamination of knowing with not knowing; to do so without seeking necessarily to reduce or always reduce these contaminating effects. The point is to recognize these effects as affects or as forces of causality, an "aesthetic causality." Here, aesthetics means "having to do with appearance," as the philosopher Timothy Morton (2012) puts it. However, for Morton, appearance refers to the sensual qualities of persons and objects, those qualities that actually make it possible for things to relate or take account of each other, and where "causality is alluring," as the philosopher Graham Harman (2007, 2009) has put it.

My reason for this brief and passing mention of a philosophical movement afoot at this time is to point to the very wide canvas it suggests upon which intimacy now can take its place. It suggests that intimacy is entwined with the sensual qualities of persons and things that allow for relations, causal relations, in the first place. An aesthetic is expressed singularly by each thing and person as its capacity to affect and be affected, so that things and persons can feel and be felt by one another and by feeling become however slightly or massively changed, caused to become different things. Here, however, there is adjustment to be made to Bollas's suggestion that each of us acquires an aesthetic beginning with the way the mother holds, the way she thereby provides an environs for the infant child, so the child does not even have to think to survive; rather he or she can just feel and survive sensually (Bollas 1987: 34–35, 64–81). The adjustment to be made is to include sibling or lateral relations and the sensual or aesthetic qualities these relations offer. The aesthetic is not given only by the mother, no matter how important her place in elaborating sensuality for the infant. Nor is it only a matter of the human; all things are alluring. Things, places, events can be affective and be affected; there is an "intimacy of things," as the philosopher Steven Shaviro (2010) puts it.

In keeping with this adjustment, I want to emphasize that the aesthetic which philosophers today are critically engaging is that of the beautiful, a matter of forces of attraction and repulsion. This is because the aesthetic of the beautiful refers to responsiveness, a repulsion or attraction of forces that is without the guide of reason, concept, consciousness or cognition. The aesthetic of the beautiful has to do with things "in the way they cannot be cognized or subordinated to concepts," as Shaviro (2010: 7) argues. However, this is not due to a failed cognition but due to the ontology of things and persons where, if they connect, they connect first affectively, below or before cognition. This connectivity is a matter of allure which, having the capacity to hold with the grip of beauty, commands responsiveness; although without concept or cognition, connectivity wants to be communicated. It is communicated aesthetically.

Now, I look back and read what I have written, what I have placed on these pages for me as much as for you. I see the way my stories hang there, connected to and disconnected from psychoanalytic theories, sociopolitical and historical specifications of relations of race, class, ethnicity, gender and sexuality. The stories, isolated and reaching for connection, are out of joint even with themselves, trembling, full of suggestion, still moving with the known that is not fully thought. They are connected to and disconnected from my sister and parents whom I am without and who are inside me; my stories are presented with an unconscious force. It is all intimate, all too intimate: the intimacy of violence and sexuality, annihilation and survival, hatred and love.

Notes

1 The line from John Donne's 1625 poem *Sermon* actually is "And God was displeased with me before I was I." The line is quoted in Juliet Mitchell's *Siblings* (2003: 59) and it appears as part of a title of a book she co-edited with Enid Balint and Michael Parsons, *Before I was I: Psychoanalysis and the Imagination* (1993).

2 Gregory is quoting from the Hart, Krisvatsy, and Stubee Report (Corona-East Elmhurst Development Committee, New York (NY) Dept. of City Planning, New York (NY) Housing and Development Administration, New York 1970).

3 I am referencing the famous distinction between private troubles and social problems offered by C. Wright Mills. However, the quotes are meant here as much as scare quotes as actual ones since the terms social and private are constructed and therefore are complicated and unstable. One of the tensions between sociology and psychoanalysis rests on how to understand those concepts that propose to distinguish outside and inside.

4 It is interesting to note one of Foucault's descriptions of power. He proposes, "My main concern will be to locate the forms of power, the channels it takes, and the discourse it permeates in order to reach the most tenuous and individual modes of behavior, the paths that give it access to the rare or scarcely perceivable forms of desire, how it penetrates and controls everyday pleasure—all this entailing effects that may be those of refusal, blockage, and invalidation, but also incitement and intensification: in short, the 'polymorphous techniques of power'" (Foucault 1979: 11). In offering this quote, it is not to be thought that power precedes its movement into channels but rather that it always is its movement and its informing that through which it moves, shapes and is resisted.

5 The team of researchers include Omar Montana, Yeong Ran Kim, Elizabeth Garcia, and Elijah Wong. Our group research so far has resulted in performance pieces. We most likely will not produce together a traditional ethnography. I will conclude this essay with some comments on writing and the unconscious that calls into question traditional ethnography.

6 Like mine, Stoler's engagement with biopolitics draws heavily on Foucault's treatment of it. While Foucault suggests the expanded view of intimacy that Stoler offers, she adds to Foucault's biopolitics a sensitivity to the constitutive role of the colonies and empire in the establishment of intimacy in Western Europe, correcting the usual presumption that Western Europe is the originary location of modern intimate relations. This expanded view of intimacy adds to, even adjusts, those critiques of intimacy that point to those who are excluded especially from forms of it guaranteed by the state. In what follows, I cannot fully elaborate the connection of empire, colonialism and Corona; however, there is scholarship about the creation of Italian Americans as racially inferior (both in the USA after mass emigration to the USA, and before that in terms of the distinction made between north and south in Italy at the time of mass emigration of mostly southern Italians), as well as the treatment of African Americans during and after slavery; in this literature, these racisms are treated as derivative of colonialism and empire—an internal colonialism and empire building. This was part of my childhood

in Corona and it is part of the relations between different populations in Corona today (see DeGenova 2007; Sexton 2007, 2010).

7 Some have argued that Mitchell's view of siblings is too dark (see Cornell in this volume). Surely Mitchell does focus on cases of disturbances in sibling relationships. However, her proposal about hate between siblings also proposes that it is the condition of their love for each other. Her proposals, of course, are a matter to be taken up in a psychoanalytic context and tested there.

8 Referencing Foucault's treatment of biopolitics is meant to be genealogical, descriptive of a certain situation of governance. It is not a dynamic treatment of governance since it does not engage in the ways in which such forms of power are taken up and transformed by those who are experiencing them—and surely they are. Here I am interested only in speculating on the way in which the psyche might be assembled with the situation of governance Foucault is describing.

9 Psychometric "hope scales" recently have become widespread as a way to calculate how much hope cancer patients have. Hope scales research the will to live, measuring it as a life capacity producing populations that are hopeful and those that are hope challenged. Hope becomes normative as a desirable investment in futurity, particularly the futurity of truth. As Nik Brown (2006) has suggested, hope scales, like marketing the "nascent but deferred potential" of biotechnologies, rather than resting on controvertible present-day facts, shift facticity toward the potential of future truths. Reason itself is challenged by this "tense shifting" from present facticity to a futural facticity.

References

Berlant, Lauren (ed.) 2000. *Intimacy*. Chicago: The University of Chicago Press.

——2011. *Cruel Optimism*. Durham, NC: Duke University Press.

Bollas, Christopher. 1987. *The Shadow of the Object, Psychoanalysis of the Unthought Known*. New York: Columbia University Press.

Brown, Nik. 2006. "Shifting Tenses—from 'Regimes of Truth' to 'Regimes of Hope'," SATSU Working Paper No. 30. Science and Technology Studies Unit, University of York.

Clough, Patricia (ed.), with Jean Halley. 2007. *The Affective Turn: Theorizing the Social*. Durham, NC: Duke University Press.

DeGenova, Nicholas. 2007. "The Production of Culprits: From Deportability to Detainability in the Aftermath of 'Homeland Security'." *Citizenship Studies* 11: 421–48.

Foucault, Michel. 1979. *The History of Sexuality, vol. 1, An Introduction*. Trans. Robert Hurley. New York: Vintage.

——2003. *Society Must Be Defended: Lectures at the Collège de France, 1975–76*. New York: Picador.

——2007. *Security, Territory, Population: Lectures at the Collège de France, 1977–78*. New York: Picador.

Frankel, Jay. 2002. "Exploring Ferenczi's Concept of Identification with the Aggressor, its Role in Trauma, Everyday Life, and the Therapeutic Relationship." *Psychoanalytic Dialogues* 12(1): 101–39.

Grand, Sue. 2002. *The Reproduction of Evil*. Hillsdale, NJ: The Analytic Press.

Gregory, Steven. 1998. *Black Corona*. Princeton, NJ: Princeton University Press.

Guglielmo, Jennifer. 2010. *Living the Revolution, Italian Women's Resistance and Radicalism in New York City 1880–1945*. Chapel Hill: The University of North Carolina Press.

Harman, Graham. 2007. "On Vicarious Causation." *Collapse II* 11(26): 187–221.

——2009. *Prince of Networks*. Melbourne: re.press.

Linke, Uli. 2006. "Contact Zones: Rethinking the Sensual Life of the State." *Anthropological Theory* 6(2): 205–25.

Massumi, Brian. 2002. *Parables for the Virtual*. Durham, NC: Duke University Press.

Mitchell, Juliet. 2003. *Siblings, Sex and Violence*. Cambridge: Polity.

Moran, Richard. 2012. "Kant, Proust, and the Appeal of Beauty." *Critical Inquiry* 38(2): 298–329.

Morton, Timothy. 2012. "An Object-Oriented Defense of Poetry." *New Literary History* 43: 205–24.

Sexton, Jared. 2007. "Racial Profiling and the Societies of Control." In Joy James (ed.) *Warfare in the American Homeland: Policing and Prison in a Penal Democracy*. Durham: Duke University Press, 197–218.

——2010. "People-of-Color-Blindness: Notes on the Afterlife of Slavery." *Social Text* 28(2): 31–56.

Shaviro, Steven. 2009. *Without Criteria*. Cambridge: MIT Press.

——2010. "The Universe of Things," paper delivered at *Objected Oriented Ontology, A Symposium*, Georgia Technological Institute, April 23.

Stoler, Ann Laura (ed.) 2006. *Haunted By Empire*. Durham, NC: Duke University Press.

11 Intimacy undone

Stories of sex and abuse in the psychoanalytic consulting room

Jeffrey Prager

Introduction

Psychoanalysis has long been caricatured as the site where a patient presents profoundly personal material to an analyst who, in turn, says almost nothing. This nearly silent analyst serves as a receptacle for the patient, who is expected to vocalize any and all memories, thoughts and desires, "whatever comes to mind." Though a caricature, Freud and classical psychoanalysis are rightly credited for this kind of weird, modern relationship that has no parallel: the consulting room as uniquely intimate space and the therapeutic bond as one that cannot be trespassed, entirely confidential, unconditional and without "legs" to the outside world. In that space, the patient offers all that he or she cares to or is able. All of this is fostered by an analyst who establishes a fee and sessions on an ongoing and regularized basis and by helping to create a conversation unique to each therapeutic couple. Efforts are made by the analyst to create a safe and secure environment, characterized by features that make both the analyst and the setting predictable, stable, reliable, accessible and inviting. At the same time and despite the intimacy fostered, professional distance is maintained so that genuine "real" intimacy between the two participants never develops. Modern therapy, of nearly every stripe, struggles to achieve some form of this impossible aspiration. Not surprisingly, the challenge to maintain appropriate legal, moral and ethical boundaries and prevent professional breaches—the problems of self-disclosure, mutual analysis, various forms of boundary crossings, personal, out-of-office and sexual contact—have also been ongoing professional preoccupations. Breaches occur more often than the profession cares to admit.

Yet now, psychoanalysts themselves also speak on behalf of a new intimacy in the psychoanalytic relationship (Levenson 1974; Ehrenberg 1992). Contemporary analysts argue that the aspiration claimed in the past for a pristine professional distance and analytic neutrality is at best impossible to achieve and, more to the point, wrong to aspire to. They recognize it is impossible for the analyst not to be known, whatever efforts might be taken to hide one's "true" self. Moreover, the reciprocal intimacy shared between the two parties, rather than disavowed, should be acknowledged and worked toward. Indeed, the relationship itself is a vehicle (for some, *the* vehicle) of therapeutic cure. Therapeutic intimacy is now described as a fluid negotiation over time achieved (*if* it is achieved) through deliberation and contestation. While there are marked asymmetries in power between doctor and patient (though that too has been seen as less unidirectional as once cast), the principal impediment to successful treatment now is conceptualized as the manifold challenges entailed in the creation of authentic, intersubjective and intimate communication jointly constructed by the two participants.

This transformation in psychoanalytic thinking, first, parallels the development among some psychoanalysts that mutual recognition, as Hegel and later intersubjectivists name it (Benjamin 1988), itself constitutes the goal of treatment. Second, an acknowledgment that two individuals interacting as analysand and analyst cannot at the same time preserve the fiction of a therapeutic intimate space while absolutely maintaining interpersonal distance—holding fast to the conviction that "we have to be ever mindful that this is not a 'real' relationship." Now the promotion of a conscious and unconscious inter-psychic exchange in the consulting room is uppermost in the thoughts of the contemporary psychoanalyst. Highlighted above all are the therapeutic benefits that derive from the deepening relationship between analyst and analysand. Gone is the language of a one-person psychology (the analysand's), of analytic neutrality (the analyst's), of discovering through interpretation the patient's instinctive, unconscious drives that generate unhappiness. No longer is the goal understood as "making the unconscious conscious" or "where id was, there ego shall be": psychic transformation, rather, occurs via the creation of this new, hard-won, intimate space occupied both by the patient and the analyst. Best understood as a two-person psychology (analyst and analysand), a relational theory conceptualizing the psychoanalytic dyad where the deepening relationship is the result of a co-construction of a bond that over time becomes particularly intense and unique, replete with its own language, grammar, idiom, method of speaking, tone, cadence and so forth unique to that particular twosome. It is a bond between two people whose mutually reflexive understanding, conscious and unconscious, yields greater insight into the needs, desires and inhibitions of the patient and, as importantly, which, through shared experience, generates in the patient new capacities for healthful living. As intimate experience, it is expected that the analyst, too, necessarily is moved and changes as a result of the relationship.

This shift in focus has penetrated every aspect of psychoanalytic theory and practice. Here are three examples: *resistance* to insight by the analysand, now in its new formulation, expresses mistrust by the patient of the therapeutic other, overcome only as intimacy between the two parties continues to build. This view is a far cry from one that once saw resistance as solely a property of the analysand and an expression of the intensity of his or her repression barrier. *Counter-transference*, feelings and sentiments by the analyst that express a distortion in perception and that interfere with the capacity to maintain neutrality toward the patient, in contemporary psychoanalysis is now considered as productive knowledge; an understanding that facilitates the required closeness sought by the dyad. Rather than being an impediment to successful work and misperceptions requiring overcoming, emotions, feelings and thoughts mobilized within the analyst now serve as additional bases of information, generated through interaction, and about the patient and the obstructions activated to greater intimacy. Similarly, unconscious behavioral actions by the analyst in the consulting room (for example, handing the patient a tissue when tears flow) were once considered enactments, a breach of the therapeutic modality. *Enactments* were understood as an unreflective action by the analyst that reduced psychic communication in the room and, therefore, were believed to interfere with understanding the unconscious wishes or needs of the patient. Now, however, enactments are seen as impossible to avoid (the act of *not* offering a tissue to the teary-eyed patient is itself an enactment). Speaking is an "enactment," as is remaining silent. Therefore, the various behaviors in the consulting room (for example, whether the patient opens the door to exit or waits for the analyst to do so) simply require sensitivity to the interpersonal forces that create that particular interaction. These revised conceptions of resistance, countertransference and enactments reflect the primacy now given to understanding better the relationship between the two parties and reveal the critical role that intimacy plays in psychic change. Similar retranscriptions of classic psychoanalytic concepts to correspond to the new intimacy have occurred throughout the field. In fact, every concept has been rethought through these new intersubjective lenses.

Where once (with Freud) the psychological life of the infant began with the fluorescence of the triangulated Oedipal conflict between self, mother and father, now psychoanalysis conceptualizes psychology as in-formation from birth (for some, even prenatally) and manifest in the earliest connection between mother and child. In many respects, the work of Melanie Klein, a child analyst who asserts the presence of powerful fantasies of love, hate, envy and greed initially organized around the infant's earliest experience of the breast, has replaced the original Freudian model. The psychoanalytic relationship is understood, when proper attention is paid to it, to reveal the pre-Oedipal and prelinguistic sources of intimate connectedness. The current presumption is that adult intimacy mimics the earliest forms of social life, between infant and caregiver. It is recovered only as bodily, or sensate, manifestations of this newly created intimate space. The psychoanalytic relationship, thus, is read as more than the development of a shared cognitive understanding of the patient's early childhood experiences as it continues to impact adult experience; it is also the recreation of infantile feelings and sensations that presently express themselves through all five bodily senses. Intimacy is the linchpin through which all these possibilities depend. The nature and character of that bond provide clues as to the sources of inhibition or unhappiness creating the need or desire for the analytic relationship in the first place.

Stages of analytic intimacy

Yet, just as in other interpersonal relationships, intimacy in the consulting room doesn't establish itself immediately and only develops and usually intensifies over time. The form intimacy takes changes over the course of the therapeutic relationship corresponding to different stages of psychosexual development. Intimacy's various expressions in the analytic relationship typically reveal themselves in reverse chronological order, only over time as regression develops. At its most intense, the regressed relationship makes it possible to observe in the analytic setting the intimacy of earliest object ties, i.e. the first forms of sociality.

The dyadic analytic relationship deepens from a mature stage, at the beginning of treatment, characterized by the interaction of two separate adults, each occupying distinctively defined roles as patient and doctor, speaking to one another in a more or less intimate, though a clearly demarcated, cognitive language of self and other. Typically, the patient enters the relationship with a desire to be relieved of suffering and, in many different ways, communicates to the analyst his or her willingness to pay the price to improve, e.g. payment of fee, conscientious attendance, production of memories, sharing of experiences. The analyst communicates through many different measures, e.g. starting and ending each session on time, establishing and adhering to a regular meeting schedule, commenting meaningfully and, otherwise, behaving predictably, responding to the expectations of the patient, and successfully communicating sincerity in wanting to assist the patient in this group work. Intimacy, here, is demonstrated by the increasing willingness and ability of the patient to share with, recover and/or hand over to the therapist his or her private, innermost thoughts and the analyst reciprocates by offering comments, thoughts, interpretations that demonstrate that both people in the room are involved in the same quest to understand and repair the patient's inner world.

Intimacy, at this stage, constitutes a shared, embodied and enacted belief in the *perfectability* of the self and a demonstrable *sincerity* by both participants to engage the therapeutic process to achieve this (Levenson 1974). Transference/counter-transference issues emerge more slowly along this intimacy continuum and, by their becoming over time more pronounced and more the focus of therapeutic attention, intimacy deepens to reflect a blurring of the demarcation of two discrete persons. Increasingly, the therapeutic agenda of using the discreet inside of the consulting room to consider events and relationships outside breaks down. Intimacy is now marked by a clouding of the two-persons' perception of their own distinctiveness from one another—as a unique idiom of discourse emerges—and a recognition of the increasing vulnerability of the one on the other. In this view, as Edgar Levenson (1974: 360) points out, transference and counter-transference are not treated principally as *distortions* requiring correction but rather as interpretable phenomena expressing the uniqueness of the interpersonal, intersubjective and deepening connection.

Finally, in time, the unfolding self-awareness results for *both* analyst and analysand in his or her own contribution to the relationship. At this third stage of intimacy (only sometimes or even rarely achieved between the two participants), the ways in which the relationship *matters* to oneself generates a *rare* relationship in which *each* party is increasingly self-accepting of who he or she remains to be. The analyst doesn't fault him- or herself for not being able to provide more to the relationship—insight, knowledge, emotion, intelligence, creativity—than he or she has, and the analysand doesn't fault him- or herself for not being more different—content, happy, productive, committed, emotional, uninhibited—at the end than when the relationship began. The connection enables an appreciation of

one's own finitude, not merely the capacity to imagine change or personal transcendence in self or in other but also the limits to one's being. It also enables a
realization of the limits of the (or any) other either to be significantly better
equipped to handle the vicissitudes of life or to provide answers to the questions
that matter to oneself. Intimacy of this kind enables, finally, a capacity to be no
more than who one is, a mutual recognition not of the possibility of each member
of the dyad for perfection but, rather, an acknowledgment of love for the other
based on mutual imperfectability. "In authentic love," as Edgar Levenson (1974:
364) writes, "one need not strive for perfection, to be more than one is. Intimacy
has now become an openness to the other person as he is." Sadly, this is the
moment when the ending of treatment clearly comes into focus, and the anticipation of mutual loss and mourning becomes the final challenge to master before
termination.

This form of intimacy might be described as a more, or the most, regressed
connection corresponding to a pre-differentiated state of infant and mother (or
caregiver), one that we know can only healthily last for a time. Therapeutically,
this connection enables greater insight into those early childhood experiences in
which the patient seeks to navigate the challenge of individuating, while nonetheless depending on the other. This state of intimacy, of mutual recognition and
unconditional acceptance, constitutes the most powerful form, the most transformative and the most dangerous. It marks the time when the analysis has
accomplished the work it has set out to do. At its most intense, it corresponds to
the state of greatest vulnerability to the other—for both parties—and the period
of treatment most threatened by the intrusion of sexual feelings threatening to
disrupt analytic work. It constitutes the genuine acceptance of love for the other
(and hatred for the vulnerability that arises). It can mark as well a resurfacing of
sexual feelings in physical form, possibly as expressions of this authentic love, or
possibly a desire (sometimes manifest as rage) through sexual enactments to ward
off the possibility that the relationship has achieved what it is able to, no more, and
is nearly over. These feelings and the desire to act on them have the possibility to
transform the therapeutic relationship into something else altogether.

Defenses against intimacy

Psychoanalysis now no longer shies away from describing the psychoanalytic
relationship as a "cure through love." There are, of course, in this guise limits to
love's modes of expression. Language continues to be the medium of communication between intimate psychoanalytic partners. As Adam Phillips puts it,
"psychoanalysis is about what two people can say to each other if they agree not
to have sex" (Bersani and Phillips 2008: 1). However, as it is made evident in
every psychoanalytic hour, words used to describe and express feelings are often
not "the thing itself." Rather, talk stands in, as best as it is able, as expression and
description of extra-linguistic experience. Both analyst and analysand contribute
to finding the apt vocabulary to capture the feeling-states that the latter is
attempting to share. Language is used to capture amorphous feeling-states,
inchoate thoughts, complex reactions, inarticulate sensations, confusing and

fragmentary dreams, powerful desires, and disturbing memories both during the analytic hour and elsewhere. Yet in the end, despite the best efforts of both parties to be precise and accurate, talk proves to be only an inadequate vehicle, though the only one, to express the range and depth of feelings mobilized in this intimate setting. Words are the only way that this developing intimate relationship can find expression.[1] A private language emerges between each dyad, various metaphors meaningful only to the analytic couple become crafted. As the relationship develops, an increasingly coherent and complex narrative emerges that links early childhood experiences and prior traumatic moments to the patient's whole panoply of present-day private feelings. From this vantage point, self-destructive behavior or patterns of failure in life are understood in part as products of the persistence of faulty linkages between past and present, resulting in the repetitive experience of living in the past *as if* it were the present.

Unlike those who work within the cognitive behavioral paradigm, psychoanalysis also focuses on, in fact privileges, the unconscious, and insists that these faulty linkages oftentimes have pre-cognitive bases, can't be remembered or accessed per se, but only discovered through the intersubjective experience and the negotiation process ideally resulting in self-acceptance and acceptance of the other, i.e. mutual recognition. Seen from this one angle, the goal of analysis is intimately to know the links between present and past so as realistically to demarcate the two, and through a narrative understanding recognize and accept one's own unique set of needs and desires, originating long ago but still seeking fulfillment. When this occurs, personal choice and individual agency rather than blind determinism are now made more possible. These are the ultimate goals of an ongoing psychoanalytic encounter, allowing for greater personal choice and freedom upon termination.

Intimacy subverted

Yet this necessary resort to language as the vehicle to deepening intimacy sometimes subverts it. This paper explores one such subversion in which both analyst and analysand may unwittingly participate. This particular "narrative trap" I will describe is a premature foreclosing of the intensifying intimate bond by the shared adoption of a biographical story, familiar in its narrative structure, that links an analysand's childhood past to the adult present. This story typically has memory and/or desire at its core, and that paradoxically preserves distance, or apart-ness, in the dyad. It serves as a way to insure the retardation of greater closeness and, also, almost by definition the intensity of eroticized feelings otherwise difficult to contain. Real analytic intimacy, as I have described, typically engages the psychically primitive in both analyst and analysand; as in any loving relationship, it often activates very compelling sensual, emotional and mental expressions. In the therapeutic relationship, these can only be talked about or, absent that, they can generate unbearable anxiety that these sense experiences will prove uncontrollable. At its most profound level and for these reasons, both analysand *and* analyst are motivated to resist and to defend against deepening intimacy despite the fact that each, likely for different reasons, is nonetheless simultaneously working toward it.[2] This is the psychodynamic conflict present right there in the consulting room. In this sense, the conflict, certainly the intensity of it, is iatrogenically produced. The task of both members of the dyad is productively to resolve a problem that did not exist prior to the beginning of treatment and to be able to tolerate the loss that termination produces. Yet to "solve" the analysand's problem by prematurely naming it or to have either member of the couple name it through language exogenous to the idiom being constructed in the analytic interaction, i.e. to insert into the dyadic relationship a culturally available narrative structure, threatens to take it off the table for investigation and resolution (cf. Wrye and Welles 1994). It may well foreclose the furthering development of interpersonal intimacy, and a premature or abrupt cessation of treatment.

In the cases that follow, I describe the discovery, in the one instance through recovered memory, of early childhood sexual abuse and, in the second, the discovery of one's homosexuality as instances the function of which in treatment was to *foreclose* intimacy and to make more possible a premature ending of the treatment (Bernstein 1994). In both instances, I identify the "tyranny of the social category," through which a narrative device is wholly imported from the (non-analytic) outside. Further, it employs a language intended to describe self-experience that creates a third-party perspective and that generates the need for specific kinds of memorial evidence to "make the case." Even the activity of recall of one's own past becomes disciplined by the narrative imperative: how to convince *oneself* and others through memorial evidence that one fulfills the requirement of, here, being the victim of childhood sexual abuse or of discovering a previously hidden truth of one's own homosexuality. In both cases, the intensity of the intimate bond does not deepen; perhaps it is lessened. As I argue, an unconscious intent of appropriating these narratives is to short-circuit the intensifying personal connection between analyst and analysand. Warding off the affect of attachment is the *aim* of the narrative, not its *cause*. These social categories are importations from the outside world. As such, they are notably absent of any psychodynamic and overtly indigenous referent. In each case, the patient defensively appropriates the language of contemporary (and non-dynamic) social discourse to contain the therapeutic experience, to treat the phenomenon generally or typically and, therefore, to remove part of oneself from the perceived dangers of analytic intimacy.

For reasons of one's own, it is not difficult for the analyst to collude in this narrative construction. In these cases, to categorize a person as having been sexually abused or as homosexual appropriates a language now widely accepted in the social world that implies self-understanding but oftentimes serves to define, or insist upon, certain limits as to how far the intimate analytic relationship, self-acceptance and mutual recognition can be taken. The distinctively dynamic character of psychoanalytic thinking organized around the concept of psychic conflict, I argue, falls prey to the more familiar language of medicalized diagnostic categories. The diagnosis comes to occupy more space in the room than the relationship itself, and the preoccupation of both patient and therapist is toward the treatment of the "disease." The result is a weakening (or a slowing, or a breaking) of a developing intimate bond, and an impaired ability to use the other person productively, i.e. through internalization, after therapeutic work together has ended.

Intimacy's undoing and sexuality. Part I: the case of Ms. A. and *acting-in* the therapeutic relationship

Ms. A. was one of my first psychoanalytic training cases.[3] She was my patient in the mid-to-late 1980s, and I saw her for approximately four years before she terminated her analysis, at that time having become engaged to be married and about to move to another city. She was an attractive, single woman in her late twenties when she was working with me, unattached, and having had several romantic relationships that ended tragically: one who had committed suicide (in which she found the body), and another who announced himself as homosexual and who, not long after their break-up, had contracted AIDS and shortly there-after died. She had been an alcoholic herself, and, during much of the time we were working together, regularly attended Alcoholics Anonymous. She was very proud of her ability to remain sober. Despite these very difficult personal cir-cumstances, she was a highly accomplished young professional woman, viewed by others as extremely competent, poised and resourceful. Many of her friends looked to her for both professional and personal guidance, which she was able to provide, despite her own sense of possessing little self-understanding, inadequate internal resources, and a personal feeling of emptiness and non-achievement.

She had learned of psychoanalysis through her professional training and, because AA was beginning to provide her with a language geared to the inner self, she was very eager to find an analyst and begin intensive work. She was already experiencing herself as a survivor of many disappointments and crises, and she thought of analytic treatment as another step on her quest to single-handedly manage very difficult circumstances. At the same time, she was increasingly convinced that no matter how accomplished she was by appearance, and how much she was admired, respected and consulted due to her achieve-ments, her internal feelings about herself would never correspond. Psychoanalysis, she hoped, would reconcile the perceptions others had of her with those she felt about herself.

Ms. A. was the youngest child and the youngest daughter of a very large charismatic Christian household. Being the youngest, she watched each of her older siblings leave home so that for the last two years of high school she was home alone with her parents. She was instructed by her mother to keep the worsening alcoholism of her father a secret, even from her older siblings. For a time, when Ms. A. was very young she recalls a very loving relationship with her grandmother who, when living in the house, died suddenly. Her aunt came to live in the house; again, she recalls a very close relationship that she described as one where her aunt cherished Ms. A. *as* a little girl. Mother, in contrast, while extremely close to her daughter, required Ms. A. to align completely with her and could not tolerate her being a little girl. Ms. A. rejected "childish" games, never played with dolls, and early on took on the preternatural role as her mother's confidante. They came to share together a palpable disdain for the father. Her father was a "quiet alcoholic" as long as Ms. A. could remember and had been relegated by her mother as a useless member of the household. While there was a rebellious, secret side to Ms. A. that her mother never knew about (though which had enabled her to leave home, have sexual relationships and attain an advanced professional degree, all at tremendous personal cost), Ms. A. always remained closely tied to her mother and fearful of displeasing her. She was actively fending off guilty feelings whenever she aspired to differentiate herself from her mother. Our analytic work largely hinged on this struggle toward her own differentiation, owning up to her own desires for separation and to be able to express freely her femininity and sexuality, both of which were experienced as dangers to the maternal bond.

About six or seven months into her analysis, Ms. A.'s mother was diagnosed with an untreatable cancer and was expected to die shortly. Our analytic work together naturally changed dramatically; nearly all attention shifted to Ms. A's experience of watching her mother rapidly decline (to the point of no longer being able to recognize her) and die. An especially intense period of grief, Ms. A. became concerned whether she would ever recover. All members of the family came together more closely, including her father, and Ms. A. felt more closely connected to her family than she ever remembered. She also came to rely more intensely on our work together to process this very difficult experience.

As Ms. A. was beginning to get her feet back on the ground, it was striking that she was beginning to pay more attention to her appearance, purchasing new clothes, allowing her fingernails to grow longer and so forth. She was experimenting with femininity and gradually emerging from the world of grief. Among the most lasting impressions she had of the last several months before her mother's death was her surprise at her father's capacity to rise to the challenging occasion, and interact with all of his children and his failing wife in ways that Ms. A. would never have predicted. He was loving, caring and responsible while himself gravely suffering his wife's loss. Both his ability to manage his wife's dying and his capacity to relate and respond to the various needs of his children resulted in Ms. A. having a regard and respect for him that never had been expressed (or consciously felt) before. Ms. A.'s inner world was being radically reconfigured as a result of these major changes occurring in her family.

Sometime during this process, Ms. A. reported a dream. It was a disturbing one where she was confronted by a large tent full of people, each lying on cots, and required to select one of them with whom she was supposed to have sex. She mentioned seeing a "cute guy" in one cot but was drawn to another that, upon closer inspection, revealed a bruised and damaged infant. The baby had the appearance, as Ms. A. described it, of being only physically present; emotionally, the baby was absent, seemingly having removed herself from the awful environment in which she found herself. It was clear in the dream that she was destined to be with this little baby and fulfill her sexual requirement through her. Ms. A. awoke when both she and baby were crying.

I suggested the dream expressed her current conflict between sexual and feminine feelings surfacing (noticing first the cute guy), on the one side, and the threat those impulses posed to her relationship to her mother—the stunted infant who forever remained under the shadow of her mother, on the other. Ms. A. heard my interpretation, seemed to accept it, and left at the end of the session. The following session (the next day), Ms. A. returned, thoroughly enraged with me, having struggled whether to return at all. She charged me with not only mis-interpreting the dream but also intentionally directing her away from the actual meaning of the dream: for her, the dream constituted a memory of having been sexually abused as a child. She described this as a worry that she for a long time held privately; as she saw it, her dream affirmed the reality of her concern. Moreover, she believed that I could never understand the experience of abuse, as I was a man, and she wondered whether I had any knowledge of all that was being reported at the time in the media and elsewhere concerning the frequency with which abuse toward little girls occurred as well as the capacity of those abused to repress memories of the experience.

Because of her hostile feelings toward me, she asked me for permission to attend a "survivors' group," constituted by women who had only recently remembered their abuse and were collectively attempting to deal with the long-term effects of that mistreatment. The assault on me continued; memories were recovered of her father committing incest at a very early age, perhaps around two years old. Over the course of several days, she dramatically decompensated, finding it very difficult to leave her apartment, report to work and otherwise function in the world. Neither openly affirming her memory nor disputing it, I agreed to meet her now six times per week. These developments, of course, concerned me greatly. At least in one respect her charges directed at me were accu-rate. I was hardly aware (as difficult as it may seem now and much as she feared) of the widespread publicity then being given to recovered memory, to the shock-ing details relentlessly coming forward describing the frequency of incest and other forms of abuse, including accounts of satanic ritual abuse where infants would be sacrificed for the pleasure of the adults. In fact, at the time of Ms. A.'s anger at me, there was no countervailing public narrative that memories are not always trustworthy. No one had yet publicly voiced the possibility that long-ago abuse and mistreatment might be made up, misremembered, or that new cultural tropes, like recovered memories of horrific trauma, themselves might influence an individual's efforts to remember and describe one's own past. In *Presenting the Past*, I address the ways in which memory is contextualized and to illustrate how pro-foundly current frameworks for understanding both shape memory and produce narratives, even ones so personal as the story of one's life.

Yet Ms. A. was also drawn to this narrative for other reasons. Understanding herself as someone whose father had sexually abused her at an early age solved a disabling intrapsychic problem with which she was presently struggling. The death of her mother, despite its tragedy, gave Ms. A. the space psychically to breathe. No longer was she forced to constrict her own personal development because of the danger it represented to her relationship with her mother. Sup-pression of her own femininity and sexuality no longer could be defended against in an effort to preserve her symbiotic tie with her mother. These newly felt emancipatory feelings and a sense of her "victory" over her mother proved to be intolerable. Her sexuality was finding expression through intensifying erotic feelings toward me and, as important, a reawakening of the loving feelings toward her father. It was no longer possible to relegate him to the abject status demanded by her mother. Yet an acknowledgement of these feelings risked, in her mind, losing the protectiveness of her mother and celebrating her death. For a time, Ms. A. resisted these developments. She did so dramatically by casting her father not as a harmless drunk and as an embarrassment to the family but rather as an aggressive predator. In fact, in very short order, she proceeded to accuse her father of incest, informed all of her siblings of his violations, and broke off all communication with the family. She suspected that I was complicit, in some sense, in the crime, imagining me as unaware of the female experience of vulnerability to the sexual appetites of others. She questioned her ability or willingness to continue to work with me. By my not validating her memories or affirming her desire to attend another therapeutic group, she saw me as refusing to take her mother's place. I was not willing to provide her intimate comfort by reassuring her that my thoughts and feelings were identical to hers. Had I corroborated her story of her past, I would have been in collusion with her. We would have been in agreement that her early victimization fully accounted for the present-day difficulties with which she was struggling.

Ms. A. was engaged in a kind of Faustian bargain with herself and needed me to go along: as a way of distancing herself from her self-affirming and erotized feelings, she instead identified as a helpless victim of childhood sexual abuse. Her hope unconsciously was that this narrative of trauma might provide relief from her dilemma: she would forever be able to preserve the protective, though stifling, role her relationship with her mother provided. In the end, after some time, Ms. A. retracted her accusations toward her father, continued to grieve her mother's death, "forgave me" for not serving the role she had hoped, and came to feel both more future-oriented and capable of living as a mature young woman. She continued to explore the new world opened to her following the death of her mother.

It bears considering what might have happened had I, being similarly impressed by the new revelations of widespread child abuse and the phenomenon of recovered memory, shared her conviction that her current difficulties derived from this early history. The "reality" of this phenomenon was all around us and, from the media, we were both suffused with one story after another corroborating the claim that early abuse explains lasting and permanent psychological damage. Indeed, the persuasiveness for Ms. A. of this explanation was a result of its capacity to account for so many features of her current life's difficulties: feelings of emptiness, depression, discordance between inner feelings and others' perceptions, sexual inhibitions, preoccupation with past events and past losses, attraction to men who were unavailable as long-term partners, and so forth.[4] Paternal incest, a diagnostic category, explained it all, and, had I acknowledged this horrific event of exploitation and betrayal, it would have eased the intensity of her present-day experience. She would have felt free to acquire close ties with other "survivors" and her felt need for me likely would have lessened. To her mind, her AA experience, prior to her work with me, would have been recreated and the sense of herself as single-handedly, secretly caring for herself would have been reestablished.

Her adoption of this narrative structure would have succeeded in serving further purposes. It elevated past events to the foreground, subordinating Ms. A's efforts to live with herself presently. Further, it would have blockaded deepening feelings for her father and me—though, in my case, my incapacity to understand girls' experiences would have allowed her to cast me both as a stand-in for her sexual, predatory father and potentially to return me to being a safe and secure mother who might help her disavow her own sexuality. There was comfort in her being able to fold into the common experience, sharing with others the role of abuse victim. It enabled her, for the time she adopted this story as her own, to feel less responsible for her feelings (including eroticized ones) and less personally accountable for her current state of unhappiness. For reasons that I detail in the book, I withheld judgment. Yet I surely implicitly conveyed to her my skepticism.

Much was riding on the process then unfolding as we negotiated this significant rupture in our relationship. Ms. A. seemed to be embracing the role of abuse victim and sought my support in giving her permission to attend a "survivors' group." Paradoxically, the assertiveness of accusing her father and challenging me were disempowering acts. Not only was she attempting to see herself as a third-party victim, but she also wanted me to do the same. We would have introduced into the room an object, i.e. the victim, who, rather than our work together, would have become the focus of both our attention. The relationship between us likely would have lost the erotic charge characteristic of every (alive) intimate relationship.

Narratives as defensive action

Being able to tell a coherent story, even one arrived at by the painstaking work of two people over a long period of time and aspiring to its veridicality, sometimes obscures rather than reveals.[5] In fact, working to find *the* narrative is a misplaced aspiration of the therapeutic dyad. It may detract from self-exploration and self-understanding.[6] Students of narrative as a literary form note the logic and the necessary kinds of evidence a particular narrative structure imposes on an unfolding story (Bernstein 1994; Morson 1994). Built into the life-history narrative form—the telling of a past in relation to one's present—is its own logic and rationale, so what is remembered and emphasized and what is seen as irrelevant and unremarkable necessarily are the result of an imposition or demand of the narrative form on the reconstructive process. The narrative form, in short, produces its own set of demands on the memorial process, generating a particular incentive and predilection to remember certain experiences, while forgetting others.

It was perhaps one of Freud's greatest insights—certainly with respect to the study of memory—that the story oftentimes cannot be constructed alone, when self-interest, shame and embarrassment, among other emotions that seemingly demand distortion, are features that limit a personal capacity for self-knowledge. The intimacy of the psychoanalytic consulting room sometimes is necessary for the intricate web of defensive patterns to become known and undone, but even that is fraught with the possibility of failure. Ms. A., for example, expected her discovery of abuse to constitute a major breakthrough in her self-understanding. Memory and the ability to recount a traumatic past would be her pathway to cure. Despite the pain the memory entailed, Ms. A. believed for a time, like others, that her emancipation would follow her capacity to narrate what had happened to her.[7] Indeed, much of the self-help literature of the time spoke of the need to speak the trauma, to allow the inner child to be heard, and not to stifle suspicions of one's own childhood abuse. To be able to tell the story—to recover the trauma and its aftermath—became widely understood as the path toward psychic health.

Yet, as I have suggested, narrative can serve unconsciously as a powerful psychic defense against intimacy. It can serve as a buffer against an understanding of oneself and an unfolding discovery of personal needs and desires in reaction to a participating other. It can develop in service to a desire to retain distance and to forestall discomforting feelings in the present. Narration risks hypostasizing experience through its use of categories of experience and, especially when shared by both members of the dyad, stands to foreclose the possibility of ever moving beyond it.

The role that "one's story" may play to distance oneself from the surrounding world of others challenges a current preoccupation with the unequivocal virtue of remembering and telling and their cathartic effects. In fact, a too-easy appropriation of the story heightens the possibility that the past continues to be lived as if it were the present. The teller of the story assumes the role of a third person, removing the lived-experience itself, replaced by the category—the typicality of experience—to which it conforms. In this sense, the reigning narratives today often succeed in offering a non-dynamic, static, conflict-free description of past experiences that yield present-day outcome. Rather than drawing the teller and the listener closer to one another as part of this "new intimacy," it resurrects old, far more patterned, stationary positions establishing third-person or traditional boundaries between one another.[8]

Specifically, in terms of the psychoanalytic relationship, such narratives, however easily available, require being guarded against. In the end, they threaten to curtail the possibility of jointly defining the terms of psychic, even physical, contact between the dyadic pair. Because the two of us, in the end, were able to tolerate the ambiguity of not knowing, Ms. A. was able to move away from her sense of having been sexually abused as a child and toward resumption of the love she originally felt toward her father (before her mother's intervention) and an acknowledgment of the strength of her feelings toward me. Equally as important, she was able to resist the temptation to view her future as ineluctably shaped by experiences suffered as a young child. I would say she learned to acknowledge her own desire for intimacy and embrace the possibility of finding it outside her family and beyond the confines of the psychoanalytic relationship.

None of this suspicion of Ms. A.'s narrative account at the time discounts the profound difficulties she faced in what must have been an often-traumatized early childhood past. By the time she came to believe that she had been abused, we had already uncovered many occasions in which the experiences with which she was confronted were too overwhelming for her as a child to handle. She did have a traumatic past, but *narratives* of past wrongs, as I have argued elsewhere, potentially externalize conflict to the outside world and, paradoxically, protect defensive denial, preserve others as villains and encourage a sense of oneself as having been a victim. Further, a too-quick imposition of a narrative account of traumatic experiences, in itself, may make more difficult trauma's undoing: remembering as a story that happened to this third person, what might be described as an *affectively distant* reporting of what happened buffered by sufficient evidentiary memories, interferes with further exploration of the affective and conflictual content, only fully revealed, as Freud originally argued, as it is re-peated in present-day relationships. "One cannot overcome an enemy," Freud (1957b: 152) writes, "who is absent or not within range." Childhood trauma's undoing, in short, is not to be achieved either purely cognitively through aware-ness of the past, nor through the premature imposition of a narrative account, either by analyst or analysand, that neatly ties all the pieces together.

Intimacy's undoing and sexuality. Part II: the case of Mr. B. and *acting-out* in the therapeutic relationship

Mr. B. had recently moved to Los Angeles after having had some success as an actor elsewhere. He moved now to try his luck in this major market for acting. He was married to a woman whom he had met through his acting, and she agreed to make the move, although this entailed giving up a job that she liked, to search for, and finally to begin a new one in an unfamiliar city. However, the strains of relocation for both and the inability of Mr. B. quickly to find satisfying work in acting led to marital difficulty. He took work as a temporary worker, working a full day while also joining a local theater group both to sharpen his acting skills as well as to make contacts with other struggling actors. His time was spent increasingly away from home and he and his wife seemed to be growing further and further apart. He contacted me for therapy just as his marriage was dissolving, a break-up largely initiated by his wife but not without an acknowl-edgment by Mr. B. that the marriage had fallen on very hard times. Early during our work together, Mr. B. moved out of their rented home and rented an apart-ment for himself. He was depressed because of the failure of his marriage, a depression surely exacerbated by his inability to find satisfying work as an actor. It seemed unlikely that, despite his unhappiness, he would have initiated the talk of separation, the moving out to another residence, and the increasing possibility of divorce.

In many respects, Mr. B. had had a conventional upbringing, raised by two parents, Jewish émigrés from World War II Europe. He was the youngest of three brothers; at the time he began seeing me, he was in his late twenties. His father was a successful professional in Europe and was required after arriving in the USA to apply again to practice his profession. The family settled in a small town in the American southeast and his parents held very high aspirations for their three sons. His mother was actively involved in the raising of her children. His older brothers complied with the expectations of high achievement and each became very successful in their professions, married appropriately, and both now had young families. One remained in the town, closely involved with his parents, while the other lived nearby in a larger city. Mr. B. also had a younger sister, close in age, who at a young age had a child out of wedlock. She remained unmarried, struggled to find satisfactory work, and depended greatly on her parents to help raise her child.

Mr. B., like his brothers, attended a highly prestigious American university but, as Mr. B. understands it, he was strongly affected by the counterculture, rebelled against conventional career choices and aspired instead to become an actor. An early marriage, an unexpected choice of occupation and living far away from home all indicated a real sense of estrangement from his family. Of all his brothers, he remained closest to and more personally involved with his sister and his nephew, now living away and independently. In his upbringing, which, as he recalls it, remained largely unremarkable, two events stand out. First, he had strong feelings of one moment in particular, when he was about 11 years old: he vividly remembers waking up and about to attend his first day of the sixth grade, only to be told by his parents that, because they were unhappy with his current school, they had unilaterally decided to change his school. That morning he would be attending a different school, placed in a classroom where he knew no one. He remembered being very unhappy and disoriented, not only because he was suddenly attending a new school but also because he came to realize how much had taken place behind his back without his being brought into the discussion or decision making. Second, he remembers being sent to an elite boarding school in a nearby large city. One of his brothers had also attended, while the other attended the public school in the town in which he grew up, but Mr. B. remembers being very homesick and longing to return home, though in time he adjusted and became quite happy there, while still feeling quite removed from his family. He also recounts how he became one of the favorites in the school, receiving special attention—first out of concern for his difficult adjustment but later because of his academic promise—and was singled out for special attention by the headmaster. He had specific memories of time alone spent with the headmaster and, now, having reflected upon it, wondered whether it might have been an inappropriate relationship, one that involved some form of sexual abuse. He had no specific memories of sexual content but his time in therapy, for reasons I will describe, made him wonder more deeply about the connection.

Prior to seeing me, Mr. B. had very little experience with therapy. He remembers speaking briefly with a therapist at the boarding school when he was so unhappy but, other than that, he, like the rest of his family, believed that individuals should be able to solve their own problems; therapy only served as a crutch. Nonetheless, he took to therapy like a duck to water. He was extremely eager to "learn" how to do therapy and was very intrigued to discover, as examples, that actions had psychological meaning, that dreams could be interpreted, that feelings could be the result of unconscious associations difficult to access. He described an increasing preoccupation with his therapy and a sense that he was always, even when outside my office, in dialogue with me. Every experience in his "outside" life was being filtered also as a story to share with me, and he described increasing excitement as our appointment time neared. We never saw each other more than twice a week, though his capacity for introspection and insight was impressive, and he became determined to take full advantage of the time spent with me. Over time, he reported increasingly uprooted feelings, particularly over the weekend and, often, I would suggest that those feelings might be connected to his feeling of my absence in his life (or, later, as some resentment for my imagined involvement with my own family). He took in this interpretation but had no ability to access those feelings toward me over the weekend, despite his confusion during that period.

After about 10 months of our working together and his still having a very difficult time adjusting to his marital separation, he began to wonder whether the reason for his divorce might not be accounted for by his being (latently) a homosexual. He described to me his admiration for the courage of gay men who "came out" and asserted their right to "be themselves." He had a few homosexual experiences in the past, largely random sexual encounters with men that he considered insignificant, but now he showed an increasing interest in the nature of his relationship with his headmaster. He thought that perhaps this was the riddle— his homosexuality—to be solved in our work together. Over time, he began to describe homosexual encounters in which he was increasingly engaging, and a greater acceptance of the fact that he was homosexual. His sexual activity was most pronounced during weekends and I continued to suggest that he was having difficulty being apart from me. Still, he felt no deep resonance to this suggestion.

His homosexual identity was developing and deepening in the next several months, first by his having successive sexual encounters with men. These were becoming so frequent and so dangerously random and impersonal that I expressed my concern to him. He also began elaborating on the physical appearance of various male actors in his company to whom he felt sexually attracted (and, oftentimes, paternal). Soon, he found a long-term lover, an older man with whom he came to spend much of his time. The two began vacationing with other gay men, his former wife was told of this turn in his life, and his sense was that this was a permanent change in his life's direction. He also felt freer to describe to me the great excitement, at times building to an almost feverish pitch, in anticipation of seeing me. He understood that his greater ease in describing the excitement to me was a result of his newfound ability to see himself as a homosexual, and therefore felt much less shame in revealing it to me. It was, for him, another indication of his homosexuality.

Mr. B. soon seemed perfectly comfortable with his homosexual identity, though he was very reluctant to share any of this with his family of origin. I had no reason to question it either, though I was skeptical, based upon what he had already told me concerning the difficulties in his marriage, that this alone was the explanation for its dissolution. There was nonetheless a maniacal quality to his embrace of this new identity, as if he was trying to make up for lost time. It seemed to me, however, that his sexual acting-out was, in part, a defense against depression and his own sense of both professional and marriage failure.

As time passed, I came to believe that his very quick embrace of a full-blown homosexual identity, in fact, served also as a superego or moral defense against his wish for greater intimacy with me. It was an intimacy, I believe, in which genital sexuality was only a small or absent piece of his fantasies. After all, the excitement he felt in anticipation of my seeing him was not only expressed through genital arousal but included a far wider range of bodily sensations. What Mr. B. was deeply longing for from me was a sense of my total acceptance of him, a love that was unconditional. He needed to be *cherished* by me, expressing his unfulfilled longing for deep connectedness (Young-Bruehl and Bethelard 2000). The plenitude of his desire was short-circuited by thinking of himself as homo-sexual and looking for that bond from other men. In this case, homosexuality was his appropriation of a social category, now fully performed. Here, he was realiz-ing his most grandiose ambitions as an actor. Yet, as a role (and here I mean it in the widest sense of the word), it served as a break in our intimate connection. It was also a way *not* to understand better his desires. To my mind now, Mr. B. was *acting-in* the treatment, attempting to sexualize, i.e. genitalize, his connection to me rather than to acknowledge the intensity of his identificatory longings, pre-genital ones, for my (perhaps male) closeness and intimacy. He desired knowing my love for him, the special regard with which I held him, but found it far too difficult to know it was that which he wanted or to ask for it. By understanding his longing for me as a homosexual one, he sought to contain his deeper, earlier, pre-genital desires. It was likely not the words I spoke but the tone of my voice that comforted him; it was a desire to feel my touch that surfaced and a wish to be back in the consulting-room setting that felt safe and familiar—to feel held— and was being experienced more and more sharply and more uncomfortably.[9] Sexualization served as a defense against knowing his yearning for this more regressed and basic pre-genital desire of closeness.

Unbeknownst to me with this "compromise-formation," Mr. B. was preparing for our work to be over. From his perspective, he now had an active social life, more friends, a lover and, perhaps most importantly, he was no longer suffering the loss of his wife and the break-up of his marriage. Life was moving on and, without much prior notice, he was prepared to end his treatment. Other life crises intervened, however, requiring him to stay in treatment.

Over the course of the next year, Mr. B. broke off with his lover and main-tained a celibate life. He decided that an acting career was likely not going to happen for him, so he went back to school and prepared for another profession, one more closely related to both his father's and his eldest brothers' and not entirely dissimilar to my own. He became very involved and excited about his professional training and also proud of his achievements. He was happy to share those achievements not only with me but also with his father who greatly appre-ciated them, and his two brothers who applauded him for his efforts. Over time, he felt himself far less estranged from his family than he could ever remember and, after some time, he met a woman through his classroom experience, began dating her and ultimately married her. Many years have passed since my work with him and I don't know the status of his marriage, though I do know that he has achieved considerable success and prominence in his new profession.

My relationship with Mr. B. never attained the degree of intimacy that I shared with Ms. A., nor did it come close to the development of mutual recognition that I described earlier as the ultimate form of intimate therapeutic engagement. His marriage to a female work colleague does not imply that homosexual impulses may not have continued to remain important in his psychic life. However, his case illustrates again the sometimes danger of premature storytelling. Mr. B. appropriated his admiration for gay men who have the courage to declare themselves as gay and claimed that courage for himself, but the homosexual narrative, at least when he adopted it as his own, served as a way of "acting-in" the treatment, attempting to establish a sexualized connection to me, absent of intimacy.

The perverse effect of memory and desire on narrative forms

Together, the clinical material presented captures how the appropriation of certain culturally available discourses may be employed as a categorical *defense* against psychoanalytic intimacy: the appropriation of a narrative of pre-destiny (Ms. A. as a victim and Mr. B. as a homosexual), and a willful subordination to the permanent status now self-assigned. For Ms. A., it was a largely unconscious strategy to ward off unwanted and dangerous feelings of sexuality, attempting to recreate the feeling of safety and intimacy without the intrusion of genital sexuality. The case of Mr. B. illustrates best, I believe, the second dimension of this defense—namely, the misrecognition of genital sexuality for deeper desires for intimate connection. To be sure, he began to establish the necessary historic credentials for his homosexual activity. He sought to construct, with my cooperation, a narrative of homosexuality currently sanctioned in the broader social world. His renewed focus on his previous homosexual encounters and, most specifically, his relationship with his headmaster, occupied much of his psychic attention. Like any good actor, he was providing a plausible backstory—his childhood and adolescent memories—to make meaningful his current homosexual behavior and identity. Stated most sharply, Mr. B. revealed the profound contribution of the narrative of the time: either one *was* a homosexual or one *was* heterosexual and, here, he presented himself as someone definitively changing sides. He thought he was heterosexual and now he realized that he was homosexual all along.

However, life narratives such as these are always fueled by memory and desire. They include selective remembering and significant forgetting, and they often express strong and regressed wishes felt to be unfulfilled in adult life, or as never having been fulfilled even as a child. An identity is assumed oftentimes with the hope that something that feels absent might be fulfilled. Just as affective intensity fuels life narratives, it is also true that powerful defenses can be activated to reject, deny and suppress these impulses. Oftentimes, the power of defense and its capacity to distort and misidentify these desires—especially in the context of an important, intense and intimate relationship in which these narratives become worked on—are sometimes underestimated. Mr. B.'s embrace of homosexual sexuality served as his unconscious defense against deeply felt longings for intimacy—a sensual desire to be enveloped by me—which felt too dangerous for him to accept. I believe, as with Ms. A., his proved to be a case of *misrecognition*, an instance where the "true" self wasn't uncovered. Rather, for a time the defensive protection against further knowing prevailed.

Said differently, Mr. B. *performed* homosexuality thinking that, in therapy, it was his sexual preference for men that became known and that revealed his "authentic self." In fact, sexual feelings of a genital nature, expressed bodily through physical arousal, stood in to protect himself from knowing his eroticized desire for a pre-genital connectedness, i.e. intimacy that predated genitality. Why was this misrecognition experienced as homosexual rather than, say, the desire simply for promiscuous heterosexuality? Because what he longed for was a deeper *identification* with important men in his life, with whom he felt insufficiently included, resulting in his own masculine identity requiring outside sustenance. I was an in-the-present stand-in simultaneously for what he longed for them to provide and for the anger he felt at their inability to furnish him with it. His conclusion, established long before any competitive, Oedipal feelings toward his father or brother may have surfaced, was his own feeling of inadequacy as the boy he understood himself to be. For that reason, his intensifying connection with me as his therapist became eroticized. His yearning for a stronger male identification— in a family of strong, older, more accomplished men—became reactivated as our relationship continued and deepened. What he yearned for was to *become me*, correspondent to his more primitive experiences developmentally *prior to* genital sexuality, expressed through strong desires for object-relatedness of a particular kind. He didn't want to have sex with me; he wanted to be me. It was simultaneously a longing fueled both by his love and by his hate.

The strength of the impulse for identification, as Borch-Jacobsen (1988: 47) puts it in *The Freudian Subject*, "induces—predicts—desire much more than it serves desire." In fact, the importance of identification for the psychological subject is the source of Borch-Jacobsen's critique of Freudianism that has become only more scathing over time—namely, that Freud, by insisting that the psychic life of an infant begins with the triangulated Oedipal triangle, asserts that desire— expressed through jealousy, competitiveness and fear of retaliation—*precedes* identification (or mimesis). The infant's first passion, Borch-Jacobsen argues, by contrast, is not to replace an other but *to become* the other, to be inside and indistinguishable. It is no wonder, as he argues, that the desire becomes mistaken for sexuality or, in this case, for homosexuality. In so arguing, Borch-Jacobsen concludes that the fundamental role of the dyad, not the triad, and the wish for a form of doubling (or merger) transforms our understanding of the subject who, in fact, expresses the actual Freudian finding that individuals yearn to be like an other, i.e. to identify, and not to be separate, distinct and self-gratifying.

Borch-Jacobsen asserts that his alternative reading of Freud's own dreams in *The Interpretation of Dreams* refutes Freud's claim that psychoanalysis represents a scientific advance over other forms of therapeutic treatment. By offering a conception of the subject who suffers from too much repression of desire and which becomes manifest only through the transference relationship, Freud claims that, when the unconscious is made conscious, the subject is able to accept his or her own unique set of subjective desires. The transference relationship is therefore resolved, and the analysand is able to live his or her independent, autonomous life. In this, Freud insists he solved the problem of overcoming a psychology of imitation and suggestion. The end result of psychoanalysis, and its goal, is not for the analysand to identify with the analyst but instead to discover him- or herself, distinct from any conception of the real features of the analyst. The capacity to overcome identification and become autonomous, for Freud, is the distinguishing feature of psychoanalysis from all other forms of therapeutic intervention. He alone developed a method of treatment where the goal was not for the patient to imitate the mental health of the doctor, where a capacity to follow the doctor's suggestion was not the end goal of treatment. Psychoanalysis, in contrast, enabled analysands to develop the capacity to differentiate from the other, to discover one's own unique set of desires and constraints.

For Borch-Jacobsen, however, the transference relationship is the result of an intensifying identification by the analysand toward the analyst, and termination of treatment represents an outcome in which the patient feels capable of operating in the world without the continued provisions offered by the analyst only because the analysand has refashioned him- or herself in the image of the analyst. Object-relatedness provides the safety, security and care necessary to promote identification, and identification with the other is manifest not only through sexual fulfillment but, developmentally before that, with a capacity to share in a common world of touch, smell, sound and sight. The therapeutic setting, when sufficient regression can be tolerated, engages the dyad in this commonly shared world of sensations that promote mutual identification. Rather than overcoming suggestion, Borch-Jacobsen argues that psychoanalysis simply provides a more intensive set of procedures better to ensure the identificatory process.

The psychoanalyst Ruth Stein, however, informed by a post-Freudian and relational psychoanalysis, suggests the possibility that the patient in the psycho-analytic dyad strengthens identification with the analyst, experienced unconsciously for a time as necessary or as needed, much as Borch-Jacobsen suggests. However, in contrast, she insists that, when identification represents the culmination of the analytic process, a failed psychoanalysis has occurred. Together, she claims, analyst and analysand possess the capacity for an acknowledgement of how analyst and analysand are different from one another, each with their own personal history and each with their specific sets of memories and desires. Stein documents just how treacherous a process this can be and, as I have been suggesting with respect to the narrative process, how subtly a post-identificatory state can be derailed. Stein (2005: 776) describes a "perverse mode of object-relatedness," by which she means an effort of the analysand to seduce and bribe the other in order to destroy his or her separateness: exploiting the other for purposes of control and "to destroy intimacy when intimacy is experienced as threatening" (ibid.: 781). She describes in particular an analytic relationship the derailment of which is possible through a "perverse pact," jointly created by both participants, enticing "false love." "Perversion," Stein (2005: 781) writes, "is a dodging and outwitting of the human need for intimacy, love, for being recognized and excited; it is the scorning of the moral imperative of coming face to face with another human being's depth and unfathomable nature, which becomes palpable when one is in touch with one's longing for the 'inside' of the other, sexually or otherwise." Stein describes what always remains possible in the analytic dyad—namely, a perverse solution experienced as genuine love and intimacy, though in service to its inhibition:

> The analyst's quasi-psychotic susceptibility to the patient's experience has to eventually be curbed, "renormalized" and exited after it has provided emotional identification and understanding of what is involved in a particular analytic relationship with a person who resorts to perverse solutions ... The perverse solution ... lies in striking a pact in which two invalids invalidate the outside world, creating their own rules, in order to validate and vindicate their mutual weakness and indulgence. So, the unsavory secret of working effectively with perversion is that the analyst is deeply and perversely implicated in the game.
>
> (Stein 2005: 792)

Stein argues that genuine analytic intimacy can be achieved once the analyst is able to understand the spell under which he or she has been cast. The achievement of a non-perverse though intimate object-tie occurs, after false love, only by first emotionally understanding the deep longings for closeness desired by the patient and the defenses erected over a lifetime so as to survive their absence, and then to navigate both oneself and the analysand up and out to a more mature understanding of those longings. What Stein points to in identifying its perverse form are the intimate connections oftentimes sought within the dyadic relationship that are different and predate genital sexuality (where sexuality can intervene defensively so as not to know these deeper forms of need), or what Young-Bruehl and Bethelard (2000) characterize as the need for "cherishment." However, as importantly, she defines a therapeutic terrain where mutual recognition can obtain, where suggestion and imitation serve their purposes, *and* where separation and individuation *with* an intimate object-tie can flourish.

Conclusion

I conclude by returning again to Ms. A., but this time describing not her need to invoke a narrative to reduce intimacy, but to consider the ways in which sexuality was unconsciously deployed as a defense in service to the same outcome. As I suggested, and as I believe the controversial dream expressed, Ms. A.'s efforts to establish herself as a victim of abuse was her unwitting attempt to foreclose an exploration of the relation of her sexuality to her desires for greater intimacy with men. This foreclosing may have been encouraged, too, by the analyst eager to short-circuit his intensifying erotic feelings toward the patient. The death of her mother enabled Ms. A. more openly to accept and explore her own sexuality. As the intensity of her closeness to two important men in her life (myself and her father) deepened (and, in her mind, threatened her relationship to her dead mother), her fantasies toward both of us took on a sexualized form. In her mind, we both became potential sexual predators—a projection of her increasing erotic and loving feelings toward us and, in addition, a belief in the dangers entailed in any opposite-sex intimate ties.

Sexuality itself, and the extraordinary potency with which it can feel as a driving force, in this instance became experienced by her not as erotic or loving but only as genital, aggressive and demanding. She remarked at one point on her wish to sit on my lap, but feared that it would be arousing to me. At the time, when the wish first presented itself, she was ashamed of it. Yet sexual arousal in the consulting room, despite its activation by the words or tone of voice or whatever, often is experienced as non-relational, as biologically- based, as instinctual, and as one-person. It is felt as inappropriate, having no place in the consulting room and requiring disavowal. Leo Bersani, paraphrasing Freud, writes, "the sexualizing of the ego is identical to the shattering of the ego" (Bersani and Phillips 2008: 66). Unconsciously, Ms. A.'s fantasy of sitting on my lap likely expressed her wish to identify with me, to become *of* me. Her sexualization of the fantasy, i.e. her imagining that I would become sexually aroused, served as her ego-defense against regression, or her shattering, to a more undifferentiated state of being.

It is quite likely that Ms. A., given her early childhood experiences, yearned for paternal intimacy in the form of safety and security, a form of relatedness that long preceded the onset of genital sexuality. She accused her father of abusing her at a very early age—she imagined around two or three years old. Though her memories remained suspect, it is quite likely that her own sense of when things went wrong for her dated to about this time. However, her sexual fantasies, this time about her father, were intended to put a brake on those feelings, displace them on to us, and ultimately destroy the deepening bonds between us. The rough waters that needed to be charted were those sexual feelings, composed of fantasies of genital sexuality, activated en route to her more primitive pre-genital longings. Her appropriation of the language of sexual abuse were the rough waters; carefully navigated, it was possible to avoid naming it as abuse and to move more deeply into feelings of closeness where loving feelings of safety and security, provided by men, could be enjoyed.

Ms. A. was seeking with me for a time, in the language of Ruth Stein, the establishment of a "perverse pact," but its avoidance could only be ensured by not succumbing too quickly to her desire to be seen as a victim. It required on her part an impressive capacity to tolerate my resistance to joining her pact, and it depended on my not becoming overly preoccupied with the question of whether the abuse had actually occurred. All of this was negotiated through a complex form of communication that occurred between us largely unspoken. Our unfolding relationship, over the span of several years, is the best instance I know of to illustrate the delicacy needed when two people desire to establish genuine intimacy and the exquisite challenges on a day-to-day (or moment-to-moment) basis that go into its preservation.

A narrative of the relation of Ms. A's past to her present became only available at the close of our work together, and even that is forever subject to her re-evaluation and revision. Only at the end of our work together, when intimacy in our relationship was most fully developed, was it possible to use our analytic relationship for a better picture of the most primitive issues besetting her, old strategies employed intended to insure survival, and new ways of establishing connections to people presently. Within an ongoing psychoanalytic relationship, in sum, a story of one's own past can't be told fully without incorporating the experience of the present; without that, the story of one's life can potentially remain as an alien object the effect of which is to constrict rather than enhance one's relationship to the world and profoundly interfere with the achievement of intimacy.

Acknowledgements

I would like to offer special thanks to my Study Group on Intersubjectivity for providing over the past 18 years the intellectual and personal environment enabling me to learn from each of them, and to encourage the development of ideas that, only in a restricted sense, can I call my own: Joseph Natterson, Ray Friedman, Frank Dines, Karen Beard, Sharon Blum, Robert Hill, Peter Schou, Wendy Smith, Chris Hrdesky and Douglas Hollan. Also, I appreciate the contributions of readers of previous drafts: Alexander Stein, Martha Slagerman, Maria Lymberis and Debora Silverman. The essay is entirely indebted to my patients, some of whom are referred to here, others not, but in very particular ways all have been influential in helping me to raise the question of intimacy and its challenges. A few especially made me aware of its treacherous side.

Notes

1 In Lecture I of *The New Introductory Lectures*, Freud (1957c), responding to one critique of "the talking cure" as "mere talking," writes that "words were originally magic and to this day words have retained much of their ancient magical power. By words one person can make another blissfully happy or drive him to despair, by words the teacher conveys his knowledge to pupils, by words the orator carries his audience with him and determines their judgements and decisions. Words provoke affects that are in general the means of mutual influence among men. Thus we shall not depreciate the use of words in psychotherapy and we shall be pleased if we can listen to the words that pass between the analyst and his patient."

2 See D.W. Winnicott's (1974) essay on defenses against the fear of breakdown, though in this essay I am describing *both* the analysand's *and* the analyst's fear. In another article, Winnicott (1960: 585) describes the impulse of the therapist to name or diagnose the problem of the patient and which fails to have any effect. He writes that "the patient is not helped if the analyst says: 'Your mother was not good enough ... your father really seduced you ... your aunt dropped you.' Changes come in the analysis when the traumatic factors enter the psycho-analytic material in the patient's own way, and within the patient's own omnipotence." Winnicott's focus is on the patient, while here I describe the necessary role that both doctor and patient share in order to know the experience "omnipotently"—i.e. to know what it would be like for the doctor to drop the patient and the doctor to be dropped by the patient.

3 The clinical material presented here is described in greater detail in chapter 1 of my book *Presenting the Past, Psychoanalysis and the Sociology of Misremembering*. In the book, I argue on behalf of the role that the present plays—both present-day personal relationships and various sociocultural narratives that have a particular currency at the time— in the reconstruction of individuals' understanding of their own past. An ever-changing present holds the potential to promote an ever-changing understanding of one's own

past. In this article, I use my work with Ms. A. to emphasize a different point—namely, the defensive potential of memories of the past, encoded narratively, to thwart changing experiences in the present, including the psychoanalytic relationship itself.

4 Ellen Bass and Laura Davis described many of these symptoms in *The Courage to Heal* (1992: 22). This book was a best-seller and very influential at the time. Ms. A. expressed concern that I may not have read the book. Encouraging women to come forth with their stories, they wrote, "often the knowledge that you were abused starts with a tiny feeling, an intuition. Assume your feelings are valid. So far, no one we've talked to thought she might have been abused, and then later discovered that she hadn't been."

5 When Winnicott (1965) cautions that only an experienced analyst, not an analytic candidate, should take on a patient who presents as a "false self," he identifies the possibility of analytic work proceeding, sometimes for years, in which a finely crafted defensive structure of the patient goes undetected. The two inadvertently collude in an elaborate self-presentation that hides more than it reveals. In this same sense, I am suggesting that the pre-mature adoption of a specific narrative concerning the events and psychic consequences of a patient's past runs the danger, too, of constricting, perhaps hiding, more germane and troubling elements that go undetected.

6 Susan Derwin (2012) analyzes many of the important testimonies written by Holocaust survivors which have been understood in terms of the positive therapeutic benefits of "telling your story," or "sharing with others your story." Yet she offers a compelling argument suggesting that their efforts to narrativize experience failed to reveal an underlying rage that each of the authors possessed and, for some, led to their own suicide.

7 I write about the non-emancipatory potential of narrative in a different context in Prager 2008: 411.

8 Once again, Winnicott's observation is central here: it isn't the fact of trauma but its experience that must be recovered in order for it to be overcome.

9 See Nancy Chodorow (2012) for a discussion of the role that sensual experiences, other than hearing and speaking, play in the psychoanalytic consulting room.

References

Bass, Ellen and Laura Davis. 1992. *The Courage to Heal: A Guide for Women Survivors of Child Sexual Abuse*. New York: Harper Perennial.

Benjamin, Jessica. 1988. *Bonds of Love, Psychoanalysis, Feminism and the Problem of Domination*. New York: Pantheon Press.

Bernstein, Michael Andre. 1994. *Foregone Conclusions, Against Apocalyptic History*. Berkeley: University of California Press.

Bersani, Leo and Adam Phillips. 2008. *Intimacies*. Chicago: University of Chicago Press.

Borch-Jacobsen, Mikkel. 1988. *The Freudian Subject*. Stanford: Stanford University Press.

Chodorow, Nancy. 2010. "Beyond the Dyad: Individual Psychology, Social World." *Journal of the American Psychoanalytic Association* (58): 207–30.

——2012. "Analytic Listening and the Senses: Introduction." *Journal of the American Psychoanalytic Association* 60: 747–58.

Derwin, Susan. 2012. *Rage is the Subtext, Readings in Holocaust Literature and Film*. Columbus: Ohio State University Press.

Ehrenberg, Darlene. 1992. *The Intimate Edge: Extending the Reality of Psychoanalytic Interaction*. New York: Norton & Co.

Freud, Sigmund. 1957a [1912]. "The Dynamics of Transference." In *The Standard Edition of the Complete Psychological Works* Vol. XII. London: Hogarth Press.

——1957b [1914]. "Remembering, Repeating and Working Through." In *The Standard Edition of the Complete Psychological Works* Vol. XIV–XV. London: Hogarth Press.

——1957c [1915]. "The New Introductory Lectures." In *The Standard Edition of the Complete Psychological Works* Vol. XIV–XV. London: Hogarth Press.

Levenson, Edgar. 1974. "Changing Concepts of Intimacy in Psychoanalytic Practice." *Contemporary Psychoanalysis* 10: 359–69.

Morson, Gary Saul. 1994. *Narrative and Freedom, The Shadows of Time.* New Haven: Yale University Press.

Prager, Jeffrey. 1998. *Presenting the Past, Psychoanalysis and the Sociology of Misremembering.* Cambridge, MA: Harvard University Press.

——2008. "Healing from History, Psychoanalytic Considerations on Traumatic Pasts and Social Repair." *European Journal of Social Theory* 11(3): 405–19.

Stein, Ruth. 2005. "Why Perversion? 'False Love' and the Perverse Pact." *International Journal of Psychoanalysis* 86: 775–99.

Winnicott, Donald. 1960. "The Theory of the Parent–Infant Relationship." *International Journal of Psychoanalysis* 41: 585–95.

——1965. "Ego Distortion in Terms of the True and False Self." *The Maturational Processes and the Facilitating Environment: Studies in the Theory of Emotional Development.* London: Hogarth Press, 140–52.

——1974. "Fear of Breakdown." *International Review of Psycho-Analysis* 1: 103–7.

Wrye, Harriet Kimble and Judith Welles. 1994. *The Narration of Desire, Erotic Transferences and Countertransferences.* Hillsdale, NJ: The Analytic Press.

Young-Bruehl, Elizabeth and Faith Bethelard. 2000. *Cherishment, A Psychology of the Heart.* New York: The Free Press.

12 Who's your daddy?

Intimacy, recognition and the queer family story

Arlene Stein

To be human requires recognition from others. Our very individuality depends upon the willingness, and capacity, of others to recognize us. "We do not survive," writes Judith Butler (2005: 12), "without being addressed." Recognition, in other words, is a basic human need. Nonrecognition or misrecognition can lead to marginality and to non-personhood. Little wonder, then, that the quest for recognition has been central to identity-based social movements, such as the movement for gay and lesbian civil rights. Since the 1970s, this quest has been defined primarily in relation to a politics of visibility, embodied in the strategy of "coming out," or openly declaring one's homosexuality. Coming out has been viewed as the first step in consolidating gay and lesbian subcultures the anticipated outcome of which was mutual recognition and visibility beyond queer worlds.

A number of analysts suggest that this strategy has largely been successful, with large segments of the queer world in the USA now "beyond the closet" (Seidman *et al.* 2002). Homosexuality is increasingly normalized and routinized, and incorporated into family life. For many families headed by gay men or lesbians, particularly those with children, managing one's identity and obscuring one's sexuality is today impossible, undesirable, or unnecessary. Far from distancing themselves from their homosexuality, members of LGBTQ (lesbian, gay, bisexual, transgender, queer)-headed families increasingly want to be identified with it, to make their ties to one another intelligible. There is, writes historian Jeffrey Weeks, a "fundamental shift in non-heterosexual communities away from a focus on issues of identity towards ones of intimacy" (Weeks *et al.* 2001: 164).

The rise of a politics of same-sex marriage, and the growing (incomplete) public affirmation and acceptance of legal protections for such relationships is indicative of this shift.[1] However, even as long-term coupled queer people, including those with children, enter what anthropologist Gayle Rubin has called the "charmed circle" of sexuality, and are accommodated by the dominant culture, non- and misrecognition persists. Institutionalized heteronormativity means that queer people are assumed not to have families, or if they have families their sexuality is often erased. Indeed, for the relatively privileged, for whom the closet is no longer salient, recognition may be the issue *de jour*.

Nonrecognition typically occurs in relation to institutions of the "straight state"— schools, post offices, legal institutions and the like—which generate stories about families, narrating understandings of what kinds of families are acceptable or desirable, while failing to acknowledge the specificity of LGBT-headed house-holds. If *nonrecognition* takes place in relation to bureaucracies, *misrecognition* typi-cally occurs in everyday interactions with neighbors and strangers. A case in point: I recently checked into a suburban New Jersey hospital for a minor surgical procedure. When I entered the recovery room, my girlfriend was ushered inside to see me. "You can go and visit your mother now," the nurse told her, as I lay in a post-anesthesia stupor. I am two years older than my girlfriend, and, while she is a young-looking 50 year old, most will agree that I do not look old enough to be her mother! In my last primary relationship, my partner and I were also roughly the same age, but were frequently mistaken for sisters—even though we do not look at all alike. Lesbian mothers also describe interactions with strangers at their local supermarket and other public places that often entail inquiries about the whereabouts of their children's biological fathers (Pascoe 2012). What these and other examples suggest is that, when heteronormativity rules, queer intimacies are often read through a heterosexual lens, transforming sexual and affectional ties into biological ones, and effacing the nature of gay and lesbian relationships.

To be recognized by others, one must be intelligible according to the codes circulating within the culture. Heterosexuality continues to be inscribed in domi-nant understandings of kinship, making queer families unintelligible, which espe-cially impacts the children of same-sex couples, along with non-biological parents, and leads to the shame of nonrecognition, as I show in the following, drawing upon some recent studies of queer families, along with vignettes and material evidence from my own. At the same time, queer families tell their own stories, representing themselves to themselves and to others, narrating their unfolding histories. In conclusion, I consider the political implications of such storytelling, suggesting that emerging hegemonic understandings of queer kinship, which focus on the primacy of the (same-sex) couple and child(ren), downplay the diversity of both homo and hetero family forms and the myriad ways same-sex couples represent themselves to themselves and to others.

Telling (queer) family stories

Family stories are central to creating, maintaining, understanding and communicat-ing personal relationships. Storytelling, communications scholar Jody Kellas (2010: 3) writes, "not only helps us make sense of family experiences, but also performs, creates, and shapes family relationships as well as individual and cultural identities." Stories "hold people together, and pull people apart," sociologist Ken Plummer (1995: 5) has written. Family storytelling is part of everyday talk, in different contexts and in mul-tiple settings: at occasions such as weddings and funerals; in interactions with neigh-bors and friends; when confronting bureaucracies and state agencies, including schools; and in family discussions over dinner and at breakfast. Through storytelling, people define who is a member of a given family, create "origin myths" that describe its genealogy and affirm a sense of unity, and manage conflicts and disagreements. The stories that people tell about their families, in effect, constitute them.

By telling stories about family, people also reflect upon the meaning of their relationships—what sociologist Anthony Giddens has described as the "reflexive project of the self." As he and others show, as intimacies are increasingly detached from reproduction, they "can be molded as a trait of personality" and are "intrinsically bound up with the self" (Giddens 1992: 2). Rising rates of divorce, among other trends, suggest that marital permanence is no longer expected, making acts of recognition even more important. "The family" is a social institution, comprising contractual ties, implicated in a web of networks, and governed by more or less public norms and codes, but it also encompasses a set of practices, and is "performed" through practices of recognition, in which people share detailed information about one another, building a common world-view. Such performances occur as families interact with institutions of the state, as well as with friends, extended family members and others. Indeed, some would argue that gay and lesbian families are paradigmatic of late modern intimacies, which are more individually oriented, more reflexive and more fluid than intimate relationships of old that were based on the "'til death do us part" script.

As advocates for the rights of gays and lesbian families argue, "love makes a family": family should be based neither on genetic linkages, nor on assumptions of permanence, nor be limited to erotic relationships, but on the capacity for caring and on the quality of relationships. Longevity is no longer the sole, or even primary, marker of kinship. As cultural critic Simon Watney suggests, perhaps idealistically, gay men and lesbians of his generation, the postwar generation of baby boomers, "defined our own forms of domesticity, perhaps a little more honest[ly] and flexibl[y] than those we fled—or that threw us out" (Watney 1991: 33). Certainly, queer families tend to be more self-conscious and reflexive about their relationships, as a gay man interviewed by Jeffrey Weeks and his research team in England in the 1990s articulated: "So much is somehow assumed in heterosexual relationships, whereas in gay relationships it has to be made somehow more explicit ... You can't slide through recognized patterns of relationships. You've got to make a more conscious decision about what you want from each other" (Weeks *et al.* 2001: 111).

Queer people do not craft families from scratch, of course. They tell stories that draw upon "old" stories of family based on blood and belonging, which emphasize continuity, and also create new notions of family which upend biology. Emphasizing choice and flexibility and affirming, utilizing and subverting representations of family life, they construct their own narratives of family life in relation to practices of the "straight state." The queer "family story" is constructed in the interstices of these hegemonic constructions and the everyday narrative practices of parents and their children. LGBTQ families negotiate visibility and invisibility by constructing narratives of family life that legitimate their own constructions of family, affording self-disclosure and intimacy. Such narrative work is an important part of the process of building connections and intimate attachments within families and gaining recognition from those outside.

Queer families, like all families, construct stories to represent themselves to themselves and to others, defining who can rightly claim membership in that family. Queer family stories begin with a myth of origins that is different from the one most heterosexual families might embrace. Blending biological and social kinship, "families we choose," as anthropologist Kath Weston described them, flout dominant notions of kinship based solely on biology and blood, refusing, at least in principle, to prioritize biological over social belonging. Studying gays and lesbians in the San Francisco Bay Area in the 1980s, Weston suggested that there is an explicit refusal to accept biological connectedness as the source of kinship. Queer families cannot completely negate the power of biology, however; though they refuse to reduce relationships of belonging to blood ties, such ties play an enduring role, as my own story suggests.

The story of us

My chosen family was established in 1988, when Nancy and I formed a relationship. We were part of the great migration of young gays and lesbians who left their natal homes (in our case, New York and Boston) and moved (in our case, to the San Francisco Bay Area) seeking independence, drawn by preexisting lesbian-feminist and gay subcultures, and the prospect of meeting others like ourselves. Though we had little interest in getting married, we expected to make our lives together over time. Five years after we met, Nancy and I moved to Oregon, where we had a child through donor insemination. Nancy gave birth to our son Lewis in 1997.

Our struggle for control over the family story began early on. The morning after our son's birth, the hospital circulated a form that would be sent to the local newspaper, which asked for the mother's name, the father's name, the baby's name and his date of birth. We filled it out, placing Nancy, his birth mother, in the box calling for the mother's name, and a gender-neutral version of my name, "A.J. Stein", in place of "father." Otherwise, we feared, they would not print the announcement; I had never seen a birth announcement in the local paper where there was not a father and a mother. (What, I wondered at the time, do single mothers do? Are their children not worthy of public acclamation?) The strategy worked: the next day, the newspaper announcement listed our son's name next to ours. We affixed a photo of Lewis, and it became his birth announcement. Through that sleight of hand, I became the putative "father," and we became "Mommy" and "Mama" to our son. At that moment, and at various points along the way, Nancy and I took some small measure of satisfaction in subverting public heteronormative expectations, and we saw ourselves as pioneers, of sorts, in the queer family project.

The newspaper notice, and the birth announcement that grew out of it, were public affirmations of our son's birth that we shared with friends and family. But how would we convey that story to our son as he became old enough to understand?

Nancy decided to put together a book that would offer a history of our family, which she entitled *The Story of Me*. It was a handmade affair through and through, with a cover showing an imprint of our newborn's feet. *The Story of Me* was brilliant in its simplicity: a stunning rebuke to the dominant biogenetic narrative of family formation, it told our family story on our own terms.

Like Gertrude Stein's narration of her partner's life, *The Autobiography of Alice B. Toklas*, *The Story of Me* narrated Lewis's early life from the period before his birth, to his parents' decision to have a child, ostensibly in his own voice. Like an early classic of queer family lit, *Heather Has Two Mommies*, it offered a matter-of-fact declaration of queer difference that announced: *this is who you are, this is who we are, this is how things are, get used to it!* First, it conveyed to Lewis how he came to be: his

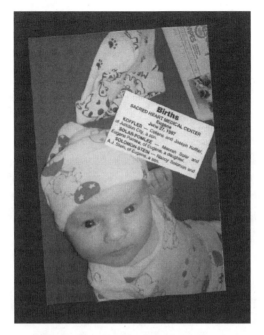

Figure 12.1 Lewis' birth announcement

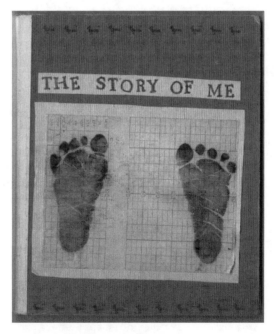

Figure 12.2 Cover of our family "album"

mothers wanted a child very much, but, since it takes a man and a woman to make a baby, they got "help" from Charles, named as the "donor." It depicts Charles feeding newborn Lewis, and suggests through that image, that he provided not only sperm, but even nurturance on occasion. The book offers its primary intended audience (Lewis) an account of his origins that subverts biogenetic constructions of parenthood, suggesting that social parenthood is just as legitimate (and sometimes even more legitimate) than biological parenthood. Charles is named as "donor"—not "father"—offering Lewis a way to identify him, purposely blurring distinctions between biology and belonging. Although a story of difference that offers a deliberate, self-reflexive narrative of family formation, *The Story of Me* also conveys a sense of sameness: you came to be, much like kids in other families, as an expression of love. It suggests that every life has value when it is embedded in a series of relationships and possesses a history, and deserves recognition.

During his first two years, as he was beginning to acquire language, we often read that book to Lewis, and it became a part of his understanding of himself, anticipating some of the questions he would ask about his own history before he was even capable of knowing what those questions were. The book assumed pride of place in the family archives, and sat on a bookshelf next to our photo albums. It tells a story of family origins, mainly focusing on the pre-history and birth of our son, and was designed to be read to him by us, his parents. It is a unique document, though there are probably other queer families who have constructed similar kinds of documents, and certainly family photo albums bear some resemblance, and serve similar roles.

Figure 12.3 From "The Story of Me"

Figure 12.4 "The Story of Me"—continued

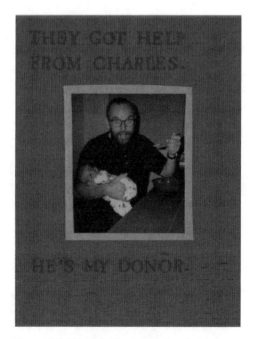

Figure 12.5 "Uncle" Charles feeding Lewis

The family album

Most family photo albums document what anthropologists and sociologists call "ritual moments" or "autobiographical occasions" for self-making (Carsten 2004: 97). They are not necessarily documents of origins, or even of everyday life, though at times they may be. Their focus tends to be on birthdays, family gatherings, milestones such as the first day of school, and leisure activities such as vacations. Technology shapes the ways photographs are organized and archived. In an era before digital photography, albums were a conventionalized objects, and displayed in bound volumes. Today, family photos are more likely to exist on computer hard drives alone, and less likely to be organized in album form. If they are organized in digital albums, there may be multiple iterations of albums, assembled by different family members, and for different audiences.

Like all narratives, family photo albums have beginnings, principles of selection, principles of connection and intended moral meanings. Every album "tells a story and makes a set of claims about who and what one was and is," writes sociologist Robert Zussman (2005: 28). They are representations of a family as the person assembling the photo album wishes it to be seen, and are, says Zussman, "a highly selective record of a life" rather than an unencumbered display of self-expression. They tell a story that is constrained by narrative conventions which operate in society, including a desire to emphasize family unity, to show individuals in relationship with one another, and to emphasize family continuity. That is, while the photo album tells a family story, it also creates family myths. Through producing, selecting, ordering and displaying photographs, feminist theorist Annette Kuhn writes, "the family is actually in the process of making itself" (Kuhn 1991: 23). The same could be said of individual photographs. Every photograph, writes Stuart Hall, is "a structure of 'presences' (what is represented, in a definitive way) and 'absences' (what is unsaid, or unsayable)" (Hall 1991: 156).

For children growing up in heteronormative families who may experience early same-sex feelings, or who are gender non-normative, there is often much that is unsayable. Cultural critic Simon Watney writes of the fact that many gay men and lesbians grow up with a sense of estrangement from the photo albums their families assemble, and a sense that the person in the photograph is not the person they "really" are. "Like many other gay men," he says, "I am acutely aware of the moment when I realized that I was not the 'nice' little boy in the holiday snaps, that a deception was being perpetrated" (Watney 1991: 27). Of course, one doesn't have to be queer to experience this sense of estrangement; many people have memories of their childhoods that signal a gap between the person they believe themselves to be and the person that appears in the photographs. Photographs are often about putting on appearances. Watney suggests that gay children are particularly vulnerable to their parents' fantasies about who they are, and these fantasies, he says, "invariably fail us." Consequently, gay children frequently lead lives of intense privacy, "knowing far more than they can ever reveal" (Watney 1991: 30). When adult gays and lesbians glance at their family photographs, they see the little budding butch girl who is awkwardly pictured in her ballet tutu, or the effeminate little boy is shown in the baseball uniform he was forced to don for Little League—but even gender-normative individuals often report a sense of estrangement from the ways their parents represent them visually.

Queer family albums begin with these foundations, but they also depart from them, creating representations of families that are more flexible and less biologically rooted. Typically, though, they do not stray too far from normative expectations about what family albums (or even gendered children) should look like. In my own queer family albums, assembled in the late 1990s and early 2000s, the images were taken with film cameras. Like all family photo albums, they tell a story of relationships, but they blur the lines between friends and family, and depict friends prominently. The refusal to limit the family to biological ties is also reflected in the ways the album depicts Lewis's two mothers: one of whom bore him biologically, and the other (myself) who assumed the role of "social mother" or, as some have called it (acknowledging the continuing primacy of biological ties) the "other mother."[2]

However, if our queer family photo albums blur the line between family and friends, they emphasize the primacy of the nuclear family unit. Like most family albums, the relationship between children and parents takes center stage, and young children are pictured far more consistently than adults—ours is no different. In terms of its intended audience, our photo album is also a rather private affair, designed to be shared primarily with family members, and occasionally with friends (though we all know how boring it can be to look at others' photos!), and to be the family archive. And like other family photo albums, ours presents the family in a highly idealized light. It is a story not of what a family is, but of what we would like it to be. Many of our photographs focus on family vacations, particularly on travels (when, like most families, we were most relaxed!), reinforcing this sense. As Zussman describes the photo albums he surveyed, closeness is emphasized, conflicts tend to be absent, and the overall impression created is that of unity. "The children's party may bring tantrums," critic Patricia Holland (1991: 8) writes, "but the pictures will show laughter." Ours were no different.

Traditionally, fathers play the role of family photographers, at least in the standard gendered division of labor of the post-war era, while mothers assemble the photo albums. Assembling a photo album is part of the work of kinship, what Micaela di Leonardo (1987) calls the "female world of cards and holidays." That's changing, particularly with technological innovations that make cameras cheaper and easier to use, and with the continued breakdown of the gendered division of family labor. While queer families blur traditional gendered divisions of labor, they do tend to have divisions of labor, though these tend to look somewhat different from heteronormative ones. In our family, for example, I was usually the photographer, while Nancy assembled the albums. That I took most of the photographs was mainly due to my interest in photography, and the fact that I don't particularly relish having my photo taken. This meant that most of the photographs of our family focus on Lewis and Nancy, and a shifting constellation of family and friends, and that I am often absent from the photographs.

It is notable that my biological parents are also absent from these albums, for the most part. This was due to a combination of familial estrangement, illness and death. (My father died before our son was born, and never met Nancy. My mother was seriously ill during Lewis's early years, and was never particularly comfortable with my sexual choices.) This inadvertently reinforced power dynamics already at work in the family, reimposing the primacy of the biological ties, and making Nancy's familial links to Lewis much more salient in the family album. Also noteworthy is that, when the three of us appear in photographs together, Lewis is inevitably by Nancy's side rather than by mine—partly by his choice.

The queer family album is, then, like all family albums, a selective rendering of family history. If the standard heteronormative family album is an idealized representation of family unity that downplays divisions and tensions, the queer album plays a similar role—perhaps even more defensively, at times—and estrangement certainly figures into it, often through absences. Still, such albums play an important role in constructing the family story, and, to the extent that they are shared with those outside the family, they call upon others to recognize the family as a family. Heterosexual families have recourse to marriage and other traditional rites as ways of symbolizing familial bonds. Marriage and commitment rituals are becoming an increasingly important part of the cultural repertoires of many same-sex couples, too, of course, but, for most queer people, the construction of the family story tends to be a somewhat more private, and certainly a less highly institutionalized (and commercialized) affair, improvised out of a mix of traditional and nontraditional elements. One could argue that, in the absence of such traditional rituals, photo albums, and increasingly video and other audio-visual records, play an even greater role in constructing and archiving the family story than is typically the case.

So, while hetero families use photo albums and videos to affirm norms of family life and togetherness, queer families do so similarly. At the same time, they are continuously producing a queer family counternarrative that refuses the mis- and nonrecognition that often occurs if viewed narrowly through biogenetic, heteronormative frameworks. If lesbian couples are at times misrecognized as mother–daughter pairs or as sisters, by telling the queer family story we affirm the value of such relationships and announce that social parenthood is equivalent to biological parenthood, and that children, products of voluntary, contingent unions, are as legitimate, and valuable, as any others.[3]

Of course, asymmetries of various sorts, including those between biological and non-biological parents continue to inscribe themselves in even seemingly egalitarian, "chosen" families. However, in asserting both sameness and difference in relation to the heteronormative family, queer family stories suggest that difference does not imply deficits, and that love and commitment make a family. The subversive quality of such family stories lies precisely in the matter-of-factness of these assertions, and their reclaiming of understandings of normality and refusal to downplay difference, and to be seen through a heterosexual lens. These stories solidify a sense of collectivity and elicit recognition from others. But when it comes to interacting with institutions of the state, such as municipal governments, post offices and schools, this search for recognition tends to be more fraught.

Queer families/straight state

Interacting with bureaucratic institutions, queer families continue to encounter a "heterosexual assumption" that shores up the heterosexual model as the norm, even as societies grow more formally accepting of difference (Weeks *et al.* 2001: 41). Indeed, even in relatively liberal areas of the USA, nonrecognition is common, as the following examples suggest. In some states (such as New York), which have legalized same-sex marriage, clerks' online forms offer only a choice of "bride" and "groom," and children of same-sex parents frequently bring home from school forms that specify "mother" and "father." Federal College Aid forms fail to accommodate same-sex families, particularly those who have undergone divorce, thereby limiting financial assistance to their children. "Married" same-sex couples often encounter curiosity when checking into guesthouses and hotels (Holson 2011; Hernandez and Flegenheimer 2011). What these and other examples suggest is that, even as institutionalized heteronormativity is fading (though slowly, in many parts of the country), a one-size-fits-all understanding of family is still culturally dominant, casting queer families into the realm of marginality, and placing the burden on them to tell their family story, and account for their difference.[4]

When my son was in middle school, for example, he was asked to fill out numerous forms that asked him for basic information, including his parents' names and phone numbers. There were spaces for his mother's first name, her last name, her work phone and her home phone, and for the father's first name, last name, work phone and home phone. The configuration of this form befits an era (and a socioeconomic context) where mothers tend to work outside the home, and when mothers and fathers often have their own phone lines. One can imagine that a similar form of 40 years or more ago might have looked very different. Yet the form assumes that each child has a mother and a father, rather than two fathers or two mothers, or even a single mother or father, and also that both parents, in a society where divorce is prevalent, share one address. When Lewis brought that form home, he placed Nancy's name in the space that requested information for his "mother," and where it asked for information about "father," he crossed out the word "father" and wrote in "mother," with my information next to it.

There are many, many mundane instances of how we went unrecognized as a family. Our mail came addressed to Mr. and Mrs. Stein, Mr. Arlene and Mrs. Nancy Solomon, The Solomon Family, Nancy and Arlene Solomon, Nancy Stein, Arlene & Solomon, and so on and so forth. Over a number of years, I collected over 20 different configurations of our names! Nancy and I laughed about the ways our little family confounded the routines of various bureaucratic agencies' software programs. However, when it came to the ways schools misrecognized our son's family story, there was little to laugh about. I cannot know how Lewis felt about having to change the forms to make his family "fit," but I can't imagine that he relished having to do so: it marginalized him, and forced him to "come out," in effect, about having same-sex parents. As Judith Butler suggests, such nonrecognition delegitimates the bond that produced the child, and by implication delegitimates the child itself. "If you're not real," she writes, "it can be hard to sustain yourselves over time; the sense of delegitimation can make it harder to sustain a bond, a bond that is not real anyway, a bond that does not 'exist'" (Butler 2002: 25).

Moreover, although children play a central role in the family story, these stories are not their creations, and children do not necessarily share their parents' narrative of family. Children have not "chosen" their family situation, and they may choose to negotiate their own sense of self and family differently than their parents. This became painfully clear to me one day when my son was about eight. He and a friend were in the attic playing one afternoon. I was working close by, unbeknownst to them, and overheard an exchange in which my son's friend asked him about his father. My son replied: "my dad is dead." His dad was not dead at all, in fact: he did not have a dad, at least not a social father. His biological father—his sperm donor—was a friend he knew well, whom we call "Uncle Charles." Lewis knew that Charles is his biological father, though we did not use that term. A contract we signed before his donation of sperm made it explicit: "Charles will not be known as daddy." But that afternoon in the attic, for the first time, I heard Lewis struggle to simultaneously explain—and hide—his family.

Parents clearly have more power to represent the family than children do, and they are frequently unaware of the struggles their children face, in part because children may choose to hide them. So, while parents may be comfortable with their sexuality, their children must negotiate a world where the "heterosexual assumption" still exists, and where their families are mis- or unrecognized. Parents often try to circumvent this, introducing themselves publicly so that their children do not have to do the emotional work of "coming out" to others. For example, once a year, Nancy and I organized a Chanukah celebration in Lewis's class, where we shared the story of the holiday and made potato latkes. Educating the predominantly gentile student body about Jewish difference, we saved Lewis the task of having to come out about his lesbian mothers—and, in fact, we did not really give him the option of *not* coming out. We treated Jewish and sexual difference nonchalantly, and also as roughly comparable "ethnic" identities that deserve to be celebrated.

So, even in our own supremely out little queer family, despite the fact that my partner and I never concealed our homosexuality from either our son or his friends, and indeed often celebrated it, he still operated in a world in which having a queer nonbiological mother—and not having a father—needed to be explained.[5] The *dominant culture is very dominant*. Dominant understandings of biological family often trumped our own efforts to tell the family story on our own terms, contravening even the most convincing efforts to perform forms of belonging that were not reducible to blood. As I've suggested, much of the work entailed in making the family story legible to others, and achieving legitimacy for it, falls on children, and, where there is only one biological parent, upon the nonbiological parent.

My nonrecognition on my son's hospital birth announcement, for example, suggests that asymmetries of power persist despite our best efforts to level the playing field. Studies that seek to assess the outcomes of same-sex parenting, and whether children of such couples fare as well as those of heterosexual couples, are incomplete if they fail to consider the impact of nonrecognition on such families, and how it can lead such families to feel illegitimate, second-class, or invisible.

Changing family stories?

We become ourselves within relationships, and in these relationships we make ourselves known and represent ourselves to others. Practices of recognition take place in relation to the dominant culture and its language, practices, political ideologies and institutional arrangements. However, even as the lived experiences of intimacy and relatedness become ever more complex, the heterosexual assumption prevails, limiting our efforts to tell our own stories, and resignify and transform dominant meanings (Benjamin 2011: 63). We see this in interactions with bureaucratic and governmental organizations, medical authorities and schools, as well as with friends, neighbors and family members.

Some suggest that, if queer families continue to be effaced, it is because homosexuality has yet to be fully integrated into the dominant culture; a thorough understanding of the fundamental moral equivalence between hetero and homo intimacies has not yet occurred. The process of incorporation, they suggest, is ongoing and frequently slow, yet progress is being made. Recognition requires educating others, which same-sex couples are doing by their very publicness, but the process of recognition takes patience, fortitude, the formation of collective will and the mobilization of resources. Indeed, the right to marry has become the predominant issue for middle-class LGBTQ people in the USA today for the very reason that, in marriage signifies and is a precondition for belonging. Marriage could make same-sex couples and their offspring immediately recognizable and intelligible, offering queer intimates public affirmation, along with legal recognition. While conferring an aura of permanence upon same-sex relationships ("'til death do we part"), legal recognition is also a reminder of the potential impermanence of such relationships, and the role that the law plays in providing some (however limited) guarantees and "intimate citizenship."

Others suggest that queer families remain unintelligible because they can never be fully assimilable. Like a square peg in a round hole, same-sex couples and their offspring can only ever be "virtually normal." While the quest for recognition may confer legal rights, it poses the threat of intensified normalization, which may exclude those who enact intimacies that do not conform to the nuclear family model: queer people who live alone, who are nonmonogamous and, perhaps even those who do not have children. Along these lines, some suggest, harkening back to an earlier wave of feminist and gay liberation writings about the family, the great contribution of queerness is to creatively up-end dominant familial structures. It is this that should be celebrated and affirmed.

Indeed, ongoing failures of recognition, some would say, suggest that queer families are ultimately untranslatable into a dominant heteronormative rubric. Judith Halberstam suggests, for example, that queer understandings of time and space are different from those of heterosexuals, urging us to reject "paradigmatic markers of life experience" in order to carve out time and space in a queer sense

(Halberstam 2005). If we associate maturity with coupledom, or with procreation, we marginalize those who do not couple or procreate. Rather than seek to be understood on others' terms, a more radical queer politic, in short, urges us to subvert dominant modes of recognition and build oppositional cultures rather than assimilating into existing ones. Maintaining illegibility or unrepresentability could be a counterweight to normalization.

While I am sympathetic to these critiques and believe they provide a necessary corrective to the rush to create what some might call "homonormative" families, it seems to me that living outside of norms is impossible—particularly for families with children. Kids attend school, and because of this, perhaps to a greater extent than their parents, they must abide by the rules of the dominant culture. Although children of gay and lesbian parents tend to exhibit greater tolerance for nonnormative gender expressions and for homosexuality, they are rarely activists on behalf of gender and sexual transgression—nor can they be expected to be (Stacey and Biblarz 2001). Moreover, queer critiques that urge a politics of non-recognition, fail to engage with the political institutions that structure our lives, distributing health insurance, codifying family law, and governing birth and death. As much as we would like to do so at times, we cannot live outside the law.

Mindful of the gap between maintaining a critique of the family and seeking to be recognized within it, Judith Butler (2002: 25) urges us to "keep the tension alive between maintaining a critical perspective and making a politically legible claim." In relation to the politics of recognition, this might lead us to argue for full marriage rights, for example, as well as for legal protections and economic benefits (such as domestic partnerships) for those who choose not to marry—and for decent healthcare for all. It might call for the simultaneous deconstruction of "the family," while shoring up its component parts—the individual, the couple, the child—regardless of sexual orientation, or biological origin. It may be tempting to see the legal recognition of same-sex marriage as the "solution" to the problem of intelligibility of queer families. Marriage is highly valued in contemporary American culture, signifying loyalty, desirability, permanence and a host of other attributes. By identifying with it, and gaining access to its cultural and legal benefits, same-sex couples become immediately legible, understandable and normative. However, while marriage rights offer one "solution" to the problem of intelligibility, they do not necessarily do justice to the myriad forms of kinship—queer and not-so-queer.

Recent economic and cultural changes are encouraging a more individualized form of family life, along with transformations of intimacy away from the privatized nuclear family, toward more temporary, flexible and unbounded forms. For example, during the last six years, according to US census data, there have been more unmarried households than married ones. At the same time, increasing numbers of same-sex couples are having children using surrogates or sperm donors, or through adoption (Holson 2011). Could it be, as Judith Stacey has declared, "all families are queer" (Stacey 2002)? Perhaps the growing convergence between queer and "straight" families will diminish the legal and cultural weight of the "heterosexual assumption" and go a long way toward alleviating the problem of non- and misrecognition many families now face.

As *The New York Times* recently reported, the "family tree today is beginning to look more like a tangled forest." As the composition of families changes, so too has the notion of who gets a branch on the family tree. Dominant understandings of genealogy privilege family defined through biological descent or marriage, failing to accommodate "chosen" families, marginalizing gay and lesbian family members. For some children, having to explain their family tree can be alienating, so some families now organize their family tree into two separate histories: genetic and emotional. Whereas charting family history has traditionally been a classroom project, some schools now skip the exercise altogether. A teacher is quoted: "You have to be ready to have that conversation about surrogates, sperm donors and same-sex parents if you are going to teach the family tree in the classroom," she said (Holson 2011: A1). If there is in fact growing acknowledgement that even seemingly "biological" families are also products of choice and contingency, this development may present the best hope of destigmatizing queer families and ensuring that they receive recognition. In the meantime, millions of same-sex parents and their children, who exist largely in relation to heteronormative family forms, will struggle to tell their stories in ways they best see fit.

Acknowledgements

Thanks to Cynthia Chris, Julee Raiskin, Steven Seidman and Nancy Solomon for their comments on an earlier draft of this essay, and to Yolanda Martinez-San Miguel and members of the Rutgers University Institute for Research on Women seminar.

Notes

1 The "public affirmation by non-heterosexuals of their importance of their chosen relationships represents a major shift in their life chances" (Weeks *et al.* 2001: 4). While same-sex parents and their families face misrecognition, for transgender individuals, particularly those who are genderqueer, the challenges are rather different. See, for example, Kellman 2012.

2 This struggle for primacy or importance characterizes two-mother families, and leads to asymmetries in which biological ties persist. I will not take up this subject here, which posed a formidable challenge to my own partnership. Ironically, the family photo albums I write about here await duplication so that Nancy and I can each have a copy in our now separate households.

3 On the construction of queer counternarratives as activism, see Vaccaro 2010.

4 Same-sex couples with children who reside in states that do not permit second parent adoptions continue to face particularly difficult legal challenges. See Bernard 2012.

5 White women who participated in a support group for children of LGBTQ parents describe tales of "coming out" that sound quite similar to the type of coming out stories white, middle-class LGBTQ youth typically tell. Children work to keep an LGBTQ parent hidden by "not telling anyone," "acting casual," "avoiding the situation," or "never explaining" things. Another way participants talk about hiding the sexual identity of their parent(s) is by "straightening up the house" (hiding anything LGBTQ or any signs of an LGBTQ relationship so parent(s) appear heterosexual). See Joos and Broad 2007: 283.

References

Benjamin, Jessica. 1988. *The Bonds of Love: Psychoanalysis, Feminism, & the Problem of Domination.* New York: Pantheon.

——2011. "Facing Reality Together." *Studies in Gender and Sexuality* 12: 27–36.

Bernard, Tara. 2012. "A Family with Two Moms, Except in the Eyes of the Law." *New York Times,* July 21: B1–B3.

Bernstein, Mary and R. Reimann. 2001. *Queer Families, Queer Politics.* New York: Columbia University Press.

Butler, Judith. 2002. "Is Kinship Always Already Heterosexual?" *differences* 13.1: 14–44.

——2005. *Giving an Account of Oneself.* New York: Fordham University Press.

Canaday, Margot. 2009. *The Straight State: Sexuality and Citizenship in Twentieth-Century America.* Princeton: Princeton University Press.

Carsten, Janet. 2004. *After Kinship.* Cambridge: Cambridge University Press.

di Leonardo, M. 1987. "The Female World of Cards and Holidays: Women, Families, and the Work of Kinship." *SIGNS* 12: 440–53.

Eng, David. 2010. *The Feeling of Kinship: Queer Liberalism and the Racialization of Intimacy.* Durham: Duke University Press.

Feagin, Joe R. 2010. *The White Racial Frame: Centuries of Framing and Counter-Framing.* New York: Routledge.

Fivush, Robin. 2008. "Remembering and Reminiscing: How Individual Lives are Constructed in Family Narratives." *Memory Studies* 1(1): 49–58.

Franklin, Sarah and Susan McKinnon. 2000. "New Directions in Kinship Study: A Core Concept Revisited." *Current Anthropology* 41(2): 275–79.

Giddens, Anthony. 1992. *The Transformation of Intimacy: Sex, Love, and Eroticism in Modern Societies.* Stanford: Stanford University Press.

Halberstam, Judith. 2005. *In a Queer Time and Place: Transgender Bodies, Subcultural Lives.* New York: NYU Press.

Hall, Stuart. 1991. "Reconstruction Work: Images of Post-War Black Settlement." In Jo Spence (ed.) *Family Snaps: The Meaning of Domestic Photography.* London: Virago.

Hernandez, Javier C. and Matt Flegenheimer. 2011. "You're Making Me the Bride? A Hiccup for Gay Unions." *The New York Times,* July 5. www.nytimes.com/2011/07/06/nyregion/seeking-marriage-licenses-gay-couples-hit-roadblock.html.

Holland, Patricia. 1991. "Introduction." In Jo Spence and Patricia Holland (eds) *Family Snaps: The Meaning of Domestic Photography.* London: Virago.

Holson, Laura M. 2011. "Who's on the Family Tree? Now it's Complicated." *The New York Times.* www.nytimes.com/2011/07/05/us/05tree.html?_r=1&emc ...

Honneth, Axel. 1995. "Patterns of Intersubjective Recognition: Love, Rights, and Solidarity." ethicalpolitics.org/blackwood/honneth.htm.

Jamieson, Lynn. 1998. *Intimacy: Personal Relationships in Modern Societies.* Cambridge: Malden, MA: Polity Press.

Joos, Kristin E. and K.L. Broad. 2007. "Coming Out of the Family Closet: Stories of Adult Women with LGBTQ Parent(s)." *Qualitative Sociology* 30: 275–95.

Kellas, Jody Koenig. 2010. "Narrating Family: Introduction to the Special Issue on Narratives and Storytelling in the Family." *Journal of Family Communication* 10: 1–6.

Kellman, C.J. 2012. "Seventeen-year-old to Facebook: I Exist, and Gender Identity is also a Civil Rights Issue." *Huffington Post,* May 22.

Kuhn, Annette. 1991. "Remembrance." In Jo Spence (ed.) *Family Snaps: The Meaning of Domestic Photography.* London: Virago.

Leonardo, Micaela. 1987. "The Female World of Cards and Holidays: Women, Families, and the Work of Kinship." *Signs* Vol. 12, No. 3 (Spring): 440–53.

Lewin, Ellen. 1993. *Lesbian Mothers: Accounts of Gender in American Culture*. Ithaca, NY: Cornell University Press.

McAdams, Dan P. 1993. *The Stories We Live By: Personal Myths and the Making of the Self*. New York: Guilford Press.

McDonald, Katrina Bell and A.M. Harvey Wingfield. 2009. "(In)visibility Blues: The Paradox of Institutional Racism." *Sociological Spectrum* 29: 28–50.

Munoz, Jose. 1999. *Disidentifications: Queers of Color and the Performance of Politics*. Minneapolis: University of Minnesota Press.

Pascoe, C.J. 2012. "Occupy the Family." *Social (in)queery*, February 17. socialinqueery. wordpress.com/2012/02/17/occupy-the-family/.

Plummer, Ken. 1995. *Telling Sexual Stories: Power, Change, and Social Worlds*. London: Routledge.

——2003. *Intimate Citizenship*. Seattle: University of Washington Press.

Rubin, Gayle. 1984. "Thinking Sex." In C. Vance, *Pleasure and Danger*. New York: Monthly Review Press.

Sedgwick, Eve. 2009. "Shame, Theatricality and Queer Performativity." In David Halperin, *Gay Shame*. Chicago: University of Chicago Press.

Seidman, Steven, C. Meeks and F. Traschen. 2002. "Beyond the Closet? The Changing Social Meaning of Homosexuality in the United States." In C. Williams and A. Stein (eds) *Sexuality and Gender*. Cambridge: Blackwell.

Spence, Jo and Patricia Holland (eds) 1991. *Family Snaps: The Meaning of Domestic Photography*. London: Virago.

Stacey, Judith. 2002. "Gay and Lesbian Families are Here—All Our Families are Queer— Let's Get Used to it!" In Christine Williams and Arlene Stein (eds) *Sexuality and Gender*. Malden, MA: Blackwell.

——2011. *Unhitched: Love, Marriage, and Family Values From West Hollywood to Western China*. NYU Press.

Stacey, Judith and Tim Biblarz. 2001. "(How) Does the Sexual Orientation of Parents Matter?" *American Sociological Review* 66.2: 159–83.

Taylor, Charles and Amy Gutman. 1992. *Multiculturalism and the Politics of Recognition*. Princeton: Princeton University Press.

Vaccaro, Annemarie. 2010. "Toward Inclusivity in Family Narratives: Counter-Stories From Queer Multi-Parent Families." *Journal of GLBT Family Studies* 6(4): 425–46.

Warner, Michael. 1999. *The Trouble with Normal: Sex, Politics and the Ethics of Queer Life*. New York: Free Press.

Watney, Simon. 1991. "Ordinary Boys." In Jo Spence (ed.) *Family Snaps: The Meaning of Domestic Photography*. London: Virago.

Weeks, Jeffrey, B. Heaphy and C. Donovan. 2001. *Same Sex Intimacies: Families of Choice and Other Life Experiments*. London: Routledge.

Weston, Kath. 1997. *Families We Choose: Lesbians, Gays, Kinship*. New York: Columbia University Press.

Zussman, Robert. 2005. "Picturing the Self: My Mother's Photo Albums." *Contexts* 5(4): 28–34.

Part V

Phenomenology of intimacy

13 The search for intimacy

Nearness and distance in psychoanalytic work

Jane Kupersmidt and Catherine B. Silver[1]

Intimacy has memorably been called "that most fragile and cherished edifice of the private sphere" (Gurstein 1996: 217). The phrase speaks volumes about the cultural and social heritage that shapes our emotions, and the idealized images of intimacy that haunt our daily lives. As psychoanalysts approaching the discussion from backgrounds in sociology (Silver) and literature (Kupersmidt), we come together in our recognition that, in clinical work, intimacy is a close-up experience with hidden referents. Because we are perhaps inadvertent guardians of the right to a private, intimate space, we hesitate to think of intimacy as a consciously sought-after construct. Our aim is rather the development of a depth of emotional experience, with and in the presence of another and with recognition of its therapeutic value. This commitment to intimately known selves in relation to others leads us to negotiate fragile territory in our work, deliberately or accidentally approaching or distancing our patients by signs and gestures that will be interpreted according to an encoding of intimacy that has been acquired, inherited and created, and for each of us that encoding will be both like and unlike our own.

Moving from one psychic and affective state to another, yet always as part of a dyad, the individual who comes to psychoanalytic work participates in an intricate process of search and discovery, finding and loss, fusion and separateness that develops and intensifies intimacy. Though we take it as a sine qua non, its role and value in psychoanalytic work has remained theoretically perplexing, even when seen as clinically essential.

Unlike empathy, a misunderstood but frequently discussed concept used to indicate a predisposition to fine attunement, intimacy in the psychoanalytic setting is a more elusive subject, bringing with it a wide range of everyday uses, and a suggestion of intensely maintained bonds of love and sexuality. That elusiveness appeared in the many case histories we found that build on the immediacy of connection in the moment. We noticed, too, the inclusion of many different characterizations of closeness as part of the analytic field,[2] but intimacy as a component of analytic work is rarely named or conceptualized as such. Our purpose, then, is to set in relief the interplay of forces involved in psychoanalytic intimacy, both verbal and non-verbal, libidinal and aggressive, and in so doing trace a theoretical lineage. Further, the tension between formal boundaries and asymmetries, on the one hand, and the protected sphere of expression offered to the patient's unconscious needs, desires and fears, on the other, constitute a dynamic of nearness and distance that lies at the heart of psycho-analytic work.

Locating intimacy in the psychoanalytic process

The dynamics of growth and rupture

The qualities of intimacy that make it essential in analytic work also make it mobile and even precarious in practice. Chief among them is its inherent excess, for, with rare exceptions, intimate connections push against constraints, exceed boundaries, are characterized by intense affective states, and are not susceptible to a discourse of reason. Even when analyst and patient would welcome an intimate connection, they may not be able to choose or tolerate the tension that necessarily comes with that territory. No matter what theoretical orientation shapes our work, we pay as much and perhaps more attention to the ebb and flow of connection in the transference as we do to the narrative. The balance is elusive:

> At bottom I think that every analysis succeeds more or less well in relation to the fact that there must be a desire, but there must not be erotization; exchanges will take place, but they must not be invasive or forced; a natural intimacy is constructed, but also a shelter against intrusion. There should be an appropriate warmth without inflammation, a communication as flowing and as fluid as possible but not overwhelming; a sufficient enduring contact, but not one that is insisted upon to the point of irritation, and so forth.
>
> (Bolognini 2008: 116–17)

This is an amiable evocation of a varied and active analytic process, one in which the movement of transference and countertransference finds a useful and mutually attuned rhythm. Ideas of sufficiency, endurance and contact do matter in the kinds of recurring intimacies we speak of here, both in terms of theoretical perspectives and within our own and our patients' cultural contexts. Often enough, inevitable discomfort and blocks also occur, so intervals of rupture and repair belong in our ideas of growth. For intimacy to thrive within a relationship, stasis needs to alternate with moments of rupture, and both require tolerance of self and other.[3] Though Bolognini's description may have a normative ring to it, he posits ways of containing the excesses of anxiety, libido and aggression that could lead to an endgame.

The diminishment of inhibition

A patient voices her expectation that therapy will make her "immune to ... fears of rejection and abandonment." For many who share this fantasy, therapy should release inhibitions and enable us to possess all we find lacking in ourselves. It seduces with the promise that one's time to be seen, valued and considered important, individually and as a member of society, has come. A further seduction is that, as Adam Phillips writes, "a psychoanalysis, like a journal, is a relatively private affair. It is a refuge for the exposure of one's life without dignity. It is neither public, nor published. One's 'childishness' is secluded" (Phillips 2002: 168).

The actuality of fulfillment plays out in quite different terms, and depends upon how and when and in what form intimacies enter the picture, and how countering forces like shame come too. Often we have a far more intimate grasp of what was wished for or feared than of the chronology of events belonging to the patient's factual history. Along the way toward sorting out the powerful fantasies that have shaped the patient's narrative, both patient and analyst submit to boundaries, a continually redefined concept that grew out of the institutional history of psychoanalysis:

> If cure is not based entirely, or even largely, on recovery of the past, on making the unconscious conscious, but, rather, on the mutative effects of the relationship between patient and analyst ... and if the therapeutic action per se is not interpretation alone ... then where does this Freudian concept of therapeutic boundary fit? And how now are boundaries to be thought about and delimited in terms of the intimacy that is a central aspect of any well-functioning therapeutic relationship, balanced by the requirement of analytic restraint?
>
> (Shane and Shane 1997: 73)

Boundaries are always in question, then. When either or both parties have been overzealous about maintaining them, or have otherwise made overly expressive use of them, they intrude. They necessarily figure in examining the environments in which intimacy is found, but also negated. The setting and frame—such elements as time limits and payment—are reminders, sometimes too insistent, that, though we care, we set the terms and are paid. Though we are available, we leave for weekends and vacations planned around our own preferences. Similar asymmetric relations of authority and power reflect the societal givens that are the context for analysis.

Other qualities differentiate analytic intimacy from what happens between you and me speaking outside the clinical setting. Uniquely, in analytic work, the persons, that is "the two parts which are its very essence are both brought together and kept apart" (Green 1979: 19). Right away, a particular tension inheres in the analytic situation. During sessions, analyst and patient generally remain in our respective, consistent positions, our voices and silences carrying the modulations of meaning and expression that will be the subject of the work. These elements may have a procedural impact, with implicit meanings not always analyzed, but generally sit in the background, part of how the prolonged and varied containing function of analytic work creates an embrace unlike any other.

Our patients may come to us expecting a transformative journey, a rite of passage to contentment, and, when their needs seem more congruent with an idealized or more acceptable image of self in relation to others, may consider the task accomplished. For others, who become more keenly aware of their desires, sexual in particular, but feel we haven't done enough to gratify the fantasies we invited, the promise remains unfulfilled, and disappointments linger.

A parable for psychoanalytic work: dreaming and deception

The Sleeping Beauty, a vivid and disturbing film by Catherine Breillat, illustrates one such rite of passage, with its heightened desire to know oneself and another intimately. Made in 2010, the film carries us, as we watch its central figure, through a bold and often phantasmagoric landscape of love, ruthlessness and tenderness, all of which seem to enrich the character's fantasies, yet, at journey's end, leave her stranded in a pallid intimacy far from her expectations.

As in the familiar fairy tale, evil and beneficent figures fight over the destiny of a young girl who will grow up both cursed and saved. Since she must sleep through her years of growing up, she will instead dream her way to womanhood, living through, in her dream life, one astonishing adventure after another. She sets off on her journey as a princess child, remote in her beauty and splendidly accoutered. When we first look down on her sleeping figure, she seems innocently at peace, expectant and unafraid, as if all she could possibly want will come to her of its own accord.

At the film's end, the young woman she has become is no longer a princess, and no longer a stranger to life's duplicities. It was a magical journey, in magical company, where she saw and sometimes thrilled to spectacles of brutality, lust and greed, passing through them seemingly untouched. She has had passionate attachments of friendship and love, and been adored, but then the enchantment fades and the scene loses its splendor. We see her reclaimed in a world like ours, and like our patients' worlds. Seen from above, as we saw her at the film's beginning, she lies unhappily enmeshed with her lover, clothes ill-fitting, a run in her stocking, the silvery sleep of her childhood perhaps only an image in her reverie, though it persists in ours.

Her dream journey through adolescent and then passionately sexual knowledge has left her a weary initiate. Though so many adventures suggest that only some ultimate form of intimacy can fulfill her desires and show a path to freedom, the colorful edifice of intimacy devolves into an illusion. Extremes of longing and disillusionment mark this girl's coming of age, and the loves lost, betrayed or abandoned inhabit her. Like the patients we speak of in describing analytic deceptions, the character described here is no more destined to escape intimacy than she is to be freed by it.

From private fantasy to public culture

We describe the film because it is an apt revisiting of classic themes of search to transcend human limitations, themes prevalent in most cultures. Fairy tales offer idealized journeys of one kind, the epic another, but, in both, a character might embark on a series of trials in order to find his (or occasionally her) way back. Often the figure encounters inequity, the injustice of political and social forces, arbitrary cruelty and the tragedy of individual fate in an impersonal world. These works are models of how the individual's journey through life carries with it the history of a culture, with its fantasies and beliefs. In many of them, the story of the journey is framed by an intimate relationship, perhaps with a confidant or sage, who mediates a mystery, of law or of the heart, and interprets to the seeker the meaning of the search.[4] Today psychoanalysis has become the space available to those who seek knowledge about themselves and their place in the world.

To consider intimacy only within the context of clinical seclusion, then, would mask the degree to which psychoanalytic views of intimacy grow out of social, political, legal and artistic contexts. With some notable and highly vocal exceptions, these considerations have not been widely incorporated in psychoanalytic theory.[5]

Before the advent of modernity, the concept of intimacy often related to conversations important to the public sphere, including the nature of one's religious life, both privately and in the public acknowledgement of a connection with God. One could have an intimate sense of innermost knowing, and one could know another intimately, and sexually. By the time Freud wrote *Three Essays on the Theory of Sexuality* (1905), intimacy had been romanticized, sexualized and detached from larger public concerns (Kristeva 1991; Oliver and Keltner 2009; Gurstein 1996).

Earlier still, in the post-Enlightenment period, intimacy and the search for personal fulfillment had developed jointly as part of a Western democratization of social relations that entered private and public spheres (Giddens 1992). Foucault (1988) made perhaps the strongest statement on the overdetermined ideology of sexual identity masquerading under the guise of personal satisfaction. According to his argument, the discourse and assumptions of the social sciences, in which he included psychotherapy, made the search for personal happiness collaborative with an ever-expanding control over sexual fulfillment. Further, sexual desire is easily titillated by consumption, and the stimulation is reciprocal. That is, to the extent that psychoanalysis flourished with the emergence of consumer societies, it also came into service as a form of consumerism.

For decades, this view has entered into the controversy about the normative impact of psychoanalysis, which appears to place individual concerns over those of society, casting therapy as an enveloping and self-perpetuating milieu in which personal freedom takes precedence over civil and social obligations. No single view of the impact of psychoanalysis can claim completeness, but, in sorting out the nature of intimate action, it has been important to us to acknowledge the widening circle our work needs to encompass.

Inside / outside

Psychoanalytic theory has traditionally used binary thinking not only in relation to gender and sexuality, but also to analyze links between the unconscious and the conscious, chief among them between id and ego, or ego and superego, between the good breast and the bad breast, true self and false self, and between self and other. This tendency to binary thinking has been challenged by Ferenczi, Lacan, Ettinger, Eigen and Bolognini, among others. Lacan's concept of *extimité*, translated as ex-timacy, points to the misleading nature of self/other boundaries. In a continuous transformation of inside to outside and back again, *extimité* works as a psychic Möbius strip. Similar conceptual weavings of inside and outside are familiar from Kleinian and Relational traditions. Such linkages in treatment have also been described through the metaphor of a mucous membrane that joins inner to outer, and lends intimacy its bodily, psycho-sensorial quality (Bolognini 2008: 116), which may be nourishing or toxic. Bracha Ettinger (2004), an artist and psychoanalyst, points to nourishing processes that take place in the move-ment of still-undifferentiated parts within porous intrauterine borders, where there is an ambiguous heterogeneity. Her theoretical model, following Winnicott's tradition, focuses on the earliest prenatal bond, and processes of "jointness-in-separation," without clear distinction between container and contained (quoted in Silver 2007). Even in the work of such widely diverse theorists as those just mentioned, intimacy arises as a form of interpenetration between inside/outside.

A language for trauma

Trauma, and the difficult work with traumatized patients, is an entire field of its own in writing and research, but it is no less part of many analyses. Beginning with the work of the neurologist and social anthropologist Dr. W.H.R. Rivers in Edinburgh during World War I, when trauma was still called shell shock, those who treat victims and witnesses of war, with its residue of unspeakable memories, have recognized the demand for treatment time and space outside the continuity of daily life. Davoine and Gaudillière (2004: 146) recounted their personal war memories to their patients, and through their telling the patients too were able to give the suppressed knowledge of what had happened representation in the lan-guage of the "therapeutic unconscious." The analyst's own experience became part of the treatment, and provided a link that broke the patient's isolation within history and society. What had until then remained unsymbolized could enter a living, shared discourse. In such trauma, the therapist awakens a willingness in the patient to speak with the voice of an "alien internal identity," in Laplanche's (1996) formulation. This voice actually constitutes the unconscious, although it has not been generated from within, and is maintained as a sealed-off external-ization, where, without symbolization, the work that takes place in the transference, closeness cannot penetrate.

Extremes and the primary object

If analytic space offers containment of unconscious and conscious need, it also accommodates overflow of many kinds—excess expectations of self-knowledge, sexual excitement and emotional intensities. Many of the facets of intimacies we explore in theoretical and clinical contexts have to do with patients' or analysts' feelings of constraint or excess, feelings of being or having too much or too little. Intimacy is linked with the struggle for separation, and with many points along the continua from language to silence, from outer to inner, from surfeit to deficit or absence, and from trauma to survival, with surges and states of intimacy that go in both directions.

It is in the extremes of the relationship with a primary object that both con-straints and excesses first occur. In *Hysteria*, Christopher Bollas sketches out how patients with differently characterized psychic structures stand in relation to a primary object, and defines what is meant by that concept:

> The primary object ... is a derivative of many experiences with actual others, some occasioned by environmental stresses ... some determined by character disorders of the mother and father that are condensed into distressed experiences of the primary, and other factors having to do with the self's own constitutional liabilities.
>
> A primary object, then, is determined by the self's psychic structure. Formed during the first years of life, this psychic structure projects the primary object that will be taken as the disposition of all others toward the self. In non-conflictual moments it may be benign, but when the self is disturbed it will reflect the structure of the self's pathology.
>
> (Bollas 2000: 7)

We have kept in mind the sense that, in many cases, it is in relation to the analyst as an embodiment of different experiences of a primary object that our patients seek intimacy. The analyst may indeed be used as a relatively new and receptive kind of object, but the traces of the past accompany every moment of relating.

Intimacy with our patients: illustrations from clinical work

We want to acknowledge, once again, the complexities and layers of meaning that define intimacy. Necessarily, our paper touches only on certain themes and theories. We could not include a number of important issues and theories that were too broad or empirical for the scope of this paper.[6] The clinical material that follows serves as illustration and sometimes counterpoint to the theoretical issues discussed thus far.

Working with a defensive surveillance: Alex[7]

Mental suffering can make life seem only a space for realization of how debased the person has become. It is not only psychotic patients who bring into treatment what the British psychoanalyst Paul Williams has called their "core psychological premise":

> Human relationships have proved to be a source of disaster and unimaginable suffering. I have fallen out of their orbit and need to be reconnected to them if life is ever to have meaning again. I fear that this is impossible as I have become so removed from people.
>
> (Williams 2010: 2)

The patient I worked with, over many years, never fully removed himself from people, but never believed he was in the same orbit inhabited by others. He thought analysis would make life livable, but the price it seemed to demand, the dependence felt toward me, felt unfair. He would suffer, and the repetition of his trauma would be unavoidable.

As a child, Alex would take apart his toys, then keep all the parts in separate boxes, sometimes adding insect wings. He would concentrate fiercely on his collection, hoping not to feel the rising tension between his parents. When something tipped his mother into one of her dangerous, near-psychotic states, his father would leave the house, and Alex would be left to try to propitiate his mother and hope she wouldn't turn on him. Usually, her destructiveness was expressed with noise-making, and she would bang on the piano, making an unbearable cacophony. Occasionally, he hid, but couldn't shut out the discordant sounds of her voice and the piano. He remains sensitive to music, and can easily become agitated when he finds it jarring.

His father, whom Alex realized should have established the rule of order, had abdicated his duty and avoided home by traveling, ostensibly for business, and Alex could not forgive him. When she was not threatening her son, his mother had made him her "advance guard," a kind of front to the world showing what a handsome family they were. The rollercoaster of being pulled in, pushed away made her staggeringly unreliable. She, too, was unforgivable. Her power as so pathological a primary object made him fear for his father's safety as well as his own (and concealed his own wish to divide them and drive his father away). Neither parent, he felt, was safe to leave out of his thoughts for a moment, and preferably not out of his sight, when all were at home. He was conscious of relief (barely so of excitement) when his parents stopped sharing a room. By the time he was old enough to go to school, the pattern of being unable to tolerate separation or connection was strongly established. He never knew, coming back, by what level of chaos he would be enveloped, or whether there would be a nothing, a no one there to relate to.

Schoolwork became something of a refuge, since knowledge, too, could be taken apart and examined, piece by piece. Learning was one thing, but, predictably, forming an autonomous endeavor quite another for him. Obsessional thought made him double back on every decision and effort, so working as part of a team became a nightmare of anxiety about losing control. His pattern would be to work under someone whom he viewed with contempt—a frequent, though unconscious defense—and then, when that person made too many demands, feel invaded and need to retreat. Similarly, he would choose women he viewed as somewhat more damaged than he considered himself to be, and interlace himself with them so closely that he would penetrate every aspect of their lives. The expectations of constancy he would set up in this way so aroused his ambivalence that he would stage a devastating rejection that left the woman in a powerless state. Seeing her so diminished would then arouse too much pity and tenderness, and he would coax her back into intimacy, promising the love and fidelity that, once again, felt too entrapping.

The pattern had its corollary with me. He made requests for more sessions, but didn't want additional regularly scheduled sessions. He speculated about the goodness of my character according to the level of pain he experienced through the work. He knew he was in trouble, knew that his treatment of others recapitulated what he had learned of first hand, and that his success at carrying his parents within him made him enact shameful and sometimes mutually humiliating scenes. All this he could bring into analysis with some honesty, acknowledging also that he was capable of striking indifference and cruelty. He had explored different therapeutic and healing modalities, and occasionally experienced some relief, but living in an intimate connection was what mattered most, and it was out of reach. For us to succeed, I needed to keep his vulnerability in the foreground, and not distance myself from his sometimes very objectionable manner, or his unerring aim when he wanted to punish the people who disappointed him.

Taking such a patient into analysis feels a bit like defying the odds, and helpfully brought to mind Freud's treatment of the Rat Man. Freud could see his patient's obsessions and fascination with perversely cruel images as a part of his character, but liked and respected other sides of his nature as well. The task with Alex also demanded that I not be distracted by perverse appearances, and understand the reparative bargaining in which he engaged, along with the circuitous efforts he made to disguise his maneuvers (Kupersmidt 2009: 9).

Alex and I, as patient and analyst, would only connect if I could receive and hold his projections and the tormented states behind them, which drove his attacks. He could be both observant and inventive, and, feeling provoked by my presence, could so easily act out of stereotypical expectations of women—whether in the role of mother, grandmother, girlfriend, spouse—and thus had many opportunities for harsh and sometimes accurate attacks on my appearance, voice, mannerisms and physical characteristics, attacks in which his fears were barely concealed. His transferential shifts recalled the way he had described dating, when he would relax his vigilance and, as he put it, "get cozy," but the next morning he would want to disappear before his companion could wake up and see him next to her. Alex didn't want to be surprised by sudden pleasure in closeness, and fantasized about creating geographical distance leaving the little stability he had in order to move as far away as possible. Aspects of the analytic frame came under fire as well—it would seem to him that the session started early, or late, or coming very early made him feel closer, or seeing other people in the waiting room made him feel excluded, or the room felt uncomfortably bright, or too dim, and revealingly the schedule inhibited his freedom but also was expected to provide more structure. He never missed a session, and told me that on days without analysis he felt adrift.

It became clear that most of his attacks defended against intimacy with others and with aspects of himself he found unbearable. His analyst had to assume "the task of managing what is dreaded within the self ... In such cases, patients cannot separate from the analyst and the internalized pathological parent" (Coen 1998: 1186). For Alex, years of work were required to begin to tolerate continued intimacy, first with me and later with a partner, with any period of calm sure to provoke a rupture that we could analyze and survive, but not prevent.

Stalled identity: Claire[8]

To articulate the identities that a patient holds internally and those displayed externally is generally a large part of the work of analysis. Claire entered analysis while she was in law school, realizing that only friendships and a friendly group environment felt motivating to her. The work itself felt irrelevant, though not terribly difficult. She had always done well in school without much effort, and believed that making an effort was a sign that something didn't fit. She herself could rely on inspiration and her ability to speak persuasively, and the impression that her own mother so idealized her. It had never occurred to her that along with the idealization came the handicap of not being invited to know herself or how she could be and have what others seemed capable of having and doing (Torok 1994; Bergmann 2000). She knew even less what she wanted, other than to impress people and make sure they liked her.

To become close with Claire meant a tricky tightrope walk. She could see that her need for specialness had become a paralyzing trap, and knew she didn't want me to be taken in by her charm or humor, because then she would be taking care of me. Once someone liked her, she had to make sure never to lose value in that person's eyes. She badly needed to recognize her aggression as a source of energy and assertiveness, but had no way safely to integrate that image of herself. If I seemed willing and interested in knowing the "dark" side of her, I would implicitly be asking her to tolerate an aspect of her identity that she had convinced herself was inauthentic, and now felt shameful. Similarly, her avowed intention was to be even more like she already appeared to be. It didn't sit well with her that I didn't have such an agenda, or in fact any agenda other than my interest in her complex, individual self.

After a long period of frustration, Claire began to speak in an almost elegiac way about the now-shaky certainties on which she thought she could rely. Prior to this moment four years into her analysis, despite her affinity for an idealized self, she had been able to speak with intelligence and insight about her dilemma. We both could see, however, that she was using her analysis as a refuge from the demands of her life, and was avoiding the positive and negative Oedipal tasks she characterized as "becoming a grown-up, like everyone else." Core infantile beliefs and fantasies still directed her actions.

With these realizations, she began to feel her identity was crumbling, and went through a period of sincere resentment against me as the messenger who had brought her to a point of knowing unwelcome truths. I understood how much loss would be involved in the passage to an identity that is hers, and not constructed by how others see her. Loss and anxiety around loss filled the sessions as her whole constellation of internal objects came into the transference.

The nature of our intimacy began to shift as well. I had been a mostly beneficent object she saw as validating her struggle, so, unlike most of her objects, I did not require her to rewrite her narratives to please me. On my part, I had admired her grace and vitality, and knew I found our sessions invigorating, as if these "good hours" were a goal in themselves. We had created an "enclave" (O'Shaughnessy 1992) where the saga of her quite varied and interesting narratives could play out without interference from the passage of time, and unfortunately also without impact on her passive surveillance of the problems in her life.

She had touched many aspects of my own nature, and, though the details of my life never entered the work in any explicit way, she felt, and occasionally said, that she counted on the "fact" that I found her perspectives, whether on the people she mentioned or on her long relationship with a man very close to her own age, sympathetic and rational. It would be a misnomer, in this treatment and in general, to call my experience of Claire "countertransference" in the traditional sense, which would imply that what I felt was only a response to what she brought in. That view of countertransference has long been considered a misrepresentation (Green 2005: 51–57), for much more is invoked than a response. Even when well analyzed, we read theory, make interpretations and are present for our patients in a neutrality that is not blank, but instead dependent on our own structures and replete with our own associations. The more clearly I understood the nature of our dyad, the more I was able to retreat and let her fill the space we created.

Claire was able to draw on this intimacy as her determination grew to do more than inhabit an enclave with me. Soon, her sense that the old ground of her identity was slipping away made her anxiety palpable, all the more so as analysis remained private but not sequestered from everyday life. One day,, she spoke of an argument with her mother, and in an unusually active way, I questioned the way she had framed her account as another example of her mother's limitations. As the session continued, I noticed that, in the slightly staccato rhythm of our dialogue, we were replicating the suppressed anger and edgy tone of the argument she was describing, as if we had to replay the music of their relationship between us and acknowledge the painfully enclosed situation it created.

The anxiety of the moment was strong for both of us. In keeping with my receptivity to our joint and separate emotional states, I had been caught up in an enactment. It was proving valuable, though I could see that I had come close to acting rather than only being seen as a dangerous object. She was able to articulate her fear that, like her mother, I might enclose her as well, and punish her for failing to meet my demands. Claire's often stated feeling of safety in the treatment had collided with an anxious sense of my potential to be dangerous. She felt exhausted, but grounded in a more honest intimacy than she had ever before achieved, and the difference felt unmistakable to her.

In such moments of connection, it may seem that the analyst's message will release the patient from the spell of being a child who cannot separate, but, of course, this is a partial account, one kind of connection, and, though as such it is powerful, it will and must be repeated in many guises before genuine integration occurs.

Psychic nourishment: Anna[9]

Anna first came to analysis with expectations of being understood, listened to and loved—very much within the socially constructed ideology of therapy as a guarantor of psychic change, if not "happiness." As a child growing up in conditions of economic hardships, abandonments and displacements, Anna had needs that could not be fulfilled. The three siblings were at times separated from their parents and from each other, and Anna, as she told her therapist quite early on, at age two had been taken in alone by another family for more than a year. The sense of displacement that she had experienced was an embedded certainty, and a part of her identity, but a part she most wished to keep at bay.

In her aloneness, Anna felt that she did not know who she was, or to whom she belonged. She wished to be known and loved, yet was afraid of being seen and acknowledged. To a striking degree, Anna initially could not accept the impersonality of the analytic situation and the asymmetry of knowledge, power and money, which for her reopened the wounds of being intellectually marginalized and emotionally ignored. Analysis, she felt, should obey different standards, tailored to fit her, not repeat the family dynamic that left her feeling dispossessed. Yet Anna kept coming, never giving up the battle for connectedness, with its oscillations between a desire to be known and acknowledged, and a desire to hide and remain anonymous.

Anna developed a strong and positive transference that echoed her observant, idealizing strategy as a child. She imbued her therapist/mother with the very virtues most valuable in his own eyes, not only hers: a finely honed poetic sensibility and, most of all, a gift for reverie and attunement (similar to what Bion (1962) describes in his observations on maternal care). As the treatment proceeded, a mutual idealization grew and proved dangerously seductive to both. For Anna, it became a defense against her desperate need to merge, a need that covered a fear of annihilation. Both sides of the therapeutic dyad felt gratified in what was initially experienced as a deep sense of connectedness. Their emotional world seemed to resonate and echo each other, and neither recognized the threat posed by resting on mutual idealization.

Anna experienced intimacy as a form of nourishment akin to the prelinguistic and pre-Oedipal experiences she had lived through with her mother in a near-merged state. She talked about her mother and herself as twins. The need to keep intact the identification of the analyst with the idealized mother became especially important after Anna's mother passed away several years later, and the analysis became part of a mourning process. During that time, words became less important than feeling close to her analyst in the silence they shared. This deep experience of emotional nearness led in the end to an impasse.

Offering nourishment for early emotional deficits is essential for analysands who have suffered early traumas and emotional deprivation (Winnicott 1971), yet this primary focus on pre-Oedipal issues of aloneness and alienation carries multiple dangers. In this case, though intimacy had provided a way to contain Anna's aloneness and fears of abandonment, at another and perhaps more complex level, it had also concealed a dissociative thought process, and Anna's use of splitting and the idealization of her therapist to defend against her suppressed anger. There were glimpses of hateful wishes, and an unforgiving, paranoid-schizoid hatred of needed objects (Klein 1957). The therapy had continued to focus on Anna's desires and fantasies[10] to fuse with and invade an object serving maternal needs, but in so doing had preempted the exploration of jealousy, anger and sexual competitive feelings, not only in the Oedipal struggles with her father but even more in the rivalries with her siblings. As Juliet Mitchell has so powerfully reminded us, it is crucial to take lateral conflicts, those within the same generation, into account (Mitchell 2003). We see how incestuous and murderous desires among siblings also shape the emergence of a social identity. In Anna's case precisely such wishes had grown out of the relationships with her siblings, and were far more prominent than Oedipal wishes, yet they never were fully identified or interpreted in the transference.

As long as the therapy couple maintained an unspoken and non-conflictual contract that bypassed the expression and interpretation of aggression towards the Other and the workings of the death drive toward the self, they had been able to maintain the general aura of Oneness (Bion 1959). Under the surface of a charmed analysis, however, were tensions and a growing sense of misrecognition as a form of symbolic violence (Bourdieu 1991) and as a fear of not knowing, which carries with it a state of non-existence (Green 1975).

Therapists as well as patients have a need to feel loved and recognized. Both are engaged in the struggle to restrain erotic and aggressive drives as well as the process of coming to terms with separation issues (Dimen 2011). In Anna's treatment, her analyst's narcissistic needs, coupled with his inwardness, made the expression of her own inner terror difficult to reveal. After many years of treatment, Anna came to realize that there was little room to express her pent-up anger, frustration and rage—the emotional nourishment had turned toxic in its effects.

With the shift away from pre-Oedipal containment and nourishment to Oedipal struggles and sibling rivalries, which brought in a very different and often erotic fantasy life, the communication process between Anna and her therapist drastically changed. The loss of the earlier intimacy, rather than being mourned, became part of a negative transference that was never analyzed, and that further stunted her emotional growth. At that point, her therapist became defensive and unable to respond impersonally to her emotional challenges and verbal attacks. The "failure of speech," to use a Lacanian formulation, made Anna feel, once more, misinterpreted, misunderstood and ignored. The promise to use language for the unrestricted expression of thoughts and feelings had come to enslave more than liberate Anna in the psychoanalytic process. Her analyst was not able to verbalize her "unspeakable" desires to be known in ways that would have made them acceptable to her, and available as a language of emotional life that could be spoken, heard and reinscribed in social discourse.

The impasse became punitive, and it seemed clear that Anna needed to see another analyst. What happened in the shift from a nurturing to a poisonous intimacy illustrates the failure of "impersonal intimacy," a concept used by Bersani and Phillips in their book *Intimacies* (2008). Impersonal intimacy refers to the role of speech in the creation of a psychic space in which the persona of the analyst becomes a virtual presence for the analysand. In such a space, linguistic exchange invites a search for intimacy with the self. "Impersonal intimacy asks of us what is the most inconceivable thing: to believe in the future without the need to personalize it" (Bersani and Phillips 2008: 117). In Anna's case, the negative transference had come to feel like a very personal rejection by the analyst that concretized the therapeutic relationship, stopping any possibility of further psychic growth. The therapeutic dialogue between Anna and her therapist never became a "conversation suspended in virtuality" (ibid.: 28) that analysis needs to offer if the patient is to thrive.[11]

In his paper on "The Uncanny" (1909), Freud observed that the greatest intimacy comes with a view of oneself that surprises by its foreignness—what we might call its "virtuality." When Anna left her analyst, she was ready to make the acquaintance of many unfamiliar and scary aspects of herself. Writing was an area blocked while she was so connected to her therapist, but, once Anna accepted her own competitive striving and creativity, she began to write.

From asymmetry to feeling equal: Sarah[12]

In her analysis, Sarah, a successful professional, wanted a dialogue, a mutual sharing of ideas and affects that would make her feel socially included and emotionally secure. Not unlike Anna, she wanted to create a shared intersubjective reality. Analysis, in her conception, deals with the expression of repressed wishes in a mutually active context that brings about greater self-awareness and a feeling of being alive. From the start, Sarah felt controlled by arbitrary authority and by the intellectual rigidity of the theoretical frame that she felt guided my interpretations. She experienced a lack of engagement and openness on my part that repeated previous family dynamics of not having been heard or considered an equal. She became increasingly needy, angry and frustrated, opening up layers of suppressed feelings. In contrast to what had occurred in Anna's therapy, the lack of idealization in the way Sarah and I worked together made it possible for me to hear and accept her struggles for recognition.

The lack of communication with her educated parents had been a source of sadness and resentment. Growing up, Sarah felt she had been brought up in total silence, ignored emotionally and intellectually. Her mother was a visual artist who did not trust words as a way to express emotions. She believed that language, as a product of the social order, could not be used to validate intimate feelings. Wordless intimacy was a condition of love for her mother. Her silence was not hostile or punitive, yet Sarah felt left out of her mother's internal world of rich and exciting feelings and thoughts. Sarah's father, out of professional habit, used language sparingly and always with ambiguous meaning. He lived in a tower of silence and used patriarchal authority to get what he wanted. Her father's silence, unlike her mother's, was hostile, dismissive and tyrannical. In her analysis, whenever Sarah asked questions or raised intellectual issues, I listened with interest but with restraint and neutrality. I knew how difficult she found it that I would not engage in an opinionated and open discussion.

At those moments, Sarah re-experienced the deep wounds of childhood, carried through in adulthood, of not having been spoken to and not having been a part of a shared, familial social discourse. Her struggle, as in childhood, took the form of silent resentment against me as a primary object, followed by outbursts of anger and even abusive language to force recognition. A pattern of oscillation between language—or its lack—as emotional expression or as a means of control led Sarah to disassociate words from feelings, making trust difficult to maintain.

As Sarah revealed more of her inner self and exposed unconscious and often, to her, shameful desires and emotions, it appeared to her that the knowledge gap between us grew. I felt that any attempt to bridge the gap would be misguided, and thus continued to listen and be present as she struggled. Over many years, Sarah came to accept the asymmetry of the communication process. She recognized that the seeming injustice of the therapeutic dialogue had actually diminished her inhibitions, and been integral to her process of psychic change as well as the emergence of a new type of "relationality ... a reciprocal self-recognition in which the very opposition between sameness and difference becomes irrelevant as a structuring category" (Bersani and Phillips 2008: 104).

Gradually, a new range of affects—acceptance, compassion and pleasure—developed between us, together with a different psychoanalytic dialogue that involved greater sharing. Paradoxically, the asymmetry against which she fought so hard brought about a deeper acceptance of separate selves and the recognition of an intersubjective space of connectedness that Bersani calls "first intimacy" (Bersani and Phillips 2008: 108). First intimacy defines the mutual connectedness and potentiality for growth within an unequal field, between the infant and the process of mothering (not the mother per se), a process that goes beyond an attachment to a subject.

The differentiated but reciprocal attachment that occurs in parenting, as in analysis, presupposes two essential components: a shared emotional language (non-verbal and verbal) and acceptance of the inevitability of loss. For Sarah, the loss consisted in relinquishing her fantasies of possessing me entirely in order to share a sense of *jouissance*[13] and being alive, as she had tried to do with her mother. Her desire to possess me was not aggressive in a Kleinian sense, but was experienced as a pleasurable invasive excess. As her analyst, I felt joy and excitement at her ability to escape from modes of thinking and feeling that had kept her a prisoner to herself. Yet, I also felt trepidation and some fear that her new feelings of empowerment would lead to disappointment in her engagement with the world.

Moments of intimacy—a smile, a look, a tear, a gesture in the silence—flourished when the gap between us became less an area of contention and gave way to a sense of trust in the analytic process. Though Sarah had long fought the boundaries of treatment as being unjust and emotionally abusive, after many years in treatment, she could experience how much her deep need for connectedness had allowed her a greater sense of intimacy with herself. When we jointly decided to end her analysis, she made use of the impending termination to explore her sense of release from the formal boundaries that had defined our relationship. A few weeks before the end of her analysis, she felt a genuine gratitude for our work together. By now, the asymmetry of the relationship between us was not experienced as a lack of recognition and an impediment to analytic work. The unspoken and unconscious exchange of feelings between us created a bridge that let us accept each other as equals.

Secrets: Emma[14]

Among patients who have been abandoned or abused as children, the struggle for intimacy is especially poignant. In their lives, the search for intimacy becomes a compulsion, part of an unending journey of hope, disappointment and self-punishment.

For Emma, the space of intimacy in analysis existed around the sharing of secrets. Her father's best friend had sexually abused her when she was a teenager. The incident shaped the rest of her life. Following a previous analysis when she was in her late teens, Emma was able to gradually move away from the feeling of being a victim and the guilt and shame attached to it. Unconsciously, however, she was repeating the trauma in many aspects of her life. Emma, now in her forties, is married to a man who provides caring and emotional support. Yet there is little or no sexual desire between them. Emma has had multiple affairs to fulfill her sexual needs. More than sexual enjoyment, the sexual encounters were a way to get back at men, to hurt them and to enjoy their impotence. In her analysis, her sexual life was revealed in great detail, but without much libidinal energy. Listening to her induced in me a feeling of deadness, which I understood as a fear of her own inner deadness being used to keep a safe distance between us. Emma kept her sexuality separate from her emotional life. Bringing them together was experienced as too dangerous. She risked being flooded with memories and the shame she had repressed.

Emma's life situation changed once she met a married man who could fulfill her emotional and sexual needs. Emma felt attached to both her husband and what she calls her "second husband." For the last two and a half years, she has been living a secret double life, achieving a remarkable but precarious emotional balance. In the transference, I became a parent from whom she needed support but also expected disapproval and punishment. The dynamics of treatment oscillated between feeling confident about herself, followed by loathing, and self-doubt. Emma wanted me to force her to make a choice between the two men and hoped that I could find a solution to her excruciating dilemma. She was terrified of the losses and rejections that would ensue whatever choice she made. I felt that Emma has come to identify me as a co-conspirator, the only person privy to her secret life. This image is bound up with expectations of loyalty that enhance a sense of emotional security, but provide no real emotional connectedness. Emma trusted me, yet she was also using me to avoid making a difficult choice. In Emma's balancing act, she was projecting her confusion, ambivalence and fears. Because of her traumatized history, the feeling of connectedness was based on a fragile equilibrium between trust and the fear of betrayal. Intimacy as a tool of treatment is double edged. In Emma's case, it was used as a resistance as well as an emotional safety net. Moving on in her life means becoming more attached to one primary object while losing another, an impossible loss. Our work at this point is very gradual. It consists in creating the conditions for a process of separation-in-jointness where emotional intimacy and safety can coexist in and outside of treatment.

Conclusion

Though psychoanalysis, and our commitment to it, privileges the inner life, our discussion of how intimacy functions in analytic work has reinforced, for each of us, a belief that the individual seen in the private sphere alone is seen apart from the lived dimensions of social and political contexts. The strength of psychoanalysis, its willingness to know the human psyche, is also its vulnerability. Hannah Arendt's urgency is relevant here:

> ... even the greatest forces of intimate life—the passions of the heart, the thoughts of the mind, the delights of the senses—lead an uncertain, shadowy kind of existence unless and until they are transformed, deprivatized and deindividualized, as it were, into a shape to fit them for public appearance.
>
> (Hannah Arendt, *The Human Condition*, cited by Gurstein: 29)

Going from the individual in isolation to the larger world, and back again, the search for intimacy thus bears irresolvable tensions which transform both participants in clinical work, functioning in destructive as well as life-enhancing ways. These tensions—around nearness and distance, the fading and restitution of perceived boundaries, and the endurance of loss and mourning—are the formative aspects of intimacy we have traced in the accounts from our practices and theoretical discussions. In that process, we have realized the richness of this concept, and how integral it is to the fluid, oscillating work of psychoanalysis.

Notes

1 Authors' names are listed alphabetically.
2 Compared to concepts like empathy and subjectivity, intimacy, with a few exceptions, is absent in psychoanalytic discourse, and in indices.
3 There are many statements of the limits of equilibrium, from Freud's *Beyond the Pleasure Principle* onwards.
4 The Sumerian *Epic of Gilgamesh* is one of the earliest, dating from the third millennium BC.
5 The early effort by Freud to set up clinics has now been compellingly described by Elizabeth Ann Danto (2005). Among current examples, Section IX of Division 39 of the APA is active in its opposition to American military uses of psychologists.
6 We have not tried to discuss how the gender, sexual orientation, racial, ethnic or religious difference between patient and analyst affect intimacies in the clinical dyad, though these are certainly important differences to investigate. We were also drawn to particular theories in relation to our subject. For example, while we talk about connectedness and attachment in the clinical setting, we do not use the literature on attachment theory that tends to be more research and data oriented.
7 Alex is a patient seen by Jane Kupersmidt.
8 Claire is a patient seen by Jane Kupersmidt.
9 This vignette of Anna's analysis is based on a case that Catherine Silver supervised. It is not intended as a discussion of the supervisory process.
10 We have used the more frequent American spelling, but, in the literature referring to Kleinian uses of the term, the spelling "phantasy" is more frequent.
11 Another helpful illustration of impersonal intimacy and its corollary, impersonal narcissism, occurs in the narrative written by a patient–analyst team several years after the therapy ended (Budick and Aronson 2007). The dual narrative shows the gradual emergence of separate identities supporting growth and change in each other through the experience of impersonal narcissism, which "whatever else it is, [is] a training in bearing frustration without recourse to [symbolic] violence" (Bersani and Phillips 2008: 109).
12 Sarah is a patient seen by Catherine Silver.

13 We are using the word *"jouissance"* to connote a sexual enjoyment that goes beyond the pleasure principle, and in doing so transgresses the very prohibition created by desire (Lacan 1992).
14 Emma is a patient seen by Catherine Silver.

References

Bergmann, Maria V. 2000. *What I Heard in the Silence: Role Reversal, Trauma and Creativity in the Lives of Women.* Madison, CT: International Universities Press.
Bersani, Leo and Adam Phillips. 2008. *Intimacies.* Chicago: University of Chicago Press.
Bion, W.R. 1959. "Attacks on Linking." *International Journal of Psychoanalysis* 40: 308–15.
——1962. "The Psycho-Analytic Study of Thinking." *International Journal of Psychoanalysis.* 43: 306–10.
Bollas, Christopher. 2000. *Hysteria.* London: Routledge.
Bolognini, Stefano. 2008. *Secret Passages: The Theory and Technique of Interpsychic Relations.* Trans. Gina Atkinson. London: Routledge.
Bourdieu, Pierre. 1991. *Language and Symbolic Power.* Boston: Harvard University Press.
Breillat, Catherine. 2011. *La Belle Endormie (The Sleeping Beauty).* Story: H.C. Anderson, C. Breillat, C. Perrault. Production: Arte France, CB Films, Flach Film. Strand Releasing, USA.
Budick, Emily and Rami Aronson. 2007. *Psychotherapy and the Everyday Life. A Guide to the Puzzled Customers.* London: Karnac Books.
Coen, S.J. 1998. "Perverse Defenses in Neurotic Patients." *Journal of the American Psychoanalytic Association* 46: 1169–94.
Danto, Elizabeth A. 2005. *Freud's Free Clinics: Psychoanalysis and Social Justice, 1918–1938.* New York: Columbia University Press.
Davoine, Francoise and Jean-Max Gaudillière. 2004. *History Beyond Trauma.* New York: Other Press.
Dimen, Muriel. 2011. "Lapsus Linguae or a Slip of the Tongue?" *Contemporary Psychoanalysis* 47(1): 35–79.
Eigen, Michael. 1993. *Flames from the Unconscious.* London: Karnac.
Ettinger, L. 2004. "Matrixial Trans-subjectivity." *Theory, Culture and Society* 23(2–3): 218–22.
Ferenczi, Sándor. 1949 [1933]. "Confusion of the Tongues between Adults and the Child (The Language of Tenderness and of Passion)." *International Journal of Psychoanalysis* 30: 225–30.
Ferro, Antonino. 2002. *In the Analyst's Consulting Room.* Trans. Philip Slotkin. New York: Routledge.
Foucault, Michel. 1988. *The Care of the Self. The History of Sexuality*, Vol. 3. New York: Random House.
Freud, Sigmund. 1905. "Three Essays on the Theory of Sexuality." In J. Strachey (ed. and trans.) *The Standard Edition of the Complete Psychological Works of Sigmund Freud*, Vol. 7: 136–49.
——1919. "The Uncanny." In J. Strachey (ed. and trans.) *The Standard Edition of the Complete Psychological Works of Sigmund Freud*, Vol. 17: 219–26.
Giddens, Anthony. 1992. *The Transformation of Intimacy. Sexuality, Love & Eroticism in Modern Societies.* Stanford: Stanford University Press.
Green, André. 1975. "The Analyst, Symbolization and Absence in the Analytic Setting (On Changes in Analytic Practice and Analytic Experience)—In Memory of D.W. Winnicott." *International Journal of Psychoanalysis* 56: 1–22.
——1979. "Psychoanalysis and Ordinary Modes of Thought." Trans. Patricia Tyrell. In *On Private Madness.* Madison, CT: International Universities Press, Inc.

———2005. *Key Ideas for a Contemporary Psychoanalysis: Misrecognition and Recognition of the Uncon-scious*. Trans. Andrew Weller. London: Routledge, New Library of Psychoanalysis.

Gurstein, Rochelle. 1996. *The Repeal of Reticence: America's Cultural and Legal Struggles over Free Speech, Obscenity, Sexual Liberation, and Modern Art*. New York: Hill and Wang.

Klein, Melanie. 1957. *Envy and Gratitude*. New York: Basic Books.

Kristeva, Julia. 1991. *Strangers to Ourselves*. Trans. Leon S. Roudiez. New York: Columbia University Press.

Kupersmidt, Jane. 2009. "Listening to the Rat Man 100 Years Later, or the Gadfly of Doubt." *The Round Robin* XXIV, 1: 3–11.

Lacan, Jacques. 1992. *Ethics in Psychoanalysis: The Seminar of Jacques Lacan, Book 7 (1959–1960)*. Trans. Dennis Porter. New York: Norton.

Laplanche, Jean. 1976. *Life and Death in Psychoanalysis*. Trans. J. Mehlman. The Johns Hopkins University Press.

———1996. "Aims of the Psychoanalytic Process." *Journal of European Psychoanalysis* Vol. 5 (Spring–Fall): 69–79.

———1999. *Essays in Otherness*. London: Routledge.

Mitchell, Juliet. 2003. *Siblings: Sex and Violence*. Cambridge: Polity Press.

Ogden, Thomas H. 1995. "Analysing Forms of Aliveness and Deadness of the Transfer-ence—Countertransference." *International Journal of Psychoanalysis* 76: 695–709.

———2005. *This Art of Psychoanalysis. Dreaming Undreamt Dreams and Interrupted Cries*. London: Routledge.

Oliver, Kelly and S.K. Keltner (eds). 2009. *Psychoanalysis, Aesthetics and Politics in the Work of Kristeva*. Albany, NY: SUNY Press.

O'Shaughnessy, Edna. 1992. "Enclaves and Excursions." *International Journal of Psychoanalysis* 73: 603–11.

Phillips, Adam. 2002. *Equals*. New York: Basic Books.

Shane, E. and M. Shane. 1997. "Intimacy, Boundaries, and Countertransference in the Analytic Relationship." *Psychoanalytic Inquiry* 17: 69–89.

Silver, Catherine B. 2007. "Womb Envy: Loss and Grief of the Maternal Body." *Psycho-analytic Review* 94(3): 409–30.

Stein, Ruth. 1998. "The Enigmatic Dimension of Sexual Experience: The 'Otherness' of Sexuality and Primal Seduction." *The Psychoanalytic Quarterly* 67: 594–625.

Torok, Maria. 1994 [1964]. "The Meaning of 'Penis Envy' in Women." In N. Abraham and M. Torok, *The Shell and the Kernel*. Trans. N. Rand. Chicago: University of Chicago Press.

Williams, Paul. 2010. *Invasive Objects: Minds Under Siege*. London: Routledge.

Winnicott, D.W. 1971. *Playing and Reality*. London Routledge.

14 Finding the addressee

Notes on the termination of an analysis

Anne Golomb Hoffman

For an analysand, the termination of an analysis involves recognition of the analyst in the present moment. That recognition entails the ability to feel the aliveness, to grasp the embodied subjectivity of the other person in the room. Working closely with that other person over time, one re-finds oneself. My experience of analysis is the history of this struggle. Given the paradoxical intimacy of the analytic relationship, rule-governed and formal on the one hand, touching on the most private and interior concerns on the other, it seems appropriate to use my own experience as the material for an investigation that draws on the analytic literature regarding termination. If analysis is itself a process of inquiry, then its grounding in the personal offers insight into the intimate pathways through which other forms of intellectual inquiry take shape.

Some years back, I sought help because I found myself experiencing massive difficulties in writing. (Far be it from me to suggest that writing is ever easy; I refer to a degree and kind of difficulty that amounted to a failure of creativity.) Looking back, I see that the analysis took up my loss of access to interiority, a loss so profound that I barely knew it had occurred. As a reader, teacher and scholar of literature, the world of texts is central to my life and it was exactly that domain of textuality that seemed to have died in me. As a provisional definition, consider textuality to be the lived space of a text, a realm possessing amplitude and depth, through which the mind can move. Although at the time I could not have conceptualized the loss, I was aware that it was becoming harder and harder for me to write: I was grinding to a halt.

From the vantage point of the present, it seems obvious now that an experience of surgery, a hysterectomy, had the impact on me, completely unnoticed at the time, of the loss of a precious internal domain, the source of life and art. In the time following surgery, I found myself expending enormous amounts of energy as I worked to overcome the distance between me and the text, and to gain access to the inner world—the body—of the text. Nevertheless, it was through the work of analysis that I came to understand the many meanings of that "juicy organ", the uterus in my emotional life. Analysis took me into a mythic universe of the body, where a hidden chamber contained the secrets of life and art.

The body in the mind

Analysis allowed me to comprehend more fully the role of the infantile body as the grounding of metaphor. My own experiences of loss and recuperation illustrate the ways in which metaphor emerges out of the earliest sensations, perceptions and fantasies of the body. In its embodied origins, metaphor transfers meaning from concrete to abstract in the life of the mind (see Borbely 1998 on metaphor). The origins of metaphor lie in the realm of infantile sexuality, inasmuch as the small child's sensations, perceptions and fantasies of its body and those bodies closest to it form the basis for unconscious mental life (Erreich 2003). From the body to the mind in the life of the subject: early experiences of embodiment inscribe the contours of subjectivity (Litowitz 2002). Those early experiences establish surfaces and openings, differentiate inside from outside, provide the foundations of subjectivity.

Yet much as one individuates and acquires a sense of self as separate from others, one never fully relinquishes the connections and confusions of inner with outer, self and other that occur prior to and during this formative process. (Perhaps it's in this sense that nothing is ever lost in the unconscious: seemingly contradictory states and perceptions coexist in the strata of mental life.) The physical and the abstract never entirely lose their connection, moreover, which is part of what gives life to our experiences of language.

The infantile body is thus a vital resource, and yet one that remains generally inaccessible to conscious awareness. Psychoanalysis acknowledges the roots of metaphor in the infantile body, but resists any suggestion that early experiences are readily available to consciousness and intentionality. Access is indirect. The physiological functions of the uterus notwithstanding, it took me years to come to terms with the fantasmatic meanings that organ had assumed in my emotional life. While medically benign, surgery was traumatic at the level of metaphor and myth: how I lived in my body unawares. My unconscious response to an otherwise uneventful surgery demonstrates the power of mythical meanings to shape bodily experience and emotional life. Analysis thus became the means through which to explore and bring to light the significations that had so profoundly disrupted my ability to write. Surgical excision of an organ amounted to loss of the source of fertility, the domain of creation and creativity, a loss too great to recognize.

Analytic intimacy

It is a paradox of analytic intimacy that the primitive body comes alive within the framework of a relationship that is governed by a prohibition on physical contact, beyond the occasional handshake. The most intimate bodily interiors come alive within this rather formal setting. Reflecting on the connection between mind and body, Marilyn Charles (Charles 2001) observes that it is precisely the prohibition on physical touch that makes it possible for analysis to carry out this work of restoring the intimate connection between fantasy, language and embodiment. The prohibition on touch makes possible the retrieval of the roots of metaphor in physical experience. It allows *touch* to come to life again in *language*.

The prohibition on physical contact makes possible the work that is specific to analysis, allowing a sense of primitive embodiment to come to life in words. Thus, Didier Anzieu observes, the possibility of an analytic cure rests on a bodily foundation: "The verbal exchange which marks out the terrain of the cure is only effective because it takes up again on a new, symbolic plane what was previously exchanged in the visual and tactile registers" (Anzieu 1989: 139). In effect, this rule-governed structure creates a dynamic space in which language registers tactile sensation and becomes the object of study.

> Psychoanalysis is only possible if the prohibition on touching is respected. One may say anything, so long as one finds words that are both appropriate to the transference situation and that express thoughts suited to the actual nature of the patient's suffering. The analyst's words symbolize, replace and re-create tactile contact, without the actual contact being necessary: the symbolic reality of the exchange is more effective than its physical reality.
>
> (Anzieu 1989: 154)

Working with Freud's observation that the first ego is a bodily ego, Anzieu develops the concept of the early "skin ego" as a way of thinking about the primitive body in the early years of life. Anzieu describes the "phantasy ... of a skin shared by mother and child" (Anzieu 1989: 59), established through touch and the maternal "surround" or "*entourage*," as common to mother and child, allowing for "direct communication between the two partners, reciprocal empathy and an adhesive identification" (ibid.: 62–63). The psychoanalytic pair recreate some of these earliest aspects of experience.

Interior space

The difficulties that I experienced after surgery ask to be understood or at least imagined on the level of primitive fantasy. My difficulties attest to the survival of those forms of primitive thinking: how else to explain the connection between the uterus and the ability to carry out literary scholarship? Or, put another way, the analytic work of excavation—carried out through dreams, associations, reflections—acquainted me with the connection.[1] Psychoanalysis offered a way to excavate the layers of thought and activity beneath which primitive images continued to operate.

I would say that a governing image in my emotional life concerns an interior domain, an enclosed space. I can look at my experience of analysis through the prism of this image, as it came up in so many different ways over the course of the work. I have experienced this enclosed space or magical interior both as something that exists inside me and as something of which I am a part, as interior to my body and as a space that I occupy, a space in which I found myself in the analytic session, together with another person. I came to understand that I was experiencing this space in multiple ways: as a chamber within my own body, as the analytic consulting room and also as the body of the analyst. It was both intra- and intersubjective.

I recall how startled I was by these interpretive possibilities, when they first began to come up. It was electrifying, for example, to identify a fantasy of the analyst's body as a chamber that I might enter. As I think back to the excitement that I felt at these fantasmatic images, they suggest the beginnings of recovery of a vitality that I had lost. Through associative work, I was stumbling upon a domain of life of which I was a part, a domain that was a part of me. It was as if I'd been given permission to be a child again and to speak.

The very flexibility, the versatility of this image of spatial structure gives the measure of its analytic importance. Images of an interior chamber, an enchanted space, undoubtedly go back to a time earlier than my awareness of the uterus as an organ and involve images of space and enclosure that are prior to language and individuation. Analytic work was excavating the layers of fantasy and knowledge that constituted the image. All of this helps to explain why a hysterectomy should have had so traumatic an impact on my intellectual creativity. The careful work of analysis brought this versatile and vital image into visibility, giving it substance in the analytic work. Through analytic work, I regained not the organ, nor its physiological fertility, but the fertility of metaphor.

Tamar Pollak (2009: 488) posits a "primal psycho-physical space" where bodily and mental experience exist prior to the subordination of the bodily to the mental. While it may be impossible to retrieve the memories or experiences of such an early time, the contained space and formal structure—the framing—of the analytic session have the effect of undoing conventional hierarchies of the mental over the physical.

Drown

Midway in my analysis, T.S. Eliot's line "Till human voices wake us and we drown" entered my thoughts. The phrase conveys my experience of the densely saturated verbal medium of the analytic session: the saturation of verbal experience for which the session served as container and frame. Eliot's phrase was an association that helped me put into words something distinctive about the medium of the session. It indicated the beginnings of my exploration of what I would recognize eventually as the inner space of the analytic consulting room and of my own body. Does "drown" have a particular meaning here? It suggests the feeling of immersion in an intimate sphere that had been lost, a realm belonging to the earliest years of life, shaped by bodily sensations and fantasies. Eliot's words gave me a verbal formulation for what I was experiencing in the session: the dense saturation of language with embodiment.

On the significance of the uterus as a "juicy organ": as an adult, I never minded menstruating. My body signaled its primacy in its periodic flows over which I could exert no conscious control. I liked that. I also enjoyed being pregnant. In particular, I recall the growing textual roundness of a first pregnancy when I was a graduate student embarking on a dissertation; working on a proposal with rounding belly offered a very satisfying sense of containment that embraced the textual along with the physical. This pleasure in a "juicy organ" gives support to Rosemary Balsam's cogent advocacy for recognizing women's pleasure in their own bodies; she argues for the importance of using specifically feminine terms that are not filtered through a male perspective (Balsam 2012: ch. 2).

Reading Balsam's work revives in me perceptions and fantasies that go back to my reactions to my mother's pregnancy when I was three. I recall a dream as an adult of a large pregnant abdomen, with drops of water glistening on it, titled in my dream the National Drinking Water Supply. Clearly, I was in awe of the power of the maternal body as a container that could swell with new life. Balsam's attentiveness to clinical detail and her refusal to hasten into conventional readings of penis envy and castration illuminate the impact of women's bodies, their contours and changing shapes, in a specifically female Imaginary. It is worth noting that I carried out this work with a male analyst: gender difference was no barrier to imaginative exploration of an embodied universe where bodies changed shape with a frequency worthy of Ovid.

Opaque vs. translucent

At a relatively early point in the analysis, when these mythical meanings of an inner-body space were just beginning to emerge, there was an interruption in the analysis, due to the analyst's illness. I mention this to trace the fate of the image at a time when I suddenly had cause to worry about the health and well-being of the analyst. Following a phone call, from a person not known to me, which aroused my deepest concerns, I found myself bereft, at risk of losing something so precious that I was only then beginning to retrieve through the shared work of analysis. I felt as though something inside of me had suddenly gone dead and I was sentenced to carry a dead object inside of me forever. I was grieving. Given the painful urgency of these feelings, I made some inquiries and learned that my analyst was not in danger. The news that he was in fact recovering produced in me a distinct and dramatic shift: suddenly the heavy dead object that I'd found inside me changed.

In a vivid and wordless moment, I felt I was perceiving this internal object as it transformed from lifeless and dark to translucent. It became textual and potentially legible, rather than inert and opaque. So grateful was I for this restoration of inner vitality that I wrote a letter to the analyst in order to share with him my understanding of what had happened: writing the letter constituted a way of grasping the moment in which that inner body object changed from opaque to readable. The letter amounted to an analytic get well card, sustaining the analytic relationship as I communicated to the analyst my sense of his ongoing presence as addressee in the work that we shared.

Framing the object

Consider the investment in language of a literary critic, or of any academic, for that matter. Language is invested as an object and thus becomes an expressive medium, registering conflict and desire. On the role of language in psychoanalysis, André Green draws attention to a "*transference onto speech*: it is the result of the conversion of all the psychic elements into discourse. It is what induces me to say that, in analysis, it is as though the psychical apparatus were transformed into a language apparatus" (Green 2005: 50). My difficulties in the aftermath of surgery played out in the domain of language. Interestingly, during a sabbatical early in the analysis, at a time when I was experiencing acute difficulty in trying to write, I did find myself able to draw. I had always liked to draw from the model, but, in those months, I became my own model and drew myself full-length in the bathroom mirror. Without consciously realizing what I was doing, I see now that I was sketching the bodily terms or at least the locus of my dilemma in what amounted to a visual elaboration (or even anticipation) of the analytic process. My sketchpad served as frame for this nonverbal exploration.

Drawing connections between analysis and painting, Milner (1952) writes:

> I had already, when trying to study some of the psychological factors which facilitate or impede the painting of pictures, become interested in the part played by the frame. The frame marks off the different kind of reality that is within it from that which is outside it; but a temporal spatial frame also marks off the special kind of reality of a psycho-analytic session. And in psycho-analysis it is the existence of this frame that makes possible the full development of that creative illusion that analysts call the transference.
>
> (Milner 1952: 184)

The framing of the analytic space makes possible this experience through its separation from the world outside the consulting room. André Green regards the session as the basic cell, or the "psychoanalytic atom" (Green 2005: 33). Paradoxes of intimacy: in this most structured of relationships, a unique form of intimacy develops, engaging language and embodied presence, in the clearly defined time-space and the frame of the session.

Can one think of the body as the first frame, or container? Didier Anzieu's concept of the "skin ego" considers the bodily grounding of a sense of self: "the Skin Ego constitutes itself as an envelope that is sufficiently 'containing' of what then become its psychical contents" (Anzieu 1989: 87). Ego develops at the surface of the organism, as does the skin. Anzieu refers to the specifically Freudian principle that "every psychical function develops by supporting itself upon a bodily function whose workings it transposes on to the mental plane," as suggested in the concept of anaclisis or propping (Anzieu 1989: 96).

Midway in my analysis, I began to think about writing in ways that would draw on my experience of analysis and connect the literary with the psychoanalytic. In an essay that explored the relationship of textuality to embodiment, I made use of a dream (Hoffman 2006). In the dream, I was in a subway car and saw a seat that was unusual, not like the familiar rattan seats of my childhood but oddly metallic, consisting of two shiny metal bands, horizontally, at its back. The train was heading into Brooklyn, where I grew up, but I wanted to be able to return to Manhattan. Sitting in that seat with the shiny metal bands, I looked towards the wall of the car, hoping to find a subway map. What I saw on the wall was a text, but printed in type so small that I could not make out any of what it said. It was a flat, densely written text that I could not read. I realize now not only that the metal bands on the subway seat were the bars of a hospital bed, but also that my dream thoughts concerned the state of being unable to read after an operation.

Looking back at the course of the analysis, I can see the point at which I began to explore space and to feel my way into thoughts of underground structures, buried pipes and waterways. During a week of vacation, I found myself absorbed in exploring excavations of sites related to the Erie Canal, in upstate towns with streets named for the canal, paved streets that were once waterways. I see now that what drew my interest was the possibility that the flat surface of the ground possessed hidden depth and structure. In retrospect, I would say that the very possibility of a history to those buried and seemingly lost structures excited me with its metaphorical implications for my own analytic inquiry into a psychic interiority with which I had lost connection.

The idea that a flat surface might give access to structures hidden beneath it indicates that correspondence between the body's interior and buried structures in the outer world that gives focus to my interest in textuality. I use my own experience in order to hold on to an intimate ground of knowing, felt as real, on a continuum that begins in the imagined inner life of the body and extends to include the active reflection that is theory. Ricoeur (1977: 836) observes that analytic theory is "the codification of what takes place in the analytic situation and, more precisely, in the analytic relationship." Following Ricoeur, I write out of a sense of the imbrication of theory with experience. These are mutually energizing sources and resources. In this instance, theory amplifies the more personal work of understanding the impact of early experience on an active sense of embodiment later in life.

A year to the day after termination, I wrote to my analyst to mark the moment and my sense of what had changed, and he wrote back to me. While our epistolary exchange affirmed connection, it also confirmed separateness in the context of termination: as much as we had shared, we were no longer inside the space of that work. Our work together had undoubtedly changed each of us, in the sense that Glen Gabbard describes as "a noncoercive collaboration involving a process of two people thinking what either alone cannot think" (Gabbard 2009: 581; Orgel 2000). Our epistolary exchange gave graphic evidence of the fact that we no longer inhabited that intimate space together, a recognition that carries with it a certain amount of sadness.

Termination, mourning and internalization

Martin Bergmann points out an important difference between termination as it occurs in psychoanalysis and in other human relationships:

> Psychoanalysis is the only significant human relationship that terminates abruptly. In real life, we encounter three types of termination of human relationships: geographical separation, transformation of a friendly or love relationship into a hostile one, and death. The analysand, however, is supposed to bring about separation under conditions of love and gratitude. All life experience runs against such a termination. To be sure, the child separates from the parent, but this separation occurs in stages and is

never complete. Psychoanalysis makes demands on internalization that are not asked for in any other human relationship.

(Bergmann 1997: 169)

Bergmann's observations help to bring analytic termination under closer scrutiny, leading to questions about its function in analytic work, highlighting the potential for change within both analysand and analyst.

Loewald advances this inquiry by considering separation and termination in light of the analytic understanding of mourning. If we follow Freud's comments on mourning from "Mourning and Melancholia" (1914) to *The Ego and the Id* (1923), we see evidence of Freud's growing awareness of the dynamic importance of internalization of an object. He shifts from regarding this internalization as a key feature of the painful experience of melancholia to recognizing it as a crucial component of psychic life, particularly in the early years of life. In the change in his position from 1914 to 1923, Freud elaborates his growing recognition that what he had previously addressed as a painful condition following loss might actually indicate a process more fundamental to development of the ego: the ego takes shape in response to early losses, he wrote. It is the precipitate of abandoned object cathexes. (Analysts have led the way for academic theorists in recognizing that the significance of mourning goes beyond its meaning as a response to loss. Academic theory, beginning with Butler's notable contributions, has made use of that understanding, recognizing mourning and melancholia as the unconscious disavowal of loss that is intrinsic to the formation of subjectivity.)

I want to explore the concept of mourning for the light it sheds on analytic termination as a moment that is marked by the sorrow of loss, but also by a recognition of inner change that involves the internalization of the analytic relationship. Termination is the occasion for a different kind of gain through introjection. It is worth noting that current analytic theorizing works from a greater sense of the mutuality of the analytic relationship, reflecting on the responses of both participants. Poland (2000: 26) observes that "the patient–analyst relationship has moved to the center of our study of the clinical process." In a recent lecture that looked back to the era of ego psychology, Francis Baudry noted the shift from the analytic emphasis on making the "right" interpretation to a focus on the relationship between analyst and analysand (Freud lecture, NYPSI, May 1, 2012). This is a shift from Freud's stance. Indeed, André Green notes Freud's distaste for personal involvement or any form of self-disclosure in the therapeutic situation and sees Freud's focus on transference, to the exclusion of counter-transference as one result. For Green, the result is that Freud attached too "little importance to all the effects of the dialogical relationship that analysis has established" (Green 2005: 50). (So, too, Orgel (2000) comments on Freud's neglect of his own countertransference and failure to see that transferential feelings continue to operate long after the termination of an analysis.)

Warren Poland addresses termination in light of a shift in the interaction between analyst and analysand that can be thought of in terms of analytic witnessing, a function that serves to connect "*self*-definition and the fabric of human *inter*connection" (Poland 2000: 18). Poland's nuanced treatment of witnessing is attentive to the awareness of separateness that lays the groundwork for the separation that is termination. He emphasizes the patient's growing ability to recognize the analyst "as a distinctly separate person, not merely as a trans-ferential object." So too the analyst perceives the patient "from a position of sepa-rated otherness" (ibid.: 21). "*Witnessing develops from holding but implies letting go.* It implies respecting the patient's essential aloneness" (ibid.: 21, emphasis in original).

Poland understands "witnessing" to be indicative of "a vital shift in that clinical relationship, a shift based on separation, with separation a negation of fantasied or desired union" (ibid.: 26). While witnessing may play a particularly important role during termination, it is also indicative of something quite fundamental to the work that involves negation and separateness. Thus, Poland underscores the function of interpretation in moving the analytic relationship from fantasies of merger to recognition of the ultimate separateness of both participants.

> No matter its helpful or even kindly quality, an interpretation implies a powerful statement of negation and separation deeply structured within it, a negation central to the analytic process. This deeper message, which the patient comes at least unconsciously to recognize, is the implication that says, "No, I am not you, nor am I one of your ghosts. Though I work with you to call up your ghosts, to put names on them, I am a different person from you. As much as we share this clinical universe, no, I am not your fantasy actualized. We share a task but are separate people with separate lives." Any interpretation moves the relationship from one of seeming union to one of separateness, where, separate people touching, contact replaces merging.
>
> (Poland 2000: 27)

Indeed, Poland recalls Freud's speculation (1915) that the ability to perceive reality, to think, originates in the act of negation: "As [Freud] speculated, at the beginning of a sense of self is the distinction that what is bad is outside and what is good is inside. Through this act of negation and separation, the mind is born into its sense of a self apart" (Poland 2000: 27). Therefore, in the context of analytic work, considered as a way of revisiting some of those earliest aspects of experience, negation figures once again as the indication of a renewed and dif-ferent sense of autonomy in the analysand: "The analyst in both interpreting and witnessing provides in interaction a model of negation, of letting go, in the shared clinical experience. The internalization of this process is key to the patient's increasing capacity for self observation and self-analysis" (ibid.: 27–28).

Ghost stories

I'd like to move towards conclusion by drawing some connections between lit-erary and psychoanalytic experience as haunted spaces for those of us who enter them and linger to think about what we are doing. Henry James's ghost story "The Third Person" lends itself to these reflections. I draw on the model of Rita Charon's reading of James's stories in an analytic context that highlights the reciprocal relationship between analyst and analysand, writer and reader. I have chosen for study "The Third Person," a story that first appeared in 1900. Interestingly, James appears to have written it just after he had moved to Lamb House, Rye, in Sussex. Was James thinking of his own ghosts as he settled into his British home?

In the story, two older ladies, cousins who had not previously known each other, Miss Amy Frush and Miss Susan Frush, come to live together in a house in Marr that they inherit from a relative. There they encounter the ghost of an ancestor, who, as they later learn, was hanged for smuggling, which was in former years a widespread practice in Marr. Each lady tries in her own way to do justice to/for this ancestral ghost. They live with their ancestor ghost for a time, but then figure out how to lay him to rest. In the context of the present discussion, my interest in this story highlights the relationship of the two protagonists to an ancestor and a house that they have inherited: their inheritance turns out to involve more than they could have known or taken into account. The notion of inheritance thus lends itself to broader speculations about what it means to come into and occupy space, to act upon an awareness of the past.

In this respect, my point is heightened by the extreme innocence of James's protagonists. Nothing could be further from their experience than the criminality of their male ancestor. Nonetheless, they act. Miss Susan Frush sends £20 to the Royal Exchequer to make up for Cuthbert's illegal gains, but it is Miss Amy who succeeds in laying the ghost to rest when she travels to Paris and returns with a copy of a Tauchnitz novel hidden "[a]bout her person" (James 1996: 286). In her own way, she has reenacted the long-dead Cuthbert's crime of smuggling. (Interestingly, Henry James was published by Tauchnitz Editions, a German firm that printed British and American fiction, but was prevented by law from selling its books in England or the USA. So there is something here for James, who did suffer in his career from pirated editions of his work, in making this smuggled book the punchline of his story.)

The ghost is the "third person" of the story's title. The two Misses Frush inhabit a space that is haunted by memories they do not share and yet it is their shared labor to reenact the crime and to carry out restitution for it. All in the gentle comedy of maiden ladies whose lives are animated by the masculine presence of a ghost. The separateness of the two ladies (although readers might be forgiven for confusing one with the other): their tidiness and propriety, the clear lines of inheritance, all are upended by the excitement generated by their discovery of the ghost with whom they share the house they have inherited.

James writes:

> The element in question, then, was a third person in their association, a hovering presence for the dark hours, a figure that … could be trusted to look at them out of unnatural places; yet only, it doubtless might be assumed, to look at them. They had it at last—had what was to be had *in an old house where many, too many, things had happened, where the very walls they touched and floors they trod could have told secrets and named names, where every surface was a blurred mirror of life and death, of the endured, the remembered, the forgotten.*
>
> (James 1996: 263, emphasis added)

In this evocative passage, the house takes on the architecture of bodily being, intimately known and felt, forgotten, yet familiar. The narrative brings two maiden ladies into a space that might be characterized as the domestic structure of embodiment. As a "blurred mirror," the house reflects both what is remembered and what is forgotten, suggesting something like Freud's conception of the *Unheimlich*, the Uncanny, as the recurrence of what was originally *Heimlich* or home-like. The *Unheimlich* is a ghostly revenant, resonating within the most homey interior.

In the sense in which our bodies contain intimate histories with which we may be unacquainted but which are nevertheless our own, this house is haunted by an ancestor whose criminal actions become the particular burden of its present occupants. They work to expiate his crime which has become their history. As a haunted or animated interior, the house carries not only the resonances of embodiment, but, going further, might be likened to the domain of textuality or the space of an analysis: like the Misses Frush, the reader or analysand enters unawares into a space that offers encounter with a lost or buried history, a ghostly ancestor. That is, the story's gentle comedy might be read as an enactment of the experiences of reader or analysand. (Charon explores this line of thought, interpreting James's "A Round of Visits" as an enactment of the risks that writers and readers, analysts and analysands, take in their encounter.)

The "third person" of James's title, in the story I am considering, might be approached in light of the notion of the "analytic third" that is a specific function of the analytic relationship. The suggestive concept of the analytic third is somewhat fluid in the literature, but can be used to identify the specific production of analytic work. Thus, André Green notes that the session engages both the intrapsychic and the intersubjective, allowing for "*transference on to speech* and *transference on to the object*" (Green 2005: 34, italics in original). Identifying the basic rule of saying whatever comes to mind as the defining condition for analytic work, Green asserts that this rule inscribes itself as *third* in the analytic space and makes possible "a mode of waking reverie during the session" (ibid.: 33). Similarly, literary experience, either writing or reading, can be thought of as the stimulus for thoughts that might not otherwise come to the surface of awareness. Along these lines, Charon comments on the symbolization, the bringing into words, that characterizes literary and analytic work. I follow Charon in observing that writing fiction works to make something visible, just as analysis functions as a way of making something visible in words in the session. The words are the making happen. They are not simply "about" something. They are that thing.

Thomas Ogden develops a conception of the analytic third as intrinsic to psychoanalysis. He characterizes analysis "as a form of human relatedness specifically designed to create conditions in which the conversations with oneself that take place at the unconscious–preconscious frontier might be rendered increasingly 'audible' to analyst and analysand" (Ogden 2001: 12). In this view, analytic work involves not only the individual productions of each participant, but the "set of unconscious experiences jointly, but asymmetrically, constructed by the analytic pair" (ibid.: 12). This is the "analytic third," "a third subject with a life of its own, generated by the analytic pair and standing in dialectic tension with patient and analyst as separate individuals" (ibid.: 12). Interestingly, in this respect, Balsam raises the concept of a "psychoanalytic body," which she identifies as "the third," created cooperatively through the interaction of analyst and analysand out of experiences of the biological bodies and inner worlds of each (Balsam 2012: 170, 174). This concept of thirdness comes up as a way of addressing the intersubjective grounding for subjective internalizations.

This story (and perhaps any story) is the equivalent of the analytic third in the relationship of reader to writer. James puts the story out there for the reader to engage. One might think of the house/ghost for the two women and the story for the reader (and writer) as structures that stimulate expression. They are the frame structure that allows for expression. The frame is the occasion for transference, as Milner observes about painting and about psychoanalysis. Through entry into the frame of the text, the frame of reading, reader joins writer in experience of potential exposure, the possibility of self-revelation through the related (and even collaborative) activities of reading and writing.

The space of analysis is perhaps by definition a haunted space. The possibility of transference is the defining condition for the analytic ghost stories that unfold within the context of the analytic interaction. Indeed, Hans Loewald develops a ghost story of his own that allows him to bring to life a vivid sense of analytic process. I follow Charon and others in citing this well-known passage for its stunning imagery:

> The transference neurosis, in the technical sense of the establishment and resolution of it in the analytic process, is due to the blood of recognition which the patient's unconscious is given to taste—so that the old ghosts may reawaken to life. Those who know ghosts tell us that they long to be released from their ghost-life and led to rest as ancestors. As ancestors they live forth in the present generation, while as ghosts they are compelled to haunt the present generation with their shadow-life. Transference is pathological in so far as the unconscious is a crowd of ghosts, and this is the beginning of the transference neurosis in analysis: ghosts of the unconscious, imprisoned by defences but haunting the patient in the dark of his defences and symptoms, are allowed to taste blood, are let loose. In the daylight of analysis the ghosts of the unconscious are laid and led to rest as ancestors whose power is taken over and transformed into the newer intensity of present life, of the secondary process and contemporary objects.
>
> (Loewald 1960: 29)

How interesting that Homer's depiction of Odysseus's journey to the underworld offers Loewald the pictorial resources for depicting the unconscious drama of the analytic encounter. What does it mean to "taste blood"? Loewald's blood imagery— the unconscious tastes the blood of recognition—conveys the power, immediacy and lack of awareness that spark analytic engagement. Literature and psychoanalysis share this interest in ghosts and psychic phenomena that cannot be accounted for in terms of physical reality, but form part of the domestic architecture of lived experi- ence. Charon observes that Loewald "seems to be suggesting that the blood to be tasted is the blood of the analyst, he or she who commits the acts of recognition in this process. The sacrifice here is not the corporeal one of vampirization but the symbolic (and dangerous) functioning as the ghosts' agent, their surrogate, their kin" (Charon 2008: 284). Charon points out the risks that are shared by the analyst and writer or teller who offers the possibility for transformative interaction to the analy-sand and the reader. I highlight the vaulted structure of the scene, the space of the underworld scene, where Odysseus encounters the figures who were most mean-ingful to him in his earlier years: this is also the textual space where writer meets reader, or the room in which analyst and analysand carry out their work.

In the days immediately following termination, at a moment when I was feeling bereft and struggling to manage painful feelings, I played a favorite piece of music and felt an immediate onrush of strong emotion, the impact of all that I'd been holding back, released in response to the music. Just as suddenly, W.S. Merwin's "Elegy" popped into my thoughts: "who would I show it to"—a poem so brief that it lacks even a final period. Thinking of the poem at that moment marked my awareness of a sudden shift within me from the tense management of strong emotion, including the effort to keep feeling at a distance, to full encounter. The moment held recognition of what I had gained through analysis, together with the pain of loss of an extraordinary working relationship.

From the distance now of several years in time, I would like to think that the moment affirmed the internalization of that relationship in me, but I am wary of so neat a formulation. Nevertheless, the internalization that is part of termination assumes a capacity to experience interiority. From a post-termination perspective, I recognize the feeling of being present in the moment and able to grasp what I might have been afraid to see before. (The physicality of the verb "grasp" resonates with bodily awareness.) In the sense of presentness lies the prospect of creative work and connection to others. I have titled this essay "Finding the addressee" to acknowledge the relationship that is at the center of analytic work, the relationship that supplies the material or the medium through which embodiment, language and subjectivity come into view, and become available for thought and reflection. Change within one person becomes possible through this interaction with another person. What I think of as *grasping* the embodied sub-jectivity of the other person thus entails a recognition of separateness, but does not deny or disavow the intimacy of shared work carried out with a certain intensity over time. This recognition of intimate connection is thus also a way of marking the fuller grasp of one's own autonomous being.

Notes

1 While the more general association of uterus with the creation of new life is obvious, I omit from this discussion the specifics of personal history and fantasy that determined the particular form of my response to a hysterectomy.

References

Anzieu, Didier. 1989. *The Skin Ego*. Trans. Chris Turner. New Haven and London: Yale University Press.

Balsam, Rosemary. 2012. *Women's Bodies in Psychoanalysis*. London and New York: Routledge.

Bergmann, Martin S. 1997. "Termination: The Achilles Heel of Psychoanalytic Technique." *Psychoanalytic Psychology* 14: 163–74.

Borbely, Antal. 1998. "A Psychoanalytic Concept of Metaphor." *International Journal of Psychoanalysis* 79: 923–36.

Charles, Marilyn. 2001. "Nonphysical Touch: Modes of Containment and Communication Within the Analytic Process." *Psychoanalytic Quarterly* 70: 387–416.

Charon, Rita. 2008. "A Momentary Watcher, or the Imperiled Reader of 'A Round of Visits'." *The Henry James Review* 29.3 (Fall): 275–86.

Erreich, Anne. 2003. "A Modest Proposal: (Re)defining Unconscious Fantasy." *Psychoanalytic Quarterly* 72: 541–70.

Gabbard, Glen. 2009. "What is A 'Good Enough' Termination?" *Journal of the American Psychoanalytic Association* 57: 575–94.

Green, André. 2005. "Transference and Countertransference." In *Key Ideas for a Contemporary Psychoanalysis: Misrecognition and Recognition of the Unconscious*. Trans. Andrew Weller. London: Routledge.

——2005. "Setting, Process, Transference." In *Key Ideas for a Contemporary Psychoanalysis: Misrecognition and Recognition of the Unconscious*. Trans. Andrew Weller. London: Routledge.

Hoffman, Anne Golomb. 2006. "Is Psychoanalysis a Poetics of the Body?" *American Imago* 63.4 (Winter): 395–422.

James, Henry. 1996. "The Third Person." In *Henry James: Complete Stories, 1898–1910*, ed. Denis Donoghue. New York: Library of America.

Litowitz, Bonnie. 2002. "Sexuality and Textuality." *Journal of the American Psychoanalytic Association* 50: 171–98.

Loewald, Hans. 1960. "On the Therapeutic Action of Psychoanalysis." *International Journal of Psychoanalysis* 41: 16–33.

Milner, Marion. 1952. "Aspects of Symbolism in Comprehension of the Non-Self." *International Journal of Psychoanalysis* 33: 181–94.

Ogden, Thomas. 2001. "Conversations at the Frontier of Dreaming." *fort da* 7: 7–14.

Orgel, Shelley. 2000. "Letting Go." *Journal of the American Psychoanalysis Association* 48: 719.

Poland, Warren S. 2000. "The Analyst's Witnessing and Otherness." *Journal of the American Psychoanalytic Association* 48: 7–14.

Pollak, Tamar. 2009. "The Body-Container: A New Perspective on the 'Body-Ego'." *International Journal of Psychoanalysis* 90: 487–506.

Ricoeur, Paul. 1977. "The Question of Proof in Freud's Psychoanalytic Writings." *Journal of the American Psychoanalytic Association* 25: 835–71.

15 The intimacy of objects

Living and perishing in the company of things

Joseph Schneider

In a *New York Times* review, dance critic Alastair Macaulay writes of the 70-year relationship, both professional and personal, between composer John Cage and choreographer Merce Cunningham (Macaulay 2012). The performances he saw included two works by Cunningham to which he had added music written by Cage, who died in 1992. Macaulay notes that, during the period when Cunningham composed these dances, he created others having "characteristic ambiguity" and that took up "aspects of death, transcendence, [and] different realms of existence." Cunningham died in 2009 and his company closed at the end of 2011. The show Macaulay writes about, early in 2012, included eight dancers from that company. He notes the many ghosts he felt that night, both on and beyond the stage, although he does not use that word.

Of the dance called "Doubletoss," Cunningham's first new major work after Cage's death, Macaulay writes that the choreographer's "own immediate sense of loss is also a constant subtext, but so is the idea that the dead accompany and inspire us," the living. The dead, he suggests, are here and help carry us forward. He felt this in Cage's music, put with Cunningham's choreography as a reproducible set of moves, sights and sounds, but also in the pairings of men dancers, one of whom he reads as "otherworldly" and who partners and, ironically, enlivens the dancer who appears more "mortal," "earthbound."

These material pasts and presents reaching out, extending to and entreating us—what Alphonso Lingis (1998) called "the imperative"—are felt in Macaulay's observation that Cunningham is present in the dancers' "every movement and every phrase": "Just the firm planting of a bare foot on the floor, seemingly as rooted as a tree, brings back a lost world of Cunningham memories," he writes. However, as Macaulay demonstrates, such memories, such objects, are hardly lost as long as other objects, events, images capable of catalyzing them in particular ways—such as Macaulay himself does in his review—intersect and add something, both old and new, to the now and to the next.

As I read his review, comfortably back in bed with coffee and the paper after breakfast on a chilly late winter morning in Des Moines, I felt this essay, then partially written, and my promise to take up in the revision how present Nancy was, and largely remains, in the innumerable objects and their arrangements that she and I and our marriage of 34 years drew together in particular ways; part of our overlapping lives, practices, psyches and worlds; all more … and surely less;

still, but not quite, present in that same third-floor apartment with a view into the massive branches of large oak trees and a busy urban thoroughfare beyond. I said that I wanted to write about what Steven Shaviro (2012: 13), drawing from Alfred North Whitehead, and others have called "the intimacy of things," and to underscore how central the seemingly impersonal materiality or "mattering" of life is to fueling that which is, on the contrary, so very personal indeed.[1] However, trying to write this story straight, so to speak, seemed to risk missing it all together, or missing the stories that seemed to press to be told. I'm thus grateful to Macaulay and others, as you will see, for their help in my attempt to write, as Nancy Chen and Trinh Minh-ha (1994) might have put it, "nearby."

Before saying more about Whitehead's help, I quote a line from Elizabeth Grosz's (2005: 44) *Time Travels: Feminism, Nature, Power*. "Nature is the ground, the condition or field in which culture erupts or emerges as a supervening quality not contained in nature but derived from it." Grosz, Patricia Clough's (2000; Clough and Halley 2007) writing on autoaffection and affect, and the work of Donna Haraway (1989, 1991, 1997, 2008) helped me see the importance of dynamic matter for an enlivened cultural theory, aided by Jane Bennett's (2001, 2010) two well-known books on this topic. Grosz's claim, that nature is culture's ground, can be misread to leave in place the crusty dualism of nature "versus" culture. That surely was, and is, not her intent, but the givenness of this division—as Whitehead made so clear—is long-lived and weighty indeed. A prime instance of this dualism is matter as separate from and other to language.

While I have learned much from and been a great fan of the insights and arguments from poststructuralism, offered especially in the work of Michel Foucault and Jacques Derrida, the proverbial "elephant in the room" at the close of arguments derived from their work seemed only more apparent the better I got in making them (or perhaps it was not "better"). That elephant can be variously named matter, materiality, or, after Pheng Cheah's (1996) trenchant commentary on the work of Judith Butler and Grosz, mattering.[2] For all the brilliance and productivity that the human cognitive capacity for language and the symbolic has enabled, these hardly could shine so brightly without the ground or "soil" of "nature" or matter from and in which it grows and with which it forever remains entwined. Grosz's choice of metaphor in the quote is key, for it insists on the inseparability of the multiple entities and dynamic processes that ground and growth, soil and emergent plantings, mark.

She notes this in her reading of Charles Darwin and Gilles Deleuze, who open thought to how matter may be seen as the provocative "outside" to what cultural theory highlights: the symbolic; meaning, language and representation, often as though they can exist in some disembodied form. This outside, Grosz (2005: 49) writes:

> is the force that disrupts, intervenes, to break down expectation and to generate invention and innovation, to enable the emergence or eruption of subjectivity or culture. The outside is the (successful or victorious) series of forces that impinge on structures, plans, expectations of the living: this outside appears to us in the form of events, natural and social, and events generate

for us the problems that our inventiveness, above all our culture's ingenuity, attempts to address or resolve. For Deleuze, this outside is the force that induces thinking, that shakes life from automatism, that generates culture. This outside, composed of competing forces, forces in the process of their composition, can be called by a number of different names: nature, time, events. It is the force of this outside that incites culture.

In this, "the past and the present are superseded and overwritten by the future." The past thus becomes not causal but rather "an index of the resources that the future has to develop itself differently" (Grosz 2005: 38).

While Whitehead would not use Grosz's "outside" to describe nature, the view she offers is one that insists on the centrality of the force of Cheah's mattering in any discussion of culture and language. Clearly, this is relevant to our thinking about objects. I was struck by her reading of "event" as having the capacity to disrupt the orderliness of an established and very sturdy "garden" of cultural growth, cutting away huge swaths of "life as we know it." That seemed to be what had happened to me with the "event" of Nancy's death.

Beyond the intimacy of objects noted by Shaviro, Whitehead's work turns on a set of concepts that read as orthogonal to dominant Western philosophy. I here draw on several of those concepts, along with others from scholars and writers who have given objects particular importance in their work and lives. For Whitehead (1978: 168), existence is the dynamic experience that entities have or are: "[T]he whole universe consists of elements disclosed in the analysis of the experiences of subjects." "Subjects" here, please note, includes stones and wasps equally as it does human beings. Whitehead's philosophy of organism thus offers a view of existence that might be called an aesthetic democracy of lively objects.[3] For him, existence is grounded in dynamic, haptic experience, and experience is thought as feeling; feeling is mostly physical or sensual, and is a quality that all entities, in varying degree, share. Here is Whitehead (1967: 262), from his *Adventures of Ideas*:

> The emotional significance of an object as "*It*" divorced from its qualitative aspects at the moment presented, is one of the strongest forces in human nature. It is at the base of family affection, and of the love of particular possessions. This trait is not a peculiarity of mankind alone. A dog smells in order to find out if the person in question is that *It* to which its affections cling. The room, or stable, may be full of odours, many of them for a dog sweeter. But he is not smelling for the pleasure of that smell, but to discover that *It* who claims his whole affection.

For Whitehead, all entities have a "mental pole" to their experience—of which we humans are so rightly proud—even though in the vast majority of cases it is secondary by far to the physical.[4]

Given this, "the intimacy of objects" could for Whitehead address the intimacy of stones and wasps themselves, that is, of stones with other stones, wasps with other wasps, and/or with each other; the "prehensions" linking a glass and an ashtray juxtaposed on a bar, human access to which is, at best, limited, the presumptuous lure of phenomenology to the contrary notwithstanding.[5] Unlike much recent work in object-oriented ontology or philosophy, I aim to think here about humans and other things, inextricably linked in a ubiquitous if not always recognized intimacy.[6] Objects are thus seen as causal and, as Timothy Morton (2012: 8) argues, "causality is wholly an aesthetic phenomenon." Taking other objects more seriously requires a shift in how we see our human-object selves. Certain grandiose claims about us humans must be tempered, while others, about a different "us," must come to the fore. In this, Whitehead is especially "good to think with."

If the experience of objects in Whitehead is relational to the core, loss is also central to his philosophy. That caught my attention. His "perpetual perishing," an idea borrowed from John Locke, is experienced by all entities and is an ending that is also the occasion for unleashing new resources for the future; that is, for novelty. Loss—death—for Whitehead (1967: 238) is then inextricably linked to gain and life; to perhaps his favorite word, creativity. "How the past perishes," he writes, "is how the future becomes." Each actual occasion or event moves toward a "concrescence of prehensions" that, when "satisfied," then becomes a "datum" of potential—the past—for a new process involving different, becoming entities. Insofar as life—but not life alone (remember rocks, and think electrons, which also have experience)—relies on this endless movement of drawing "food" from its particular environment, Whitehead (1978: 105) has written, provocatively but with ecological pathos: "life is robbery."[7] The perpetual perishing is also, and at the same time, a perpetual becoming, moving along multiple and varied vectors; the latter requires the former. Drawn from another thread of my life, as Douglas Brooks (2011), scholar of South Asian Philosophy and Religion has put it, characterizing Hindu cosmology, "all is food and everything is hungry." Efficacy guides but in no sense controls an entity's experience.

Whitehead's ontology is not one of dualisms but rather of duality or, better, multiplicity. From his earliest philosophical work, he writes against the dominant Western tradition that he calls the bifurcation of nature, from the Greeks through Locke, Descartes, Hume and Kant. This is why Grosz's "outside" would not work for him. Rather, he sees a world of endless relational complexity: of "both/and, and ..." rather than "either/or." This is not a vision, an abstraction, of differences erased or forever blurred, but rather of a moving complex of difference, affectively entwined and modulated according to the particularities of the locale within which the becoming concrescence of entities, of objects, becomes. The past in the present beyond itself in the future. Experience, Whitehead (1955: 43–44) insists in *Symbolism*, is complex:

> One part of our experience is handy, and definite in our consciousness; also it is easy to reproduce at will. The other type of experience, however insistent, is vague, haunting, unmanageable. The former type, for all its decorative sense experience, is barren. It displays a world concealed under an adventitious show, a show of our own bodily production. The latter type is heavy with the contact of the things gone by, which lay their grip on our immediate selves.

Actual and potential, always and inevitably together, in real timespace. The always moving capacity to affect and be affected.[8] Intimacy written as not only "up close," but also at a distance, but arguably nonetheless personal.

Steve Goodman (2010) reads this aspect of Whitehead's philosophy as offering a solution to the either/or stalemate visible in the critique by Gaston Bachelard of Henri Bergson on the question of continuity in duration and time, a circular and unproductive debate that still infuses much contemporary thought. Put here too simply, Goodman argues that Bachelard saw Bergson's emphasis on continuity as a product of his focus on human perception, which elides or erases the recognition of nodes or forms of intensity that are thought, if not seen (like the quantum), as discontinuous. "[F]or Bachelard," writes Goodman (2010: 88), "time is fractured, interrupted, multiple, and discrete." For Bergson, by contrast, the notion of the singular instant or moment of time is illusory. With his concept of the extensive continuum, which Goodman characterizes as a "rhythmic break flow or (dis) continuum," Whitehead dissolves the dualism of space versus or distinct from time, of form versus or distinct from process or movement, and, as with William James, Goodman (2010: 91) says, "the relation between things assumes as much significance as the things themselves." It is from this sense that Whitehead (1978: 35) insisted, "There is a becoming of continuity, but no continuity of becoming."

Macaulay, of course, alludes to the personal intimacy between Cunningham and Cage. I read his sense of that intimacy in the allusion to the sound of Cage's music and the dancers' moves, although both men insisted on the independence of music and choreographed movement; and to the linked movements of arms, heads, torsos and the "planted feet" of the dancers, on the one hand, and Cunningham himself, on the other; in the otherworldly-and-the-mortal. The presence of love, loss, joy, pain, difference; "stubborn fact"—a term Whitehead takes from his reading of Descartes and Locke—and potential that Macaulay brought to me, from his own experience of a public event far away, served as a relay to my project (Whitehead 1978: 219–20). His phrase "a bare foot on the floor," put just so—I *felt* this image, having seen Cunningham on stage—leads me to think of how, when I am with Nancy's brother John, a few years older than she (we had no children, in whom this point might be made even more clearly, or not), a certain tilt of his head, a chuckle punctuating a phrase, feeds an ineffable sense of recognition that is a presence of "Nancy herself"; not so much a memory of her if we think of memory only as ideational, but rather memory as a bodily experience called forth in, solicited from, me of her presence in the details of her brother's movements and how they touch me in the here and now or the then and there of those strands of timespace. Imperativity; evocation; vectors of affectivity coming my way. A force.

It is as though one timespace opens up inside another, moving along a different vector; the distinctive head, the same chuckle, the shape of the nose draw me along without words. I read Macaulay's sense of a foot put just so is also less about memories as solely representational and more a matter of feeling, of the aesthetic; of being touched and reaching to touch back; a question of the promise of thinking together intimacy, body and—to use words that have become so important in recent writing on materiality and life—the aesthetic of objects' linked experience and of their affect. This is memory in the Whiteheadean sense of nature understood as "of a piece," erasing the bifurcation that he decried, here into cognition—arguably memory as usually thought—and what Haraway might call "fleshly matter." Bergson, on whom Whitehead drew, wrote of "true memory" as distinct from and in connection to perception. The latter occurs, he held, in the unfolding present project pursued by the embodied and sentient being, moving through the world. It has an agenda, one might say. The former interrupts perception and slows its linear project as part of the presence of the past in the human's now and its particular relevance to the object perceived.[9]

In reference to Bergson, Grosz (2005: 97) suggests that "If memory directs me to the past and to duration, then it is linked not only to my body and its experiences but to the broad web of connections in which my body is [and has been] located." Perception, says Grosz, links to location, while memory is about duration. And "[t]he more immersed we are in memory," she writes, "the less our actions can be directly invoked and prepared for [by us]; but the more directly and instrumentally we act, the less our reflection, memories, and consciousness intervene into and regulate our actions" (Grosz 2005: 97).[10] When Macaulay sees the Cunningham foot, because he knows it and has been with it in the past, true memory, through his body and the seen foot, come together and the present opens elsewhere, even if ever so fleetingly, to the past, on its way forward to the future. "Minimally," writes Morton (2012: 13), "action at a distance is just the existence-for-the-other of the sensual qualities of any entity."

"Nancy Claire Harper Schneider, 62, died Saturday, 18 November, at home from complications associated with a recurrence of breast cancer first diagnosed in 1999." That's what I wrote in the obituary. Nancy died very suddenly and, I hope, very quickly, at about 3:10 a.m. that morning in 2006 as she sat on my lap on the bed—the same bed I mention above, where I first read Macaulay's review—and as I struggled unsuccessfully to lift her into a wheelchair nearby. She had awakened me and asked if I could help her to the bathroom. She had become so weakened from the endless chemotherapy and the cancer that we had turned to the chair for help. She clasped my neck and I held her under the arms to stand, but when she stood up she collapsed under the effort. As her body fell back onto the bed, I somehow turned us and slid under her, ending up facing her back, seated with her on my lap. The spreading warm wetness on my thighs and running down my legs—"I need to go to the bathroom but I can't get up. Can you help me?"—stopped my breath. "Oh, God. No!" I think I cried.

The phone. 911. Hurry, hurry please! But I knew or thought I knew it couldn't matter now. Holding and feeling and living her dying in that very "intimate" way—I can't think of a more fitting word—was a break of some kind in my life; the event dividing time and place into a before and an after. To see death on a face that you know and love and have studied for such a long time is—to say the least—disconcerting and even frightening. Freud's "uncanny." She was just here, but the face here now is not hers. Miles from "home," for sure. I tried CPR and, as Shakespeare's Juliet cried at her last Romeo kiss, "Thy lips are warm!"

Two and a half months later, on February 3, 2007 in Sarasota, Florida, my mother's body, or my second mother's body, lay still and lifeless from the victory of another life, related but of a different sort, called lung cancer. Her face and body had been becalmed by the hospice staff: hair combed, mouth and eyes drawn closed, bedcovers smoothed, and the room ordered—it was indeed a "viewing" that my brother and I did as we sat beside her last bed, where, just hours before, the life called Sara Schneider—"bare" though it then was—was still nonetheless present. That is not how it was with Nancy and me at 3:10 a.m. on November 18, 2006. The word trauma easily comes to mind or to bodymind. There was no sitting nearby.

I was invited to submit a proposal for this collection because one of the editors heard me present a conference paper that seemed relevant to its theme. That first, brief essay was written for a panel to honor a new book by a former colleague, Allen Shelton (2007), titled *Dreamworlds of Alabama*, which draws centrally on memories of his early life growing up and living there. Allen knew Nancy since he and I were in the same department for a time. When I think of him, I can easily think of the three of us, seated at a table in a favorite coffeehouse, talking and laughing about our everyday lives and pasts. It's the same coffeehouse, and perhaps the same table at which I have written much of this essay. I gave the conference paper in 2008, a little more than two years after Nancy's death. That writing and reading were accompanied by feelings of sorrow and pain, but also a sense of relief at being able to write and speak from those feelings and that experience. Not, surely, a matter of "getting beyond" or banishing them so much as a way to acknowledge or "voice" and weave them into the shifting story of myself. Cathartic, I think, would be a fitting term for that writing/performance, but that perhaps overcodes for offloading, when it seems, even now, more an expansion, an affirmation of a becoming that I felt so deeply but that no one or few could see when they saw "me."

The conference panel asked us to choose a paragraph from Allen's book that resonated with us and that he then would read aloud before we spoke. I did not set out then to write about Nancy's death and how important objects would be in bringing her back into my life and giving it ground. As I looked through Allen's book to see what bits I had marked, I chose his comments about a very complex and lively backyard garden—another figure of ground and growth-from—where he once lived:

> The garden is a border between a series of interlocked structures, which are twined together like honeysuckle around a sapling. The bare branch stretched like a network of arms about to bud across the kitchen window. The flat, white cut of the pruner visible on the branches, a red wagon turned on its side on a gravel path, through the glass to a bowl of Honey Nut Cheerios and an Oneida spoon. The garden retains a history and the accumulation of debris and markings on the ground. The spade cut, the pruned branch, the scar on the hand, the rotting compost retains the compositional structure of Freud's simile but gives it a more personal, smaller radius. The garden stands for an aboresque and more human vegetative mind alongside Freud's metropolitan equation. The intertwining of the family with the commercial and bureaucratic triangles begins as soon as the doorknob is

turned and the man mistakes his wife for a straw hat. At the same time a floral surrealism blooms in the margins. Instead of following streets and monuments in an archeological dig, the garden simile develops the lilac into a new patient for analysis. The lilac has a history that is personal as well as genetic. It is an actant with stories to tell ... Plants, objects, and bodies are not separate but are wrapped systems with stories originating as much out of the actant as the actor. The shovel gardens. The gardener is another tool in an oedipal archeology.

(Shelton 2007: 24–25)

Allen's passage evoked my own sense of how memories of Nancy were and are so entwined with, even in, things, objects—commodities or not—and particular places, that/where, when I find myself around/in them, draw me to her or her to me. In the presence of those things, there is—I have—a bodily *resonance* that this essay seeks to foreground. These experiences often *also* (but not always) have memory in the more familiar sense of cognition, images and particular culture-shaped emotions, instances of the human-elaborated "mental pole" to which bifurcation typically gives priority. However, for Whitehead, these *too* are physical and that is my point. A bare foot, planted just so.

However, this essay really started with a book by the well-known non-fiction writer Joan Didion. Before Whitehead there was Didion; at least for me. I knew the name Joan Didion from her reputation as an incisive and critical observer of contemporary American politics and society, but, when I noticed a brief account of her book *The Year of Magical Thinking*, I read on, primed by age and circumstance (Didion 2005). I mean, I was already more than 60 and had plenty of experience with death and illness of those dear to me. Nancy had been diagnosed with a recurrence of the cancer that was discovered in 1999 but that we thought/hoped was "cured"—a word that the beloved oncologist apparently believed in since he had used it to describe my own cancer experience (admittedly, with the quotes in place)—until Nancy's cancer wasn't and was back five years and several months later, growing in her right lung "in an inoperable place," they said. I remember her saying that day, as we sat waiting to "take more pictures" of her lung, "But I feel so good." Life itself; but not, as it turned out, hers.

Didion tells the story of her life after the sudden "cardiac event" that brought the death of her husband, life partner, muse, colleague, beloved, John Gregory Dunne; at dinner at home on the upper east side of Manhattan at about nine o'clock on the night of December 30, 2003. I was drawn to the book because I knew Didion would not shy from the dark and difficult that I feared would come to me. She would face the pain straight, with no "pretty words" and with skepticism for the received wisdom about how to go on ... after. She did not disappoint:

> Life changes fast.
> Life changes in the instant.
> You sit down to dinner and life as you know it ends.
> *The question of self-pity.*

(Didion 2005: 3)

Life as you know it ends, but of course she does not mean that *she* died. She lived on, but life as the Joan Didion she was before this event had ended. Let's start at the beginning of that ending (although Whitehead might remind us that being itself is the beginning of that ever-ending, which isn't after all a final end; all of which strikes me now, almost six years on, as somewhat comforting, although it would not have done so then, as I lay in bed reading Didion, catching myself not breathing; Nancy asleep beside me). Whitehead also might respond to Didion's claims about life by saying, *sotto voce*, that is the way it is with life, with existence: it often changes fast and is indeed never as it was, just a moment ago. Living-and-existence: a perpetual creation and perishing; things never quite what they seem.[11] No surprise then that my classical yoga text advises *aparigraha*, non-grasping or non-hoarding; "not to collect things one does not require immediately." Non-stealing (Iyengar 1979: 35). Then, Whitehead reminds, life, even existence, is robbery, and we do not easily give up what we thus have taken and think is ours.

So here, below, is Didion, starting at the beginning of the end, when they had just returned from seeing their critically ill daughter Quintana in intensive care. She interrupts the recounting of Dunne's sudden heart attack and death to reflect on her experience of "being there" across a series of events involving a range of objects and places that had helped constitute her life with John Gregory Dunne, the most important of which was of course Dunne himself. Her disdain for the professional knowledge, so distanced and abstract (about which Whitehead had much critical to say), is palpable. As I reread her words later, after Nancy died, I felt she spoke what might have been my own, both about her death and grief.

> Unusual dependency (is that a way of saying "marriage"? "husband and wife"? "mother and child"? "nuclear family"?) is not the only situation in which complicated or pathological grief can occur. Another, I read in the literature is one in which the grieving process is interrupted by "circumstantial factors," say by "a delay in the funeral," or by "an illness or second death in the family." I read an explanation by Vamik D. Volkan, M.D., a professor of psychiatry ... of what he called "re-grief therapy," a technique developed ... for the treatment of "established pathological mourners" ... But from where exactly did Dr. Volkan ... derive ... [his] unique understanding of "the psychodynamics involved in the patient's need to keep the lost one alive," their special ability to "explain and interpret the relationship that had existed between the patient and the one who died"? Were you watching Tenko with me and "the lost one" in Brentwood Park, did you go to dinner with us at Morton's? Were you with me and "the lost one who died" at Punchbowl in Honolulu four months before it happened? Did you gather up plumeria blossoms with us and drop them on the graves of the unknown dead from Pearl Harbor? Did you catch cold with us in the rain at the Jardin du Ranelagh in Paris a month before it happened? Did you skip the Monets with us and go to lunch at Conti? Were you with us when we left Conti and bought the thermometer, were you sitting on our bed at the

Bristol when neither of us could figure out how to convert the thermometer's centigrade reading to Fahrenheit?

(Didion 2005: 54–56)

No, of course, she says, Vamik Volkan was not there, acknowledging her own questions as unreasonable. Still, she insists, the kind of knowledge she has of what transpired that night at her dinner table and after is of a sort distinct from that contained in the "literature." She was in and of Dunne's death—and something of her own as well; she was there.

Didion goes on to note the extent to which death in our variously modern world has been further removed, erased from the everyday of life—unless of course you also were "there," as I was—along with, especially, mourning and the embodiment of grief. We are enjoined from creating circumstances that spoil the "enjoyment" of others and even of ourselves; and death, surely, can do that. We are supposedly good at "moving on," "getting closure" (see Berns 2011). As the mid-20th-century Chinese anthropologist Fei Xiaotong (1993) once wrote of the USA, we are—sadly, he thought—a "land without ghosts," in no small part because we, he felt, discard the past and deny its presence in us, truncating what the future might bring.

So, what about that part of Didion's life that ended that night at dinner, in an instant? That part of her that was him that was her that remains at Brentwood Park? At the Punchbowl in Honolulu? What about that part of her in his shoes in their closet? In his favorite pen, left next to his favorite chair after he wrote that note last night when they discussed a problem he was having with an essay (perhaps before they went to the hospital to see their daughter)? His fingerprints would still be there; his DNA perhaps, if he had chewed on the pen absent-mindedly. There was his smell as she stepped into his side of their closet. In all of these, Didion registers her aesthetic experience as a ground for knowing that takes precedence over the cognitive knowing that the experts offer. She was there.

I have a Nancy's closet that carries her smell and that saddens me to the core each time I step in to get something I've stored there in this rather sealed-off space that, nonetheless, I can't quite bear to make into something else. The bed is still here, the pillows, the sheets and mattress pad; the lamp, the table. Her dresser, now acting as a storage unit for things I can't decide what to do with. The carpet near the bed is here as well, where two large stains of Nancy's blood had fallen when the medics put a tube down her throat, trying to give her breath. One of the giant fire fighters said to me—they all seemed so big; I felt so small, shivering barefoot in my bathrobe—"there was blood in her lungs when we put the tube in," as if to say hopeless. After several days, I covered the stains with a towel and finally, weeks later, washed them away one night as Meiling, the white cat Nancy gave me, sat looking on. The white cat is a whole other story of intimacy and affect ... and fear of more loss (Schneider 2012). All of these things, for sure, were there with me that morning.

Some of them, like the blood, were or bore such a part of her and that 22-month period of cancer's relentless return that I could not bear to have them when I never would have her again. After the funeral home men took her that morning, I could hardly look at and touch her toothbrush, her make-up brushes, the hairbrush, offering me strands of her chemotherapy-shocked hair. Un-bearable, literally.[12] Other of these things that were part of that terrible morning and remain seem to comfort me; they carry her to me when I am with them and are thus precious. I have a version of this same response to some of Nancy's dear friends who also loved her. Although I do not see these women much, when our paths cross, we always conjure Nancy, almost without words, and our tears are suddenly there as well. That brings me back to the uncanny and to ghosts.

While Freud's (1955) *unheimlich* or uncanny (literally, un-homely; thinkable as the un-familia-r) seemed right when Nancy's face was no longer the face I knew, or was not quite, it carries too much a sense of fear and menace to describe my connection to these other objects. Living with—in the company of—these things has been, admittedly, full of nostalgia but not at all frightening. Even my dreamscape, to which I ordinarily have only the dimmest waking connection, brings no disturbing narratives or images of Nancy (at least that I can read).

If the uncanny codes too negatively, the presence of ghosts and haunting have a distinct resonance. I had forgotten that I once wrote about living in a land of ghosts, that is, in China (Schneider and Wang 2000). While focused then mostly on how the ghost of the *xiaozi* or filial son haunts boys and men in their relationships with parents even today, I learned that ghosts, primarily in the form of "ancestors" and their particular places and things, could be very comforting presences, helping humans remember who they are and what they owe. While of course frightful if angered by disrespectful behavior from the living, these Chinese ghosts seemed to provide those same living with an ongoing sense of connection and embrace with the past.

This is what the anthropologist Fei felt was missing in America. He once visited at the University of Chicago, where he occupied the temporarily vacant office of the famous Chicago School sociologist Robert Park, who had been Fei's teacher many years before when Park visited China. He was particularly concerned to maintain its material details just as the professor had left them, as if better to draw, respectfully and with efficacy, from their accumulated Parkian resonance.

> I was secretly happy that, sitting in the chair he had used, I would surely absorb something of his spirit ... I felt that if the nameplate, the old books lining the walls, even the air in the room were not disturbed, then, surrounded by this lingering past, perhaps in a few months I would see a draft of [my book] ... on the table. But that if these were disturbed, all might be lost.
>
> (Fei 1993: 176)

There is the very long history in Chinese thought and practice, on which Fei no doubt draws, that takes what Jane Bennett has called "the enchantment" of the world; its very liveliness, as Donna Haraway might put it; or its mattering, as a given.[13] My Chinese friends, I felt sure, would understand the intimacy of objects.

Christopher Bollas (2009: 6) claims that psychoanalysis "concentrates on the daily 'trip' which we all take," as embodied beings in real timespace, "stimulated by desire, need, memory and emotional life." He credits Freud's attention to our experience of the quotidian that is recalled during free association as one of his greatest contributions to understanding psychic processes. In his *The Evocative Object World*, Bollas summarizes much of his prior work on this intersection of objects—primarily, but not only, other humans—and patients seeking therapy. His use of the adjective "evocative" takes us to the heart of my essay. As you have seen, I am suggesting that, while we know humans have amazing capacities to evoke, to call or summon forth—to affect—to "make happen," we are less aware of or prepared to consider the claim that such evocative capacity comes to us humans from non-human and especially non-living objects.

In a chapter that takes the book's title as its own, Bollas stories a thread of his late work as reaching toward such an appreciation. Sounding a bit like some of the object-oriented scholars noted earlier, Bollas (2009: 79) writes, "The object world— its 'thing-ness'—is crucial to our use of it. As we move about, we live in an evocative object world that is only so because objects have an integrity of their own." Here and subsequently Bollas seems to grant these other objects with which or whom we share context—and Whitehead would insist on this foundational relationality—an "in itselfness" from which comes the capacity to affect us, in the sense of an initiatory movement or vector not beginning only in the human. However, it turns out that is not quite the case: "Those objects leave an imprint in our unconscious that is partly the property of the thing-itself and *mostly* the result of the meaning within our individual self" (Bollas 2009: 83, my emphasis). Writing specifically about what he calls the destiny drive, he notes "how after one passes away we leave behind 'personal effects': the trace of those objects *we used* in our life that *fulfilled* (or perhaps did not) the needs of *that drive*" (Bollas 2009: 87, my emphasis).

The object that seems most interesting to Bollas then turns out to be the internal object, either in its conscious meaning for us or in its play in the unconscious. While he has much interesting to say about objects, psychoanalysis, of course, does not—fortunately—set out to treat the turbulence of rocks and humans equally. Such a reading of my experience around and after Nancy's death would be valid on its own terms and perhaps even helpful to me in my life, but it would not shine as bright a light on the non-human objects in themselves as I have tried to do.

Sherry Turkle, who writes with more than a little insight into psychoanalysis, has edited a collection of essays called *Evocative Objects: Things We Think With*, and contributes the introduction, titled "The Things that Matter" (Turkle 2007).[14] She locates the collection of papers relative to a long scholarly "reticence to examine objects as centerpieces of emotional life," and adds that Western "knowing" itself codes strongly as abstract (Turkle 2007: 6). For Turkle (2007: 10), Freud and the psychodynamic tradition enable us to see more clearly "the intensity of our connections to the world of things" and "how we relate to the animate and inanimate" in similar ways. Perhaps because she is not a clinician but rather a scholar of the person-in-society culture, Turkle's comments seem to give more warrant to the object in itself than those from Bollas, even if, finally, she also turns to the "internal object" as the object of interest.[15]

She speaks of a "memory closet" in her grandparents' Brooklyn apartment that had a "smell and feel" all of its own and that contained a collection of family things—mementos, photographs, trinkets, postcards, jewelry—that she was allowed as a child to take down and hold, arrange and be with. These objects, she says, helped her know who her grandparents, parents and she herself were. In the collected essays, Turkle (2007: 5) says, the authors write stories of objects as "companions" to their own "life experience." Although only as an aside, she connects this work to a late 20th-century line of scholarly writing that emerged before the object-oriented work noted here and which opened thinking about objects truly in their own right. In that footnote reference, Turkle unwittingly brings us back to Whitehead.

This is so not only because of Whitehead's attention to objects but also because Turkle references the late 20th-century tradition of writing in science studies that takes "the concrete" as having, to use Karen Barad's (2007) term, an "agential" capacity. However, before Barad there was Haraway and Bruno Latour, two science studies scholars whose work has importantly shaped that field of study from 1980 forward. Both Latour and Haraway acknowledge thoroughgoing insight gained from reading Whitehead, insight that is apparent in Latour's trenchant critique of the social and sociological concepts and his actor-network theory, giving central place to his term "actant" (rather than "actor"), and in Haraway's rejection of the bifurcation of nature, insisting on "natureculture" and the promiscuous and messy relationality from her famous cyborg to her dog-human and other companion species amalgams.[16]

We can draw a line from this Whitehead-Haraway-Latour work that touches what Bollas and Turkle, for instance, have to say about objects. However, the risk of doing so is that precisely the point so important to the object-oriented and -related scholars and to the story I tell here of living in the company of things, namely, the "in-itselfness" first of non-human and then non-living objects—their affectivity as generators and receptors of Whitehead's "feeling" or the aesthetic—is obscured by the shadow of the human and of life. I have tried here to avoid that dominating presence even as I have insisted on the connection thereto as the matter at hand. My experience of Nancy's death and, no doubt, the almost two years before it during cancer's return (or new arrival—I was never sure) has been full of an abiding awareness of how important the intimacy of a range of objects has been in supporting my life into the now from the then, which is also here. I don't know if it would have been different if she had died without warning in a car crash and/or our relationship had been deeply fraught. Would "our" objects then have acted differently in their aesthetic connection to me? Whitehead likely would say of course.

The question of going on, of becoming—as if it were really a question about which there could be a question at all. For even in death, life, existence, continues. As Didion (2005: 5) writes, perhaps more poignantly than she could know, quoting the Episcopal *Book of Common Prayer*, "In the midst of life, we are in death."[17] Of course, we think we already know this. Life and death are entwined as each other's limit; a provocative, sophisticated idea, but knowing it and living it, in the midst, in the flesh, with the *matter* of life and death breathing and pulsing together—and then not: that's another matter. Here, the verb to know doesn't quite convey how it *feels*. Whitehead's insistence that existence is aesthetic before it is cognitive strikes me as compelling. So perhaps it is precisely the liveliness of these particular "Nancy things" in my life—and of things, matter, more generally—that he and others who have written on/for objects have foregrounded, that bring me comfort and a sense of existential enmeshness.[18] If, as Bollas suggests, with his notion of aesthetic dejection, certain objects bring only aversive experience for other human objects (for him, apparently, one such is the city of Copenhagen), we might then think of a whole realm of connections between objects that could be called, using Whitehead's term, "satisfying," which carries a flavor of intensity that he might applaud.

Just as I am finishing this final draft, I have looked again at a short (unpublished) essay by Nancy's brother John Harper, called "The End of the Dock." Resonant with memories of the past and the summers he spent growing up at a family cottage on a northwest Iowa lake, he tells of a private and secret place at the end of the family boat dock where, only at night and alone, he often searched the dark and starry sky to glimpse his future from the details of his life so far. The figure of a sweet younger sister who always seemed to be the emotional rudder of his family moves in and out of the frame. He writes, some 50 years after he first found/made this private place, of the two of us, making our way to the end of the dock on a chilly and drizzly September day. We were there with the last portion of Nancy's ashes to say our final goodbye and to leave some part of her at a place that she also loved. His words bring my story of the intimacy of objects to a close:

> Joseph opens the bag, digs a hand into it, and then passes it to me. Cremains are invariably filled with sharp edges and bone fragments, and are a dull grey color. But Nancy's are all a fine ivory-color powder, such a delicate consistency. They adhere to my palms and fingers as I toss several handfuls into the choppy water below. We stand there in silence for a while, sharing a good cry ... [then] drive back into town to eat lunch before the long journey home. But I can't bring myself to wash my hands ... Nancy is present, a part of me in a way she hasn't been since her death more than ten months ago. I resolve that I must come back to my special place one more time, but at night.

Acknowledgements

Conversations with Patricia Clough about materiality and theory have been enormously important in thinking this essay. Thanks also to Richard Abel, Barbara Hodgdon and Janet Wirth-Cauchon for helpful comments on earlier drafts.

Notes

1 See Shaviro (2009). "Mattering" is Pheng Cheah's (1996) term, titling his critical review of Judith Butler and Elizabeth Grosz on this question of the material in their work.
2 Vicki Kirby (2011) has written specifically to these issues of materiality from a Derridean and poststructuralist view.
3 Levi Bryant (2011) titles his recent book *The Democracy of Objects*.
4 See, for instance, Whitehead (1978: 56).

5 See Ian Bogost (2012).

6 On object-oriented thought, see Bryant *et al.* (2011); Harman (2002, 2005); Bryant (2011); Bogost (2012); and Morton (2012).

7 After which he writes: "It is at this point that with life morals become acute. The robber requires justification."

8 These capacities as the definition of affect are traceable back through Clough and Halley (2007), and Massumi (2002), to Deleuze and Spinoza.

9 See Bergson (1991); and see the films of Agnès Varda, especially *The Beaches of Agnès*, for another sense of this.

10 As Grosz notes, Bergson was fascinated by this space between the cognitive or ideational/representational of memory, on the one hand, and the body and bodily matter required for memory to exist, on the other—a division Whitehead would erase in his critique of bifurcation, a point Goodman (2010) addresses.

11 Morton argues that objects should be seen as dialetheic, embracing the claim that some contradictions can be true and that appearance and reality not only can be at odds but in fact are. That is, an object in its complex dynamism is both what it seems and not; its essence is not its appearance. "An object is therefore both itself and not-itself, at the very same time" (Morton 2012: 17).

12 Psychoanalyst Christopher Bollas (2009: 91) uses the term "aesthetic dejection" to refer to "an irresolvable mismatch between self and object." Here, the distinct and separate object "out there" stands forth as having qualities that are separate from its internal version in the psyche.. Of course, while it is an object that brings depression and dejection "for me"—underscoring its joint production—Bollas (2009: 91) allows that in such cases "The only solution [for the patient] is to be removed from the object itself."

13 Beyond Bennett and Haraway, see, on ancient Chinese thought made relevant to this discussion, Jullien (2007).

14 Much of Turkle's work looks at the relationship between humans and machines, especially computers; see also her recent discussion of personal robots or PARO (Turkle 2011).

15 On Freud's internal object, see Freud (1953).

16 See, for instance, Latour (1987, 1999) and Haraway (2008).

17 Some 16 months after Dunne's death, Didion was to face another personal tragedy in the death of their daughter Quintana Roo Dunne Michael, from the relentless infection alluded to in the long quote I include from *The Year of Magical Thinking*. In *Blue Nights*, Didion (2011) writes the story of life after her daughter's death, with characteristic force.

18 This is Morton's (2012) term, from "Objects in Mirror are Closer than they Appear."

References

Barad, Karen. 2007. *Meeting the Universe Halfway: Quantum Physics and the Entanglement of Matter and Meaning*. Durham, NC: Duke University Press.

Bennett, Jane. 2001. *The Enchantment of Modern Life: Attachments, Crossings, and Ethics*. Princeton, NJ: Princeton University Press.

——2010. *Vibrant Matter: A Political Ecology of Things*. Durham, NC: Duke University Press.

Bergson, Henri. 1991 [1908]. *Matter and Memory*. Trans. Nancy Margaret Paul and W. Scott Palmer. New York: Zone.

Berns, Nancy. 2011. *Closure: The Rush to End Grief and What It Can Cost Us*. Philadelphia: Temple University Press.

Bogost, Ian. 2012. *Alien Phenomenology, or What It's Like To Be a Thing*. Minneapolis, MN: University of Minnesota Press.

Bollas, Christopher. 2009. *The Evocative Object World*. New York: Routledge.

Brooks, Douglas R. 2011. "Yoga Mantra." Unpublished lecture, July 28. Srividyalaya Yoga Summer Camp. Gell Center, Naples, New York.

Bryant, Levi. 2011. *The Democracy of Objects*. Ann Arbor, MI: Open Humanities Press.

Bryant, Levi, Nick Srnicek and Graham Harman (eds). 2011. *The Speculative Turn: Continental Materialism and Realism*. Melbourne: re:press.

Cheah, Pheng. 1996. "Mattering." *Diacritics* 26: 108–39.

Chen, Nancy N. and Trinh T. Minh-ha. 1994. "Speaking Nearby." In Lucian Taylor (ed.) *Visualizing Theory: Selected Essays from V.A.R. 1990–1994*. New York: Routledge, 434–51.

Clough, Patricia Ticineto. 2000. *Autoaffection: Unconscious Thought in the Age of Teletechnology*. Minneapolis: University of Minnesota Press.

Clough, Patricia Ticineto and Jean Halley (eds). 2007. *The Affective Turn: Theorizing the Social*. Durham, NC: Duke University Press.

Didion, Joan. 2005. *The Year of Magical Thinking*. New York: Knopf.

——2011. *Blue Nights*. New York: Knopf.

Fei, Xiaotong. 1993. "The Shallowness of Cultural Tradition." In R. David Arkush and Leo O. Lee (eds) *Land Without Ghosts: Chinese Impressions of America from the Mid-Nineteenth Century to the Present*. Berkeley: University of California Press, 171–81.

Freud, Sigmund Freud. 1953. "Mourning and Melancholia." In James Strachey (ed. and trans.) *The Standard Edition of the Complete Psychological Works of Sigmund Freud*, Vol. 14. London: Hogarth, 239–58.

——1955 [1919]. "The 'Uncanny'." In James Strachey (ed. and trans.) *The Standard Edition of the Complete Psychological Works of Sigmund Freud*, Vol. 17. London: Hogarth Press, 217–52.

Goodman, Steve. 2010. *Sonic Warfare: Sound, Affect, and the Ecology of Fear*. Cambridge, MA: MIT Press.

Grosz, Elizabeth. 2005. *Time Travels: Feminism, Nature, Power*. Durham, NC: Duke University Press.

Haraway, Donna J. 1989. *Primate Visions: Gender, Race, and Nature in the World of Modern Science*. New York: Routledge.

——1991. *Simians, Cyborgs, and Women: The Reinvention of Nature*. New York: Routledge.

——1997. *Modest_Witness@Second_Millennium: FemaleMan©_Meets_Oncomouse^{TM}: Feminism and Technoscience*. New York: Routledge.

——2008. *When Species Meet*. Minneapolis, MN: University of Minnesota Press.

Harman, Graham. 2002. *Tool Being: Heidegger and the Metaphysics of Objects*. Chicago: Open Court.

——2005. *Guerrilla Metaphysics: Phenomenology and the Carpentry of Things*. Chicago: Open Court.

Iyengar, B.K.S. 1979. *Light on Yoga*. New York: Shocken.

Jullien, François. 2007. *Vital Nourishment: Departing from Happiness*. New York: Zone Books.

Kirby, Vicki. 2011. *Quantum Anthropologies: Life at Large*. Durham, NC: Duke University Press.

Latour, Bruno. 1987. *Science in Action: How to Follow Scientists and Engineers through Society*. Cambridge, MA: Harvard University Press.

——1999. *Pandora's Hope: Essays on the Reality of Science Studies*. Cambridge, MA: Harvard University Press.

Lingis, Alphonso. 1998. *The Imperative*. Bloomington, IN: Indiana University Press.

Macaulay, Alastair. 2012. "Cage and Cunningham, Reunited, Restaged." *The New York Times*, March 24: C1.

Massumi, Brian. 2002. *Parables for the Virtual: Movement, Affect, Sensation*. Durham, NC: Duke University Press.

Morton, Timothy. 2012. "Objects in Mirror are Closer than they Appear." In Tom Sparrow and Bobby George (eds) *Another Phenomenology: Exploring the Sensuous Earth*, Vol. 1 of *Singularum: Lessons in Aesthetics*, 2–35.

Schneider, Joseph. 2012. "Whitehead, White Cat, Aesthetic Experience, Affect: Scenes from a Relationship." Paper presented at meetings of Society for Literature, Science, and the Arts, Milwaukee, Wisconsin, September, 27–30.

Schneider, Joseph and Wang Laihua. 2000. "The Ghost of the Xiaozi." In *Giving Care, Writing Self: A "New" Ethnography*. New York: Lang, 199–226.

Shaviro, Steven. 2009. *Without Criteria: Kant, Whitehead, Deleuze, and Aesthetics*. Cambridge, MA: MIT Press.

——2012. "The Universe of Things." Unpublished PDF manuscript. www.shaviro.com/Othertexts/articles.html.

Shelton, Allen. 2007. *Dreamworlds of Alabama*. Minneapolis: University of Minnesota Press.

Turkle, Sherry (ed.). 2007. *Evocative Objects: Things We Think With*. Cambridge, MA: MIT Press.

——2011. *Alone Together: Why We Expect More from Technology and Less from Each Other*. New York: Basic Books.

Whitehead, Alfred North. 1955 [1927]. *Symbolism: Its Meaning and Effect*. New York: Fordham University Press.

——1967 [1933]. *Adventures of Ideas*. New York: The Free Press.

——1978 [1929]. *Process and Reality. An Essay in Cosmology*. Ed. D.R. Griffin and D.W. Sherburne, corrected edition. New York: Free Press.

Index